Games and Simulations in Online Learning:
Research and Development Frameworks

David Gibson
CurveShift.com, USA

Clark Aldrich
SimuLearn Inc., USA

Marc Prensky
games2train, USA

Information Science Publishing

Hershey • London • Melbourne • Singapore

Acquisition Editor: Michelle Potter
Senior Managing Editor: Jennifer Neidig
Managing Editor: Sara Reed
Development Editor: Kristin Roth
Copy Editor: Kim Berger
Typesetter: Marko Primorac
Cover Design: Lisa Tosheff
Printed at: Integrated Book Technology

Published in the United States of America by
            Information Science Publishing (an imprint of Idea Group Inc.)
            701 E. Chocolate Avenue
            Hershey PA 17033
            Tel: 717-533-8845
            Fax: 717-533-8661
            E-mail: cust@idea-group.com
            Web site: http://www.idea-group.com

and in the United Kingdom by
            Information Science Publishing (an imprint of Idea Group Inc.)
            3 Henrietta Street
            Covent Garden
            London WC2E 8LU
            Tel: 44 20 7240 0856
            Fax: 44 20 7379 3313
            Web site: http://www.eurospan.co.uk

Library of Congress Cataloging-in-Publication Data

Games and simulations in online learning : research and development frameworks / David Gibson, Clark Aldrich and Marc Prensky, editors.
      p. cm.
   Summary: "This book examines the potential of games and simulations in online learning, and how the future could look as developers learn to use the emerging capabilities of the Semantic Web. It explores how the Semantic Web will impact education and how games and simulations can evolve to become robust teaching resources"--Provided by publisher.
   ISBN 1-59904-304-1 (hardcover) -- ISBN 1-59904-305-X (softcover) -- ISBN 1-59904-306-8 (ebook)
   1. Education--Simulation methods. 2. Computer games. 3. Computer-assisted instruction. I. Gibson, David. II. Aldrich, Clark, 1967- III. Prensky, Marc.
   LB1029.S53G36 2007
   371.33'4--dc22
                              2006019128

British Cataloguing in Publication Data
A Cataloguing in Publication record for this book is available from the British Library.

Games and Simulations in Online Learning:
Research and Development Frameworks

Table of Contents

Foreword

By using design-based research (Dede, 2005), the next generation of games and simulations has the potential to dramatically improve students' motivation and educational outcomes, as well as generating new insights about the nature of learning. To accomplish these goals, proponents of these interactive media must recognize some lessons learned from prior research on many types of learning experiences. These include:

- No educational design is always powerful for all participants, because learning strengths and styles, as well as sources of engagement, vary greatly among people.
- As with all other types of learning experiences, games and simulations will not result in educational benefits unless their design is excellent along multiple dimensions.
- To the extent that games involve competition (e.g., winners and losers based on uni-dimensional scoring systems, as in professional sports), some participants' motivation will increase, while others' will diminish.
- To be effective for learning, simulations must walk a tightrope between authenticity and validity to the real world (which makes learning more difficult, because reality is complex) and oversimplifications that introducing misconceptions, which in turn make later, deeper learning more difficult.

At the moment, the media are touting games and simulations as the latest panacea for education's problems, but today's hype will inevitably turn into tomorrow's disillusionment unless designers and scholars think deeply about these issues, are principled in their studies, and are cautious in their claims.

In our work on the River City multi-user virtual environment (http://muve.gse.harvard.edu/rivercityproject/), a game-like immersive simulation for middle school students, we are constantly reminded of how many powerful options for sophisticated information and communication technologies now enable. Designers can easily lose their way in developing virtual settings that are fascinating and fun, but fall short of conveying deep content, higher order skills, and complex ethical perspectives. The various contributions to this volume reflect the leading edge of work in games and simulations for learning. Together they exemplify the current strengths and limits of this emerging field, and collectively the authors convey a sense of what is possible, what is desirable, and what we now can attain.

Like the contributors to this book, I am very excited about the potential of the next generation of games and simulations for education. Over the next decade, immersive, mediated, situated learning experiences may open up transformative types of learning in and out of academic settings. I hope that reading this book will inspire you to join all of us in exploring these powerful interactive media.

Reference

Dede, C. (2005). Why design-based research is both important and difficult. *Educational Technology, 45*(1), 5-8.

Chris Dede, the Timothy E. Wirth Professor in learning technologies at the Harvard Graduate School of Education, is deeply interested in the expanded human capabilities for knowledge creation, sharing, and mastery that emerging technologies enable. His teaching models the use of information technology to distribute and orchestrate learning across space, time, and multiple interactive media. His research spans emerging technologies for learning, infusing technology into large-scale educational improvement initiatives, policy formulation and analysis, and leadership in educational innovation. He is currently conducting funded studies to develop and assess learning environments based on modeling and visualization, online teacher professional development, high-bandwidth telementoring, wireless mobile devices for ubiquitous computing, and multiuser virtual environments. Dr. Dede also is active in policy initiatives, including creating a widely used State Policy Framework for Assessing Educational Technology Implementation and studying the potential of developing a scalability index for educational innovations. From 2001 to 2004, he served as chair of the learning & teaching area at Harvard Graduate School of Education.

Preface

Whenever one plays a game, and whatever game one plays, learning happens constantly, whether the players want it to, and are aware of it, or not. And the players are learning "about life," which is one of the great positive consequences of all game playing. This learning takes place, continuously and simultaneously in every game, every time one plays. One need not even pay much attention. (Prensky, 2002)

Games are serious learning tools. But can games teach exactly what and when you want them to? What about simulations? Are they like games? Why talk about games AND simulations in online learning…and why in "online learning?" How do these fit together and to what end?

Rather than thinking about games and simulation, it is more productive to think about the distinct elements, namely:

- *Simulation elements*
- *Game elements*
- *Pedagogical elements.* (Aldrich, 2005)

Research and development of digital games and simulations in online learning is in its infancy. Digital games and simulations explicitly designed for education have only been available on disks and CDs since the 1980s and available on the Internet since the 1990s. Now in 2006, two decades into their evolution, games and simulations are beginning to show new promise for the future of learning.

The old promise was that when a computer is involved in playing a game or running a simulation, a lot of the slowness and drudgery is taken out of score keeping, rolling dice, marking positions, operating a model, and replicating causes. This allows players to concentrate on strategy and tactics, which is good, because concentrating on higher order skills brings people closer to the essence of learning how to learn.

Beyond efficiency and focus, the old promise was also about the enhancing effect of integrated multimedia: snazzy graphics, exciting sounds, compelling stories, and interactivity! Games without computers involve dice, spinners, paper, markers, game boards, and cards. Digital game-based learning involves highly engaging hypermedia often including player-defined nonlinear texts with audio and video. These media elements motivate players through experiences that have the gripping force of a first-person story.

But the new promises are even more exciting. We are just beginning to understand and document, through a blend of IT and social research, how game and simulation elements can take advantage of the global network infrastructure to add live data, new social contexts, and distributed processing on far-flung knowledge databases. These promising new capabilities allow the player to be part of an extended, living community of inquiry and practice.

Can these elements be brought together by design without, as Prensky, Clark, and others warn, "sucking the fun out of everything?"

The field of educational and serious games is strewn with a mixture of entrepreneurs and academicians who are experimenting, building prototypes, and laying the foundations for future research and development. Not all is clear in the dust kicked up by this activity, but there is plenty to think about and several promising leads. We have gathered some of it here for you to scan and spend time with as your interests lead you.

Since you are reading this, you must be among those who are curious to find out what others are thinking and doing with games and simulations in education. For you, we do not have to talk about "why games?" or "why simulations?" You already know that they are valuable pursuits. Playing them or experimenting with them leads to learning. Including them in online learning, you sense, will add excitement at least, and at best, more powerful and effective experiences that deeply engage learners and create memorable, lasting impressions.

For you, it is clear that advanced information technologies should be more aggressively exploited to improve education. You know that educators are underutilizing the vast potential of information technology to transform schooling, teaching, and learning. While current educational policies seem bent on subjugating people into submission to standards, you understand that we need to better understand how students learn with advanced technologies. Then we need to design and use better tools to take advantage of this understanding. It is perfectly clear to you that games and simulations are central to the future of education.

But we are not "there yet." The touted promises of a new learning society founded upon easy access to educational resources on the telecommunications infrastructure seem to have faded. Where is the "sprawling, wired city full of researchers, teachers, students, and members of the community" pursuing diverse directions (Johnson, 2002)?

Many people have not yet made the connection between computational science, which has completely changed how science is conducted, and education that could be using those same computational and informational technologies. Yet, this is where simulations live and breathe. In addition, many people seem to be afraid of what would happen if all learning were as effective and fun as possible. Yet, this is where most of early learning takes place and where, if the truth be told, we would all rather spend our time than in a didactic "course" with a test at the end of the tunnel. What can be done to help these people see a path to the future of learning?

These people need to be shown, convinced, and supported in their consideration of the promise of games and simulations in education. They need to see research and development frameworks that are grounded in generally accepted educational theories. They need to read about prototype projects that are experimenting their way to the future, and they need to develop a hunger to have their own institutions engage in this work.

The kinds of questions on their minds are: What sort of new research and development is emerging around games and simulations? What kinds of learning are involved, and how do we know if users are "getting it?" What is the unique added value and potential for learning and assessment in the digital environment? Are there examples that can inspire researchers to think more deeply, and see a new horizon for e-learning?

We hope that this book provides some food for thought concerning these questions. We hope the book contributes to your thinking by presenting themes for research and development of educational games and simulations from a variety of perspectives, stretching you in new ways perhaps, or confirming your own creative ideas and insightful hypotheses about how games and simulations are changing education. Here is a brief overview of the chapters in this collection.

Göknur Kaplan Akilli, in **Chapter I**, *Games and Simulations: A New Approach in Education?,* provides a brief review of the literature, which she organizes around questions that define games, simulations, instructional design, and instructional development models. Her review situates the problem of instructional design models as out-dated frameworks that came into being before the age of ubiquitous games and simulations. She criticizes the current state of design, points to more promising theories, and ends by introducing us to the FIDGE model as a possible framework for a more game-like instructional design model.

Katrin Becker, in **Chapter II**, *Pedagogy in Commercial Video Games,* after tying games to deep learning and urging educators to "learn about learning from games," gives a point-by-point overview that relates game and simulation elements to several well-known learning theories. For example, Gagne's nine "events" are reviewed, with examples from popular games; Riegeluth's "elaboration" theory is presented with Becker's reflections. Bruner's psycho-cultural tenets of learning and Merrill's principles of instruction receive similar treatment. Learning style and intelligence theorists like Gardner, Keirsey, Felder, Kolb, and Gregoric are included in her argument that "good games are good for learning." But, Becker warns, a demonstration of good pedagogy in games does not add up to a prescription for creating good learning games. We should not impose instructional design onto a game or we will get what Prensky calls the "dancing banana" effect—game-like trappings on drill and kill pedagogy. Games are a completely new technology calling for completely new instructional design approaches.

Several writers present social analyses of multi-user virtual environments, which leaves us with a growing sense that networked virtual worlds are a new kind of learning ecosystem waiting to be tapped for education. The next four chapters explore this idea.

Joel Foreman and Thomasina Borkman share their experience in in **Chapter III**, using a commercial off the shelf game—The Sims—to teach a Sociology course. They wonder what would happen if colleges staged more of their large introductory courses within massively multiplayer virtual environments.

In **Chapter IV,** Lisa Galarneau and Melanie Zibit extend the theme of the new social environment of MMOGs by outlining the 21st century skills that are promoted through online games. The skills for the new millennium are shaped by global ubiquitous access to the tools of communication, collaboration, and creative decision-making needed by knowledge workers. They first discuss the new skills from a variety of perspectives—the SCANS report in the U.S. and Perelman's *School's Out* in the 1990s, the international OECD competencies, and Goleman's "emotional intelligence" in 2000. They then demonstrate how online games in MMOGs can serve as a "practice arena" for the skills.

James G. Jones and Stephen C. Bronack, in **Chapter V,** *Rethinking Cognition, Representations, and Processes in 3D Online Social Learning Environments,* take the social analysis of 3D spaces further by pointing out their tendency to encourage peer-based informal learning. The elements of immediacy, movement, artifacts, and multimodal communications are highlighted within a larger conception of learning known as "social constructivism." The theory provides numerous core concepts such as cognitive scaffolding, situated learning, and authenticity, which are provided in 3D virtual reality spaces. The authors then provide a framework for creating and sustaining an effective learning environment in such spaces, by outlining how various users and roles relate and interact. Two case studies are presented that give concrete life to their ideas.

In **Chapter VI,** Karen Barton and Paul Maharg use another case example, the Glasgow Graduate School of Law's simulation "Ardcallough" to frame what they see as a new "trading zone" in virtual space. Their chapter *E-Simulations in the Wild: Interdisciplinary Research, Design, and Implementation* points out that a simulation is more than a likeness of reality; it is a purposeful, focused view that presents the user with a complex conceptual, as well as operational, challenge. They present a spectrum framework that at one end is "bounded" and at the other, an "open field of practice" and is consistent with discovery learning that guides the learner through self-directed activity to construct their own understanding. The trading zone of the 3D space provides a variety of transactions, which other authors in this volume "mine" for assessment information. Perhaps most refreshing, the student experience is largely absent the "normal academic forms of study and communication." Now that is progress!

What do the users think of MMOG spaces, games, and simulations as learning tools? The next two chapters provide different views.

In **Chapter VII,** Jonathan Beedle and Vivian H. Wright offer us *Perspectives from Multiplayer Video Gamers,* a research report based on a survey of gamers. Their literature review provides a synopsis of a familiar narrative. Games are big and are growing fast. Unfortunately, research thus far has focused mostly on the potentially detrimental aspects, and many of the "educational titles" are just bad teaching. However, a growing body of theory, research, and experience indicates that people learn in brand new ways when interacting with games and simulations. If you believe this and want to teach with games and simulations, there are "modding" tools that allow you to customize the applications to some extent. The list of potential benefits of learning with games leads to four questions about motivation, problem solving, communication, and creativity. Will video game players say that they believe that games increase critical thinking skills via these four avenues? Their results speak for themselves.

As we worked to build a classroom simulation—a flight trainer for future teachers—we began to wonder if the generation of teachers coming through the system at this point in time shared attitudes and experiences with the "gamer generation" as talked about by Prensky in "Digital Game-Based Learning" and by Beck and Wade in "Got Game." **Chapter VIII,** by and David Gibson, William Halverson, and Eric Riedel, titled *Gamer Teachers* gives a preliminary answer of yes. The literature review outlines the major concerns that seem to block or hinder the use of games and simulations in teaching and includes our take on a self-test (you can take it and give it to others) that was suggested by Prensky's list of cognitive styles of the gamer generation. The chapter provides a handful of hints for designing games-based learning experiences, organized to coincide with a cognitive science summary framework from Bransford, Brown, and Cocking. Our results tend to corroborate what others have found, not so much as an age gap between generations, but a "playing gap" depending on one's game experiences. A big unanswered question is whether gamer teachers—and there are quite a few—will turn to games to teach once they are in the classroom.

Continuing with the theme of "teaching teachers how to teach," Brian Ferry and Lisa Kervin relate their experiences in **Chapter IX**, *Developing an Online Classroom Simulation to Support a Pre-Service Teacher Education Program*. Their chapter presents a straightforward step-by-step account of building a software prototyping team in higher education. The team developed a virtual kindergarten teaching application that has shown promise for engaging future teachers in the complexities of teaching decisions. The chapter will be valuable to any group that wants to develop a teaching application, especially a game or simulation about teaching. They provide a glimpse into budgets, planning processes, people, and roles in the development effort, and share the teaching framework at the heart of their simulation. A notable stage of their development included the use of a complex systems representation tool—STELLA—to explore dynamic relationships among the variables they were proposing to model.

Gerald R. and Mark Girod (father and son) and programmer Jeff Denton give us **Chapter X**, *Lessons Learned Modeling "Connecting Teaching and Learning,"* provides a second example of a development process in teacher education. Their effort is based on the "teacher work sample methodology" developed at Western Oregon University over 30 years ago. A classroom simulator called "Cook School District" models how students learn as a result of instructional strategy choices made by users. The chapter presents an informative look into the logic structure of the application and highlights eight lessons the team learned during the development process. For development teams wishing to make a contribution to teaching through a game or simulation, this team's work is a "must read."

Sara Dexter, in **Chapter XI**, *Educational Theory Into Practice Software*, presents a new perspective on teacher development by sharing a unique and powerful case-based reasoning application that has both game-like and simulation elements. The core of the application is a problem space or case, which is a collection of multimedia elements that collectively present a narrative of a specific simulated school Web site. The chapter outlines how the application works and shares some of the challenges and directional changes faced during its development. Among the lessons learned, and shared with other projects in this book are new learning and assessment theories, and a rapid prototyping approach to programming.

The next two chapters use real space as part of the virtual experience for players by integrating wireless and GPS technologies into the game and simulation. From their experience at the Swiss Federal Institute of Technology in Zurich, Steffen P. Walz and Odilo Schoch talk about *Pervasive Game Design as an Architectural Teaching and Research Method* in **Chapter XII**. The game they designed grew from the idea that architectural students of the future should be able to design both physical and virtual "hybrid reality" spaces. Their development story centers on a place-based game designed in collaboration with architectural students. The game transforms the university's campus into a giant wireless game board. Key positions in physical space issue forth questions that are best answered in collaboration with other players in the real space.

Across the Atlantic at the Massachusetts Institute of Technology, Karen Schrier built a place-based game that uses the city of Lexington, Massachusetts as the trigger for events and interactions that help players revisit and relive the Revolutionary War. Players of "Reliving the Revolution" seek to answer the question "who fired the shot heard 'round the world?" Players experience a different version of history depending on their role as well as the places they visit as they seek to piece together a coherent story of that fateful event in American history. Becker calls this an "augmented reality game" that is focused on teaching critical thinking and historical inquiry. Her story in **Chapter XIII** relates valuable lessons about game development and redesign in the service of giving players opportunities to develop complex thinking skills. She offers a design summary as part of her lessons to pass along to others.

The last five chapters explore machine learning, network-based assessment, and intelligent agents. Related by today's experimenters and developers, these provide glimpses into tomorrow's potential for games and simulations in education.

Richard Van Eck, in **Chapter XIV**, *Building Artificially Intelligent Learning Games*, presents a two-part chapter. The first part reviews pedagogical principles in games and covers ground that will be familiar to this book's readers. He asserts that games employ elements that engage and teach through problem solving that embodies the tenets of learning theory and social constructivism. Traditional approaches to instruction are insufficient for game-based learning, but fortunately, new principles are available to form a framework for research and development. He then outlines four principles of learning in games and uses them as a foundation to raise key questions that guide the second part of the chapter. Artificial intelligence, pedagogical agents, and intelligent tutoring systems are offered as mechanisms for presenting content in ways that support the four principles of learning. He ends by calling for the creation of new authoring tools that will help guide the creation of principled learning games.

Chapter XV, *simSchool and the Conceptual Assessment Framework* (CAF), by David Gibson, uses the "simSchool" flight simulator for teachers as an example of building a game-like learning application with assessment in mind. Assessing learning that potentially occurs as a result of playing a game or working with a simulator requires a formalization of everyday reasoning. The CAF (Mislevy, Steinberg, & Almond, 2003) formalizes some of the key assessment issues involved in the process of making an inference based on the evidence gathered from artifacts created by a learner. These artifacts can be intended, as is the case of an essay, or unintended, for example, the order, timing, and configuration of resources used during a game or simulation session. Details are given about how simSchool embodies the formalized student, task, and evidence model features of the CAF. In simSchool, the CAF framework is used to organize the logic of the simulation model as well as to assess the user—a case that may best fit when the goal is to "teach a user by modeling a learner."

In **Chapter XVI**, *Designing Online Games Assessment as "Information Trails,"* Christian Sebastian Loh discuss some of the specific ways that user artifacts can form the basis for assessment. Comparative examples from online commerce ("cookies," "user profiles," "targeted marketing") help make the case that tracking technology is already used to build records over time, assess user preferences, and sell new ideas to users. He introduces the reader to the idea of "agent-detectable markings" left by a "moving agent in an information-ecology." Designers of game-based assessments will need "event hooks" that need to be worked into the instructional design processes and will need to learn to construct automated analyses, teacher modifiable conditions for analysis rules. The hooks themselves will need to be adaptable so that as users make choices within the boundaries of a game, the meaning of an analysis can be adjusted. According to Loh, teachers may one day be seen as game masters who are co-constructing the world of inquiry and discovery, like a dungeon master leading a party to adventure.

Ron Steven's work on the UCLA IMMEX project has led to **Chapter XVII**, *Machine Learning Assessment Systems for Modeling Patterns of Student Learning*. As a concrete example of using player artifacts in assessment, Stevens presents a layered analytic model of how high school and university students construct, modify, and retain problem-solving strategies as they solve science problems online. Item response theory modeling provides initial estimates of problem solving ability at the individual level. Later, self-organizing artificial neural networks analyze hundreds of performance instances to form clusters of solution strategies. Hidden Markov Modeling is then used to develop "learning trajectories" across sequences of performances and to stochastically represent problem solving progress. He has found that students quickly zero in on preferred strategies, which remain stable for long periods of time, and that students working in groups do so quicker and use a more limited repertoire of strategies than do students working alone.

In **Chapter XVIII**, *Shaping the Research Agenda with Cyber Researcher Assistants,* Lyn Henderson concludes the collection with a reflection about the possibilities and open questions of using the powerful tracking, analytic and interactive aspects of games and simulations to empower learners and teachers.

We hope that these chapters promote increased serious use of games and simulations in online learning by offering new possibilities for framing research and development efforts.

David Gibson
Clark Aldrich
Marc Prensky

References

Aldrich, C. (2005). *Learning by doing: The essential guide to simulations, computer games, and pedagogy in e-learning and other educational experiences*. San Francisco: Jossey-Bass.

Johnson, D. (2002). The university of the future. *The Futurist, 36*(3), 7-8.

Mislevy, R. J., Steinberg, L. S., & Almond, R. G. (2003). On the structure of educational assessments. *Measurement: Interdisciplinary Research and Perspectives, 1*, 3-67.

Prensky, M. (2002). *What kids learn that's positive from playing video games.*

Acknowledgments

I'd like to thank the growing number of people who use digital games and simulations in teaching, training and self-development. Their interest and motivation to provide learners with the most highly engaging environments is leading to a revolution in teaching and learning. They drive game and simulation producers to invent, advocates to celebrate, and even by-standers to wonder.

I'd also like to thank my wife, the violinist Mary, and my two children, Molly and Michael. They were patient and understanding with me when I was absent-minded, focused on this distant goal, and ruminating, probably mumbling, as I thought about the book.

A special thanks to co-editors Clark Aldrich and Marc Prensky for the meetings and calls that circled around the difficulty of pulling together several author's voices on a complex topic. Their openness to the idea of the book propelled it forward. Their advice and soundings expanded and shaped the collection into a much more powerful group of chapters than I could have accomplished alone. Their availability and willingness to assist was invaluable. I'm humbled (but I'll grab the chance and be very proud!) to be associated with them and their leading-edge work in this emerging field.

Finally, all of us editors would like to thank the thoughtful designers, users and producers of digital games and simulations who contributed proposals and chapters. The Serious Games online community, the Society for Information Technology in Teacher Education, and the International Society for Technology in Education all helped put us in touch with the authors. And we thank our editors, development experts, and publishers, who advised us and worked tirelessly to make the book a reality.

Section I

Situating Games and Simulations in Education

Chapter I

Games and Simulations:
A New Approach in Education?

Göknur Kaplan Akilli, Pennsylvania State University, USA

Abstract

Computer games and simulations are considered powerful tools for learning with an untapped potential for formal educational use. However, the lack of available well-designed research studies about their integration into teaching and learning leaves unanswered questions, despite their more than 30 years of existence in the instructional design movement. Beginning with these issues, this chapter aims to shed light on the definition of games and simulations, their educational use, and some of their effects on learning. Criticisms and new trends in the field of instructional design/development in relation to educational use of games and simulations are briefly reviewed. The chapter intends to provide a brief theoretical framework and a fresh starting point for practitioners in the field who are interested in educational use of games and simulations and their integration into learning environments.

Introduction

It is unanimously acknowledged that we are living in the information age, taking part in the information society (Bates, 2000; Reigeluth, 1996). What makes these two emerging concepts possible is technology, or rather, the rate of progress that has been achieved in technology over the past 50 or so years (Molenda & Sullivan, 2003). Throughout this period, technology has been both the generator and the transmitter of information with an increasingly faster speed and wider audience each and every day. It now dominates most facets of our lives, penetrating into the conduct of normal daily life.

The field of education is not an exception in the permeation of technology. On the contrary, education has always been considered as potentially one of the most productive breeding-grounds for technology, where it would perhaps find its finest resonances and lead to revolutionary effects. Yet, high expectations regarding the revolutionary impacts of technology on education have hardly been realized so far. More specifically, instructional technology, or the use of technology in educational environments, has not contributed significantly to the realization of these expectations (Molenda & Sullivan, 2003; Russell, 2003). It may be argued that the relative ineffectiveness of instructional technology thus far has been caused by the application of the same old methods in new educational media—"New wine was poured, but only into old bottles" (Cohen & Ball, 1990, p. 334). The inconclusiveness of the research is illustrated by the Clark and Kozma debate, started by Clark's 1983 statement that media do not influence students' learning (Clark, 1983). Kozma (1991) counter-argued that learning and media are complementary and that interrelationships of media, method, and external environment have influence on learning. Both of them rationalized their arguments by calling on Russell's (2003) study on, so called, "no-significant-difference" research. Clark (1983, 1994a, 1994b) uses this phenomenon as evidence for his argument, whereas Kozma (1994) uses this phenomenon as indicative of insufficient evidence for his debate.

Current models and methods of instructional technology are insufficient to meet the consequences of the paradigm shift from industrial age to information age (Bates, 2000; Reigeluth, 1996, 1999). Consequently, instructional designers are faced with the challenge of forcing learning situations to fit an instructional design/development model rather than selecting an appropriate model to fit the needs of varying learning situations (Gustafson & Branch, 1997).

One of the possible novelties in instructional methods is the use of games. Indeed, it may possibly be wrong to call games a novelty in education, since young children, by nature, begin to learn through games and playing from their earliest years (Rieber, 1996). However, as they grow up, their play and games are being replaced by formal education, the transition of which does not always—especially nowadays—seem to be a sharp one to the extent that games are being used also in some educational environments, yet their success is questionable or at least not rigorously established. In another sense the use of games in education is not so much a novelty, because its history may be traced back well over a thousand years (Dempsey, Lucassen, Haynes, & Casey, 1998). It is now known that even in times before history, games and dramatic performances as representations of real life were effective as teaching tools. In our modern day, with the new technological advancements, I strongly believe that traditional games have been replaced by electronic games, and, in a similar manner, dramatic representations of old have been transformed into role-playing in simulation environments. Hence, electronic games and simulations have begun to enter contemporary formal education. In addition, the "already-present" new generation of learners have grown up with ever-present games. Prensky (2001) refers to them as the digital natives of the "game generation" (p. 65). He states that this new generation is different from the "digital immigrants" (people born before games were digital and ubiquitous) resulting from their different life experiences with games as a part of the "new media socialization" (Calvert & Jordan, 2001; Prensky, 2001, p. 65). Digital natives who play a lot of games are provided with skills, such as dealing with large amounts of information quickly even at the early ages, using alternative ways to get information, and finding solutions to their own problems through new communication paths. The new "game generation" prefers doing many things simultaneously by using various paths toward the same goal, rather than doing one thing at a time following linear steps. They are less likely to get stuck with frustration when facing a new situation; on the contrary they push themselves into a new situation without knowing anything about it and prefer being active, learning by trial and error, and figuring things out by themselves rather than by reading or listening. Lastly, they want to be treated as "creators and doers" rather than "receptacles to be filled with the content." Hence, the game generation is also referred to as the "intellectual-problem-solving-oriented generation" (Prensky, 2001, p. 76).

When the above issues are considered, it leads to three main bodies of questions, which shape the main focus and scope of this chapter:

1. What are games and simulations? What makes something a game or simulation? What are their educational uses? Do they really have an effect on learning?

2. What is happening in the instructional design/development (IDD) field? Is there a place for games and simulations in both the theory and the practices of IDD?

3. If games and simulations are useful educational tools, how can they be used in education? How can instructional designers take them into account, while designing learning environments? Are there any instructional design/development models (IDDMs) that would light up an instructional designer's path, guiding their journey to integrate games and simulations into their designs?

Games and Simulations: What are They?

Games and simulations are often referred to as experiential exercises (Gredler, 1996), in which there is "learning how to learn" that provides something more than "plain thinking:" beyond thinking (Turkle, 1984). Prensky (2001) defines games as "organized play" (p. 119). Heinich, Molenda, Russell, and Smaldino (2002) define a game as "an activity, in which participants follow prescribed rules that differ from those of real life [while] striving to attain a challenging goal" (p. 10). Dempsey, Rasmussen, and Lucassen (1996) define gaming in a basic sense as "any overt instructional or learning format that involves competition and is rule-guided" (p. 4). In my opinion, (except for Prensky's [2001] later and incessant emphasis throughout his book) these definitions are lacking two vital elements: fun and creativity. So my own definition of "game" becomes "a competitive activity that is creative and enjoyable in its essence, which is bounded by certain rules and requires certain skills."

As put forth by many researchers, several game genres can be distinguished, such as action, puzzle, educational, fighting/combat, sports, racing, role play/adventure, flight, shoot'em, platform games, business, board, word, general entertainment, fantasy violence, human violence, non-violent sports, sports violence, and simulation games (Alessi & Trollip, 2001; Funk, Hagan, & Schimming, 1999; Media Analysis Laboratory, 1999; Prensky, 2001; Yelland & Lloyd, 2001). Many researchers also assert that games have some characteristics such as "one or more players (decision makers), rules of play, one or more goals that the players are trying to reach, conditions introduced by chance, a spirit of competition, a strategy or pattern of action-choices to be taken by the players, a feedback system for revealing the state of the game, and a winning player or team" (Price, 1990, p. 52), "turn-taking, fantasy, equipment, and some combination of skill versus luck" (Alessi & Trollip, 2001, p. 271). Furthermore, Price (1990) categorizes "educational" games as academic games, which aim to teach and provide practice, while motivating the learners, and life simulation games, which are context simulation games including strict rules in real-life contexts, or open-ended life simulation games including flexible rules and goals in social science contexts.

A simulation is defined as an interactive abstraction or simplification of some real life (Baudrillard, 1983; Heinich et al., 2002), or any attempt to imitate a real or imaginary environment or system (Alessi & Trollip, 2001; Reigeluth & Schwartz, 1989; Thurman, 1993). It is "a simulated real life scenario displayed on the computer, which the student has to act upon" (Tessmer, Jonassen, & Caverly, 1989, p. 89).

Although both games and simulations are terms that refer to different concepts, they have common characteristics, too. On the surface, both contain a model of some kind of system, and in both of them learners can observe the consequences of their actions, such as changes occurred in variable, values, or specific actions (Gredler, 1996; Jacobs & Dempsey, 1993). Jacobs and Dempsey (1993) state that the distinction between simulation and games is often blurred, and that many recent articles in this area refer to a single "simulation game" entity. One of them is Prensky (2001), who argues that "depending on what it is doing, a simulation can be a story, it can be a game, [and] it can be a toy" (p. 128).

Gredler (1996) identifies three important differences between the deep structure of games and simulations. Instead of attempting to win the objective of games, participants in a simulation are executing serious responsibilities with privileges that result in associated consequences.

Secondly, the event sequence of a game is typically linear, whereas, according to Gredler (1996), a simulation sequence is non-linear. The player or a team in many games respond to a content-related question and either advance or do not advance depending on the answer, which is repeated for each player or team at each turn. However, in a simulation, participants are confronted with different problems, issues, or events caused mainly by their prior decisions made at each decision point.

The third difference is the mechanisms that determine the consequences to be conveyed for different actions taken by the players. Games consist of rules that describe allowable moves, constraints, privileges, and penalties for illegal (non-permissible) actions. The rules may be totally imaginative, unrelated to real world or events. In contrast, a simulation is based on dynamic set(s) of relationships among several variables that change over time and reflect authentic causal processes. That is, the processes should possess, embody, and result in verifiable relationships.

According to Prensky (2001) simulations and games differ in that, "simulations are not, in and of themselves games. In order to become games, they need additional structural elements—fun, play, rules, a goal, winning, competition, etc." (p. 212). Depending on these definitions and characteristics, as an attempt to derive a general term, I will use *game-like learning environments*, which will be defined as "authentic or simulated places, where learning is fostered and supported especially by seamless integration of motivating game elements, such as challenge, curiosity, and fantasy."

Effects of Games and Simulations on Learning

Although the literature on games and simulations is accumulating day by day, the issue of whether games influence students' learning in a positive way is still vague. For instance, Molenda and Sullivan (2003) state that among problem solving and integrated learning systems, games and simulations are among the least used technology applications in education. However, there are some studies that describe the effects of games and simulations on discovery learning strategies; problem solving skills and computer using skills; and effects on students' intellectual, visual, motor skills and indicate how games and simulations impact student engagement and interactivity, which are important for learning environments.

Cole (1996) has shown that long-term game playing has a positive effect on students' learning (cited in Subrahmanyam, Greenfield, Kraut, & Gross, 2001, p. 16). Gredler states that intellectual skills and "cognitive strategies" are acquired during academic games (1996, p. 525). However, she also states that certain games require only simple skills such as recall of verbal or visual elements rather than higher-order skills and as a result, provide environments for winning by guessing (Gredler, 1994). Similarly, Prensky (2001) admits that especially with the non-stop speedy games, the opportunity to stop and think critically about the experience is lessened (Prensky, 2001; Provenzo, 1992). Csikszentmihalyi (1990) also supports the belief that during an enjoyable activity, insufficient amount of time is devoted for thinking and reflection.

Games are claimed to have cognitive development effects on visual skills including "spatial representation," "iconic skills," and "visual attention" (Greenfield, 1984, cited in Prensky, 2001, p. 45; Subrahmanyam et al., 2001, p. 13). Greenfield, deWinstanley, Kilpatrick, and Kaye (1994) claim that as players become more skilled in games, their visual attention becomes proportionally better.

Critical thinking and problem-solving skills (Rieber, 1996), drawing meaningful conclusions (Price, 1990), some inductive discovery skills like observation, trial, and error and hypothesis testing (Gorriz & Medina, 2000; Greenfield, 1984, cited in Prensky, 2001; Price, 1990), and several other strategies of exploration (Prensky, 2001; Provenzo, 1992) were other positive effects of games on learning.

Subrahmanyam et al. (2001) articulate that playing computer games can provide training opportunities for gaining computer literacy, which is consistent with Prensky's (2001) statement that games can be used in order to help people gain some familiarity with the computer hardware.

Games motivate learners to take responsibility for their own learning, which leads to intrinsic motivation contained by the method itself (Rieber, 1996). Malone (1980) and Malone and Lepper (1987) define four characteristics of games that contribute to increases in motivation and eagerness for learning. These are challenge, fantasy, curiosity, and control. Challenges in a game tend to fight students' boredom and keep them engaged with the activity by means of adjusted levels of difficulty. Fantasy in a game increases enthusiasm by providing an appealing imaginary context, whereas curiosity offers interesting, surprising, and novel contexts that stimulate students' needs to explore the unknown. Finally, the control characteristic gives learners the feeling of self-determination.

According to Rieber (1996), gaming elements have a relationship with enjoyable activities that enable the "flow" stage, a term coined by Csikszentmihalyi (1990). Thus, gaming activities have the potential to engross the learner into a state of flow and consequently cause better learning through focus and pleasant rewards (Prensky, 2001), while increasing their motivation and attainment (Rosas, Nussbaum, Cumsille, Marianov, Correa, Flores, et al., 2003).

Other characteristics that ensure the effectiveness of game-based learning are their engagement and interactivity, and active participation (Gredler, 1996; Prensky, 2001; Price, 1990; Provenzo, 1992). Games provide a great deal of highly interactive feedback, which is crucial to learning (Gredler, 1994; Malone, 1980; Prensky, 2001; Rieber, 1996). "Practice and feedback, learning by doing, learning from mistakes, goal oriented learning, discovery learning, task-based learning, question-based learning, situated learning, role playing, coaching, constructivist learning, multi-sensory learning" are applicable interactive learning techniques, when learning through games (Prensky, 2001, p. 157).

Educational Use of Games and Simulations

There is evidence that the use of games as instructional tools dates back to 3000 B.C. in China (Dempsey, Lucassen, Haynes, & Casey, 1998). Nevertheless, games and simulations did not become a part of the formal field of instructional design until the early 1970s, despite their entrance into the educational scene in the late 1950s (Gredler, 1996). Seels and Richie (1994) report that in those times audio-visual specialists saw the potential of games and simulations but not of video or electronic games.

Although computer games can be considered powerful tools for increasing learning (Dempsey, Lucassen, et al., 1998; Dempsey, Rasmussen, & Lucassen, 1996), there are two major problems that instructional designers encounter. One is that there are no available comprehensive design paradigms and the other is the lack of well-designed research studies (Gredler, 1996). Since the first problem will be handled in the following sections, at this point, it is proper to proceed with a discussion on the second problem.

While the literature on games and simulations is growing, a majority of the research studies report on perceived student reactions preceded by vague descriptions of games and simulations or on comparisons of simulations versus regular classroom instruction (Gredler, 1996). The more important questions that need further research remain unanswered (Dede, 1996; Dempsey, Lucassen, et al., 1998): How to incorporate games into learning environments? How do students learn best through games and simulations? What are the significant impacts of games and simulations on learning that differentiate them from other forms of online teaching?

Rieber (1996) argues that technological innovations provide new opportunities for interactive learning environments that can be integrated with and validated by theories of learning. Prensky (2001) underscores the need for change in instructional design by claiming that much of the instruction currently provided through computer assisted instruction and Web-based technologies does not contribute to learning, rather it subtracts. People do not want to be included in such learning "opportunities" offered via "new wine into old bottles" innovative technologies, unless they have to, since these learning "opportunities" possess still the same boring content and same old fashioned strategy as traditional education (pp. 92-93). Prensky (2001) puts forth that learning can best take place when there is high engagement, and he proposes "digital-game-based learning," which has potential for achievement of the necessary "high learning" through "high engagement" (p. 149). He states that high engagement, interactive learning process, and the way the two are put together will guarantee the sound working of digital game-based learning (Prensky, 2001).

Rieber (1996) states that, "Research from education, psychology, and anthropology suggests that play is a powerful mediator for learning throughout a person's life" (p. 43). In line with this statement, Prensky (2001) further claims that, "Play has a deep biological, evolutionarily important, function, which has to do specifically with learning" (p. 112). However, despite some important psychological and cultural relationships to games, the education profession has long been hesitant about the value of games as an instructional tool or strategy (Rieber, 1996). For instance, as the prevailing philosophy in education has changed over time, the attitude toward play changed accordingly, too. "In one era, play can be viewed as a productive and natural means of engaging children in problem-solving and knowledge construction, but in another era it can be viewed as wasteful diversion from a child's studies" (Rieber, 1996, p. 44).

The *seamless* integration of beneficial elements of games and simulations into learning, in an endeavor to create "game-like learning environments" seems promising and worth trying. Before discussing the instructional designer's concerns and reviewing instructional design/development models, I will first provide a brief look into the "instructional design/development" field to catch a glimpse of what is going on there.

Instructional (Systems) Design/Development (IDD)

The need for the development of a linking science and the need for a "middleman" between learning theory and educational practice was first asserted by John Dewey in 1900 (as cited in Reigeluth, 1983), yet, when the origins of instructional design procedures are traced, it is seen that the first research efforts date back only to the time of World War II (Dick, 1987). Moreover, the need for a "middleman" was also put forth by Glaser (1971), who stated that an instructional designer must perform the interplay between theory, research, and application.

As the title seems to imply (i.e., is it "design" or "development," and is it "instruction" or an "instructional system"?), there is no consensus about the name and the definition of, what I choose to call "instructional design/development (IDD)." Basically, my concern here is "instructional design" as an activity rather than the most accurate name that refers to this activity. However, the term IDD is used here as a term of convenience, since it encompasses the width and the depth of these activities in a fairly acceptable manner. The literature shows an interchangeable use of instructional design, instructional systems design (ISD), instructional development (ID), and even instructional technology (IT) (Gustafson & Branch, 1997; Reigeluth, 1983; Schrock, 1995; Seels & Richie, 1994). Even though several attempts have been made to derive standardized definitions and terms (Gustafson & Branch, 1997; Schiffman, 1995; Seels & Richie, 1994), the results have not been widely adopted and used in the literature.

Reigeluth (1983) characterizes his views on instructional design as "concerned with understanding, improving and applying methods of instruction" (p. 7), contrasted with instructional development as being "concerned with understanding, improving and applying methods of *creating* [italics added] instruction" (p. 8). Furthermore, he states that instructional design produces knowledge of optimal blueprints about methods of instruction, whereas instructional development optimizes the process of developing the instruction and encompasses design, implementation, and formative evaluation activities. He also emphasizes that design theories are different from descriptive theories due to their prescriptive nature, in the sense that they offer guidelines, without attempting to spell out every detail and allow no variation (Reigeluth, 1983, 1997, 1999). On the other hand, Gustafson and Branch (1997) accept the Seels and Richie (1994) definition, which is "an organized procedure that includes steps of analyzing, designing, developing, implementing, and evaluating instruction" (p. 31). However, they declare that Seels and Richie (1994) have coined this definition for ISD, instead of instructional development. Shrock (1995) has also made a definition similar to that of Seels and Richie's (1994), yet for instructional development. Gustafson and Branch (1997) further characterize instructional development as "a complex, yet purposeful process that promotes creativity, interactivity and cyberneticity [communication and control processes]" (p. 18).

What is an Instructional Design/Development Model (IDDM)?

Gustafson and Branch (1997) define model as "simple representation of more complex forms, processes, and functions of physical phenomena or ideas" (p. 17). It provides a visual representation of an abstract concept (Schindelka, 2003), helps people to "conceptualize representations of reality" (Gustafson & Branch, 1997, p. 17), and "explains ways of doing" (Gustafson & Branch, 1998, p. 3).

In line with Reigeluth's (1983) opinions about instructional development, Gustafson and Branch (1997) have gone a step further and stated that instructional development models have at least four components, which are "analysis of the setting and learner needs; design of a set of specifications for an effective, efficient and relevant learner environment; development of all learner and management materials; and evaluation of the results of the development both formatively and summatively" (p. 12). They have also added that a fifth activity could be the distribution and monitoring of the learning environment across various settings, over an extended period of time. These components help instructional development models serve as "conceptual and communications tool" (p. 13). Gros, Elen, Kerres, Merriënboer, and Spector (1997, p. 48) state that, "instructional design models have the ambition to provide a link between learning theories and the practice of building instructional systems."

The origins of instructional design procedures can be traced to the first research efforts dating back to World War II (Dick, 1987). Gustafson and Branch (1997) state that instructional development models first appeared in 1960s and since then an increasing number of models have been published in the literature. Seels and Richie (1994) highlight the simplicity of the first instructional design models, which had only to master a few techniques and a fundamentally linear theory, since instructional science was an infant and many of the tools and theories of today were not conceivable. Since then, a variety of developments and trends have impacted instructional design practices (Reiser, 2001). However, the introduction of microcomputers in the 1980s has exerted the most significant effect on instructional design practices. With the advent of desktop digital media and the subsequent arrival of worldwide Internet access, discussions began for the need to develop new models of instructional design to accommodate the capability and interactivity of this technology (Merrill, Li, & Jones, 1990). Wide variations have emerged in models in terms of their purposes, amount of detail provided, degree of linearity in which they are applied, and quantity, quality, and relevance of the accompanying operational tools (Gustafson & Branch, 1997). This paradigmatic change has contributed to the instability of the terminology and shows that the field of IDD is not static; it has evolved in time and is still evolving. This is good, since a field that becomes static and uncreative is likely to become less prominent (Seels & Richie, 1994).

Since the 1990s, six factors have had significant impact on instructional design practices (Reiser, 2001). These are performance technology movement, constructivism, Electronic Performance Support Systems (EPSSs), rapid prototyping, increasing use of Internet for distance education/distance learning, and knowledge management endeavors. However, to provide an account of these factors is out of the scope of this chapter, and Reiser's work should be consulted for a comprehensive discussion.

Criticisms About the Current State of IDD and IDDMs

Gustafson and Branch (1997) assert that there has been a cumulative increase in the number of published instructional development models since the 1960s. However, there seems to be little uniqueness in the structure of these models, although they are abundant in number. In other words, as time passes, models are enhanced in quantity, but not in quality (Gustafson & Branch, 1997, 1998).

Some writers have argued that the traditional instructional design models are resistant against substantial changes (Rowland, 1992) and are only fit to narrow, well-defined, and static scenarios, because they are process-oriented rather than people-oriented, and use clumsy, bureaucratic, and linear approaches (Gordon & Zemke, 2000; Jonassen, 1990; McCombs, 1986; Tripp & Bichelmeyer, 1990; You, 1993; Zemke & Rossett, 2002). Contrasting with these criticisms, others contend that over time, problems become apparent in the traditional ISD model and important and permanent modifications and additions are performed (Clark, 2002; Schiffman, 1995; Shrock, 1995).

The procedural stratifications and time-consuming practices of traditional ISD models have drawn much of the criticism. As an alternative, thinking of instructional development as a set of concurrent, overlapping procedures might help both to speed up the process and to overcome many limitations of the traditional instructional design models. One of the most well known examples is "prototyping" or "rapid prototyping," which is a design approach borrowed from the discipline of software engineering (Tripp & Bichelmeyer, 1990).

Both Prensky (2001) and Rowland, Parra, and Basnet (1994) assert that often instructional design is done by the book or by using an overly rationalistic view, which in turn produces "boring cookie-cutter outcomes" (Prensky, 2001, p. 83). These writers emphasize that a move toward more creative methodologies is necessary, in order to lead to flexible, creative solutions to unique situations.

Since the existing design theories have not reached perfection, there is need for new theories and models that will guide instructional designers in the use of ideas about learning founded in human development and cognitive science, and in taking advantage of new information technologies as tools for feedback and assessment or for instruction in general (Reigeluth & Frick, 1999).

Table 1. Key alterations with the shift from Industrial Age to Information Age

Industrial Age	Information Age
Industrial Society (Bates, 2000)	Information Society
Bureaucratic organization	Team-based organization
Centralized control	Autonomy with accountability
Adversarial relationships	Cooperative relationships
Autocratic decision making	Shared decision making
Compliance	Initiative
Conformity	Diversity
One-way communications	Networking
Compartmentalization	Holism
Parts-oriented	Process-oriented
Planned obsolescence	Total quality
CEO or boss "King"	Customer (learner) as "King"

Apart from technological changes, Reigeluth (1999) discusses a paradigm shift in education and training, a major shift from Industrial Age to Information Age thinking, which implies shifts in various attributes for instruction (see Table 1).

The change in paradigms, according to Reigeluth (1996), requires a shift from standardization to customization. New models of IDD need to make possible a unique learning experience for each learner, rather than trying to produce a single, clearly defined outcome for all learners. The need for customization is also consistent with Winn's (1997) and Jonassen Hennon, Ondrusek, Samouilova, Spaulding, Yueh et al.'s (1997) criticisms about the positivist basis of ID models. Both disapproved the way that a linear design process assumes the predictability of human behavior, the closed and isolated nature of learning situations, the responsibility for learning belonging to the instructor rather than the learner. New IDD models need to reflect the dynamic, complex, and non-linear nature of the design process, the changing contexts of learning in digital game-based environments, and the many and varied cognitive, emotional, and social differences in abilities among learners.

New Trends in IDD and IDDMs

This section explores a number of new alternative approaches that have been suggested for the improvement of the IDD process. Jonassen et al. (1997) suggest adapting new scientific models, such as hermeneutics, fuzzy logic, and chaos theory. Reigeluth (1996, 1999) suggests customized, learner-centered and social-contextual design conducted by user-designers, which is also articulated by Winn's (1997) matched timing of design and use of instructional material and Winn's (1996) statement of necessity to get help from the Human Computer Interaction discipline. Lastly, Hoffman (1997) offers the ideas of plasticity and modularity as a result of linking Reigeluth's (1983) Elaboration Theory (ET) and hypermedia. There are further suggestions, such as Gros et al.'s (1997) multimedia-facilitated IDD models that depend on multi-perspectival presentation of knowledge or Wilson, Teslow, and Osman-Jouchoux' (1995), and Wilson's (1997) adaptation of postmodernism to IDD field, which need to be further explored.

Hermeneutics emphasizes the importance of the socio-historical context in mediating the meanings of individuals creating and decoding texts; this implies that IDD must strive to introduce gaps of understanding, which allow the learner to create his/her own meanings (Jonassen et al., 1997). Other chapters in this book introduce the idea that new massively multiplayer online learning environments entail new social processes that align well with social constructivist, hermeneutic philosophy, and methods.

Chaos theory finds order in the chaos of natural structures through looking for self-similarity and self-organization, patterns that are repeated at different levels of complexity through a structure, for example, a fractal. It can offer two alternatives to IDD: first complex, dynamic IDDMs that adjust to learners on the fly, and secondly due to its sensitiveness to initial conditions, consideration of learners' emotions, and related self-awareness, besides cognitive skills and self awareness (Cagiltay, 2001; Jonassen et al., 1997).

The last alternative that Jonassen et al. (1997) suggest is fuzzy logic. Fuzzy logic is based on the idea that reality can rarely be represented accurately in a bivalent manner. Rather, it is multivalent, having many in-between values, which do not have to belong to mutually exclusive sets. It is a departure from classical two-valued sets and logic, that uses "soft" linguistic (e.g., large, hot, tall) system variables and a continuous range of truth values in the closed interval [0, 1], rather than strict binary (True or False) decisions and assignments. Since the sequence of events within a project depends on human decisions, which is based on approximate reasoning of human beings, fuzzy logic can be well applied to IDD process.

The fuzzy logic perspective implies for IDD that behavior can be better understood probabilistically, using continua, rather than binary measures. Instead of having strictly bounded and sequenced phases, having intertwined phases, which have flexible and fuzzy boundaries, would be more advantageous in that it would allow designers to move freely in between phases throughout the entire IDD process. Jonassen et al. (1997) state that the more one moves away from deterministic approaches to thinking and designing toward more probabilistic ways of thinking, the more useful it becomes in providing methods for assessing "real-life" issues, where things are not black-and-white, but rather any number of different shades of color across the spectrum. Jonassen et al. (1997) further state that it is impossible to predict, let alone describe, what will happen in learning situations due to the elusive and complex nature of human consciousness, which is also consistent with Winn's (1996) opinion that although instructional designers would like them to do otherwise, people think "irrationally," and reason "implausibly." Both of these statements support the main definition of fuzzy logic. However, both researchers' studies lack more specific facets of fuzzy logic. More specifically, the set-theoretic facet of fuzzy logic implies the non-linear, dynamic IDDM phases, which have "fuzzy" rather than strict boundaries. This provides freedom for instructional designers to move back and forth throughout the design process and even conduct more than one activity at a time.

Depending on the previously mentioned shift to Information Age, Reigeluth (1999) also suggests an alternative to the linear stages of the ID process. The entire process cannot be known in advance, so designers are required to do "just-in-time analysis" (p. 15), synthesis, evaluation, and change at every stage in the ID process. However, this is not a newcomer to the field, since learner-centeredness and parallel process have been articulated by Heinich (1973) a long time ago (cited in Winn, 1996). Reigeluth (1999) further states that to be capable to meet the demands of the Information Age, the instructional designer should become more aware of the broader social context, within which the instruction takes place, and a point that is also made by various researchers as well (Dede, 1996; Jonassen et al., 1997; Kember & Murphy, 1995; Richey, 1995; Tessmer & Richey, 1997). For example, the instructional designer might consult more broadly with stakeholder groups to reach a common vision of the final instruction and the means to develop it. The social context can expand to include the learners, consistent with Kember and Murphy's (1995) suggestion that linking the learners to designers supports iterative improvement.

Lastly, Hoffman (1997) offered plasticity and modularity as a result of linking Reigeluth's (1983) Elaboration Theory (ET) and hypermedia. He states that the Web-like linking of ideas that characterizes hypermedia is more alike to the functioning of human cognition than is the traditional linear structure found in much educational programming. He further asserted that this kind of model for IDD could lead to the possibility of modularity and plasticity, which would bring along the ease to make changes in response to learner needs without changing the overall structure of the product and rapid development. It could also allow the customization from the user end to allow a more feasible learner control in like manner to that of a Web structure.

To sum up the whole discussion, IDD and IDDM should find alternative ways to catch up with the changing world of education due to changes in the world itself. The previously mentioned alternatives are thought to be useful and helpful to renew and strengthen the IDD field against the criticisms. It also reveals the fact that like the other disciplines, IDD also begins to evolve into a multidisciplinary discipline. Indeed, Jonassen et al.'s (1997) statement summarizes the main idea:

Like the chiropractor who realigns your spine, we might become healthier from a realignment of our theories. If we admit to and attempt to accommodate some of the uncertainty, indeterminism, and unpredictability that pervade our complex world, we will develop stronger theories and practices that will have more powerful (if not predictable) effects on human learning. (p. 33)

Design Models for Educational Use of Games and Simulations

Theories that inspire game design include "Flow Theory of Optimal Experience" developed by Mihaly Csikszentmihalyi (1990) and "Activity Theory" developed by Alexey Leontiev, a student of Lev Vygotsky (Kaptelinin & Nardi, 1997). Moreover, there are some myths and principles to be taken into consideration during preproduction and production stages of game design proposed by Cerny and John (2002). Yet, there seem to be hardly any design models except for the instructional design/development model tailored for the creation of game-like learning environments, which is called the FIDGE model (Akilli & Cagiltay, 2006). Hence it is clear that there is a need for IDD models that will help and guide educators to design game-like learning environments, "which requires the ability to step outside of a traditional, linear approach to content creation—a process that is counter-intuitive to many teachers" (Morrison & Aldrich, 2003).

This section offers a brief review of different design principles and lessons learned from game design processes before briefly reviewing the FIDGE model. For instance, Amory, Naicker, Vincent, and Adams (1999) identified game elements that students found interesting or useful within different game types, which were the most suitable for their teaching environment and presented a model that links pedagogical issues with these identified game elements.

Prensky (2001) presents various principles for good computer game design and other important digital game design elements. For instance, he claims that good game design is balanced in terms of challenge, creative in terms of originality, focused in terms of fun, and has character in terms of richness and depth that make you remember it, tension that keeps the player playing, and energy that keeps you up all night (pp. 133-134). In addition to these elements, he further asserts that a game should have a clear overall vision with highly adaptive, easy to learn but hard to master structure offered via a very user-friendly interface. It

Table 2. Summary of the FIDGE model (Source: Akilli & Cagiltay, 2006, p. 110; reprinted with permission from IOS Press)

Issue	Its Property
Participants	All of actively participating learners and experts
Team	Multidisciplinary, multi-skilled, game-player experience
Environment	Socio-organizational, cultural
Process	Dynamic, non-linear, fuzzy, creative, enriched by games' and simulations' elements (fantasy, challenge, etc.)
Change	Continuous, evaluation-based
Evaluation	Continuous, iterative, formative, and summative, fused into each phase
Management	Need for a leader in the team and a well-planned and scheduled time management
Technology	Suitable, compatible
Use	By (novice/expert) instructional designers and educational game designers for game-like learning environments and educational games

should have a constant focus on the player experience that keeps the player within the flow state providing exploration, discovery, and frequent rewards, not penalties. It should provide mutual assistance, which means achieving one thing in the game helps to solve another, and the ability to save this progress (pp. 134-136). Lastly, as for digital game-based learning, he provides five questions to be asked during the process of designing, again with his emphasis for fun followed by learning. These five questions can be summarized as the appeal of games in terms of fun for other people too, who are not targeted as audience; the self-perceptions

Figure 1. The overall appearance of the FIDGE model (Source: Akilli & Cagiltay, 2006, p. 112; reprinted with permission from IOS Press; reprinted with permission from IOS Press)

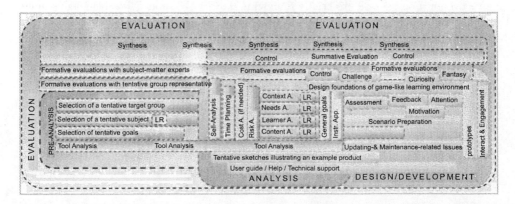

of users as "players" not as "students" or "trainees;" the level of addiction and prominence of the game among the players; the level and rate of improvement at player's skills; and the level of encouragement and enactment for players' reflection on their learning (p. 179).

The "Games-to-Teach" project carried by Massachusetts Institute of Technology proposes design principles for successful games design (MIT, 2003). These are designing educational action games by turning simulations into simulation games; moving from parameters to "power-ups [adjustments made on some traits of the character in the game, such as shifts in player speed, height, and so forth to enhance their attributes];" designing game contexts by identifying contested spaces, identifying opportunities for transgressive play [that enables players to experience new roles via "temporarily letting go of social/cultural rules and mores"]; using information to solve complex problems in simulated environments; providing choices and consequences in simulated worlds; and differentiating roles and distributing expertise in multiplayer games.

The most recent study on the subject with a promising design/development model is the "FIDGE model" (Akilli & Cagiltay, 2006). The model consists of dynamic phases with fuzzy boundaries, through which instructional designers move in a non-linear manner. The model's foundation in the fuzzy logic concept leads to a visualization of the model that is unlike traditional "boxes-and-arrows" representations (see Figure 1). There are two other sets of principles that underlie the model, which are related to socio-organizational issues for the design team and to the instructional design/development process itself. Table 2 summarizes the model in its essence.

All of these studies deserve appreciation, since educational games are mostly classified as "boring" by students. Moreover, they also show that endeavors are being suffered for and steps are being taken toward what Kirriemuir (2002) emphasized: "Computer games provide a medium that engages people for long periods of time, and gamers usually return to the same game many times over. There are obvious lessons here for the developers of digitally-based educational, learning and training materials."

Conclusion

This chapter has provided a brief theoretical framework for the educational use of games and simulations and their effect on learning. It reviewed and addressed some of the main criticisms and new trends in the IDD and IDDM fields.

The characteristics of the "game generation," the importance of games for education, and criticisms about IDDMs' failure to meet these changing needs lead to the conclusion that instructional designers should strive to seamlessly integrate game elements into their designs and to create game-like learning environments, so that they can armor students for the future and build powerful learning into their designs. However, there seems to be a little number of design guidelines, and only one IDD model exists in the literature, to guide instructional designers through this painstaking process, which at the same time provides an already existent but newly discovered playground for the practitioners in the field.

New IDD models are needed to help designers create game-like learning environments that can armor students for the future and build powerful learning into their designs.

References

Akilli, G. K., & Cagiltay, K. (2006). An instructional design/development model for game-like learning environments: The FIDGE model. In M. Pivec (Ed.), *Affective and emotional aspects of human-computer interaction game-based and innovative learning approaches* (Vol. 1, pp. 93-112). Amsterdam, The Netherlands: IOS Press.

Alessi, S. M., & Trollip, S. R. (2001). *Multimedia for learning: Methods and development* (3rd ed.). Boston: Allyn and Bacon Publication.

Amory, A., Naicker, K., Vincent, J., & Adams, C. (1999). The use of computer games as an educational tool: Identification of appropriate game types and game elements. *British Journal of Educational Technology, 30*(4), 311-321.

Bates, A. W. (2000). *Managing technological change. Strategies for college and university leaders.* San Francisco: Jossey-Bass.

Baudrillard, J. (1983). *Simulations.* New York: Semiotext[e].

Cagiltay, K. (2001). A design/development model for building electronic performance support systems. In M. Simonson & C. Lamboy (Eds.), *Annual Proceedings of Selected Research and Development [and] Practice Papers presented at the 24th National Convention of the Association for Educational Communications and Technology*, Atlanta, GA (pp. 433-440). Bloomington, IN: Association for Educational Communications and Technology. (ERIC Document Reproduction Service No: ED 470175).

Calvert, S. L., & Jordan, A. B. (2001). Children in the digital age. *Applied Developmental Psychology, 22*(1), 3-5.

Cerny, M., & John, M. (2002, June). Game development. Myth vs. method. *Game Developer Magazine*, 32-36.

Clark, R. C. (2002). The new ISD: Applying cognitive strategies to instructional design. *Performance Improvement Journal, 41*(7), 8-14.

Clark, R. E. (1983). Reconsidering research on learning from media. *Review of Educational Research, 53*(4), 445-459.

Clark, R. E. (1994a). Media will never influence learning. *Educational Technology Research & Development, 42*(2), 21-29.

Clark, R. E. (1994b). Media and method. *Educational Technology Research & Development, 42*(3), 7-10.

Cohen, D. K., & Ball, D. L. (1990). Relations between policy and practice: A commentary. *Educational Evaluation and Policy Analysis, 12*(3), 331-338.

Csikszentmihalyi, M. (1990). *Flow: The psychology of optimal experience.* New York: Harper Perennial.

Dede, C. (1996). The evolution of constructivist learning environments: Immersion in distributed, virtual worlds. In B. G. Wilson (Ed.), *Constructivist learning environments: Case studies in instructional design* (pp. 165-175). Englewood Cliffs, NJ: Educational Technology Publications.

Dempsey, J. V., Lucassen, B. A., Haynes, L. L., & Casey, M. S. (1998). Instructional applications of computer games. In J. J. Hirschbuhl & D. Bishop (Eds.), *Computer studies: Computers in education* (8th ed., pp. 85-91). Guilford, CT: Dushkin/McGraw Hill.

Dempsey, J. V., Rasmussen, K., & Lucassen, B. (1996). *The instructional gaming literature: Implications and 99 sources* (Tech. Rep. No. 96-1). Mobile, AL: University of South Alabama, College of Education. Retrieved May 30, 2002, from http://www.coe.usouthal.edu/TechReports/TR96_1.PDF

Dick, W. (1987). A history of instructional design and its impact on educational psychology. In J. Glover & R. Ronning (Eds.), *Historical foundations of educational psychology.* New York: Plenum.

Funk, J. B., Hagan, J., & Schimming, J. (1999). Children and electronic games: A comparison of parents' and children's perceptions of children's habits and preferences in a United States Sample. *Psychological Reports, 85*(3), 883-888.

Glaser, R. (1971). The design of instruction. In M. D. Merrill (Ed.), *Instructional design: Readings* (pp. 18-37). Englewood, NJ: Prentice-Hall.

Gordon, J., & Zemke, R. (2000). The attack on ISD. *Training Magazine, 37*(4), 42-53.

Gorriz, C. M., & Medina, C. (2000). Engaging girls with computers through software games. *Communications of the ACM, 43*(1), 42-49.

Gredler, M. E. (1994). *Designing and evaluating games and simulations: A process approach.* Houston, TX: Gulf Publication Company.

Gredler, M. E. (1996). Educational games and simulations: A technology in search of a (research) paradigm. In D. H. Jonassen (Ed.), *Handbook of research for educational communications and technology* (pp. 521-539). New York: Macmillan.

Greenfield, P. M., deWinstanley, P., Kilpatrick, H., & Kaye, D. (1994). Action video games and informal education: Effects on strategies for dividing visual attention [Abstract]. *Journal of Applied Developmental Psychology, 15*(1), 105-123.

Gros, B., Elen, J., Kerres, M., Merriënboer, J., & Spector, M. (1997). Instructional design and the authoring of multimedia and hypermedia systems: Does a marriage make sense? *Educational Technology, 37*(1), 48-56.

Gustafson, K. L., & Branch, R. M. (1997). *Survey of instructional development models* (3rd ed.). Syracuse, NY: ERIC Clearinghouse on Information Resources.

Gustafson, K. L., & Branch, R. M. (1998). Re-visioning models of instructional development. *Educational Technology Research and Development, 45*(3), 73-89.

Heinich, R., Molenda, M., Russell, J. D., & Smaldino, S. E. (2002). *Instructional media and technologies for learning* (7th ed.). Upper Saddle River, NJ: Merrill Prentice Hall.

Hoffman, S. (1997). Elaboration theory and hypermedia: Is there a link? *Educational Technology, 37*(1), 57-64.

Jacobs, J. W., & Dempsey, J. V. (1993). Simulation and gaming: Fidelity, feedback and motivation. In J. V. Dempsey & G. C. Sales (Eds.), *Interactive instruction and feedback* (pp. 197-228). Englewood Cliffs, NJ: Educational Technology Publications.

Jonassen, D. H. (1990). Thinking technology: Chaos in instructional design. *Educational Technology, 30*(2), 32-34.

Jonassen, D. H., Hennon, R. J., Ondrusek, A., Samouilova, M., Spaulding, K. L., Yueh, H. P., et al. (1997). Certainty, determinism, and predictability in theories of instructional design: Lessons from science. *Educational Technology, 37*(1), 27-33.

Kaptelinin, V., & Nardi, B. A. (1997). *Activity theory: Basic concepts and applications.* Retrieved October 11, 2003, from http://www.acm.org/sigchi/chi97/proceedings/tutorial/bn.htm/

Kember, D., & Murphy, D. (1995). The impact of student learning research and the nature of design on ID fundamentals. In B. Seels (Ed.), *Instructional design fundamentals: A reconsideration* (pp. 99-112). Englewood Cliffs, NJ: Educational Technology Publications.

Kirriemuir, J. (2002). Video gaming, education and digital learning technologies [Online]. *D-lib Magazine, 8*(2). Retrieved May 12, 2003, from http://www.dlib.dlib.org/february02/kirriemuir/02kirriemuir.html

Kozma, R. B. (1991). Learning with media. *Review of Educational Research, 61*(2), 179-211.

Kozma, R. B. (1994). Will media influence learning? Reframing the debate. *Educational Technology Research & Development, 42*(2), 7-19.

Malone, T. W. (1980). *What makes things fun to learn? Heuristics for designing instructional computer games.* Paper presented at the Joint Symposium: Association for Computing Machinery Special Interest Group on Small Computers and Special Interest Group on Personal Computers, Palo Alto, CA.

Malone, T. W., & Lepper, M. R. (1987). Making learning fun: A taxonomy of intrinsic motivations for learning. In R. E. Snow & M. J. Farr (Eds.), *Aptitude, learning, and instruction, III: Cognitive and affective process analysis* (pp. 223-253). Hillsdale, NJ: Lawrence Erlbaum Associates.

Massachusetts Institute of Technology (MIT). (2003). Design principles of next-generation digital gaming for education. *Educational Technology, 43*(5), 17-22.

McCombs, B. L. (1986). The instructional systems development (ISD) model: A review of those factors critical to its successful implementation. *Education Communication and Technology Journal, 34*(2), 67-81.

Media Analysis Laboratory, Simon Fraser University, B.C. (1998). Video game culture: Leisure and play of B.C. teens [Online]. Retrieved June 11, 2003, from http://www.mediaawareness.ca/eng/ISSUES/VIOLENCE/RESOURCE/reports/vgames.html

Merrill, M. D., Li, Z., & Jones, M. K. (1990). Limitations of first generations instructional design. *Educational Technology, 30*(1), 7-11.

Molenda, M., & Sullivan, M. (2003). Issues and trends in instructional technology: Treading water. In M. A. Fitzgerald, M. Orey, & R. M. Branch (Eds.), *Educational Media and Technology Yearbook 2003* (pp. 3-20). Englewood, CO: Libraries Unlimited.

Morrison, J. L., & Aldrich, C. (2003). Simulations and the learning revolution: An interview with Clark Aldrich. *The Technology Source.* Retrieved August 11, 2003, from http://64.124.14.173/default.asp?show=article&id=2032

Prensky, M. (2001). *Digital game-based learning*. New York: McGraw-Hill.

Price, R. V. (1990). *Computer-aided instruction: A guide for authors*. Pacific Grove, CA: Brooks/Cole Publishing Company.

Provenzo, E. F. (1992). The video generation. *The American School Board Journal, 179*(3), 29-32.

Reigeluth, C. M. (1983). Instructional design: What is it and why is it? In C. M. Reigeluth (Ed.), *Instructional-design theories and models: An overview of their current status* (pp. 3-36). Hillsdale, NJ: Lawrence Erlbaum Associates.

Reigeluth, C. M. (1996). A new paradigm of ISD? *Educational Technology, 36*(3), 13-20.

Reigeluth, C. M. (1997). Instructional theory, practitioner needs, and new directions: Some reflections. *Educational Technology, 37*(1), 42-47.

Reigeluth, C. M. (1999). What is instructional-design theory and how is it changing? In C. M. Reigeluth (Ed.), *Instructional-design theories and models (Vol. II): A new paradigm of instructional theory* (pp. 5-29). Mahwah, NJ: Lawrence Erlbaum Associates.

Reigeluth, C. M., & Frick, T. W. (1999). Formative research: Methodology for creating and improving design theories. In C. M. Reigeluth (Ed.), *Instructional-design theories and models (Vol. II): A new paradigm of instructional theory* (pp. 633-652). Mahwah, NJ: Lawrence Erlbaum Associates.

Reigeluth, C., & Schwartz, E. (1989). An instructional theory for the design of computer-based simulations. *Journal of Computer-Based Instruction, 16*(1), 1-10.

Reiser, R. A. (2001). A history of instructional design and technology: Part II: A history of instructional design. *Educational Technology Research & Development, 49*(2), 57-67.

Richey, C. (1995). Trends in instructional design: Emerging theory-based models. *Performance Improvement Quarterly, 8*(3), 96-110.

Richey, R. C. (1997). Agenda-building and its implications for theory construction in instructional technology. *Educational Technology, 37*(1), 5-11.

Rieber, L. P. (1996). Seriously considering play: Designing interactive learning environments based on the blending of microworlds, simulations, and games. *Educational Technology Research and Development, 44*(2), 43-58.

Rosas, R., Nussbaum, M., & Cumsille, P. (2003). Beyond Nintendo: Design and assessment of educational video games for first and second grade students. *Computers & Education, 40*(1), 71-94.

Rowland, G. (1992). What do instructional designers actually do? An initial investigation of expert practice. *Performance Improvement Quarterly, 5*(2), 65-86.

Rowland, G., Parra, M. L., & Basnet, K. (1994). Educating instructional designers: Different methods for different outcomes. *Educational Technology, 34*(6), 5-11.

Russell, T. (2003). *The "No Significant Difference Phenomenon."* Retreived December 10, 2005, from http://teleeducation.nb.ca/nosignificantdifference/

Schiffman, S. S. (1995). Instructional systems design: Five views of the field. In G. Anglin (Ed.), *Instructional Technology: Past, present, and future* (2nd ed., pp. 131-144). Engelwood, CO: Libraries Unlimited.

Schindelka, B. (2003). A framework of constructivist instructional design: Shiny, happy design. *Inoad e-Zine, 3*(1). Retrieved August 18, 2003, from http://www.inroad. net/shindelka0403.html

Seels, B., & Richie, R. (1994). *Instructional technology: The definitions and domains of the field.* Washington, DC: AECT.

Shrock, S. A. (1995). A brief history of instructional development. In G. Anglin (Ed.), *Instructional technology: Past, present, and future (2nd ed.)* (pp. 11-19). Engelwood, CO: Libraries Unlimited.

Subrahmanyam, K., Greenfield, P., Kraut, R., & Gross, E. (2001). The impact of computer use on children's and adolescents' development. *Applied Developmental Psychology, 22*(1), 7-30.

Tessmer, M., Jonassen, D. H., & Caverly, D. (1989). *Non-programmer's guide to designing instruction for microcomputers.* Littleton, CO: Libraries Unlimited.

Tessmer, M., & Richey, R. C. (1997). The role of context in learning and instructional design. *Educational Technology Research and Development, 45*(2), 85-115.

Thurman, R. A. (1993). Instructional simulation from a cognitive psychology viewpoint. *Educational Technology Research and Development, 41*(4), 75-79.

Tripp, S. D., & Bichelmeyer, B. (1990). Rapid prototyping: An alternative instructional design strategy. *Educational Technology Research and Development, 38*(1), 31-44.

Turkle, S. (1984). Video games and computer holding power. In *The second self: Computers and the human spirit* (pp. 64-92). New York: Simon and Schuster.

Wilson, B. G. (1997). The postmodern paradigm. In C. R. Dills & A. A. Romiszowski (Eds.), *Instructional development paradigms* (pp. 63-80). Englewood Cliffs, NJ: Educational Technology Publications.

Wilson, B. G., Teslow, J., & Osman-Jouchoux, R. (1995). The impact of constructivism (and post-modernism) on instructional design fundamentals. In B. B. Seels (Ed.), *Instructional design fundamentals: A reconsideration* (pp. 137-157). Englewood Cliffs, NJ: Educational Technology Publications.

Winn, W. (1996). Cognitive perspectives in psychology. In D. H. Jonassen (Ed.), *Handbook of research for educational communications and technology: A project of the Association for Educational Communications and Technology* (pp. 79-112). New York: Macmillan Library Reference.

Winn, W. (1997). Advantages of a theory-based curriculum in instructional technology. *Educational Technology, 37*(1), 34-41.

Yelland, N., & Lloyd, M. (2001). Virtual kids of the 21st century: Understanding the children in schools today. *Information Technology in Childhood Education Annual, 13*(1), 175-192.

You, Y. (1993). What can we learn from Chaos theory? An alternative approach to instructional systems design. *Educational Technology Research and Development, 41*(3), 17-32.

Zemke, R. E., & Rossett, A. (2002). A hard look at ISD. *Training, 39*(2), 26-34.

Chapter II

Pedagogy in Commercial Video Games

Katrin Becker, University of Calgary, Canada

Abstract

Books, film, television, and indeed every other medium that came before them have been used and sometimes studied as media for the delivery of instruction. Outstanding examples of each medium have been applied to educative purposes with enduring results. Digital games are now also receiving attention in this context. A first step to gaining an understanding for just how a particular medium can be used in education is to study the outstanding examples, regardless of their original purpose. This chapter examines numerous well-known and commercially successful games through the lens of several known and accepted learning theories and styles, using the premise that "good" games already embody sound pedagogy in their designs even if the incorporation of those theories was not deliberate.

Introduction

In spite of their having been around for more than a generation now, video games have still not gained wide acceptance as legitimate media. Perhaps it is worthwhile to raise this argument here, though it would be for neither the first nor the last time, to be sure. Games are a medium of communication and expression and possess some parallels with other forms of media, like film. As Henry Jenkins likes to point out (as in Palmer, 2004), the early days of film were little more than chases and pies in the face, yet just a few years later we see the likes of Chaplin's *The Tramp* (1915) and Griffith's *Birth of a Nation* (1915). Thirty years after the beginning of film we already had recognized works of artistic merit, popular appeal, and lasting significance, such as *Tarzan of the Apes* (1918), *Nanook of the North* [1](1922), *The Jazz Singer* (1927), and *Steamboat Willie* (1928). We also have "stars," such as Charlie Chaplin, Rudolph Valentino, Mary Pickford, and Douglas Fairbanks. Radio and television may have started with somewhat more sombre offerings insofar as their early shows were somewhat less extreme, but they too had both classics and stars within a few years of their introduction, as well as a broad range of offerings in several genres, both fictional and not.

Is it so radical to suggest that early gems of the game industry might already be out there, and we just are not recognizing them? The average age of video game players in 2005 was 30[2] (ESA, 2005), so we can't honestly claim that video games are in the same category as children's toys. Actually, those who are gamers already recognize game "classics," such as *Pong* (1972), *Donkey Kong* (1983), *Tetris* (1988), *Monkey Island* (1990), and others. There are also "stars": some, such as Mario, Lara Croft, and Link from *Zelda* belong to a category that would include Mickey, while others such as Will Wright and Peter Molyneux are more tangible. Although each medium has its own unique qualities, each also shares qualities with the others, making it possible to compare as well as contrast. When we examine media such as radio, film, television, and even popular music, we see some similarities in the ways they have been accepted into society and the objections and resistances that were raised along the way (Williams, 2005). Given that, it must be argued that the medium of the video game deserves a place among these others as a medium of human expression and communication.

Each of the other media mentioned have, in their turn, been applied to educative goals. Each also has, to a greater or lesser extent, been studied as a medium for the delivery of instruction, and although we are far from finished with this study, each has left us with a better understanding of how we might approach a new medium if our primary goal is to educate. Even though many offerings in film, on radio, and in television are designed primarily to entertain, there are also many that are intended to deliver a message—to *teach us something*—and that intent lies at the very heart of instructional design. When looking at how the different forms of modern media have been used this way and which particular instances have been chosen, one notion stands out—the majority of the most remarkable and effective "lessons" taught to us have been created by extraordinarily talented writers, directors, and producers together with their teams. They have, by and large, *not* been created by professional educators or instructional designers. Now, before we go too much further down this particular path, permit me to make a point. Far from trying to sell educators and instructional designers short, we should recognize the opportunities afforded us in studying these outstanding examples of "educational" objects, and try to learn why they have the impact they do. Why do many of Spielberg's movies move us so? Why did the radio show *Amos 'n Andy*'s enjoy such lasting popularity? Why have so many people learned more about American politics and government from the television show *The West Wing* [1999] than they ever did in school? While we are on the subject of the appropriation of media objects for the purposes of education, it might be enlightening to note that the same can be said of literature. It is unlikely that Charles Dickens, Harper Lee, or Miguel De Cervantes had the classroom in mind when they wrote *A Christmas Carol*, *To Kill a Mockingbird*, or *Don Quixote*. They had a lesson or two in mind when they produced these works to be sure, but none were teachers or instructional designers. There is much we can learn from them, not only from the lessons they were teaching, but also from how those messages were crafted.

When we turn our attention to computer and video games, the puzzle climbs to a whole new plane. Not only can we ask what makes this medium's finest examples so compelling, but, what could possibly motivate an individual to log thousands of hours in a game that, when reflected upon, does not appear to offer more than time spent? After watching players for a time, it becomes blatantly obvious that it is not done just for the fun. In fact, games can be excruciatingly frustrating (Johnson, 2005). Clearly there is something else at work beyond pleasure or entertainment. Could it possibly be that at least some of these games fulfill some fundamental human need to learn or to be challenged? While there are exceptions (such as Tetris), modern videogames are often extremely complex, requiring many hours to learn how to play. Somehow, these games manage to hold the players' attention while they fumble through the "learning curve," and then *continue* to hold the players' attention as they approach expertise, all in the same game, sometimes for millions of players[3]. How?

Games are so engaging precisely because they tap into some of the most effective approaches for learning. Successful games teach us to play in the manner we learn best. This is worth study.

With a bit of effort, it is possible to find examples of computer and videogames that embody every single worthwhile learning theory in existence. Whether the "instructional design" was intentional or not, game designers have had to figure out how to keep their audiences interested while they learn the games—and judging by the number of people who willingly pay money for the experience, they appear to have been far more successful than formal education has.

On the other hand, it is one thing to retrofit a learning theory onto a successful game, or even analyze a bad game to see where it fails, and another thing entirely to try and do this in the other direction, namely, to use some learning theory to design a successful game. Although some of us still mean to try and come up with ways to do exactly that, I also suspect we are going to experience similar problems to those experienced in other disciplines (software engineering, film, and fiction come to mind). Some in the field of software engineering have been trying to formally specify "good" software design for 30 years—the dream seems to be that if we can only specify everything (requirements, metrics, documentation, etc.) well enough, we will be able to hire *anyone* to produce sound software, and the specifications and tools will compensate for human lack of skill and talent. The film industry and fiction writers have not taken the same "engineering" approach, but even though movies have been around for over 100 years and books for 500[4], we still have no sure-fire formulas for creating blockbusters and bestsellers. Anyone who thinks we will be able to do this for learning, whether it is using games or not, has not been paying attention.

On Motivation

The will to learn is an intrinsic motive, one that finds both its source and its reward in its own exercise. The will to learn becomes a 'problem' only under specialized circumstances like those of a school, where a curriculum is set, students are confined, and a path fixed. The problems exist not so much in learning itself, but in the fact that what the school imposes often fails to enlist the natural energies that sustain spontaneous learning. (Bruner, 1966, p. 127)

Many factors influence engagement, and in educational contexts teachers have little control over much of this (Lumsden, 1994). However, it is also known that high motivation and engagement are linked to student success (Dev, 1997), or as Donald Norman puts it, "Students learn best when they are motivated, when they care" (Norman, 2004, p. 205). So it behooves us to examine ways in which motivation and engagement can be maximized. Examining games known to be engaging is one way to accomplish this.

It has been established that motivated learners are desirable. "Motivated learners are easy to describe. They are enthusiastic, focused, and engaged. They are interested in and enjoy what they are doing, they try hard, and they persist over time. Their behavior is self-determined, driven by their own volition rather than external forces. Skinner and Belmont (1993) noted that although motivated learners are easy to recognize, they are hard to find, and they are, we would add, hard to create" (Garris, Ahlers, & Driskell, 2002, p. 444). The preceding description fits video gamers quite well, so it would seem reasonable to conclude that video games do in fact motivate players. But then the question becomes, are motivated players also *learners*? At the very least, it could probably be claimed that players learn how to play (and often to beat) the game, but we know that they also learn a great many other things in the process (Gee, 2003; Jenkins, 2002; Koster, 2004; Prensky, 2001a; Squire, 2003). Players are also learners.

Both Piaget (1951) and Bruner (1962) have said that play is important for deep learning, so perhaps they might (have) agree(d) with the previous assertion that players are also learners. In his work on the development of an Australian tall forest game, Bruce Leyland concludes that an important criterion for deep learning in games is the sustained imaginative immersion of the player, and that too many interruptions, either from the game or from external sources interfere (Leyland, 1996). This in turn would suggest that casual (i.e., surface?) play would not necessarily lead to deep learning, but that immersive play would. Once again, games fit the description. No discussion of immersion, of course, would be complete without at least some mention of Csikszentmihalyi's concept of "flow" (1991). Flow is a state that today might be referred to as "being in the zone"—it involves absolute concentration on a task. But flow is not necessary for deep learning. Although flow is sometimes used in connection with fun, having fun is not a requisite condition for being in a state of flow, nor is learning. Raph Koster, in describing his theory of fun suggests that flow is often cited in relation to the exercise of mastery, rather than the original learning (Koster, 2004).

While they may not always be having fun, video game players generally enjoy what they do. It is why they keep doing it. The following is a list of qualities associated with the enjoyment of games. See how well they fit when viewed in the context of learning. Generally speaking, people enjoy games (and learning?) when:

- They can achieve the specified goal, but not too easily.

- The task is perceived to be fair: all participants have a similar chance of "winning," at least at the start.

- The stakes (risk) for failure are not too high, but still present.

- There is sufficient positive feedback (rewards for achievement), which must occur *during* the process and must be *in context* or at least measure progress toward goal.

- There exists negative feedback as well (which also ties in to the idea of fairness).

- There is some element of chance (among other things, this allows people to minimize, or off-load "guilt" of failure to a certain extent, which in turn encourages people to keep trying or to try again).

The approach to be used for a good learning application is in many ways the same as the approach that is used for a successful game[5]. Even though there are some significant differences, the chances that the similarities turn out to be purely coincidental are slim. One key difference often raised is that games are consumer driven, and learning, by and large, is not. When looked at from a different perspective, this is no longer true. In games, the consumer is the player, and yes, the shelf life of a game is determined by the player/consumer. In games, the primary source of funding is the consumer. Even though much has changed in formal education in the last decade or two, and learning may often be student-centered, it is still educator-*driven*. Drawing a closer parallel between who drives games and who drives education requires us to identify the body in the "education business" that is the counterpart to the games business' player, and in formal education that distinction falls in two places: first to government, and only indirectly, tax-payers, and second to the learners (and sometimes teachers). This is an important distinction to be sure, and a thorough examination of this issue is not within the bounds of this chapter, yet at least one notion is worth identifying here: when looking at key ideas for player-driven design of games, "don't waste the player's time" is important (Walpole, 2004), yet the counterpart in education, "don't waste the student's time" is not normally considered. There is much we can learn about learning from games.

The first principle described by James Gee in his discussion of what we can learn about learning from games is that, "all aspects of the learning environment (including the ways in which the semiotic domain is designed and presented) are set up to encourage active and critical, not passive, learning" (Gee, 2003, p. 49). Players then, are also active learners, and games (good ones, at least) embody all of those qualities that Thomas Malone and Mark Lepper (1987), in their landmark work on intrinsic motivation claim are necessary for creating such a state.

How are Video Games Educational?

When taken as a group, those things educators say are important in the design of effective instruction have already been put to practice in "good" commercial games. "Good" here is a bit of a tautology—these games are good because they embody sound learning theories.

However, it turns out that finding examples of good games defined in this way is not very hard. People like Jim Gee (2003) have already said that good games embody sound learning principles (as have various others), but few have actually connected well-known (and loved) existing theories with what is found in games.

Games, Learning, Theories, and Models

Support for the use of games in learning contexts seems to be picking up speed, and the body of research examining the contexts and conditions for the effective use of games as an instructional technology is growing along with it. Some people, like game designer, Raph Koster, have even suggested that learning is really what games are all about (2004). For most of us who are interested in this field, the claim is not, as some may fear, that games are the panacea for all that ails education, but that what we have here is a new instructional technology with exciting potential. One way to substantiate this argument is to demonstrate how effortlessly good games can be shown to fit into multiple widely known and well-accepted instructional approaches. Existing game pedagogy is sound but often unrecognized: good games *already* possess the major components necessary to meet the requirements of sound instruction. The following pages will demonstrate this through an examination of several specific learning theories: Gagné's Nine Events (Gagné, Briggs, & Wager, 1992), Reigeluth's Elaboration Theory (Reigeluth, Merrill, Wilson, & Spiller, 1980), and two more recent works: Bruner's Socio-Cultural Approach to Education (Bruner, 1996), and Merrill's First Principles of Instruction (Merrill, 2002).

Gagné's Nine Events of Instruction

Like many others, Gagné's theory spans both learning and instructional principles. On the learning side, Gagné claims that there are five kinds of learning capabilities: (1) verbal information, both oral and written, (2) intellectual skills involving the manipulation of information in symbolic forms and problem solving, (3) cognitive strategies that involve creativity and control over one's own learning process, (4) motor skills encompassing physical activities, and (5) attitudes that influence personal choice. Each type of capability requires a different approach to instruction. Good games already do this. If for no other reason than to reach the broadest range of consumers, game designers must employ multiple approaches to both aid and challenge players. According to Gagné, "an instructional plan can generate both appropriate environmental stimuli and instructional interactions, and thereby bringing about change in the cognitive structures and operations of the learner" (Anglin, 1995, p. 147). If we were to restate this in plainer terms and superimpose the same ideas onto games, it might sound something like this[6]: the game design must offer both appropriate ingame triggers and hints, and thereby supporting progress in the knowledge and skill of the player so they can complete the game.

Each of Gagné's five categories of learning is well supported in most good games. Verbal information is provided both orally and textually, and even games like *Pokémon* that are targeted at young children (pre-readers), still present information textually. In fact, a growing number of children claim that it is precisely games like *Pokémon* that have helped them to develop their reading skills. Intellectual skills, such as the use of concepts and rules to solve problems (Aronson & Briggs, 1999), are the cornerstone of most strategy games, from Sid Meier's *Civilization* series to games with far less educational appeal, like *Deus Ex*. Cognitive strategies pretty much sum up how players win games: by finding novel solutions to problems, the acquisition of skills and knowledge, and practice and perseverance. A still small, but growing genre of games, like *Dance, Dance Revolution* (DDR) supports the development of gross motor skills. All games require the use of some sort of controller or keypad, thereby helping to develop fine motor skills. However, except in specific areas of need, like perhaps rehabilitation for people recovering from injuries or people with specific disabilities in fine motor control, there is no longer a need to encourage the use of games for the purposes of fine motor skill development—children are doing this for themselves. The last category, that of attitudes (also recognized as the affective learning domain), is central to role-playing games, and it is the essence of most "god games[7]." Sir Peter Molyneux's *Black & White* has not only incorporated ethical and moral dilemmas into the gameplay, the consequences of the player's choices even affect the appearance of the player's onscreen pet.

Direction for the design of instruction that supports the development in these five categories lies in Gagné's well-known "Nine Events of Instruction" (Gagné, 1985; Gagné et al., 1992). Not only do these events provide the necessary conditions for learning, but they also offer guidelines for the appropriate selection of media. Good games meet virtually all the criteria listed. As in all good instruction, the nine events need not be distinct, separately identifiable tasks, as often elements of one "event" can be combined or intertwined with another. This also holds true for other well-accepted instructional technologies, such as goal-based learning (Schank, Kass, & Riesbeck, 1994) and story-telling (Brown, Denning, Groh, & Prusak, 2001; Schank, 1990). For example, gaining attention, explaining the objective, and stimulating recall are often all combined as part of the initial "set-up." The connections between goal-based and story-telling scenarios and the first three events are strong, and exist in full measure in many games.

Gagné's Nine Events Applied to Games

1. **Gaining Attention (Reception):** One implementation of this event in games is what is known as "attract mode;" this is what one sees when a game appears to be playing by itself—it shows elements of the game play and is intended to entice players to play. In arcades, this is necessary to entice players to choose this game over others. It is assumed that once the player inserts his or her money to begin playing, you already *have* the player's attention. At home, this aspect is also addressed through the game's introduction when one begins to play; it is often accompanied by prepared video clips, which are typically of high production quality. This is where the game is set up. An idea borrowed from film and television, and one that works for all kinds of games, the trailer also fulfills the role of gaining attention.

2. **Informing Learners of the Objective (Expectancy):** Explaining the objective is typically part of the back-story and description of the victory condition (how one wins the game). These days, players often know quite a bit about the back-story and the objective long before they start to play. It is presented in various forms—in the

trailer, through advertising, and at the start of the game. If the game is a "numbered game" (a sequel) there is usually an assumption that the basic premise will be similar to the previous game. *Pikmin*, for example, is about Captain Olimar, who crashes on an alien planet and must find and reassemble the parts of ship so he can return home. He, of course, must face various challenges and take advantage of opportunities along the way. The sequel, *Pikmin 2*, has Captain Olimar returning to the same planet (since, presumably he succeeded in his earlier mission) to collect treasures to bring home.

In the case of licensed games, that is, those where the story line and/or characters are based on a pre-existing story, movie, cartoon, comic, and so forth, the back story is usually pre-determined also. It would be assumed, for example, that a game based on the *Spiderman* comic book character (or movie) would involve fighting crime, and that the main character would look and act in a particular way and have particular abilities as well as weaknesses.

Given the culture that already exists around video games, information about the objectives of games and approaches for play are becoming part of what could be described as basic game literacy. In the same way that most school children know what to expect from a math text by the time they reach middle school, they also know what to expect from a strategy game, a first-person shooter, a puzzle game, and so on. Children become encultured to the format and basic premise that goes along with the genre and character of a game. Those who are not yet familiar quickly become informed by their peers, or by learning about the game in advance on the Internet.

3.   **Stimulating Recall of Prior Learning (Retrieval):** Again, the back-story associated with the introduction to a game typically provides the frame of reference: sequels and new levels may refer back to things learned, achieved, or discovered in previous levels/versions. Even when it is not explicitly noted in the game, by now virtually all game players are aware of the concept of levels (basic game literacy again), where each level requires players to build on knowledge and skills acquired in the previous level. In fact the notion of levels has made its way into the general popular culture to the point where even my own mother (who is most emphatically *not* a fan of video games) knows what it means. Stimulation of recall can be both explicit, and implicit. At the start of a game, the opening sequence describes some thing that players are expected to know. Some games provide both subtle (a glow around an object) and not-so-subtle clues (a voice actually tells you).

4.   **Presenting the Stimulus (Selective Perception):** This aspect is controlled within the game and is designed to provide encouragement as well as challenge, but a key element is that it must be presented in a manner that keeps the player in the game. If a player cannot easily determine what he or she needs to do in a given situation, the player will become frustrated and eventually give up. If I choose to wander aimlessly about on the alien planet in *Pikmin*, I will eventually receive a message reminding me of my ultimate goal, and offering a hint—where to look, something to do or examine that may help me. A game that is insufficiently stimulating for the target audience will fail to hold their attention, receive a poor rating, and eventually fail economically.

5.   **Providing Learning Guidance (Semantic Encoding):** Games must be self-contained; players do not use manuals, and players often do not have a "facilitator" to help them learn how to play. Learning how to play is accomplished within the game itself. In

effect, games act as the tutor, often employing a multitude of sophisticated "just-in-time" approaches to providing help. Verbal or written hints, items that glow briefly as they come into view, and NPC's[8] that tell you something or offer help are all ways in which guidance can be provided. On the other hand, some games take advantage of the fact that many players are by now quite sophisticated when it comes to understanding the genres and basic gameplay. They rely on the real world communities to help new players get up to speed.

6. **Eliciting Performance (Responding):** This is, of course, an essential component of interactivity—without this, there really *is* no game. While the physical interface for most games is limited and tends to remain the same from game to game and console to console, *how* one actually plays the game can vary.

7. **Providing Feedback (Reinforcement):** Feedback is also provided in many ways, including scores; displays (the head up display, or HUD being a common approach); queries; and verbal feedback. Again, this is one of the imperative elements of every game: without timely and appropriate feedback, the player has no way of knowing whether or not they are progressing toward their goal. Characters within games typically have various attributes that the player can monitor throughout the game: strength, magic, health, and so forth. It is like keeping track of the vital signs of your patient—if the patient's heart-rate goes up, we may have to do something to bring it back down before continuing with whatever else we were doing.

8. **Assessing Performance (Retrieval):** Feedback and assessment are integral to any game, and games that do this poorly are often panned. Since virtually all games are contests on some level, achieving a favorable assessment is what the game is about. The journey is important, to be sure, but even in a game like *Dance, Dance Revolution* where there are no opponents to fight, no treasure to find, and no puzzle to solve, a running "score" of how closely the players' moves approximate perfection is essential.

9. **Enhancing Retention and Transfer (Generalization):** On a small scale, moving through levels within a single game requires players to remember skills, knowledge, and strategies learned in the previous level and use them to overcome obstacles and solve problems in the next. Once again, games that fail to provide a logically understood progression of difficulty and challenges through the levels of the game tend to get poor reviews and fewer players. If the skills required to reach the end of one level are completely different from those acquired in the previous level, it is not a good game. On a larger scale, skills and strategies learned in one game are often applicable to sequels, other games, and even entire genres.

When looking at "good" games through the lens of Gagné's Nine Events, we find that they do indeed possess the necessary conditions for learning and facilitate the required events.

Reigeluth's Elaboration Theory

Jean Piaget gave us the notions of the pre-, concrete, and formal operational stages of development, and both John Dewey and Herbert Spencer advocated that the organization of learning should progress from simple to complex as it does for all human development.

Ausubel and Bruner advocated the organization of learning in increasing order of complexity; Ausubel used this notion to help form his subsumption theory and the concept of advance organizers, and for Bruner this took shape in the notion of constructivism—one of the most significant learning theories of the late 20th century.

All of these contributed in laying the groundwork for Reigeluth's elaboration theory. A key argument for this approach is that learners need to develop meaningful contexts to which they can anchor new ideas and skills, and that this will in turn aid in transfer and retention. One of the most critical components in this scheme is the proper sequencing of instruction, which increases learner motivation and allows for the formation of stable cognitive structures. When this theory is viewed in the context of video games, once again, the organization and design of good games *already* meet many criteria for well-organized instruction.

Elaboration theory proposes seven major strategy components, and when they are applied to the design of good games we find:

- **An Elaborative Sequence:** Good games follow a well-paced sequence progressing from simple (and easy) to complex (and hard). A game explains its own context (theoretical), requirements to operate (procedural), and goals for play (conceptual).

- **Learning Prerequisite Sequences:** Many games offer a tutorial or practice mode that involves some simplifications as well as suggestions. Actions carried out in this mode count neither for nor against the player once he or she enters the game "for real." Once inside the game, there are clear distinctions between various grades of action—a "boss-battle" for example, is one where the player goes up against the most powerful adversary in the game. Often, before it even becomes possible to enter into such a battle, the player must have earned a particular status by meeting other challenges that could include having to beat various other opponents. It may not even be possible to instigate a boss fight before attaining certain status. In other games, you can try any time you like, but without adequate preparation, you will be instantly defeated.

- **Summary:** Virtually all games provide some form of "tab-sheet," or means of checking on progress with respect to what has been accomplished and discovered up to a particular point in a game. Driving games often show tiny maps in one corner or along one edge of the screen that show where on the track the player currently is. Fuel gages, point tallies, current position in the race—all these statistics are routinely displayed somewhere on the screen, and most players learn to be aware of them even while their concentration is primarily focused on keeping the vehicle from crashing.

- **Synthesis:** The implementation of this criterion tends to be fairly game-specific, and is typically evident in the way many games progress through various levels of play, each building on knowledge gained from the previous one, but can also come in the form of strategic hints. Often players are defeated many times before finishing a game. Each time they try again, they do so having gained some knowledge or understanding that they will apply correctly this time in order to progress a little further.

- **Analogies:** These are sometimes not evident in any one particular game, but games of similar genres have enough in common that players create their own. Players very quickly learn to look for approaches or tactics that are similar to some other game they have played, and will try to apply these in any new context that looks like it might favor this approach.

- **Cognitive Strategies:** These exist by the very design of games and are one of their great achievements: the ability to force the player to use strategies invented by the designers in order to achieve their goals. A significant part of the challenge, enjoyment, and attraction of games is the desire to uncover the requisite strategies that allow the player to reach the "victory condition" in a game.

- **Learner Control:** Player (learner) control is an obvious requirement of all games: without this it stops being categorized as a game. This is one area where good games positively excel. A good game gives the impression of providing the player with infinite choices at almost every turn. The reality cannot possibly allow for this degree of complexity, but the *design* of the experience is such that most players do not notice or do not care. Either way, we win. The player feels in control, while experiencing the encounter the designers planned.

Bruner's Psycho-Cultural Approach to Education

Bruner's accomplishments in helping to shape the notion of constructivism are perhaps among the best known of all of major advances in education of the 20th century. This work is of prime significance when looking at pedagogy in games, as the kind of learning that occurs in games is almost entirely constructive. In one of his more recent works, "The Culture of Education" (1996), Jerome Bruner discusses the importance of narrative to the development and maintenance of culture. While some believe the debate about narrative versus gameplay still rages and others feel it is a non-issue (Frasca, 2001), the importance of narrative remains a recurring theme in many discussions of games (Beavis, 1999; Kafai, 2001; Wolf & Perron, 2003). Bruner's approach is very much a culturalist one, believing that "education is not an island, but part of the continent of culture" (1996, p. 11). Education serves several roles in his view, and the information processing, or computationalism role, is just one part of that. Bruner's approach embraces the view that "'external' or 'objective' reality can only be known by the properties of mind and the symbols systems on which it relies" (ibid. p. 12). Bruner further outlines a number of tenets to guide such a "psycho-cultural" approach to education, and as the others already mentioned, this too lends itself easily to description through the lens of games.

A Psycho-Cultural Approach to Games

- **The Perspectival Tenet:** Meaning making is relative to its frame of reference. One of the aspects of games that keep players involved with the same game for extended time is the ability to play it again from a different angle. One can play the *Lord of the Rings, The Two Towers* from the perspective of any of six different characters, and in a game like *Black & White*, your choice is quite fundamental: do you wish to be good, evil, or somewhere in between? Each has consequences.

- **The Constraints Tenet:** Forms of meaning making are constrained by human mental functioning and by semiotics, including the Whorf-Sapir hypothesis, which states that the thoughts you can think are shaped by the language you speak. Good games can push you to the outer edges here. While other technologies facilitate role-playing, good games can place you in the virtual skin of someone you could not otherwise be—your choices and actions are largely constrained by the design of that character.

- **The Constructivism Tenet:** Our reality is a constructed one ascribed to the worlds we inhabit. There is no reason that this cannot be applied to virtual worlds. I am not trying to imply some *Matrix* like existence, in fact quite the contrary. The scenario presented in *The Matrix* was one that had humankind living entirely in an artificially constructed reality, while their real bodies served as fuel for the machines that supported them. The realities that can be constructed in virtual worlds can be both dream-like and fantastic, but also a hybrid of societies and relationships that exist partly in a gameworld, but anchored to real people and bolstered by real relationships and real sharing.

- **The Interactional Tenet:** Passing on knowledge involves a subcommunity in interaction. One has only to visit the Web site of *Apolyton University* (http://apolyton. net/) to see how strong this tenet is for some games. *Apolyton.net* is a site devoted to discussion, tutorials, and all manners of support for players of Sid Meier's *Civilization*. Web sites such as this have grown to become a vital element for many games, without which the kinds of challenges and the complexity of some games would make them unwinnable by all but a select few.

- **The Externalization Tenet:** Externalization is evidenced by the production of "works" that can help produce and sustain group solidarity. Once again we turn to the Internet. Fan art and fan fiction thrives in the "shadow" of a successful game. People become exited by the characters they encounter and the stories they experience. They eagerly build and share. Within the game itself, the notion of "modding," which is the ability to add custom elements to a game, has resulted in such feats as a racing game developed exclusively by the players that exists completely *inside* of another game. The track and vehicles are built entirely out of elements provided in *Warcraft III*, a game, which, by the way, has nothing to do with racing on a track. *Warcraft III* is a medieval dungeons and dragons type of role-playing game. There are not many racetracks in the game as it was originally conceived and designed by Blizzard entertainment—none, in fact.

- **The Instrumentalism Tenet:** Education has consequences that are instrumental in the lives of individuals. We all hope that formal education has a lasting effect, not only of the knowledge imparted, but also of the creation of good citizens. As Marc Prensky claims (2001b), by sheer numbers, the amount of time spent playing video games is bound to have an effect on brain development. It is beginning to become clear that there exist other consequences in the later lives of gamers, some of which appear to be quite promising. According to a study performed by Beck & Wade (2004), instrumentalism for gamers includes confidence in taking reasonable risks, teamwork, a willingness to listen to advice before making decisions, and an ability to cope with failure. Formal education should be so lucky.

- **The Institutional Tenet:** Education behaves as an institution. The institutions of a society help to shape the roles that its members take up and what shape those roles take. In Bruner's view this is not necessarily a benefit, but it is a reality. Although it would be nice to be able to report that neither game designers nor game communities follow this tenet, as it turns out, they sometimes do. However, while formal educational systems tend all to follow very similar institutional forms, game communities often evolve in a manner befitting the theme of the game.

- **The Tenet of Identity and Self-Esteem:** This tenet speaks to agency and self-evaluation. This is just too easy. Will Wright said, "interactive entertainment is a fundamentally different proposition than its linear cousins, involving quite different psychological mechanisms" (Wright, 2003, p. xxxii). Games are almost entirely dependent on agency. "Agency is our ability to alter the world around us, or our situation in it. We are able to act, and that action has effects" (Wright, 2003, p. xxxii). Brenda Laurel, in a speech delivered during the first Education Arcade Conference in 2004 stated that agency is one of the places where formal education has, by and large, failed. Students are not especially encouraged to exercise personal agency, except within very controlled boundaries. Games, on the other hand would not be games if not for the players ability to make choices, alter situations, and be subjected to the resulting consequences. While self-evaluation may be one area where games could be improved, the study conducted by Beck and Wade (see Instrumentalism Tenet) would imply that, at least indirectly, games have the effect of helping to foster the development of strong self-esteem.

- **The Narrative Tenet:** People make sense of the world and their place in it in two ways: through logical, scientific thinking and through narrative. Games overwhelmingly do what they do through the use of narrative. Although many games require players to solve elaborate problems, it is primarily done within the context of a story. Even one of the quintessential puzzle games, namely, *Myst*, is set in the context of an elaborate story with an extensive history. This gives it context and a way for the player to connect with the experience. Humankind has been teaching this way, well, pretty much always. It encourages us to identify with the characters in the story and learn through empathy. "This is important because this empathic ability we seem to exercise so seamlessly is also the psychological engine that drives the thing we call 'story.' Story (in its many forms) seems to be an 'educational technology' of sorts that we have developed over millennia that allows us to share experiences with one another across great distances of time and space. We can learn to avoid failures or achieve successes from people who are long dead across the world or who never existed at all. It's a technology that's entirely dependent on our ability to empathize with other beings" (Wright, 2003, p. xxxii). It is also key to our cultural evolution.

Merrill's First Principles of Instruction

After a highly successful and productive career in the development of instructional design theories and models, David Merrill has returned to the basics. Merrill claims that the success of a given instructional program will be directly proportional to how well and how deliberately the first principles are implemented (Merrill, 2002). Given that, if we can demonstrate that these first principles have been implemented in games, we should be able to conclude that the learning from this "program" was indeed facilitated by the design.

1. **Activation:** Start where the player is. Recall relevant experience. In games, the backstory gives clues as to the kind of knowledge that will be needed to accomplish the mission. This gets reinforced throughout the game (gameplay is typically monitored,

and certain actions on the part of the player trigger intervention by the game with more information, offers of help, etc.). In a sequel game it is even easier: it is a given that the sequel will expand upon what the players learned in the previous version. In fact, sequels that do not do that are typically panned (==> no sales ==> game fails ==> developer does not do *that* again).

2.   **Demonstration:** This principle tells us we must show people what we want them to learn, not simply tell them. Games are often quite clear about what the player will need to be able to do or achieve in order to accomplish the mission. Media often plays a starring role here with prepared animation clips, audio, flashbacks, and so forth.

3.   **Application:** New knowledge must be applied to solve problems. Skills are learned and knowledge is gained, and as the player becomes more competent, the difficulty level gets ramped up—eventually culminating in a "level up," where new challenges are presented, twists in the challenges require variations on skills and knowledge already learned, and so forth. Players have constant feedback ingame — statistics on their progress, vitals on their avatars, remaining resources, and so forth. Merrill (2001, p. 464) says, "Appropriate practice is the single most neglected aspect of effective instruction." You cannot rush Mother Nature. (Was it not the Green Giant who said that?) Here is where good games absolutely shine—just imagine what we can do if we can entice people to willingly spend 5-10-30 or more hours practicing?

4.   **Integration:** Learners are motivated to apply what they have learned. In augmented reality games, as many as several hundred thousand players must learn new skills in order to work together and solve the problems and puzzles presented to them. Once the game is finished, players actively seek out ways to use the knowledge and skills they have learned. In other games, both online and off, players like to publicly demonstrate their new skills. This is part of the need that game communities fulfill. Around every popular game (whether it be a multi-player game or not) people create Web sites, chat rooms, wikkis, offer screenshots, hints, tips, cheats, discoveries, and so on. This has other side effects, too. For example, some people have learned to create Web pages and use html just so they can contribute to the games community of their choice. There is reflection aplenty—also invention, exploration, practice, analysis, discussion, argument, and so forth.

Games and Learning Styles

The total mental efficiency of a man is the resultant of the working together of all his facul-ties. He is too complex a being for any one of them to have the casting vote. If any one of them do have the casting vote, it is more likely to be the strength of his desire and passion, the strength of the interest be takes in what is proposed. Concentration, memory, reasoning power, inventiveness, excellence of the senses,—all are subsidiary to this. (James, 1983, p. 57)

The previous section looked at how games embody various learning theories and some of the instructional strategies that go with them. This section takes a slightly different perspective to look at how games adapt to the learning styles of their players. The styles to be examined here include Howard Gardner's theory of multiple intelligences (Gardner, 1983), the Keirsey temperament sorter (Keirsey & Bates, 1984), Felder's index of learning styles (Felder & Silverman, 1988), Kolb's learning styles (Kolb & Fry, 1975), and The Gregorc system of learning (Gregorc, 1985).

The commercial games industry is just that: commercial. In other words its primary goal is to be profitable. Just like books, movies, television, and other media are targeted at particular demographic groups, so are games. There are fantasy books, non-fiction, historical epics, and so forth. In games, there are sports games, fantasy games, slower paced strategy games, and high-action adventure games, to name just a few. Some games are intended for younger audiences, and some for older audiences, but in order to sell well, the differences in the games must go beyond mere narrative and imagery. If the setting, characters, story line, gameplay, or any other aspect of the game is not appropriate to the audience, the game will not sell. One thing that is not overtly taken into account is that the targeted audiences will invariably include individuals with various learning styles. From that, it follows that in order to be successful the gameplay must address these learning styles, whether it is done deliberately or not. Modern games are expensive to produce, so an adequate return on investment is essential—all individuals in the targeted demographic must be able to engage with the game.

In his seminal work on intrinsic motivation, Thomas Malone, together with Mark Lepper, outlined four criteria that can be used to examine how to engage learners (Malone, 1981; Malone & Lepper, 1987). Using Malone's criteria, in order to be successful a game must incorporate the right amount and kinds of challenge, curiosity, fantasy, and control. Although beyond the scope of the current work[9], there exist direct parallels between those elements considered to be important to engagement and motivation by Malone and Lepper, and most, if not all of the learning styles described in this paper. Games that are highly engaging according to Malone's criteria will also be found to meet the criteria necessary to engage learners of different learning styles.

Many games are intended to appeal to a fairly specific audience, such as *Half-Life II*, *Halo*, and *Grand Theft Auto*, while others appeal to a wide range of ages, skill levels, backgrounds, and even genders, such as the *Phantasy Star* series, *Pikmin*, *Harvest Moon*, *Animal Crossing*, and the *SIMs*. These games are *not* designed with specific learning styles in mind, yet they are very successful at capturing the desired demographic. As has been stated before, many games have a steep learning curve and must be well designed to support players while they learn the game, or they will loose the player, yet once the player is acclimatized, the gameplay must change. Missing the mark in either case (during acclimatization, or during play) results in a game that that does not sell. Inadequate player support while they learn the game discourages novices, while too much "support" during gameplay is obnoxious to experienced players. Designers accomplish this feat of meeting both requirements in a number of ways, which are often employed simultaneously in the game. For beginners, many different learning approaches are exploited that keep people engaged and help them learn the game. A player who remains in one area too long may be offered a hint about a direction they might try, or one who is supposed to be searching for a particular item may be given more information about how to obtain that item. Rarely do games simply give the player the "answer." These hints sometimes come in the form of images, text, narrative, or just sounds. As players become better at using the game, the amount of support offered automatically is reduced, by monitoring the players' actions in ways very similar to what educators call assessment, and responding appropriately. As the players' skills increase, so do the challenges. Players are also often given direct control over the amount of support they receive and can choose among various modes (beginner, expert, etc.).

Support for various learning styles is obviously better in some games than others, and this has implications for how children who play games are "learning to learn." If nothing else, games train people how to play them. This "training" often begins before they even start school and continues all through school and beyond. The average age of gamers is increasing steadily as time progresses (ESA, 2005), which implies that gamers are not abandoning their games as they get older. Whether games will eventually be found to influence learning styles in individuals, and to what extent, remains to be discovered. There are indications that this also has an effect on how they learn and work once they get older (Beck & Wade, 2004), so early indications are that at least some aspects of an individual's learning style may be affected through gameplay.

Gardner's Theory of Multiple Intelligences

By several measures, Gardner's Theory of Multiple Intelligences (Gardner, 1983) is one of the most significant developments in learning theories to come out of the last quarter of the 20th century. Certainly in the school districts surrounding the author's home, one would be hard pressed to find an elementary school child who could not tell you something about his or her "kinds of smart."

The foundation of this theory is that we all employ different strategies for learning, and that these strategies relate to internal strengths and capabilities that can be classified into eight categories or "intelligences" (Armstrong & Association for Supervision and Curriculum Development, 2000). Gardner proposes eight primary forms of intelligence: (1) linguistic (oral and written), (2) musical (sound, rhythm), (3) logical-mathematical (symbolic and rule-based), (4) spatial (2-, and 3-dimensional), (5) body-kinesthetic (physical), (6) intrapersonal (insight, metacognition), (7) interpersonal (social skills), and (8) naturalistic (sensitivity to natural phenomena and classification skills). The implication of this theory is that learning can be facilitated if we focus on and develop instruction for these intelligences. Generally speaking, assessment of learning should include more than one "intelligence," as each is more than simply a content domain; it is also a learning modality. It is known that cultural differences play a key role, as each culture tends to value and emphasize particular intelligences in favor of others.

Gardner's Seven Intelligences

Connecting Gardner's ideas with the design of games is particularly effortless, as almost every one is evident in almost every successful game—in fact, it could be argued that one of the features of games that make them so engaging is precisely their success in addressing each one of these forms, and in providing players with an especially rich experience, where each player has an opportunity to take advantage of his or her own particular strengths.

- **Linguistic:** This intelligence coincides nicely with Gagné's Verbal Information category, and thus what was said there also applies here. Games often include written and spoken elements—for game play, as well as for direction and help (Rosas, Nussbaum, Cumsille, Marianov, Correa, Flores, et al., 2003). Many games combine verbal cues with written ones, and the topic of conversation is additionally supported with other visual queues. This is one reason why children often experience success in learning to read through games like *Pokémon*.

- **Musical:** Virtually all games include sound to enhance play—there are sound-effects, both diegetic (sounds that the characters could hear, like gunshots or radio) and non-diegetic (most typically the musical score, as well as music to set the mood or provide feedback about game states). In some cases musical scores for games are as sophisticated as they are for film. Sounds are used as feedback and reinforcement as well as for cinematic effect and enjoyment. Some games, like *Electroplankton, Donkey Konga*, or *Karaoke Revolution* feature sound as the main attraction.

- **Logical-mathematical:** Strategy is one of the key elements in the play of many games—the extent to which this intelligence is exercised depends heavily on the genre and specific game played. Puzzle games rely heavily on logical and mathematical intelligences to win. The management type games, like *Zoo Tycoon* also involve reliance on and further development of this intelligence, for it is virtually impossible to manage the zoo well without an ability to plan and manipulate a fairly complex set of resources. Simpler games, such as *Pikmin*, still require counting and arithmetic. Moving an object often requires a minimum number of *Pikmin*, and even very young players quickly learn to do simple calculations in order to get the optimal number of *Pikmin* into position to complete a task. Very young players, who may still be struggling with basic sums, can get reinforcement from the heads up display, which very often includes a thermometer-style gauge.

- **Spatial:** Most games are of course highly visual, providing a rich and colorful 2- or 3-dimensional environment, which is always at least partially under the player's control in terms of what is visible on the screen at any given point in time. Thus it can be quite common to be shown multiple simultaneous first- and third-person views on the screen, which not only tap into one's spatial intelligence, but at the same time actively help players learn to use these views in their gameplay.

- **Kinesthetic:** Although games cannot yet place their players physically in the game, most games do require players to "insert themselves" virtually into the game in one way or another, and all involve movement and action that can be realized through physical movements of the players' hands. Watching players as they play quickly confirms that there is indeed more going on than just hand motions—they tense, lean forward, jump up, punctuate choices with head motions, and so on. Some games are specifically designed to involve mild to heavy physical activity, such as *Dance, Dance Revolution*, and, to a lesser extent, games like *Donkey Konga*. In spite of the fact that these games are marketed on their "Kinesthetic Intelligence" attraction, they still provide musical, visual, and linguistic stimulation, as well as requirements for logical thinking and strategizing. There are very few games indeed that rely on only one or two modes for eliciting responses and engaging the user.

- **Intrapersonal:** Games force players to discover and practice various skills, and although reflection is probably one of the weakest elements of games, the communities that evolve around popular games often more than compensate. Other aspects of metacognition, such as considering what one wants to do, how one reacts to things, which things to avoid, and which things to gravitate toward are integral to most games, even first-person shooters that do not purport to be much more than target practice. Many games, such as *Black & White* or *Fable* present scenarios that involve ethical dilemmas, and have moral (or immoral) themes.

- **Interpersonal:** This is again an area where games excel. Many of the most popular games include multi-player modes, many online games massively so. Even single player games typically include multiple NPCs (non-playable characters) and often require varying degrees of both competition and cooperation in order to win. Sports games demand teamwork, but even games without multiplayer modes encourage the formation of game communities, where players help each other and share information.

- **Naturalistic:** Games with naturalistic themes are common—whether they include purely realistic flora and fauna, purely fantastical ones, or some combination of the two. Clearly, games like *Zoo Tycoon* call upon one's natural intelligence in order to be able to identify various animals' requirements for housing and care. Beyond that, any game that creates a world with geography and a variety of inhabitants requires classification, as well as naturalistic skills and understandings. Once again, even a game like *Pikmin* includes several distinct kinds (species?) of *Pikmin*, each with its own strengths and weaknesses.

Although not all games embody every kind of intelligence, most embody the majority of them, and it is always possible to find a specific game that favors one or another. And even though it can be claimed that the different genres of games, as well as variation within are not always designed to appeal to broad audiences, that same condition has not prevented us from making effective use of classic novels or movies in education.

Keirsey's Temperament Sorter

The Keirsey temperament sorter is based on the Jungian model that was developed by Isabel Briggs Myers and her mother (Myers & McCaulley, 1985). It uses four different scales, which are used to classify personalities into four different basic types. Even a superficial examination of the types described conjures up images befitting many role-playing games. Each can be seen as symbolic, perhaps even mimetic, and can easily be represented as an avatar in a game. One could even envision each as a description for an entire race of beings in some epic strategy game. See for yourself:

- **Artisans** value freedom and spontaneity: They tend to be impulsive, playful, and creative.

- **Guardians** value belonging to a group or community: They tend to be traditional, responsible, and conservative.

Table 1. Kiersey's temperment types

Kiersey's Temperament Types	
E = Expressive (extrovert)	I = Reserved (introvert)
S = Observant (sensation)	N = Introspective (intuition)
T = Tough-Minded (thinking)	F = Friendly (feeling)
J = Scheduling (judgment)	P = Probing (perception)

- **Idealists** value personal growth, authenticity, and integrit: They tend to try and encourage these traits in others. This group includes people labeled as "teachers."
- **Rationals** value competence and intelligence: They strive for knowledge, predictability, and control (Keirsey & Bates, 1984).

The results of a test that asks participants about various preferences categorize traits into one each of four groups. The results allow for 16 possible combinations: four for each personality type.

As has been mentioned before, the degree of choice permitted in games is largely an illusion; the *appearance* of virtually unlimited choice exists. As a consequence, Artisans get their freedom, and through the non-linear play and exploration possibilities built into most games, their need for spontaneity is met. Additionally, there is usually a relatively "linear" (sequential) path through the game that can be taken, which will comfort Guardians and Rationals, but the choice remains with the player. Many games cannot be won without some form of cooperative effort, either with other players (as in most MMOGs[10] and some multiplayer console games), or with the non-playable characters that are part of almost every game. A game like *Pikmin 2* requires the player to enlist the help of dozens of tiny "Pikmin" as they are essential for everything from picking up objects to defence from attack.

For the Idealists, aspects of personal growth, authenticity, and integrity are inherent in many games too. Transgressions, and playing the "bad guy" are permitted, but many games implement character attributes such as "health" and "wisdom," which are often diminished as a direct result of these actions. A moral code exists in most games, but it is one defined by the designers rather than outside forces.

One of the key aspects of successful games is how well they balance between randomness and predictability—a game that is too predictable quickly becomes boring even for most Rationals, yet one that is too unpredictable appears random, and players do not feel in control. Most games allow users to adjust the degree of randomness, and so stout Rationals can reduce the element of chance, while Artisans can "dial it up."

Felder's Index of Learning Styles

Felder's ILS model is based on the theory that students learn best when material is presented in a manner best matching their own style, so for each learning style, there is also a teaching

Table 2. Felder's index of learning styles

Felder's Index of Learning Styles	
Active (doing) *Medal of Honor, Star Wars, Super Mario Kart*	**Reflective (thinking)** *Black & White, Syberia, Myst*
Sensing (facts, processes) *Civ III, SIMs, Age of Empires*	**Intuitive (concepts, relationships)** *Pikmin, Katamary Damacy, Harvest Moon*
Visual (seeing, picturing) *Super Mario Kart, Super MonkeyBall*	**Verbal (hearing, reading, saying)** *Elecrtoplankton, Karaoke Revolution*
Sequential (step-wise) *Roller Coaster Tycoon, Myst*	**Global (leaps, random)** *Psychonauts, Grim Fandango*

style to match (Felder & Silverman, 1988). The original model has been altered in recent years to exclude the original aspect of inductive versus deductive style as the authors have come to believe that the "best" method of teaching is inductive regardless of which style the learner prefers. However, the fundamental tenet remains (Felder, 2002).

As with other theories and models, the one aspect of the model that is not especially well supported within most games is that of reflection. This seems to be a shortcoming for which the players themselves see a need, as it is often found to be thoroughly supported through the communities of players that can evolve outside of the game (Galarneau, 2005). One of the qualities of games that makes them both distinct from other educational technologies that have come before, and intrinsically suited to experiential approaches to learning, is that they are highly interactive. ALL games require players to "do." Most modern games are highly visual in presentation, and yet they almost always include narratives and text to either augment visual information, or provide extra information not available in other forms. They require players to learn facts and understand processes, but they also require them to understand concepts and synthesize relationships. Games have sequential aspects, which are balanced by global requirements.

Kolb's Learning Styles

David A. Kolb (with Roger Fry) outlined four elements in his model: concrete experience, observation and reflection, the formation of abstract concepts, and testing in new situations (Kolb & Fry, 1975). These four elements form the nodes of a connected circle of experiential learning, with learners able to enter, as it were, at any point along the circle. Ideally, learners will posses balanced abilities in each of the four areas, but in reality, they tend to polarize toward one of four "poles." These four poles are summarized in Table 3. Note that as we continue to examine additional descriptions of learning styles, many common descriptions

Table 3. Kolb's learning styles

Kolb's Learning Styles	
Learning style & Characteristic	**Description**
Converger: Abstract conceptualization (AC) + active experimentation (AE) *Myst, SIMs, Railroad Tycoon*	· **Practical application of ideas** · **Focus on hypo-deductive reasoning on specific problems** · **Unemotional** · **Narrow interests**
Diverger : Concrete experience (CX) + reflective observation(RO) *Gitaroo-Man, Katamari Demacy, Myst*	· **Imaginative ability** · **Generates ideas and sees things from different perspectives** · **Interested in people** · **Broad cultural interests**
Assimilator : Abstract conceptualization (AC) + reflective observation (RO) *Metroid Prime, SIMs*	· **Can create theoretical models** · **Excels in inductive reasoning** · **Abstract concepts rather than people.**
Accommodator : Concrete experience (CX) + active experimentation (AE) *Need for Speed, Far-Cry, Phantasy Star Online*	· **Doing** · **Risk taker** · **Can react to immediate circumstances** · **Solves problems intuitively**

become evident. Similarly, the same games can be used as exemplars for these common descriptions.

The primary argument being made here is that many games already include elements to meet the needs of various learning styles, so if true, it should not be surprising that many of the games listed could just as easily have been listed in different columns. It is all a matter of perspective, and how the player chooses to take up the game.

In more traditional settings, once an individual's style is identified, instruction can be organized to support his or her strengths, which can give confidence, while still encouraging the further development of the others. In games, the need to appeal to a broad audience ensures that the Converger can remain unemotional, yet imaginative exploration is encouraged and rewarded. Theoretical models can be devised and tested with minimal risk, yet risks *can* be taken, and normally the worst that will happen is that the player must start over.

This bears repeating: a key aspect of good games is that the player can take up the game in many different ways: as a neutral orchestrator, or as an impassioned participant. Games encourage Accommodator abilities of immediate reaction to circumstances and Converger abilities of the application of ideas, and both can remain within the bounds of the "magic circle" of play (Huizinga, 1950) because the usual rules and consequences of reality do not apply. Divergers can identify with other players or NPCs as if they are people, and assimilators can relate to them using whatever conceptual frameworks they like. Some strategies will lead to greater success within the game than others will, but the fact remains that *it is only a game*—exploration and experimentation are actively supported in most good games.

Table 4. Gregorc's learning styles

Gregorc's Learning Styles		
Concrete-Sequential	Linear and sequential.	*Super MonkeyBall, Pikmin*
Concrete-Random	Concrete and intuitive Thrives on problem- solving.	*Syberia, Myst*
Abstract-Sequential	Abstract and analytical Thrives on a mentally challenging but ordered learning environment.	*Myst, Syberia*
Abstract-Random	Emotional and imaginative, Prefers an active, interesting, and informal learning environment.	*Katamari Damacy, Electroplankton*

Gregorc System of Learning

Based on left/right brain studies, Gregorc's system of learning takes into account different ways of perceiving and ordering information. Perceptual preferences can be Abstract, which involves reason, intuition, and deduction, or Concrete, which involves the senses. The ordering preferences indicate how individuals are most comfortable organizing the information they incorporate. The two ends of the spectrum here are the Sequential (or linear and systematic) and the Random (less organized) (Gregorc, 1985).

Good games support the approaches of concrete learners by design, through a myriad of feedback mechanisms: visual, auditory, textual, progress charts, and so forth, while Abstract learners can ignore whichever feedback mechanisms they choose—often by simply switching them off. Abstract learners can develop theories and test them out within games in ways not feasible in real life. The "reset" button remains available to both whenever they get into trouble.

Sequential learners can progress through games in an orderly fashion; they can strategize about which tasks to complete first when there are choices, and follow through. Most games also permit a fairly ordered progression through the challenges, yet for more Random learners, the option exists to choose from among various "next steps." Although some games require some tasks to be completed in certain orders (good for Sequential learners), most also allow for a substantial degree of freedom for Random progressions.

From Commercial Games to Educational Game Design

A demonstration of how "good" games already seem to embody sound pedagogy in their designs accomplished several things. First it may help to put our minds somewhat at ease to know that some of the games we are playing appear to be designed on sound instructional principles. These games are not twisting our minds to a wholly foreign way of learning. Second, entities that could be viewed as implementations of some of our favorite and best-loved theories appear to be highly successful. The theories and principles that have been accepted by scholars and teachers can lead to highly engaging artefacts—in other words, following best practices in the design of instructional articles can have immensely compelling results.

A caution, however: there remains an awfully big step between showing how existing games employ "best practices" in instructional design, and turning that around in order to be able to develop instructional design strategies for creating good learning games. A useful analogy again comes with film. We can often elaborate on why great movies are so great, and a portion of most film studies curricula concerns just that, but we still have not come up with a formula for generating them. Understanding what makes a great game what it is, is but the first step. One hope is that we will eventually be able to articulate what kinds of elements comprise a "good" learning game—one that is both compelling *and* delivers on its instructional goals. Another is that we will never undervalue the contribution made by the talented people involved.

I remain convinced that the work is worthwhile and important. If we can better understand why games are so good at teaching the things they do, we may still not be able to *generate* sure-fire winners using the same principles, but we should be able to evaluate designs based on them. It can help us to avoid some of the bad stuff. I think the design of games for learning is one of the biggest challenges that instructional designers have had to face—games are, in many ways, a completely new technology. Knowing how to build Web sites, or e-learning may help, but cannot fully prepare one to design good games for learning[11], nor does knowing how to design traditional games. These may help, but games for learning are still orders of magnitude more complex.

Finally, instructional design for games must come ***out of*** the games design itself and cannot be imposed upon it. When we try and spread ID on top of games, you get the likes of *Mathblaster*, but when the ID "becomes one with the games design," you get games like *CivIII* and *Black & White*.

Much work remains to be done before we can begin to use games for learning with the same confidence we currently enjoy for text-based and other learning technologies. That players are already learning a great deal through gameplay is clear. Whether or not we can leverage this learning to other objectives is less clear. One body of knowledge that must be developed before we can truly conclude that the strategies employed by games designers can be used effectively in the design of intentional instruction is to study gamers in order to determine if particular learning styles are found to be more common than would be expected in the general population. If so, we will need to determine whether specific genres of games are preferred by people with specific learning styles, or all games have similar attractions. This information can be significant in deciding if, and how, games can be effectively used in instructional settings.

Just as Felder now finds it appropriate to advocate for inductive teaching styles for all types of learners, it may also be appropriate to now advocate for supported learner control for all. That learning is more effective and learners more amenable and responsive when they are given greater control over their learning environment is now a widely endorsed tenet.

Games already do this. Control over one's environment is a key aspect of virtually all popular games, from *Lord of the Rings*, to *Paper Mario,* and *Metroid Prime.*

Perhaps it is appropriate to close with Lev Vygotsky, who believed that with new technologies come new human capacities and a need for new approaches to learning. "The invention of new methods that are adequate to the new ways in which problems are posed requires far more than a simple modification of previously accepted methods" (1977, p. 58).

References

Anglin, G. J. (1995). *Instructional technology: Past, present, and future* (2nd ed.). Englewood, CO: Libraries Unlimited.

Armstrong, T., & Association for Supervision and Curriculum Development. (2000). *Multiple intelligences in the classroom* (2nd ed.). Alexandria, VA: Association for Supervision and Curriculum Development.

Aronson, D. T., & Briggs, L. J. (1999). Contributions of Gagné and Briggs to a prescriptive model of instruction. In C. M. Reigeluth (Ed.), *Instructional-design theories and models* (pp. 75-100). Hillsdale, NJ: Erlbaum.

Beavis, C. (1999). *Magic or mayhem? New texts and new literacies in technological times.* Paper presented at the Joint Meeting of the Australian Association for Research in Education, New Zealand.

Beck, J. C., & Wade, M. (2004). *Got game: How the gamer generation is reshaping business forever.* Boston: Harvard Business School Press.

Brown, J. S., Denning, S., Groh, K., & Prusak, L. (2001). Storytelling: Passport to the 21st century. Retrieved June 30, 2004, from http://www.creatingthe21stcentury.org/Intro0-table.html

Bruner, J. S. (1962). *On knowing; essays for the left hand.* Cambridge, MA: Belknap Press of Harvard University Press.

Bruner, J. S. (1966). *Toward a theory of instruction.* Cambridge, MA: Belkapp Press.

Bruner, J. S. (1996). *The culture of education.* Cambridge, MA: Harvard University Press.

Csikszentmihalyi, M. (1991). *Flow: The psychology of optimal experience.* New York: Harper Perennial.

Dev, P. C. (1997). Intrinsic motivation and academic achievement: What does their relationship imply for the classroom teacher? *Remedial and Special Education, 18*(1), 12-19.

ESA. (2005). Essential facts about the computer and video game industry: 2005 sales, demographics, and usage. Retrieved September 25, 2005, from http://www.theesa.com/files/2005EssentialFacts.pdf

Felder, R. M. (2002). Author's preface to: Learning and teaching styles in engineering education. Retrieved March 12, 2005, from http://www.ncsu.edu/felder-public/Papers/LS-1988.pdf

Felder, R. M., & Silverman, L. K. (1988). Learning and teaching styles in engineering education. *Engineering Education, 78*(7), 674-681.

Frasca, G. (2001). Ludology meets narratology: Similitude and differences between (video) games and narrative. Retrieved October 31, 2004, from http://www.ludology.org/articles/ludology.htm

Gagné, R. M. (1980). Learnable aspects of problem solving. *Educational Psychologist, 15*(2), 84-92.

Gagné, R. M. (1985). *The conditions of learning and theory of instruction* (4ᵗʰ ed.). New York: Holt, Rinehart and Winston.

Gagné, R. M., Briggs, L. J., & Wager, W. W. (1992). *Principles of instructional design* (4ᵗʰ ed.). Fort Worth, TX: Harcourt Brace Jovanovich College Publishers.

Galarneau, L. (2005). *Spontaneous communities of learning: A cross-cultural ethnography and social network analysis of player-learner social networks in massively multiplayer online games.* Paper presented at the DiGRA 2005 Changing Views: Worlds in Play. Retrieved July 18, 2006, from http://www.gamesconference.org/digra2005/viewabstract.php?id=364

Gardner, H. (1983). *Frames of mind: The theory of multiple intelligences.* New York: Basic Books.

Garris, R., Ahlers, R., & Driskell, J. E. (2002). Games, motivation, and learning: A research and practice model. *Simulation & Gaming, 33*(4), 441-467.

Gee, J. P. (2003). *What video games have to teach us about learning and literacy* (1ˢᵗ ed.). New York: Palgrave Macmillan.

Gregorc, A. F. (1985). *Inside styles: Beyond the basics: Questions and answers on style.* Maynard, MA: Gabriel Systems.

Huizinga, J. (1950). *Homo ludens: A study of the play element in culture.* New York: Roy Publishers.

James, W. (1983). Talks to teachers on psychology and to students on some of life's ideals. Cambridge, MA: Harvard University Press.

Jenkins, H. (2002). Game theory: How should we teach kids newtonian physics? Simple. Play computer games. *Technology Review.* Retrieved June 11, 2004, from http://www.technologyreview.com/index.asp

Johnson, S. (2005). *Everything bad is good for you* (Hardcover ed.). New York: Riverhead Books.

Kafai, Y. B. (2001). *The educational potential of electronic games: From games-to-teach to games-to-learn.* Paper presented at Playing by the Rules. Cultural Policy Center, University of Chicago. Retrieved July 18, 2006, from http://culturalpolicy.uchicago.edu/conf2001/papers/kafai.html

Keirsey, D., & Bates, M. M. (1984). *Please understand me: Character & temperament types* (5ᵗʰ ed.). Del Mar, CA: Distributed by Prometheus Nemesis Book Co.

Kolb, D. A., & Fry, R. (1975). Toward an applied theory of experiential learning. In C. Cooper (Ed.), *Theories of group process* (pp. 33-58). London: John Wiley.

Koster, R. (2004). *Theory of fun for game design* (1st ed.). Scottsdale, AZ: Paraglyph Press.

Leyland, B. (1996). *How can computer games offer deep learning and still be fun?* Paper presented at the ASCILITE 96, Adelaide, South Australia.

Lumsden, L. S. (1994). *Student motivation to learn (eric digest no. 92)*. Eugene, OR: ERIC Clearinghouse on Educational Management.

Malone, T. W. (1981, May 20-22). *What makes computer games fun?* Paper presented at the Proceedings of the Joint Conference on Easier and More Productive Use of Computer Systems (Part II) on Human Interface and the User Interface, Ann Arbor, MI.

Malone, T. W., & Lepper, M. R. (1987). Making learning fun: A taxonomy of intrinsic motivations for learning. In R. E. Snow & M. J. Farr (Eds.), *Aptitude, learning and instruction: Conative and affective process analysis* (Vol. 3, pp. 223-253). Hillsdale, NJ: Lawrence Erlbaum Associates, Inc.

Merrill, M. D. (2001). First principles of instruction. *Journal of Structural Learning & Intelligent Systems, 14*(4), 459-466.

Myers, I. B., & McCaulley, M. H. (1985). *Manual: A guide to the development and use of the Myers-Briggs type indicator*. Palo Alto, CA: Consulting Psychologists Press.

Norman, D. A. (2004). *Emotional design: Why we love (or hate) everyday things*. New York: Basic Books.

Palmer, G. (Director). (2004). *The video game revolution* [Television Special]. G. Palmer & M. Finnila (Producer). Seattle, WA: KCTS Television and Palmer/Fenster.

Piaget, J. (1951). *Play, dreams, and imitation in childhood*. New York: Norton.

Prensky, M. (2001a). *Digital game-based learning*. New York: McGraw-Hill.

Prensky, M. (2001b). Digital natives, digital immigrants, part II: Do they really think differently? *On the Horizon, 9*(6), 1-6.

Reigeluth, C. M., Merrill, M. D., Wilson, B. G., & Spiller, R. T. (1980). The elaboration theory of instruction: A model for sequencing and synthesizing instruction. *Instructional Science, 9*(3), 195-219.

Rosas, R., Nussbaum, M., Cumsille, P., Marianov, V., Correa, M. N., Flores, P., et al. (2003). Beyond Nintendo: Design and assessment of educational video games for first and second grade students. *Computers & Education, 40*(1), 71.

Schank, R. C. (1990). *Tell me a story: A new look at real and artificial memory*. New York: Scribner.

Schank, R. C., Kass, A., & Riesbeck, C. K. (1994). *Inside case-based explanation*. Hillsdale, NJ: Lawrence Erlbaum Assoc.

Skinner, E. A., & Belmont, M. J. (1993). Motivation in the classroom: Reciprocal effects of teacher behavior and student engagement across the school year. *Journal of Educational Psychology, 85*(4), 571-581.

Squire, K. (2003). *Replaying history: Learning world history through playing civilization III*. Unpublished doctoral dissertation, Indiana University.

Vygotskii, L. S., & Cole, M. (1977). *Mind in society: The development of higher psychological processes*. Cambridge: Harvard University Press.

Walpole, S. (2004). *Designing games for the wage slave*. Retrieved July 12, 2004, from http://www.gamedev.net/reference/design/features/wageslave

Williams, D. (2005, June 16-20). *A brief social history of game play.* Paper presented at the DiGRA 2005 2nd International Conference, "Changing Views: Worlds in Play," Vancouver, B.C.: Digital Games Research Association.

Wolf, M. J. P., & Perron, B. (2003). *The video game theory reader*. New York: Routledge.

Wright, W. (2003). Forward. In D. Freeman (Ed.), *Creating emotion in games: The craft and art of emotioneering* (p. xxxi-xxxiii). Indianapolis, IN: New Riders Games.

Endnotes

1   While a certain degree of controversy surrounds this film regarding the legitimacy of the footage, it is credited with being the first documentary, and is included for its status, dubious as it may be, as the first documentary film.

2   It might be interesting to note that in 2004, the average age was 29.

3   In 2004, 12 games were listed as having sold over one million units (ESA, 2005). Nine of those games were rated for teens or everyone.

4   Not to mention the ever-popular story-with-a-moral, which predates literate cultures by a considerable amount.

5   For an example of elements important to a successful gaming experience, see Walpole (2004) on designing games for the wageslave (i.e., people who must work for a living).

6   Admittedly, this still sounds far more like something an educator would say than like something a game publisher would.

7   A *god game* is one where the player controls the actions of the game and the characters within, normally without being one of the characters. They are generally played from a third person perspective, and often the player has only indirect control over other characters in the game. One can build buildings, create a storm, or move armies, but the player is not any single character.

8   NPC = non-playing character. These are characters that act within the game but are not controlled by the player. Also known as "bots" (for robot).

9   I am sure we will have seen enough of this sort of comparison by the end of this chapter.

10   MMOG = Massively Multiplayer Online Games

11   By the way, I am avoiding the term "learning games" because it has a specific meaning in AI — namely games that learn, as opposed to games that are used as vehicles to help people learn, but most people outside of CS will not get the distinction.

Section II

Social Analyses of Games and Simulations

Chapter III

Learning Sociology in a Massively Multistudent Online Learning Environment

Joel Foreman, George Mason University, USA

Thomasina Borkman, George Mason University, USA

Abstract

Is it possible to enhance the learning of sociology students by staging simulated field studies in a MMOLE (massively multi-student online learning environment) modeled after success-ful massively multiplayer online games (MMOG) such as Eve and Lineage? Lacking such a test option, the authors adapted an existing MMOG—"The Sims Online"—and conducted student exercises in that virtual environment during two successive semesters. Guided by questions keyed to course objectives, the sociology students spent 10 hours observing online interactions in TSO and produced essays revealing different levels of analytical and inter-pretive ability. The students in an advanced course on deviance performed better than those in an introductory course, with the most detailed reports focusing on scamming, trashing, and tagging. Although there are no technical obstacles to the formation and deployment of a sociology MMOLE able to serve hundreds of thousands of students, such a venture would have to solve major financial and political problems.

Introduction

Sociology 101 is one of those ubiquitous general education courses taken annually by a million or more disinterested undergraduates who frequently cram and forget rather than form a deeply learned ability to see their lives through the lens of the sociological perspective. Part of the problem is the large lecture and the academic preference for paper based displays of learning, both of which enfeeble sociology's great potential for learning by doing.

As is the case with all college courses, the teaching of sociology is a loosely regulated cottage industry that lacks any national standards and is in the hands of personnel who rarely have had any formal training as instructors. It comes as no surprise that the quality of instruction is variable and inconsistent. The typical introduction to sociology is a conventional and familiar dosage of lecture, textbook reading, term paper, and written examinations—a mix that encourages short-term learning and rote repetition of the course content. The better versions feature small classes and teacher orchestrated discussions that encourage students to make connections between what they already know and what they are learning and thereby increase the likelihood of a more meaningful and enduring experience. Better yet are those classes that use simulations and other similarly engaging devices to ensure that students understand the material well enough to apply it analytically to real or fabricated social situations. Such classes are, unfortunately, in a small minority.

What to do about it? The success of online learning management systems (LMS) where students are able to "meet" and interact in cybernetic space suggests to some that we will one day see a convergence between such spaces and the much more sophisticated (from a functional and technological perspective) massively multiplayer online games (MMOG) like Lineage, Eve, and Guild Wars. With that possibility in mind, one can begin to imagine sociology courses that convene online in pedagogically designed spaces (a massively multi-student online learning environment or MMOLE) where students would spend much (if not all) of their time learning by doing.

Why Sociology?

For those who believe a college education should have demonstrable utilitarian benefits (rather than the vague "intellectual enrichment" of late adolescents), the study of sociology is a promising competitor for continuation in the general education requirements. Sociology studies how and why people behave as they do. It deconstructs naïve beliefs about the organization of human relations and replaces them with the ability to "see" the systematic ways that social systems distribute power and wealth and enable individual actions. Students endowed with such a vision and having to interact every day with other humans in small groups and complex bureaucracies are better able to make their social systems work for, rather than against, them. A student who is able to describe the relationship, say, between values, social status, and the reward system in a college fraternity, takes from a course on sociology benefits unavailable to a student who can define these abstract terms but not recognize them embodied in action.

Despite these formidable benefits and our high regard for them, we would not cede a permanent general education requirement to sociology. These valuable slots should be earned—through consistently excellent instruction. That is, the potential of the sociological perspective flows from what students have learned, retained, and are able to apply in their lives outside the classroom. And we have no reason today to believe that most (or even many) Sociology 101 students leave the course with its lessons secured in long-term memory.

As such, Sociology 101 is a perfect candidate for reformation as an MMOLE modeled after successful massively multiplayer online games. Immersed in such an MMOLE (one that predictably and consistently achieves a set of appropriate learning goals), students would develop their understanding of sociological principles as the result of their structured inter-actions within a set of simulated social scenarios. Rather than read in a textbook (or hear from a lecturer) about social mobility or the effect of gender on employment or the rela-tion between caste and success, the student would experience, study, and have to negotiate controlled simulations of these social issues.

The Online Sims (TSO) and the Sociological Field Study

Following this line of reasoning, we considered how we might employ the extant online learning environments like WebCT and BlackBoard, and concluded that they are at this time relatively primitive systems informed more by the prevailing print technology of the past than the immersive audio/visual animations of the future. As we lacked a generous patron who could underwrite the $10 million plus cost to build and deploy a sociology MMOLE, we decided to figure out how to adapt an existing MMOG for pedagogical purposes.

The Online Sims seemed like a good candidate. It is the massively multiplayer online ver-sion of the extremely successful Sims gaming franchise. It is not violent, and thus appeals to female students; its "gameplay" is mostly about the kind of ordinary social interactions that characterize the housebound leisure of contemporary Americans. TSO allows geo-dis-tributed players to build houses; to visit and interact with others through chat and a limited repertoire of physical behaviors (like kissing and dancing); to earn "Simoleans" and spend them on house furnishings and "games within the game;" and to develop skills that serve mainly to distinguish between the serious and casual players. Moreover, it is not difficult to learn the rules of engagement. About 20 hours of online exploration confirmed this judg-ment and convinced us that the environment could support an engaging and novel student exercise in the application of sociological principles.

After selecting an avatar body type and clothing, a newbie player sees a 30,000 foot view of the Sims world, selects a region, then a neighborhood, and then a specific building. This is rather like a visual descent that concludes with the player's avatar at the front door of a dwelling. As the dwellings in this view have no roofs, the player can see into them and then move about freely to take advantage of whatever amenities and activities are provided by the dwelling "owners." The TSO management system provides popularity lists that catego-rize the nominal intent of a property (which owners can define in terms such as "romance" and "skill building") and indicates which ones are open and accessible at a given time of the day. Since owners earn Simoleans just by attracting visitors, it is easy for newbies to "teleport" into numerous properties where they may observe or interact with diverse groups of other player avatars.

As such, TSO is an accessible (if limited) social system that can provide a constrained field study for sociology students at any time of their choosing. Although we would have preferred to microdesign the student exercise to assure predictable outcomes, to do so would have required far more time, online exploration, and imagination than we were able to devote to the project. We felt certain that the students would be engaged by and benefit from a simulated field study guided by a few questions keyed to course objectives, and we subsequently conducted two iterations. The first took place in fall 2003 with a single class of Sociology 101 students who gained access to The Sims Online with the free one-month subscription EA was offering at the time as a lure for new customers. The second iteration took place a year later (fall 2004) with participation from another group of Soc 101 students and a more advanced group in a Sociology of Deviance course. For this iteration, EA provided three months of free access.

Sociology 101

The assignment instructions for the Sociology 101 exercise are as follows:

- Install the TSO software and spend approximately 10 hours exploring the online social system.
- Keep a journal in which you note the times you log on to the game, sites visited, what you did, friends you made, and skills you developed.
- Analyze your game experience in relation to the sociological ideas and concepts in the textbook and course lectures.
- Write a 5-page report that:
    o Describes the game as a constructed society. For example, what values of American society are exhibited explicitly or implicitly in the game? What aspects of social structure, social interaction, social networks, or group dynamics does TSO manifest? How are marriage and family handled? How is social class exhibited?
    o Suggest ways that the game might be used by students to apply sociological principles in future semesters.
    o Critique the game, given what you have learned about American society and sociology.

Our expectation, that 10 hours would be sufficient for students to learn how to navigate the game interface and still have time for substantial observer participation, proved to be correct. This was true for both iterations, though more so for the second because we included in-class demonstrations of the game experience. The real time demo, projected on a large screen, not only eased the student's entry and orientation experience, it motivated interest. Quite a few of the students had never seen an MMOG before and were fascinated to see the avatars moving independently through the game space and communicating with one another (via chat) even though the actual players were widely removed from one another in "real" space.

The student produced reports revealed several levels of analytical or interpretive ability. At the base level of achievement, common to all the participants, students matched distinct sociological terms with their instantiations in TSO. Most of the introductory students operated at this level and picked terms from a list of 15 American values that included progress, achievement and success, individualism, material comfort, democracy, humanitarianism, equality, and racism and group superiority. The terms identified most often were achievement, individualism, material comfort, and humanitarianism.

The students rarely dealt with the issue of racial/ethnic diversity or discrimination, which are major topics in sociology and to which the course instructor paid extensive attention. A few students remarked that they found all the Sims they encountered to be "white" even though colored skin tones were available as a choice of avatars, but that was the extent of their analysis. The tonal variation in the avatar skins is the game designers' only concession to the physical distinctions that are so important in stratifying real world social systems. Otherwise, the avatars are uniformly "attractive" in that they are of medium height; are in a 19-30 year age range (approximately); are slender, fat free, and well toned; and have no physical detractions, neither small ones like pimples nor more significant ones like deformed appendages. While one student (herself full bodied) observed that the TSO designers' decisions in this regard efface the discrimination in jobs, education, and leisure social relations faced by the overweight, many of the students claimed uncritically that TSO was "true to life."

TSO is, in fact, a simplified and idealized world lacking the diversity, complexity, and organizational elaboration of real life. The world contains no aging process, no old people, no fixed social classes, no unavoidable health problems, no adverse climatic conditions, no pain, and no irreversible death. It contains no government (other than the controls of the game monitors), no police, no military, and no corporations. Running out of money does not matter, and the rudimentary economy allows players to earn "Simoleans" mainly through entry level manufacturing jobs. Without any occupational diversification (other than manual labor and property ownership), the social system simply will not generate the job prestige hierarchies one finds in real world social systems. TSO is basically a classless meritocracy in which anyone willing to work hard enough can acquire the material accoutrements (large and well-furnished homes) of an upper class. Although the TSO management system publishes popularity lists and provides eight different lot sizes (thus differentiating between the sizes of dwellings), these distinctions benefit visitors as much as owners since attracting and entertaining the former is what increases the wealth of the latter. This structure—along with the general irrelevance of education, family history, income level, ethnicity, and occupational prestige—inhibits the formation of status hierarchies and the social complications wrought by such matters as income discrepancy and its systematic effects on homelessness, upper class status, and the like. Had TSO exhibited such social complications, we believe our introductory students would have had an easier time applying concepts learned in class.

A notable exception is the student who applied what he had learned about social networks, which the instructor discussed and illustrated in class and in an extra reading on the well known Milgram Small World Phenomena experiment. Social networks are integral to the game and may be used to advance a player's mobility in TSO (as this student pointed out) through the agency of "friendship webs." When one player becomes friends with another player, that friend is added to the player's friendship web, which is always available for any player, upon contact, to access and read. As in Milgram's small world experiment, players can see how connected they and their group of friends are to others in the game. The student observer in question reports that he spent his online time tracing the social network connections linking the friendship webs of the people he met. He visited the people listed in the friendship webs of his first encounters, looked at their webs for other contacts, and proceeded in similar fashion through the network. His application is the most sophisticated of any introductory student in that he understood how social networks applied in TSO and then used his knowledge to further his understanding of and action in the game. Such a learning experience, we believe, can be transferred to the real world social networks that successful people navigate so well.

Sociology 310: Sociology of Deviance

In 2004, our second iteration of the TSO simulated field study included the students in an advanced course—Sociology of Deviance. The course, which defined deviance as behavior that a social group regards as unacceptable and attempts to prohibit with negative sanctions, required students to enter at least three TSO properties and to observe to what degree and in what situations a controlling group defines and sanctions deviant behavior. The juniors and seniors in the course performed, as one would expect, on a much higher level than the students in Soc 101 and earned a higher percentage of A's (7/15) on their papers. They received these grades for several reasons. (1) They were able to distinguish between the rules of the game (i.e., "terms of service") and the deviance constructed by various actors in local circumstances within the game. (2) They described deviant behaviors and sanctions invoked at specific properties where they visited and observed. (3) They generalized appropriately (using the course definitions) about social control and transgressions.

In performing these sorts of observation and analysis, the students were acting within the long-standing tradition of social science and empirical research. What follows is an aggregate description of the more interesting instances of deviance observed and documented by the members of Soc 310.

Some Student Findings

Most students found it easy to distinguish between the TSO instituted regulations and those maintained and enforced at specific properties developed by gamers themselves. The TSO institutional regulations (known as the "terms of service") are formally published on the Web site and must be agreed to as part of the enrollment process. The terms of service are diverse and include such matters as the illegal publication online of copyrighted material, the improper use of complaint submission buttons, and unwelcome harassment of other players. None of the students directly witnessed or produced violations so flagrant as to warrant the major means of enforcement available to TSO—banishment from the game. TSO is, after all, a virtual world. Since its virtual inhabitants are not subject to the kinds of physical damage or deprivations encountered in the real world, it is hard to imagine a form of deviant behavior that would count as more than a slight and passing emotional disturbance. Accordingly, there is no police force visible in the game and the monitoring and reporting of perceived infractions is generally up to the players themselves.

A case in point is the scamming, which often victimizes newly arrived players, who are sometimes referred to as "newbies." One such newbie reported being flattered and pleased when another Sim asked him to be his roommate, with the provision that the newbie buy some expensive appliances for the household—at a cost of 5,000 Simoleans, the amount of "money" with which each newbie starts the game. The next time the newbie logged on, he learned that the property was up for sale and that all the profits (including his 5,000 Simolean investment) would go to the owner.

This sort of random and individualized predation, which is more of a *caveat emptor* than a punishable transgression, depends on a discrepancy between the knowledge of the scammer and the victim. A group that refers to itself as the "F.U. Mafia" exploits such discrepancies on a much larger scale through their "scam houses." Scam houses are rather like a small Las Vegas casino where Sim visitors can play the "games of chance" permitted by TSO's terms of services. In one such game, a Sim pays 1,000 Simoleans to pick a card describing an activity he must perform in order to increase his stake. The problem is, the Sim does not know that the activity (in this case, eating 10 virtual snacks in 20 TSO minutes) cannot be performed successfully because of speed limitations built into the system. When the victim Sim predictably fails the challenge, the scam house owner pockets the 1,000 Simolean stake plus the cost incurred for the snacks. And the victim Sim often leaves without even realizing he or she has been scammed.

Sim Sex

TSO property owners can control deviant behavior within the confines of their domiciles by banishing perceived offenders and preventing them from returning. Our students observed property owners who invoked their banishment privilege for a variety of relatively minor infractions when visitors or roommates broke the house rules, disturbed the peace, quarreled with other members, used profane language, or engaged in deviant sexual behavior.

Simulated sexuality drew attention from a number of student observers, surely because of its inherent interest, but also because of its ambiguous status online. Although lacking the kinesthetic and consequences of real world sex, Sim sex remains an emotionally charged social interaction marked by various degrees of deviance and negative sanctions. The TSO designers have been quite careful to limit sexual activity to fully clothed hugging and kissing. But players have discovered, for example, that it is possible for two avatars (the player's online representatives) to get into the same bed together, an act that counts as a metaphor for intercourse. The more inquisitive players are likely to discover a hack produced by a rogue software company that allows a user to see other Sims in various states of nudity. Sims can also join each other in a hot tub where they can wash each other, kiss, and play. The latter activity, as witnessed by one student, entailed one Sim submerging while another moaned suggestively. It is not entirely clear whether this exploitation of game enabled behaviors to simulate sexual activity constituted a deviation from the game developer's intentions. However, a female Sim who was in the hot tub at the time was apparently offended (as one might be when witnessing a real world enactment in such a situation) and left the hot tub.

Since Sim coupling and Sim sex is not graphic or consequential, negative sanctioning, as in the case immediately above, usually takes the form of verbal admonishment or avoidance. One student observed an interaction in which a male Sim approached a female Sim and asked her to marry him. When the conversation revealed that the male was 14, the female (who was the house owner) wrote, "You're too young to be in this property." Nevertheless, she allowed the early adolescent to "marry" and "have sex with" another female Sim who was present. This is a clear deviation from what would be acceptable in the real world, but given the absence of real world physicality and consequences, the owner apparently felt that sanctions were unnecessary. What did strike her as an unacceptable transgression, however, was one couple's on screen publication of a sexually explicit conversation. This immediately elicited from her the threat of banishment from the house.

Trashing and Tagging

One of the more activist student observers inadvertently discovered two artfully practiced forms of social deviation when he attempted to find out what would trigger sanctions at a particular property. In the first instance, he was ejected from a property after maliciously displacing some of the owner's virtual laptops. This act, he later learned, was a mild form of "trashing"—a deviant behavior practiced systematically by a local group calling itself the Irish Mafia. (The Irish Mafia and similar groups have formed spontaneously and are not game elements devised by TSO designers. More about this will follow.) In his second provocation, when his insults directed toward a female Sim failed to elicit a negative response, he "marked" her as his enemy. "Marking," more commonly known within TSO as "tagging," exploits the part of the game interface that displays a Sim's network of associates—the "friendship ring." Most Sims cultivate a completely positive "friendship ring" (one without any enemy "tags") because it affects their desirability as friends and roommates.

In tagging, the mafias can add a message, so when a user hovers over the enemy's name, it usually bears the stamp of the mafia, further spreading the group's infamy. The red links created by enemy tags are stigma symbols for innocent Sims and function as status symbols for the mafias.

The self-styled "Irish Mafia" reportedly uses both tagging and trashing to control neighborhoods and burnish its notoriety. A typical *modus operandi* entails the issuing of an extortion threat (pay us part of the revenue generated by your business or we will make trouble for you) when a new property owner enters an Irish Mafia neighborhood. If the new owner resists, the gang "tags" the property to deter potential visitors—thus depriving the owner of revenue generated by visitors. The red links created by the enemy tags and visible to others, simultaneously serve to stigmatize the innocent Sim while spreading word of the dubious achievements of the F.U. Mafia. Should this tactic fail to motivate a property owner, Mafia members known as hydras (derivation unknown) conceal their criminal associations, befriend the owner in the hope that he or she will eventually trust them enough to share "building privileges." Property owners' building privileges, as the term indicates, allow them to erect an edifice and furnish it with all of the items one would expect to find in a typical house plus a number of specialties that are unique to the TSO world. Building privileges also allow those who have them to delete any and all of the objects in and parts of the house, which is exactly what the Mafia "hydras" do (in effect, destroying the house) when a deceived and unsuspecting property owner is off-line. One particularly malicious variation of this Sim crime occurs when the Mafia "hydras" use a house's floor tiles to spell out profanities that are visible to any Sim exploring the terrain from a high-level neighborhood view. The Mafia then reports this infraction to the TSO management, resulting (supposedly) in the termination of the innocent property owner's account.

Conclusion

The student observations we have been describing persuade us that enough forethought, expertise, and money could produce a viable sociology MMOLE that would utterly transform the student learning experience. It would cost a lot to build (perhaps as much as $20 million) and to upgrade periodically (like Sim City or the Madden football game franchise) so that successive versions maintain a technological edge year after year. But because so many students take sociology every year, a potentially robust market exists to manage the costs.

What is the likelihood that this form of experiential learning would produce enduring conceptual skills for participating students? The answer is that the structure of the MMOLE would have to be designed to assure substantial, specific, and significant learning. It would do so by combining the content of sociological research (i.e. its empirical findings) with the relevant elements from videogames produced purely for leisure time activity and that have competed successfully for hundreds of hours of their users' attention. These elements include competition, sociality, graphic dynamism, and reinforcement systems—to mention but a few. Perhaps most important would be the organization of learning activities into a "level progression" whereby students would have to complete one level (requiring a demonstration of learning) before moving on to subsequent higher levels. As the student advances, the learning would accumulate and aggregate in a hierarchy leading to sociological competence. Winning the game, that is, ascending to and exiting from its highest level, would be the same as a very active demonstration of the desired sociological know-how. No external assessment would be required.

There are, of course, significant political obstacles to massive student participation in a sociology MMOLE. First, the professors and universities whose services could be displaced by a digital learning environment would surely object. The second political problem arises from the wide range of sociological studies. Sociology (along with anthropology) is probably the most inclusive social science as it covers governments and political behavior, economic behavior, history, as well as family relations, education, religion, small groups, bureaucratic organizations, social movements, social identity, race/ethnic relations, and social stratification. It ranges from the most macro level (global societies, individual societies, communities, neighborhoods, families, social networks) to the most micro (interactions between two people). Because of the breadth, depth, and inclusiveness of sociology, typical introductory courses vary widely in their content. As a consequence, a major political effort would have to be undertaken within the sociology profession itself to build agreements about the specific learning goals of an MMOLE catering to students in all parts of the nation. We believe that such an effort would be difficult but salutary.

Whether such an MMOLE would stand alone or serve as a component in a hybrid course is uncertain because sociology is a set of concepts that form a very specific perspective from which a researcher observes, collects data, and theorizes about social life. It is true that any successful member of a social order must have learned about the way it operates, but concepts and theories are needed in order to test that knowledge, to make it explicit, and to reproduce it uniformly for others to use. Under the best of circumstances, sociological concepts migrate into the public realm where we can see that terms like "siblings," "significant others," "reference group," and "sandwich generation" inform the way that the masses think about and act upon the raw data of their experience. Any game that would teach sociology would have to work in a similar manner. It would have to build conceptual structures or lenses through which the students would come to understand such matters as race relations, social stratification, and family relationships. The construction of the lenses (i.e., the delivery of conceptual information) could be done in a conventional fashion, externally through lectures or class discussions with a sociology professor. Or, the concept building activity could be built into the game as a help function or set of intellectual power-ups. For example, student players unable to solve a particular social problem might have recourse to in game functions that teach them how to design and use, say, a survey in order to get ahead in the game.

Assuming that these problems could be addressed, we can imagine an annual group of 200,000 student users whose semesterly subscription fees (say $100/student—a very reasonable figure) would generate $20 million every year. In a non-profit model, that should be enough to cover the cost of the initial construction of a sociology MMOLE, pay for annual maintenance, and an upgrade every few years. Far fetched though this vision may now appear, we believe it will be realized one day.

Chapter IV

Online Games for 21st Century Skills

Lisa Galarneau, University of Waikato, New Zealand

Melanie Zibit, Boston College, USA

Abstract

20th century visionaries foresaw that mastery of the dynamic processes underpinning the acquisition and manipulation of knowledge would be critical in the 21st century. Formal educational systems have not yet changed to facilitate the development of these necessary capabilities, and so people of all ages are developing them through a variety of digitally mediated mechanisms. Online games offer one area in which to examine patterns of spontaneously occurring phenomena that represent the natural development of such capabilities. This chapter reviews the character of, and need for, 21st century skills. It also illuminates existing digital domains in which these skills develop organically. Peering through the window of the present into the future, we see that envisioning change in education means taking a long look at what activity produces those skills, regardless of whether that activity is taking place in a formal setting or within entertainment-based worlds where the skills are learned incidentally through play.

Introduction

The approach of the 21ˢᵗ century has brought a chorus of pronouncements that "the information society" both requires and makes possible new forms of education.

We totally agree with this. But we do not agree that tardiness in translating these declarations into reality can be ascribed, as it often is, to such factors as the lack of money, technology, standards, or teacher training. Obviously there is need for improvement in all of those areas. But the primary lack is something very different—a shortage of bold, coherent, inspiring, yet realistic visions of what education could be like 10 and 20 years from now.

What we mean by vision is not a blueprint but a compelling view of the "look and feel" of the future—its needs, its opportunities, and how we can prepare ourselves now to act on them. Vision allows us to look beyond the problems that beset us today, giving direction to our passage into the future. Even more important, vision energizes that passage by inspiring and guiding us into action. (Seymour Papert and Gaston Caperton at the 91ˢᵗ Annual National Governors' Association Meeting, St. Louis, Missouri, August 1999)

In recent years there has been no shortage of well-intentioned talk in educational circles about the critical role of vision in the creation of educational systems that properly address 21ˢᵗ century needs. A Japanese proverb says, "Vision without action is a dream; action without vision, a nightmare." This is how many of us feel about our current education systems: we have far too much action without vision and quite a lot of rhetoric-based vision without action, but not enough of the two combined into a cohesive and effective result. There are, and have been for decades, many visions as to the "look and feel" of the future of education, but they have been largely stymied by an inability to translate via pragmatic means the here-and-now into that ideal. And we have had a great deal of "action" that creates a sense of activity and accountability in the short term, but minus a vision that translates that activity into long-term success. Actionable vision is a problem of connecting the dots, of understanding how the present converges into the future, and what we can do to affect and smooth that passage.

It is a common mistake to overlook the fact that our future is not as mysterious as it might seem, but nor is it a point to which we arrive without first journeying through our present. As author and futurist Bruce Sterling (2003) has commented, the future is already being written in our present, if only we know where to look for the hints of what is to come. This chapter will argue that the vision for learning in the 21ˢᵗ century already exists and is being acted upon by millions of people around the world who engage in digital activity such as sharing online information or collaborating with peers, but most notably in the complex but little understood worlds of online gaming.

Learning in the 21st Century

The world is now coming to grips with the idea that 21st century people require a different set of skills made mandatory by the complexity and pace of life and work in the face of amazing new communications technologies just beginning to entrench themselves in the social, cultural, and economic fabric of our lives. These skills for 21st century, as they are often called, are those that are necessary to succeed in an ever-changing, global society where communication is ubiquitous and instantaneous, and where software tools allow for a range of creative and collaborative options that yield new patterns and results that we are only beginning to see. The skills include critical thinking, teamwork, problem solving, collaboration, facility with technology, information literacy, and more; they are all fundamental to the success of knowledge workers.

But although we have traveled great distances technologically, these needs are not being met in today's schools, where high-stakes testing and No Child Left Behind (NCLB) policies leave little time for anything besides the standard, highly measurable, content-oriented curriculum. It is striking that many people today are not acquiring 21st century skills through structured learning environments that anticipate these needs, but rather through various "cognitively-demanding leisure" activities they choose to engage with, including to a larger and larger extent, videogames (Johnson, 2005b). Of particular note is the increasing popularity of massively multiplayer online games (MMOGs), a relatively recent videogaming phenomenon enabled by burgeoning broadband penetration[1] and a new generation of computers and consoles that allow rich worlds with thousands of participants to be rendered in real time. Literally millions of people are now playing these games world-wide.

Many of the games are referred to as "virtual worlds" (Bartle, 2003) as they are not simply games in the traditional rules-based sense, but rather "persistent social and material worlds, loosely structured by open-ended (fantasy) narratives, where players are largely free to do as they please" (Steinkuehler, 2004). Still, they are games in the sense that players come to them with a certain expectation to engage in achievement-oriented activity, often in collaboration with other players. It is notable that while we tend to think of videogames as competitive spaces, players are encountering intensely cooperative practices in these online gaming environments. The process of play itself leads to, and at the higher levels requires, a high level of achievement across various dimensions of both cognitive and social intelligence. Our perspective is that players of MMOGs develop 21st century skills in a spontaneous and holistic way as a by-product of play, even though learning these skills is not a direct goal of these games. Unlike an educational or "serious" game, where learning objectives are designed into the game, these skills are developed organically, and often quite unintentionally, as a consequence of playing the game.

This chapter looks at how we can build visions for the future of education by understanding how technology has challenged our learning process, leveraged our capabilities, and increased the demands on our skills. It also contends that young people, socialized into a digital culture, are developing 21st century literacies as they play MMOGs and engage in other digital activity. Reading the seeds of change in his own present in the early 1990s, author Lewis Perelman (1991) foresaw the possibilities of these types of interactions in his seminal book, *School's Out*:

The potential impact of advanced simulation and visualization technology on hyperlearning has not yet even been scratched. Einstein developed the special theory of relativity by "riding" a light beam in his mind's eye—those with less vivid imaginations could share Einstein's "thought experiments" through VR [virtual reality] imagery. The possibilities exceed imagination (at least most adults'). Kids hundreds or thousands of miles apart could act out Macbeth with computer-generated costumes—or even simulated adult bodies and voices—in a camera-captured and video re-created scen e that duplicates the actual Birnham Wood or Dunsinane castle. (p. 49)

Outside of school in myriad online game environments, children and adults "hundreds or thousands of miles apart" are already taking on the roles of simulated characters with a variety of bodies and voices, and learning important skills through participation in fantastic endeavors just like in Perelman's vision. The difference is that this is not occurring in an educational context at all, but through the entertainment activities of millions of people around the world. It is, in a way, an unwitting grassroots movement to learn the skills necessary to life in the 21st century, regardless of whether they are encountered within the context of one's formal education.

The Educational System and 21st Century Skills

The affordances of modern communications technologies have brought about a transformation that is readily apparent in day-to-day life across the developed world. They have taken us from the industrial revolution to the information age, and now promise a knowledge society of interconnected people who are fluent in the intricacies of online interactions and in the ways to access the information they need, when and where they need it. The world is increasingly more complex and that complexity brings rapid change that is at once unpredictable and nonlinear. No longer can the set of skills we learned in school last a lifetime. Success depends on being mentally agile and willing to embrace new ways of doing things. This factor is increasingly mandatory in light of the challenges we face on the world stage. Author Thomas Friedman (2005a), in his book *The World is Flat*, contends that failure to develop such capability could irreparably damage the American economy, given a greater propensity in developing countries like China and India to make moves in this direction.

Yet American schools have not caught up with the changes infused into our society by these technological innovations and the cultural shifts that have inevitably followed. As Marshal McLuhan (1967, p. 8) said, "Our age of anxiety is largely the result of trying to do today's job with yesterday's tools." We need students to learn the skills necessary for the 21st century, yet we teach them with yesterday's tools and measure outcomes using yesterday's assessments. In fact, our current educational system was designed over one hundred years ago to prepare students for the industrial age. It was incredibly successful at the task of churning out homogeneous, individualistic, and conformity minded factory workers to fuel the rapid, mechanistic, and linear pace of the industrial revolution's assembly lines. Yet today's increasingly complex, global world demands that students be outfitted for the unique needs of the 21st century. Initiative, teamwork, decision-making ability, problem-solving, and resourcefulness are the keys to success. Conformity is no longer desirable. Innovation, collaboration, and can-do attitudes are highly valued.

However in too many schools, students sit passively listening to teachers talk or repeat de-contextualized facts in direct response to teachers' questions, working individually on problems at desks that are lined up in neat rows. This anachronistic tendency is of grave concern to visionaries like Microsoft co-founder and chairman Bill Gates, who recently told America's governors:

Our high schools were designed 50 years ago to meet the needs of another age. Until we design them to meet the needs of the 21st century, we will keep limiting—even ruining—the lives of millions of Americans every year. (Friedman, 2005b, p. 25)

Gates is not alone in this criticism. Many government officials, not to mention untold numbers of parents and objective onlookers, have called for a "radical redesign of the nation's antiquated education system" (Murray, 2005, p. 1). High school students themselves are also asking for change. In a national survey in which high school students reflected on what is important, what is needed, and what is missing in their education and in their lives, 90% reported not seeing a connection between what they do in school today and what they might do in the future (NCSA, 2005). Employers, too, have their doubts about today's schools. A total of 67% of employers believe that "schools are not equipping young people with vital work skills such as team working, communication, and time keeping as cited in a UK survey" (Guardian Unlimited, 2005).

Employers are frustrated that young people of all abilities are finding it harder to cope in their early years at work because they have been stifled in the classroom and textbook learning rather than seeing and experiencing how they learn is applied in the world outside. (Guardian Unlimited, 2005)

It is worth noting that good commercial games, unlike textbook learning, "are already state-of-the-art learning games" that can prepare people for employment (Gee, 2005). Regarding the potential for learning through games, Gee states:

A good instructional game, like many good commercial games, should be built around what I call "authentic professionalism." In such games, skills, knowledge, and values are distributed between the virtual characters and the real-world player in a way that allows the player to experience first-hand how members of that profession think, behave, and solve problems.

Not only are young people not learning the relevant skills for a knowledge society in school, but their fluency with modern technologies is often disparaged as frivolous or a waste of time. So instead of learning the skills for the 21st century in school, young people are becoming fluent in important communication technologies outside of school, engaging in informal learning online through their communities of interest, via blogs, instant messaging, chats, discussions—and through playing online games.

Information and communication technologies are raising the bar on the competencies needed to succeed in the 21st century, and they are compelling us to revisit many of our assumptions and beliefs. (Burkhardt, Monsour, Valdez, Gunn, Dawson, Lemke, Coughlin, Thadani, & Martin, 2003, p. 49)

To ignore the groundswell of activity among technologically literate children is not simply a missed opportunity, but means ignoring a huge problem in the making. The issue will no longer be the "digital divide," for nearly all American children will have some kind of access to technology soon enough, but rather a "digital-capability divide" in which the monikers "haves" and "have-nots" refer to kids who have or have not grown up developing both the technological and socio-cultural skills necessary to succeed in a complex, digital world:

But what about the children who do not have these opportunities, opportunities now readily available to, and sometimes put to good use by, privileged families? Can they get this in school? Can they get this sort of modern learning system, directed towards preparation for future innovative work, in school? Not in a lot of the public schools we've seen. Today's popular culture has great potential to be recruited into such high value learning systems. But this doesn't happen all by itself. Kids need a network of parents, teachers, and other mentors to use popular culture as a tool for long-term growth into complex thinking, complex language, complex content, and innovative work. In other words, this ability to leverage modern technologies and popular culture for learning is creating a new and massive equity crisis, a crisis not mitigated by—and perhaps even compounded by—today's technologically impoverished schools. So the looming crisis—our surrender to the challenge of preparing public school children for innovative work—is going to hit the poor harder than the rich. But that's cold comfort, since everyone will get to suffer amply unless something is done. (Gee & Schafer, 2005, p. 11)

As the barriers of distance and time dissolve, one crucial question is whether formal learning can stay confined inside a classroom. And as new online forms of collaboration emerge, can we still expect students to work in isolation or to think that there is a benefit to such practices? As interactive programs that actively engage the learner become pervasive, can we still expect students to be passive recipients of information?

In today's world, everyone is both a learner and a teacher, for learning is facilitated by "a globe-girdling network that links all minds and all knowledge" (Perelman, 1991, p. 22). Not to throw the baby out with the bathwater, but if we are to challenge our old assumptions about education and schools, can we then look at the possibility that what young people are doing online, or through games and simulations, may in fact help prepare them for the 21st century? The next few paragraphs provide an overview of what experts—economists, academics, government officials—define as 21st century competencies from various perspectives.

Competencies for the 21st Century

1991 was a watershed year. The nation was confronting globalization. Multi-national corporations were moving complex production outside the United States, and the demands of the workplace were changing quickly. Experts voiced concerns about U.S. ability to maintain competitiveness in a fast-paced world economy intricately connected through telecommunication networks. The National Science Foundation lifted its restrictions on the commercial use of the Internet, and various businesses began to take advantage of the network and its commercial opportunities. In 1991, just like in the 1950s Sputnik era, the government was concerned about the need to improve our educational system and undertook a study that resulted in the Secretary of Labor's Commission Achieving Necessary Skills (SCANS) report:

The need to keep abreast of technological change and to participate effectively in today's high-performance workplace requires each worker to possess a set of basic competencies and a foundation of skills and personal qualities. (SCANS, 1991, p. vii)

The basic skills described went far beyond the traditional reading and math to include a whole range of capabilities such as thinking creatively, making decisions, solving problems, knowing how to learn, and reasoning, as well as interpersonal skills like working on teams and teaching others (SCANS, 1991, p. vii).

It was the same year that Robert Reich wrote *The Work of Nations* citing the end of economic nationalism and defining a new type of job for the 21st century: symbolic analysts, those who could use technology to solve problems.

The skills people need to develop have to do with problem solving and identification, developing critical facilities, understanding the value of experimentation, and the ability to collaborate... (Reich, 1992, p. 177)

And in 1991, Perelman's book *School's Out* and its vision for hyperlearning served as a wake-up call for educators. For even though it was highly controversial, many of his observations rang true with a range of individuals. He saw the potential of technology to bring new "knowledge-packed porta-tools" that allowed personal "just-in-time" learning wherever and however the opportunity warranted (Perelman, 1991, p. 48). He went so far as to forecast the dissolution of concrete and mortar schools, to be replaced with virtual education. Although Perelman provocatively labeled our educational system obsolete, he was not so far from the SCANS report's call for educational reform where "learning to know" should not be separated from "learning to do" and should link what students are taught and how they learn to the realities of the work world.[2] After the SCANS report, schools did attempt educational reform as evidenced by the 1997 President's Committee of Advisors on Science and Technology (PCAST) report on the *Use of Technology to Strengthen K-12 Education in the United States*. According to the National Center for Education Statistics, computers were added to classrooms so that by the year 2002, 99% of schools had access to the Internet and 84% of students used computers in schools (NCES, 2003).

Fast-forward 10 years to the 21st century. Countries like Australia and New Zealand have integrated softer standards into their curricula, initiating a focus on core life skills in addition to traditional literacies. The International Organization for Economic Co-operation and Development (OECD) has developed five key competencies in education that underscore a global initiative to broaden the scope of education to include skills needed for "a successful life and well-functioning society" (OECD, 2005). However, in the U.S., attempts at reform were short-lived. Educational priorities have shifted from long-term—focused reform to short-term—focused high stakes testing, now the core of the Bush administration's No Child Left Behind (NCLB) program. But while American schools are still using traditional methods and are now more than ever focusing on testing, in the world outside schools the pace of change has accelerated. Our increasing use of the computer and other electronic devices, as well as the "enormous effects of instantaneous electronic communication and universal access to knowledge, have pushed the envelope of what is possible, and concomitantly our capacity to perform" (Haste, 2001, p. 94). Again reports call for 21st century skills that echo those in the SCANS report (1991): "digital age literacy, inventive thinking, effective communication, and high productivity" (Burkhardt et al., 2003, p. 49).

Of promise are one-to-one computing initiatives—classrooms in which every student has a computer. The computers allow students access to different modes of learning—sound, pictures, and movies, as well as text and animations. One teacher said, "It's making us think about what makes things interesting for kids, and instead of just memorizing a bunch of facts, we're learning there are better ways to teach them and they really retain the concept" (Zucker & McGhee, 2005, p. 18). These projects are leading to very positive gains in student engagement, interest, increases in academic performance, group, and independent work (Bebell, 2005; Zucker & McGhee, 2005). Still in the early phases, it will take some time and effort before teachers can use these 21st century tools to facilitate the learning of 21st century skills, for example, thinking creatively, decision making, and problem solving. Nonetheless, it is progress. Teachers use the computers to enrich the curriculum, for example, accessing current information on the Internet instead of using outdated textbooks, using tools for visualization or manipulation of data to deepen student understanding resulting in increased student interest and, consequently, better retention of the material (Zucker & McGhee, 2005).

Outside the educational system, the corporate world is also coming to grips with the importance of 21st century skills. Referred to by a range of monikers, "soft skills," "emotional intelligence," or "enterprise skills," recognition is now arising that competent employees are a combination of content expertise and skills and capabilities that help them function well in a social, networked world. As Daniel Goleman (2000), author of *Working with Emotional Intelligence,* has commented:

The rules of work are changing. We're being judged by a new yardstick: not just how smart we are, or our training and expertise, but by how well we handle ourselves and each other. This yardstick is increasingly applied in choosing who will be hired and who will not, who will be let go and who retained, who passed over and who promoted. (p. 1)

Goleman's perspective, while somewhat controversial because of its alleged lack of support for "legitimate, empirical construct" for emotional intelligence (Daus & Ashkanasy, 2003), is based, at least loosely, on a well-established psychological tradition looking at emotional intelligence, as well as myriad studies involving tens of thousands of workers in real workplaces. And his core argument is more or less universally accepted: what people know is taking a back seat to how people work together. The star performers are those who display literacy in social practice and interpersonal communication, as well as knowledge of the specific tasks at hand.

The world is definitely waking up to these ideas. In 2005, a news headline announced that North Carolina is the first state with an initiative to infuse 21st century skills into its schools. Although this initiative has admirable goals, "to ensure every child's success as citizens and workers in the 21st century," the competencies suggest those outlined 10 years ago: "information and communication technology (ICT) literacy, critical thinking, communication, collaboration, global awareness, and business, economic, and civic literacy." Today's requirements go "beyond discrete skills such as literacy and numeracy" (Haste, 2001, p. 94) and beyond those outlined in the SCANS report. The competencies and skills needed for today are about learning; those that help us "learn something, do something or reach an aim," and they "involve creativity, ability for innovation, mobility, flexibility, endurance, reliability and precision" (Sperber & Dupuy, 2001, p. 75.). "These competencies show an ability to learn from unforeseen situations and circumstances and to cope with life situations" (Sperber & Dupuy, 2001, p. 76). The need for change in America's educational system is palpable.

The sheer magnitude of human knowledge, world globalization, and the accelerating rate of change due to technology necessitates a shift in our children's education—from plateaus of knowing to continuous cycles of learning. (Burkhardt, 2003, p. 5)

Learning is a 21st Century Competency

The rapid pace of change and the need for continuous cycles of learning puts the ability to learn at the center of today's competencies.

The most valuable skills someone can acquire are the skills to learn rapidly and efficiently and to go into almost any situation and figure out what has to be learned. (Morrison, 2001)

Technology has, in a sense, caused a cognitive earthquake. With the introduction of each new technology, the techno-plates shift, requiring us to learn new skills and develop new competencies. There is an ongoing relationship between our increasing innovation with technology and the need and development of these competencies. One begets the other. As each technology is mastered, new possibilities are revealed. Tools are enhanced or modified, each requiring further refinement of our skills. These cycles bring ever-increasing levels of complexity with them. For most of us, e-mail was our first experience with Internet-based communication. After obtaining a level of comfort with it, some branched out to e-mail distribution lists (listservs) or bulletin boards, followed by synchronous discussions or chats and conferencing systems. For the adventurous, there were the text-based collaborative games referred to as multi-user dungeons (MUDs) and MUD object oriented (MOOs). Now in our communications portfolio are also instant messaging (IM), blogs, Webcasts, social software, and "folksonomies" (social meta-tagging services), as well as combinations of all of them.

Although technology is impacting all areas of skill and competency, Harvard's Christopher Dede (2000), in a chapter titled "A New Century Demands New Ways of Learning" has identified three specific abilities that are of growing importance:

- Collaborate with diverse teams of people—face-to-face or at a distance—to accomplish a task

- Create, share, and master knowledge by assessing and filtering quasi-accurate information

- Thrive on chaos, that is, be able to make rapid decisions based on incomplete information in order to resolve novel dilemmas

The following paragraphs describe what has happened to make these three abilities so important, as well as explore their implications for learning and provide examples of how young people who have grown up with digital technologies have already developed these abilities. Later in this chapter, we take these same three categories of abilities and show how playing online games can lead to their development.

21st Century Skills: Knowledge-Sharing and Collaboration

The advent of computer and network technology has been both a blessing and a burden in terms of the information that it makes available. The amount of information in the world is increasing so rapidly that the storage of new information increases at a rate of over 30% per year.[3] The results of this growth have raised the level at which we need to think critically about information: its authenticity, its value, and its embedded assumptions, whether on the Web, or through various media, or through face-to-face and online communication. Both explicit knowledge "know-what" and tacit knowledge "know-how" can be distributed widely among people as shared understandings or network-based resources (Brown & Campione, 1994; Gee, 2003). No one person can have enough expertise to master or assess broad categories of information or have access to enough knowledge to go it alone. Siemens (2005) states:

In a knowledge economy, the flow of information is the equivalent of the oil pipe in the industrial economy. Creating, preserving, and utilizing information flow should be a key organizational activity. The new reality is that it takes the collaborative efforts of people with different skills and different expertise to create innovative solutions (Schrage, 1990). Learning, although seemingly an individual accomplishment, is a social process, today more than ever influenced and accomplished through a network of peers, colleagues, friends, and family. (Riel & Polin, 2004; Seely-Brown, 2002b)

As our need for collaboration grows, so too have the tools that connect us in social networks and support the creation of online communities (Haste, 2001; Schrage, 1990). Online communications facilitate groups of people coming together over the network to discuss any issue imaginable, to ask questions, and share provocative insights to which others can respond (Educom Staff, 1997; Lessig, 2001). These online social environments can evolve into "online learning communities" when they foster participants to actively engage in sharing ideas with others, furthering their own learning while at the same time advancing the collective knowledge of the group (Bielaczyc & Collins, 1999; Bruner, 1973; Cole, 1988; Lave, 1988; Mehan, 1983; Norman, 1980; Riel & Polin, 2004; Rogoff, 1994; Scardamalia & Bereiter, 1994; Wertsch, 1997). These learning communities support social constructivist learning in which:

Knowledge is generated through social intercourse, and through this interaction we gradually accumulate advances in our levels of knowing, theories derived from Dewey and Vygotsky. (Anderson & Kanuka, 1998)

People come together with varying levels of skills, providing an opportunity for novices to learn effective techniques and approaches from skilled practitioners who impart "tricks of the trade" (Bielaczyc & Collins, 1999; Brown & Campione, 1994; Collins & Bielaczyc, 1997; Collins, Hawkins, & Carver, 1997; Lave & Wenger, 1991; Riel & Polin, 2004). Over time, roles change as novices increase their skills and they, in turn, share their knowledge with new members, serving as a vehicle for passing on expertise and competence as well as norms and cultural expectations of the community (Haste, 2001; Riel & Polin, 2004).

Scardamalia and Bereiter, educational researchers who have worked extensively with students to build knowledge communities using a tool they developed called CSILE, have found that knowledge communities in schools foster "the progressive problem-solving that generates the vast informal knowledge that has been found to characterize expert competence" (Scardamalia & Bereiter, 1994). Bielaczyc and Collins (1999) articulate a vision for the redesign of schooling around learning communities:

Classroom situations where students learn to synthesize multiple perspectives, to solve problems in a variety of ways, and to use each other's diverse knowledge and skills as resources to collaboratively solve problems and advance their understanding. (p. 272)

Yet with all that we know about the benefits of using learning communities to foster the social construction of knowledge, their use is the exception. The routines and structure of schools are not conducive to supporting learning in this way. In schools today, students learn in chunks of 45 to 90 minute periods, subjects are taught in isolation of each other, learning happens only inside the school walls, and students lack the option to participate or not, making it difficult to characterize students as active participants in learning communities (Riel & Polin, 2004). In fact, when learners do collaborate and share knowledge with one another, more often than not we call it "cheating." But in fact, the modern world requires that knowledge not be limited to one individual's thinking, but rather shared and accessed in a variety of ways. It is our collective intelligence and the communication bridges from one individual to another that represent the possibility of an exponential leap forward in terms of knowledge capability on a large scale.

21st Century Skill: Thriving on Chaos

The third ability listed by Dede involves the ability to thrive on chaos and make rapid decisions. This echoes the competency defined by Haste as the "ability to learn from unforeseen situations and circumstances" (Canto-Sperber & Dupuy, 2001, p. 46). A person has to have creativity to thrive on chaos, to make sense of disparate ideas and make decisions based on incomplete information. Our creativity is of growing importance in the quest to harvest the potential from these new and ever changing innovations. Daniel Pink (2005) argues in his *Wired* article "Revenge of the Right Brain" that today's world calls for people who not only have the ability to think logically and sequentially as traditionally taught in school, but also to use their creative "right brain" facilities:

In a world upended by outsourcing, deluged with data, and choked with choices, the abilities that matter most are now closer in spirit to the specialties of the right [brain] hemisphere— artistry, empathy, seeing the big picture, and pursuing the transcendent. (p. 1)

In *Got Game: How the Gamer Generation is Reshaping Business Forever*, authors John C. Beck and Mitchell Wade (2004) describe this capability as a unique characteristic native to many gamers: the tendency to "go meta" or view problems or situations from a variety of angles, allowing for a range of creative solutions that might not be obvious to those limited to particular points-of-view.

In a time when nothing stays the same for long, business needs people who can creatively organize what at times is overwhelming amounts of information, who can use their creative insight to find patterns, analyze, and synthesize disparate facts, who can take what exists and discover new directions, and apply ideas and tools in new ways. So-called right-brainers are those people we turn to for solving hard problems, who invent one solution and when that does not work invent another, or search through collections of data looking for a spark of insight, hypothesize and then create a way to test and verify their hypothesis. This kind of thinking and creativity is now evident in the way the younger, digital generation lives and thinks. Seely-Brown (2002a) compares the learning process of adults who "do not want to try things unless we already know them to young people who like to get in and muck around, and see what works. Today's kids get on the Web to link, lurk, and watch how other people are doing things, then try it themselves" (p. 19). Seely-Brown points out that this is learning in situ: learning situated in action.

The gamer generation lives in a world "where anything is possible. Gamers have amassed thousands of hours of rapidly analyzing new situations, interacting with characters they don't really know, and solving problems quickly and independently" (Beck & Wade, 2004, p. 12). The learning process that gamers use sounds strikingly similar to three of Bloom's higher levels of learning:

- **Application:** Uses a concept in a new situation;
- **Analysis:** Separates material or concepts into component parts so that its organizational structure may be understood;
- **Synthesis:** Builds a structure or pattern from diverse elements (Clark, 2000).

Speaking at the Front End of Innovation Conference in 2004, Seely-Brown aptly compared the creative process for adults who have grown up without technology to today's digital generation:

We [adults] think of consciously designing things, but ... today's kids are so busy multi-tasking that they "smell" their way through the Web rather than navigate, and for them the Internet is like breathing, they don't think of it as technology. In today's networld, you pull stuff off the Web and co-create new stuff and put it out there with your name on it and gain identity thereby. (Seely-Brown as quoted in Tucker's Blog, 2004)

This "smelling" one's way through the digital world is an internalized capability that reflects an extreme level of comfort with the dynamic nature of knowledge. It is also a fundamental and intuitive part of the larger activity of sensemaking, the "process by which individuals (or organizations) create an understanding so that they can act in a principled and informed manner" (Palo Alto Research Center [PARC], n.d.), or as immortalized by Douglas Rushkoff (1994) in the book *Cyberia: Life in the Trenches of Hyperspace,* that ability to "ride the crest of the informational wave" (p. 60).

Recent research has highlighted the competencies and work habits of today's digital generation documenting how they align with the competencies necessary for the 21st century. Gamers are more social, readily learn through chats and online learning communities around videogame playing, and use technology tools transparently as productivity aids. The skills gained from interacting in the complex, multi-leveled worlds of simulations and games transfer to using decision-support systems that analyze complex problems such as global warming, terrorist threats, and long-term investments in infrastructure (Beck & Wade, 2004). The vice president of Charles Schwab's call center commented on his employees:

The people who play games are into technology, can handle more information, can synthesize more complex data, solve operational design problems, lead change and bring organizations through change. (Antonucci, 2005)

The Opportunity: Online Games as a Practice Arena for 21st Century Skills

Of the myriad communications platforms available today, none of them demonstrate the complexity of 21st century social interaction strategies quite like massively multiplayer online games. As "the first interactive mass medium to unite entertainment and communication in one phenomenon" (Filiciak, 2003, p. 88), MMOGs present a tremendous opportunity to explore a nascent area of media convergence, while possibly understanding how the naturally occurring phenomenon of self-motivated, social learning and collaborative problem-solving reflects the growing need and understanding of 21st century skills.

In many respects, massively multiplayer online games are a graphical extension of the text-based MUDs, MOOs, and so forth that peaked in popularity in the 1980s and 1990s. The MUDs led to a variety of new paradigms in social interaction that are now flourishing and evolving in massively multiplayer environments. Many MMOGs rely on traditional role-playing and gameplay within familiar fantasy and science fiction universes and involve classic pursuits like building up characters, defeating enemies, and fulfilling quests, all classic elements of traditional pen-and-paper and digital role playing games (RPGs). MMOGs, sometimes referred to as MMORPGs (massively multiplayer online *role playing* games) are graphically similar to many contemporary single-player games in the role-playing game (RPG) genre where the player's character is represented by a player-selected, and often player-designed, avatar that has point-based characteristics and a range of skills and abilities. These games are unique, however, in that they also require an Internet connection and an account on one of many game servers to be played. At any one time, hundreds of thousands of people might be playing. Because of technological constraints, however, players are typically limited to one server, where still a few thousand players might be in the accessible game universe at any one time. The most popular of these games to date, World of Warcraft, has approximately 6.5 five million subscribed players (IGN Entertainment, Inc., 2006). Other popular games, Lineage and its successor Lineage 2 have over four million players world-wide. Other popular MMOG titles include Everquest and Everquest 2, Guild Wars, the Matrix Online, Star Wars: Galaxies, City of Heroes, and City of Villains.

The process required to achieve game goals and reach the pinnacle of achievement, typically a high-level character, can result from a range of approaches and quite often involves hundreds of hours of collaborative play in a multi-user environment. For while they can be played individually to greater or lesser degrees depending on the game, the game play mechanics are generally such that true mastery of the game can often only be achieved by

Figure 1. Players lined up for a player-organized costume contest in Atlas Plaza in the game City of Heroes; these games are complex worlds that exhibit many of the characteristics of physical worlds, including a range of emergent social behaviors and in some cases, robust economic activity

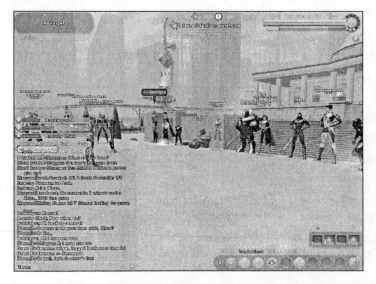

working cooperatively with other players. In fact, some of the games are designed specifically to require interdependence between players:

The game [Everquest] is designed in a way that makes grouping essential for achieving success, a concept that has been central in role-playing games since the days they were played with rulebooks, pen and paper… It is only through working with other players that individual gamers achieve maximum results. (Jakobsson & Taylor, 2003, p. 88)

The development of "soft" skills such as collaboration, cognitive, and social intelligence are not the desired end, but are a form of collateral learning (Johnson, 2005b), the means that allow players to be successful in these environments. Players that do not achieve mastery in navigating the social terrain of the game are often unable to find grouping partners or maintain relationships, and therefore unable to tackle some of the more difficult missions in the game.

The social complexity of massively multiplayer online gaming environments is often unmentioned in discussions about the possibility of videogames for learning. In the past, the majority of attention on videogames, when positive at all, has focused on the possibility of using games to achieve certain predetermined objectives related to established curricula. Yet the opportunity with game environments like MMOGs is far greater than motivating apathetic learners or transferring information in a somewhat more engaging fashion. The play activity that learners engage in is, in fact, the learning opportunity, though our established institutions may struggle with the "fuzziness" and organic nature of this learning:

Important knowledge (now usually gained in school) is content in the sense of information rooted in, or, at least, related to, intellectual domains or academic disciplines like physics, history, art, or literature. Work that does not involve such learning is "meaningless." Activities that are entertaining but that themselves do not involve such learning are just "meaningless play." Of course videogames fall into this category. (Gee, 2003, p. 21)

Yet this is precisely the point. People are learning tremendous skills and developing important real-world capabilities in these games, but somehow this is all occurring outside our educational system. Game environments are "learning cultures consisting of shared and contested meanings whose perpetual evolution lies at the very heart of [the] learning processes. Learning cultures move beyond the popular conception of learning as an activity that is bounded by teaching, educational institutions and learning prescriptions to one which recognizes that learning invariably transcends such boundaries" (James & Bloomer, 2001, p. 9).

In fact, "the level of skills [players] achieve in the pursuit of active and committed citizenship in virtual communities may exceed expectations of teachers in schools." For example, "the literacy skills children attain through playing *Gathering of the Elves*, as evidenced by their written role-playing language, reflects a high lexical density and complexity, detailed descriptive nominal groups, and a high degree of symbolism and figurative expressions" (Thomas, 2005, p. 31). This sense of citizenship is not limited to online environments, either.

Researcher Dmitri Williams (2005) found that his participants were more likely to engage in off-line civic activity after experiencing the agency of activities in virtual worlds.

John Seely-Brown (2004) has commented on the sophistication of the learning environment afforded by massively multiplayer games:

Understanding the social practices and constructivist ecologies being created around open source and massively multiplayer games will provide a glimpse into new kinds of innovation ecologies and some of the ways that meaning is created for these kids—ages 10 to 40. Perhaps our generation focused on information, but these kids focus on meaning—how does information take on meaning?

Perhaps the dissonance between our expectations of school and the realities of digital life boils down to the puritanical notion that learning must involve hard work and certainly no fun. Yet play may be the thing that prepares us best for navigating our increasingly complex lives, social spaces, work environments, and personal relationships. Play theorist Brian Sutton-Smith (2004) has suggested that play represents a "consoling phenomenon" that prepares the player for dealing with life, offering a mechanism for psychologically and cognitively navigating the challenges and difficulties of life. In the past, many of these needs were met through physical play. But in a world where opportunities for physical play are dwindling, it is likely that virtual worlds are emerging as a way to fulfil some fundamental human needs. Henry Jenkins (1998) explains this phenomenon even more fully, arguing that videogames represent an "intensity of experience" and "complete freedom of movement"

Figure 2. A Christmas gathering in City of Heroes. Players regularly congregate to acknowledge off-line occasions, as well as strictly online events like weddings; funerals and memorials marking real-life passings are commonplace, as well

that has disappeared as children (and adults) have less physical spaces to play in. As Sutton-Smith (2004) describes it, play is a way of achieving both competence and confidence in the world. Play is a refuge, but it is also more than that; it is a fundamental necessity for many aspects of human development. Or, in the words of Howard Rheingold (1992), "play is a way of organizing our models of the world and models of ourselves, of testing hypotheses about ourselves and the world, and of discerning new relationships or patterns in the jumble of our perceptions" (p. 374).

We are now seeing a shift toward play in virtual environments. But how does one learn to play? And what does "learning to play" really mean? It has been observed that videogames are often designed as "learning machines" (Gee, 2004) that rely on intuitive, convention-based game design to scaffold a player's learning of the mechanics of gameplay and the game environment as player "curiosity takes the form of explorative coping" (Grodal, 2003, p. 149). But in the dynamic, sophisticated, and collaboration-based MMOG environments also emerges a rich culture of learning support. Not only is interdependence designed into the games, but the flexible parameters specified by game designers involve creating an interactive world where environments are in constant flux: rules change, documentation is scarce, and the mastery of the game relies on a host of skills well beyond the game's manual. Indeed, these games and the strategies for playing them are exercises in co-creation where players, as co-producers, can influence the rules, affect the outcome, and create a rich universe of social interactions and culture that ultimately become the core of gameplay, rather than the periphery.

The learning support mechanisms are underpinned by flexible and ever-changing social networks of senior and junior players who engage in a symbiotic relationship, exchanging game tips and artifacts, scaffolding the learning of less experienced players and allowing more senior players to make their knowledge explicit. Further, there is an ongoing process of behavior modelling that allows players to continue to evolve their social approaches within the game and understand the shifting nuances of an emerging culture. This aspect also allows for legitimate peripheral participation where players learn from proximity to learning in the game, often in a very explicit manner as they observe conversations between players. And even beyond the necessary interactions wired into games through designing interdependence, there are a variety of sociocultural mechanisms at work for helping people through the game, "as people's intentions to learn are engaged and the meaning of learning is configured through the process of becoming a full participant in sociocultural practice" (Lave & Wenger, 1991, p. 29).

One way to look at it is that players self-organize into communities of practice united around the activity of gameplay, yet this self-organization results in the development of a range of capabilities toward which the players are not directly striving, yet are fundamental to mastery within the environment:

Players acquire knowledge in context and in pursuit of immediate goals. Learning is done in the service of game goals... players are immersed in an environment and the learning is done incidentally through problem solving... Players have to figure out everything they need to know to feed themselves, stay safe, rise in experience, acquire the items they covet, and navigate the world around them. But, in this game, they do it by picking up some knowledge that actually has some use in the real world. The game's design is not meant to trick people into learning. It's meant to give players the tools they need to succeed in the virtual world, but tools that might be useful in the real world, as well. (Kelly, 2004, p. 185)

These self-organizing and collaborative communities are what Robert Putnam (1995) in his article "Bowling Alone," describes as networks of "social engagement, fostering sturdy norms of generalized reciprocity and encouraging the emergence of social trust. Such networks facilitate coordination and communication, amplify reputations, and thus allow dilemmas of collective action to be resolved" (Putnam, 1995). Putnam's work is a lamentation on the absence of civic engagement in contemporary society, yet MMOGs are increasingly a powerful form of such engagement. Contrary to popular concern about media and games decreasing social and civic interactions, MMOGs have been found to foster bridging ties (broad but weak social networks), while having little of the perceived negative impact on stronger ties like family (Steinkeuhler & Williams, 2005). Indeed, many nuclear families and romantic couples are playing together, and extended families and social networks are finding it a practical and fun way to keep in touch (Yee, 2005b). A digital futures project (2005) study reveals that more than 40% of respondents say that use of the Internet has increased or greatly increased contact with family and friends.

But aside from developing a deeper sense of community, players develop competency in the three areas that Dede outlined as critical to long-term success in modern work environments:

Collaborate with Diverse Teams of People

When groups form in MMOG environments, they are initially quite often chaotic and disorganized. But over a period of time, a spontaneous order emerges as players learn to sync their behaviors to the behaviors of other players. This is akin to the activity undertaken by musicians in a band finding their collective rhythm, or fireflies lighting up synchronously after a short period of each adjusting to their neighbors' patterns (Strogatz, 2004). Just as "learning is done incidentally through problem-solving" (Kelly, 2004, p. 185) in these environments, increased social capability is a by-product of practice.

As people playing MMOGs span age groups, gender, and cultures, diversity is also a fundamental aspect of play. While certainly not always the case, it is extraordinary how well such a diverse group of people manage to play together, and how well they can self-manage conflicts when they do arise. Many types of intolerant behavior are self-disciplined within the context of play groups, or players who do not "play nice" are simply marginalized, sometimes an equally effective "punishment."

Create, Share, and Master Knowledge

In order for players to be successful in these environments, they must share knowledge, access available resources, and navigate their social milieu successfully in order to get the answers they need when they need them. Players often become expert nodes, available to be questioned about in-game particulars or strategies. Often these players opt to set up

Figure 3. A 16-year-old Japanese school-girl controls the avatar SlumbrousCat from her computer in Tokyo; she is unable to speak English, but having become fluent with the norms of play is still able to contribute to cooperative activities in the American version of City of Heroes

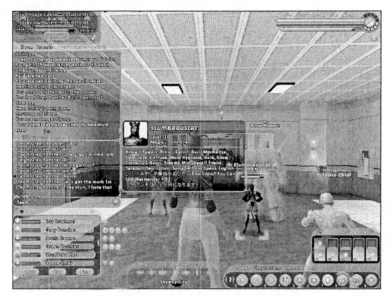

permanent resources in the form of Web sites, lists, FAQs (frequently-asked-questions), and other reference materials. They are not compensated for these activities other than in the form of increased social capital and the fulfilment of their desire to contribute to the game environment in some way. In fact, it is not uncommon for these contributors to see their contributions ripple through the player population as some previously unknown bit of knowledge makes it way into the larger player consciousness and into gameplay practice. As Gee says, "the effectiveness of the circulation of information among peers suggests that engagement in practice, rather than being its object, may well be a condition for the effectiveness of learning" (Lave & Wenger, 1991, p. 93).

Of key importance is the idea that individuals learn within this environment, but so too do their contributions and learning impact the learning of the groups and in-game communities to which they belong. The players take it upon themselves to devise and share strategies that help them master the game. Sometimes these strategies include the discovery of game "loopholes," exploited by players contrary to the intent of the game designers. As such, there is no documentation about these opportunities, yet players pass the knowledge from one player to another, until a "tipping point" is reached and a majority of players begin engaging in the activity.

Information literacy is the flip side of the knowledge-sharing coin and perhaps the most difficult 21st century skill to master. If many people are sharing information, how does one distinguish what is valid and useful from what is erroneous or irrelevant? Gamers learn to understand the importance of context in online environments. Who authored the information? Who are they affiliated with? What agenda might they have? Do they really know what they are talking about? These are all key questions in any critical assessment of the possible validity of an information source.

These skills will become increasingly important in a world that accommodates massive amounts of information, much of which is resident and accessible through the network. Gordon Bell and Jim Gray are quoted in the *Social Life of Information* with the prediction:

By 2047... all information about physical objects, including humans, buildings, process and organizations, will all be online. This is both desirable and inevitable. (Seely-Brown & Duguid, 2002, p. 1)

Thrive on Chaos

To an outsider, MMOGs are profoundly chaotic environments, but as with chaos in biological systems, a structure and logic can be found if one looks closely enough. For instance, it is common practice within MMOG environments that players have to self-organize into playgroups. This process involves self-marketing and negotiation, as well as knowledge of the subtleties of etiquette within these environments. Groupings may occur on a casual or longer-term basis. The more permanent groupings involve organization into often massive guilds or clans, often subject to all the intricacies of politics in any human social settings.

In a self-organized environment it is often imperative that someone manage the chaos by stepping, even temporarily, into a somewhat more directive role. This is especially common when things do not appear to be going well within the context of a battle, or when a

Figure 4. A screenshot from the City of Heroes community site on Allakhazam; players continuously share gameplay tips with one another on hundreds of sites like this one

Figure 5. A screenshot from the MMOG, City of Heroes, shows hundreds of players cooperating to take down a large nemesis

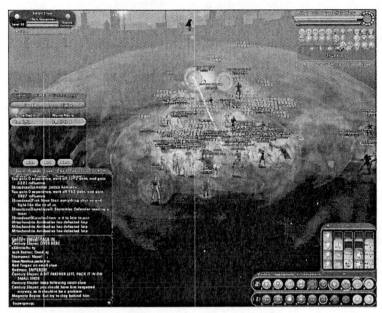

conflict requires mediation. The particularly extraordinary thing about this phenomenon is that the leaders often come from unexpected corners. Even young players can step into this role, and as long as they are making a productive contribution and behaving maturely, their self-selection is rarely challenged. This aspect of meritocracy allows many players to explore facets of themselves that may have gone unexplored in their real lives, sometimes leading to quite significant changes in their careers or perspectives.

This ability to thrive on chaos is also apparent in the rapid decision making capabilities that players exhibit. MMOG environments are dynamic and complex, often requiring players to share strategies and discuss moves, both well in advance and in the heat of battle. Players are continually analyzing and interpreting variables, making rapid decisions based on just-in-time information. Gee (2003, p. 70) characterizes players as being pushed to "operate at the outer edge of their regime of competence causing them to rethink their routinized mastery and move, within the game and within themselves to a new level."

It is the U.S. military, interestingly, that has taken the most interest in the idea of massively multiplayer online games as a practice arena for important military skills. In a recent report, *Massive Multiplayer Online Gaming: A Research Framework for Military Training and Education,* developed by the U.S. Department of Defense (DoD) in collaboration with researchers from Indiana University and Florida State University, the seriousness of interest in the phenomena surrounding these games becomes explicit:

With this focus on emerging technologies, the military is clearly interested in exploring the use of online collaborative games to train staff on the modern day intricacies of combat and noncombat operations. At the same time, the increasing focus on remote-controlled agents has raised expectations and excitement for realistic simulations and games—especially MMORPGs. The military is developing games that could host thousands of networked players. In these games, players potentially could participate for months or years in different roles and later reflect on the consequences of their decisions and actions. Debriefings or reflective processing of these games could help the user understand the purpose of the game and generalize it to different situations. The immediate goal, of course, is to enhance decision-making, problem solving, and reflection skills in the context of a military operation. (Bonk & Dennen, 2005, p. 11)

This is not to say that there are not areas of concern when it comes to videogames generally and online games in particular. There has been a tremendous amount of media coverage in recent years that concerns itself with possible media "effects" of videogame play. And while these effects have never been strongly proven, having relied on loose correlation studies with a notable lack of reliable long-term data, it seems intuitive that having kids interact with violent imagery cannot possibly be good for them. But even apparently violent squad tactics games like Counter-strike can offer many benefits in terms of skill development because they are fundamentally cooperative games where one team must work together to defeat another, just like in most sports activities. For those parents and educators concerned about violence, it is useful to consider studies that suggest that for most players, the ability to use videogames as an outlet for aggression can have a positive outcome on feelings after a gameplay session. Many young male players, while experiencing elevated heartbeats during play, appear and report being much calmer after play, thus substantiating the idea of catharsis put forth by some researchers (Ivory, 2001).

Regardless of what the effects data look like, parental involvement in videogame play is an incredible opportunity to engage kids and ask them tough questions about their violent play, for instance, mediate or maintain a watchful eye when appropriate over their relationships with online friends (especially in the case of younger children), or provide jumping off points to areas of interest that might have been cultivated by the play.

But the other area of grave concern is so-called online game "addiction," a phenomenon that researcher Nick Yee (2005a) prefers to term "problematic usage." This is a tricky area, as a small percentage of players do exhibit undesirable behaviors when they neglect real-life needs as a result of their enthusiastic gameplay. But this is certainly the exception rather than the rule, and really only proves the point that given the opportunity, certain individuals will take any behavior to an extreme. Again, adult involvement is critical here. Parents and educators can help kids avoid the issue of problematic usage by helping them to moderate the amount of time they spend playing, an important consideration given the highly rewarding nature of online game environments, especially for the socially withdrawn. And for both kids and adults, it is critical that we help people learn to transfer the skills that they develop in virtual worlds to off-line environments, as well. Otherwise it can be too easy for some players to withdraw into those worlds, lacking the perspective that an online game need not be the only vehicle for meaningful social relationships.

Preparing Ourselves for the Future

Is it conceivable that massively multiplayer online games might be officially leveraged into practice arenas for 21st century skills? As the platform evolves, it seems likely that production and maintenance costs will be lowered and we might see "the splintering of MMORPG environments into hundreds of different forms, each aimed at a very particular audience" as they move "out of the pure entertainment space" and into educational and business uses." We may even see that "many kinds of employee training will be done in virtuo using corporate and public MMORPGs as training grounds" (Kelly, 2004, p. 185). But will this possibility result in the social and cultural shift needed, or merely result in shoving the square peg of traditional curricula into the round hole of open-ended, self-organized, egalitarian environments? Will our institutions be willing and able to relinquish control to make self-organization and respect for individual autonomy a reality?

For what the world really needs is a shift in the way we view people and their contributions. In our workplaces, we need to engage in a process of "seeing people as resources, not job descriptions," recognizing that "valuable talents, knowledge and experience" "often remain concealed and untapped" as people stick to their "job descriptions and chains of command" (Kline & Saunders, 1997, pp. 132-152). But what we also need is a shift away from thinking of learning as stuffing information into individual heads with the hope that it somehow manages to be actionable. In fact, a major shift is to understand that people are part of a network of resources, distributed across the vastness of physical and virtual space:

The power of distribution—of storing knowledge in other people, texts, tools and technologies—is really the way in which all of these things are networked together. The really important knowledge is in the network—that is, in other people, their texts, their tools, and technologies, and crucially, the ways in which they are interconnected—not in any one "node" (person, text, tool or technology), but in the network as a whole. Does the network store lots of powerful knowledge? Does it ensure that this knowledge moves quickly and well to the parts of the system that need it now? Does it adapt to changed conditions by learning new things quickly and well? These are the most crucial knowledge questions we can ask in the modern world. They are hardly reflected at all in how we organize schooling and assessment in schooling. (Gee, 2003, p. 185)

There is a big lesson from MMOG environments. People are enormously capable when given the space and motivation, even through simple gameplay, to flex their cognitive and social muscle in an environment where anything is possible and experimentation is safe, permissible, and desirable. Among the many equalizing phenomena of virtual worlds, players describe a complex meritocracy in which they are "judged by their characters' actions," enjoy "spontaneous kindness" leading to "genuine friendships," and most importantly, feel like "they are making progress on an emotional level. They're not just getting ahead in the virtual world, but actually maturing, growing, learning from their experiments with behavior, and reformulating their views of themselves and their fellow human beings as a result of their experiences in the virtual world" (Kelly, 2004, pp. 62-85). These experiences represent opportunities for growth, expression and personal transformation that may not be available elsewhere. Yet this type of growth is exactly what a world focused on soft skills and emotional intelligence requires. In many respects, MMOGs represent the ideal state for any organization, one in which "each individual makes a unique contribution by marching to a different drummer but with an underlying common sense of purpose and direction" (Kline & Saunders, 1997, p. 139). Is this to say that classrooms should be replaced with MMOGs? Not at all. It is only to say that we should be paying close attention to the complex social structures and learning mechanisms that are inherent in such environments, rather than dismissing them as a "waste-of-time" or mere child's play.

Paying close attention means funnelling resources into official studies of emergent phenomena and spontaneous learning in a range of digital environments. With this data in hand, we may find ourselves better equipped to envision a future where learning is a natural, yet guided process that fits the curves and nuances of our complex lives.

Conclusion

Imagining things being otherwise may be a first step toward acting on the belief that they can be changed. (Greene, 1995, p. 19)

Modern communication technologies, and the knowledge economy, have brought unprecedented change requiring both new skills and competencies. For over a decade, young people have been increasing their socio-cultural literacy through their participation in online digital worlds. The lessons we are learning are inherent in the social structures and dynamics of online learning. Whether in communities of practice or through games and simulations, online environments can be an effective means for obtaining essential 21st century competencies. Instead of trying to close the gap between the U.S. and other nations based on test scores, we could be taking a leadership position and developing creative solutions to replace our outdated schools with the knowledge and technology-based models so needed to meet 21st century demands. In many respects education and learning are about breaking down barriers of what is known to bring understanding of what is possible. It is time to break down the boundaries of today's schooling and build the models made possible through the advances of technology and online learning environments.

In a way, these models for the future are what the younger generation follows as they embrace modern communications technologies and play in virtual environments. As Dede argues, necessary skills in the 21st century revolve around forging connections, handling information and thriving in chaotic environments. Learning is about achieving those competencies, not memorizing and repeating facts out of context. It is about confidence and competence in the face of uncertainty, novelty, chaos and fuzziness. A new world order is being wrought by younger generations who understand the skills that are relevant to their current worlds, and to the world they will help create in the future. It's time for us all to catch up.

References

21st Century Literacy Summit. (2002). *21st century literacy in a converent media world* (White Paper). Berlin, Germany: Bertelsmann Foundation and the AOL TIme Warner Foundation. Retrieved from http://www.21stcenturyliteracy.org/white/WhitePaperEnglish.pdf

Anderson, T., & Kanuka, H. (1998). Online social interchange, discord, and knowledge construction. *Revue de l'enseignement à distance [Journal of Distance Education],* 13.1. Retrieved July 4, 2006, from http://cade.icaap.org/vol13.1/kanuka.html

Antonucci, M. (2005, June 11). Game skills pay off in real life. Research finds benefits of video games in unexpected areas. *Mercury News.* Grand Forks, ND: Herald. Retrieved July 4, 2006, from http://www.freerepublic.com/focus/f-news/1400817/posts

Bebell, D. (2005). *Technology promoting student excellence: An investigation of the first year of 1:1 computing in New Hampshire middle schools.* Technology and Assessment Study Collaborative, Boston College. Retrieved July, 2006, from http://www.bc.cdu/research/intasc/studies/nhLaptop/description.shtml

Bartle, R. (2003). *Designing virtual worlds.* Indianapolis, IN: New Riders Games.

Beck, J., & Wade, M. (2004). *Got game: How the gamer generation is reshaping business forever.* Boston: Harvard Business School Press.

Bielaczyc, K., & Collins, A. (1999). Learning communities in classrooms: A reconceptualization of educational practice. In C. M. Reigeluth (Ed.), *Instructional-design theories and models: A new paradigm of instructional theory* (pp. 269-292). Mahwah, NJ: Lawrence Erlbaum Associates.

Bonk, C. J., & Dennen, V. P. (2005). *Massive multiplayer online gaming: A research framework for military training and education.* Retrieved from http://www.aldnet.org/downloads/files/186.cfm

Brown, A. L., & Campione, J. C. (1994). Guided discovery in a community of learners. In M. In K. McGilly (Ed.), *Classroom lessons: Integrating cognitive theory and classroom practice* (pp. 229-270). Cambridge, MA: MIT Press/Bradford Books.

Bruner, J. S. (1973). *Beyond the information given.* New York: Norton.

Burkhardt, G., Monsour, M., Valdez, G., Gunn, C., Dawson, M., Lemke, C., et al. (2003). *enGauge 21st century skills* (Report). North Central Regional Educational Laboratory and the Metiri Group. Retrieved July, 2006, from http://www.ncrel.org/engauge/skills/skills.htm

Canto-Sperber, M., & Dupuy, J. (2001). Competencies for the good life and the good society. In D. D. Rychen & L. H. Salganik (Eds.), *Defining and selecting key competencies: Organization for Economic Co-operation and Development (OECD)* (pp. 67-91). Kirkland, WA: Hogrefe and Huber Publishers.

Chomicz, N., Moulton, C., Simons, E., & Stekloff, M. (1997). *The SCANS.* Retrieved July, 2006, from http://literacytech.worlded.org/docs/maththing/ny1p9.htm

Clark, D. (2000). *Learning domains or Bloom's taxonomy.* Retrieved from http://www.nwlink.com/~donclark/hrd/bloom.html

Cole, M. (1998). Cross-cultural research in the sociohistorical tradition. *Human Development,* (31), 137-157.

Collins, A., & Bielaczyc, K. (1997). *Dreams of technology-supported learning communities.* Paper presented at the Proceedings of the Sixth International Conference on Computer-Assisted Instruction, Taipei, Taiwan.

Collins, A., Hawkins, J., & Carver, S. (1997). *Cognitive apprenticeship and the changing workplace.* Paper presented at the Fifth International Conference on Postcompulsory Education and Training, Queensland, Australia (pp. 13-25).

Commission, S. C. W. (2000). *A nation of opportunity: Building America's 21st century workforce.* Washington DC: Digital Commons, Cornell University. Retrieved July, 2006, http://digitalcommons.ilr.cornell.edu/key_workplace/21/

Daus, C. S., & Ashkanasy, N. M. (2003). *Will the real emotional intelligence please stand up? On deconstructing the emotional intelligence "debate."* Retrieved from http://eqi.org/real_ei.htm

Dede, C. (2000, December 1). A new century demands new ways of learning. In D. T. E. Gordon (Ed.), *The digital classroom.* Cambridge, MA: Harvard Education Letter. Retrieved July, 2006, from the Harvard Graduate School of Education [Online], http://gseweb.harvard.edu/news/features/dc_dede12012000.html

Dede, C. (2004, September). Enabling distributed learning communities via emerging technologies: Part One. *T.H.E. Journal.* Retrieved July, 2006, from http://thejournal.com/articles/16909

Dede, C. (2005). Planning for neomillennial learning styles: Implications for investments in technology and faculty. *Educause, 28*(1), 1.

Digital Futures Project. (2005). *Fifth study of the Internet by the Digital Future Project.* Center for the Digital Future, CA. Retrieved from http://digitalcenter.org

Educom Staff. (1997). Brainstorming with Lewis Perelman. *Educom Review, 32*(2). Retrieved July 17, 2006, from http://www.educause.edu/pub/er/review/reviewArticles/32218.html

Filiciak, M. (2003). Hyperidentities: Postmodern identity patterns in massively multiplayer online role-playing games. In M. J. P. Wolf & B. Perron (Eds.), *The video game theory reader* (pp. 87-102). New York: Routledge.

Friedman, T. (2005a). *The world is flat.* New York: Farrar, Straus, and Giroux.

Friedman, T. (2005b). "What me worry?" *New York Times,* Editorial Desk, Late Edition, Section A, p. 25. Retrieved from http://select.nytimes.com/gst/abstract.html?res=F10E10FA3A550C7A8EDDAD0894DD

Gee, J. P. (2003). *What video games have to teach us about learning and literacy.* New York: Palgrave-McMillan.

Gee, J. P. (2004). *Learning by design: Good video games as learning machines.* Paper presented at the Proceedings of the Game Developers' Conference, San Francisco.

Gee, J. P. (2005). What would a state of the art instructional video game look like? *INNOVATE, 1*(6). Retrieved July 7, 2006, from http://www.innovateonline.info/index.php?view=articleandid=80

Gee, J. P., & Shafer, D. W. (2005). *Before every child is left behind: How epistemic games can solve the coming crisis in education.* University of Wisconsin-Madison, Academic Advanced Distributed Learning Co-Laboratory.

Goleman, D. (2000). *Working with emotional intelligence.* New York: Bantam.

Greene, M. (1995). *Releasing the imagination.* San Francisco: Jossey-Bass.

Grodal, T. (2003). Stories for eye, ear, muscles: Video games, media and embodied experience. In M. J. P. Wolf & B. Perron (Eds.), *The video game theory reader* (pp. 129-155). New York: Routledge.

Guardian Unlimited. (2005). *School 'doesn't prepare pupils for work.'* Press Association. Retrieved December 19, 2005, from http://education.guardian.co.uk/schools/story/0,5500,1670853,00.html?gus

Haste, H. (2001). Ambiguity, autonomy, and agency: Psychological challenges to new competence. In D. D. Rychen & L. H. Salganik (Eds.), *Defining and selecting key competencies: Organization for Economic Co-operation and Development (OECD)* (pp. 93-120). Kirkland, WA: Hogrefe and Huber Publishers.

IGN Entertainment, Inc. (2006). Official news. *World Warcraft Vault.* Retrieved July 18, 2006, from http://wowvault.ign.com/View.php?view=Columns.Detail&id=158

Ivory, J. D. (2001). *Video games and the elusive search for their effects on children: An assessment of twenty years of research.* Paper presented to the Mass Communication and Society Division at the Association for Education in Journalism and Mass Communication's Annual Convention, Washington, DC. Retrieved from http://www.unc.edu/~jivory/video.html

Jakobsson, M., & Taylor, T. L. (2003). *The Sopranos meet Everquest: Social networking in massively multiplayer online games.* Retrieved from http://hypertext.rmit.edu.au/dac/papers/Jakobsson.pdf

James, D., & Bloomer, M. (2001, September 13-15). *Cultures and learning in further education.* Paper presented at British Educational Research Associations Annual Conference, University of Leeds, September 2001. Retrieved from http://www.education.ex.ac.uk/tlc/docs/publications/EX_BR_JMB_DJA_PUB_13.09.01.doc

Jenkins, H. (1998). *Complete freedom of movement: Video games as gendered play spaces.* Retrieved from http://web.mit.edu/21fms/www/faculty/henry3/pub/complete.html

Johnson, S. (2005a). Dome improvement. *Wired.* Retrieved from http://www.wired.com/wired/archive/13.05/flynn.html

Johnson, S. (2005b). *Everything bad is good for you.* New York: Touchstone.

Kanuka, H., & Anderson, T. (1998). Online social interchange, discord, and knowledge construction. *Revue de l'enseignement à distance [Journal of Distance Education],* 3.1. Retrieved from http://cade.icaap.org/vol13.1/kanuka.html

Kerka, S. (1992). *Higher order thinking skills in vocational education* (Report No. 127, p. 4). Columbus, OH: Office of Educational Research and Improvement (ED). (ERIC Document Reproduction Service No. EDO-CE-92-127).

Kelly, R. V. (2004). *Massively multiplayer online role-playing games: The people, the addiction and the playing experience.* Jefferson, NC: McFarland and Company.

Kline, P., & Saunders, B. (1997). *Ten steps to a learning organization.* Arlington, VA: Great Ocean.

Lave, J. (1988). *Cognition in practice.* New York: Cambridge University Press.

Lave, J. E., & Wenger, E. (1991). *Situated learning: Legitimate peripheral participation.* Cambridge, MA: Cambridge University Press.

Lessig, L. (2001). *The future of ideas: The fate of the commons in a connected world.* New York: Random House.

McLuhan, M. (1967). *The medium is the massage: An inventory of effects.* New York: Bantam Books.

Mehan, H. (1983). Social constructivism in psychology and sociology. *Sociologie et Societes, XIV*(2), 77-96.

Morrison, J. (2004). The future of learning technologies: An interview with Chris Dede. *INNOVATE, 1*(1).

Morrison, T. (2001). The work of nations: Interview with Robert Reich. *Aurora Online.* Retrieved July 4, 2006, from http://aurora.icaap.org/archive/reich.html

Murray, C. (2005). North Carolina governor announces 21st century center. *eSchool News.* Retrieved from http://www.eschoolnews.com/news/showStoryts.cfm?ArticleID=5627

National Center for Education Statistics (NCES). (2003). *Digest of educational statistics for 2003.* Retrieved from http://nces.ed.gov/programs/digest/d03/list_figures.asp

NCSA. (2005). *National Center for Student Aspirations: Student speak survey, University of Maine at Orono.* Retrieved from http://www.studentaspirations.org/data.htm

Norman, D. (1980). Twelve issues for cognitive science. *Cognitive Science,* (4), 1-32.

Organization for Economic Co-operation and Development (OECD). (2005). *The definition and selection of key competencies: Executive summary.* Retrieved from http://www.pisa.oecd.org/dataoecd/47/61/35070367.pdf

Palo Alto Research Center (PARC). (n.d.). *Sensemaking.* Retrieved from http://www2.parc.com/istl/groups/hdi/hdisensemaking.shtml

Partnership for 21st Century. (1994). *National models of 21st century education.* Retrieved from http://www.21stcenturyskills.org/index.php?option=com_contentandtask=viewandid=31andItemid=33

President's Committee of Advisors on Science and Technology PCAST. (1997). *Report to the President on the use of technology to strengthen K-12 education in the United States.* Retrieved from http://clinton4.nara.gov/WH/EOP/OSTP/NSTC/PCAST/k-12ed.html

Perelman, L. J. (1991). *School's out.* New York: Avon Books, Hearst Publishing.

Pink, D. (2005). Revenge of the right brain. *Wired,* 13.02. Retrieved July 4, 2006, from http://www.wired.com/wired/archive/13.02/brain.html

Prensky, M. (2002). *What kids are learning from playing video games that's positive.* Retrieved from http://www.marcprensky.com/writing/default.asp

Putnam, R. (1995). Bowling alone: America's declining social capital, an interview with Robert Putnam. *Journal of Democracy, 6*(1), 65-78. Retrieved July 11, 2006, from http://xroads.virginia.edu/~HYPER/DETOC/assoc/bowling.html

Reich, R. (1992). *The work of nations: Preparing ourselves for 21st century capitalism.* New York: Vintage Books.

Rheingold, H. (1992). *Virtual reality.* London: Mandarin.

Riel, M., & Polin, L. (2004). Online learning communities. Common ground and critical differences in designing technical environments. In S. A. Barab, R. Kling, & J. H. Gray (Eds.), *Designing for virtual communities in the service of learning.* New York: Cambridge University Press.

Rogoff, B. (1994). Developing understanding of the idea of communities of learners. *Mind, Culture, and Activity,* (4), 209-229.

Rushkoff, D. (1994). *Cyberia: Life in the trenches of hyperspace.* Retrieved from http://www.rushkoff.com/cyberia/

SCANS. (2000). *Learning a living: A blueprint for high performance. A SCANS Report for America 2000.* Washington, DC: US Department of Labor. Retrieved from http://wdr.doleta.gov/SCANS/lal/lal.pdf

Scardamalia, M., & Bereiter, C. (1994). Computer support for knowledge-building communities. *The Journal of the Learning Sciences, 3*(3), 265-283. Retrieved July 4, 2006, from http://carbon.cudenver.edu/~bwilson/building.html

Schrage, M. (1990). *Shared minds: The new technologies of collaboration.* New York: Random House.

Seely-Brown, J. (2002a). Growing up digital: How the Web changes work, education, and the ways people learn. *United States Distance Learning Association, 16*(2). Retrieved from http://www.usdla.org/html/journal/FEB02_Issue/article01.html

Seely-Brown, J. (2002b). *Learning in the digital age.* Forum for the Future of Higher Education. Retrieved from http://www.educause.edu/ir/library/pdf/ffp0203s.pdf

Seely-Brown, J. (2004). *Digital culture and learning in the digital age (abstract).* Retrieved July 7, 2006, from http://cosl.usu.edu/conference/2005/program/

Seely-Brown, J., & Duguid, P. (2002). *The social life of information.* Boston: Harvard Business School Press.

Siemens, G. (2005). Connectivism: A learning theory for the digital age. *International Journal of Instructional Technology and Distance Learning, 2*(1). Retrieved from http://www.itdl.org/Journal/Jan_05/article01.htm

Steinkuehler, C. A. (2004). Learning in massively multiplayer online games. In Y. B. Kafai, W. A. Sandoval, N. Enyedy, A. S. Nixon, & F. Herrera (Eds.), *Proceedings of the Sixth International Conference of the Learning Sciences* (pp. 521-528). Mahwah, NJ: Erlbaum. Retrieved from http://website.education.wisc.edu/steinkuehler/papers/steinkuehlerICLS2004.pdf

Steinkeuhler, C., & Williams, D. (2005). *Where everybody knows your (screen) name: Online games as "Third Places."* Paper presented at the Digital Games Research Association

(DIGRA) Changing Views: Worlds in Play International Conference. Retrieved from http://www.gamesconference.org/digra2005/download/DiGRA_2005_Program.pdf

Sterling, B. (2003, December 2). *Audio interview. Massive Change Radio.* Retrieved from http://www.massivechange.com/interviews.html

Strogatz, S. (2004). *Sync: The emerging science of spontaneous order.* New York: Hyperion.

Sutton-Smith, B. (2004). *Video conference with Brian Sutton-Smith and Eric Zimmerman.* Presented at the Digital Games Research Association (DIGRA), Level Up International Conference, Utrecht, The Netherlands.

Thomas, A. (2005). Children online: Learning in a virtual community of practice. *E-Learning, 2*(1), 27-38. Retrieved from http://www.wwwords.co.uk/elea/content/pdfs/2/issue2_1.asp#4

Tucker, R. (2004). *John Seeley Brown at the Front End of Innovation Conference, 2005, Blog.* Retrieved from http://www.innovationtools.com/weblog/innovationblog-detail.asp?ArticleID=450

U.S. Department of Labor, The Secretary's Commission on Achieving Necessary Skills (SCANS). (1991). *What work requires of schools.* Washington, DC: U.S. Government Printing Office.

Wertsch, J. (1997). *Mind as action.* London: Oxford University Press.

Williams, D. (2005). *A brief social history of game play.* Paper presented at the Digital Games Research Association (DIGRA) Changing Views: Worlds in Play International Conference. Retrieved from http://www.gamesconference.org/digra2005/papers/d3ca6639d9bbfb3d36beea8b34f4.doc

Yee, N. (2005a). Problematic usage. *The Daedalus Project.* Retrieved from http://www.nickyee.com/daedalus/archives/00336.php

Yee, N. (2005b). Who do you play with? *The Daedalus Project.* Retrieved from http://www.nickyee.com/daedalus/archives/00468.php

Zucker, A., & McGhee, R. (2005). *A study of one-to-one computer use in mathematics and science instruction at the secondary level in Henrico County Public Schools, SRI International.* Retrieved from http://ubiqcomputing.org/lit_review.html

Endnotes

[1]   Pew/Internet Reports. (2004, April). Technology and Media Use. Retrieved from http://www.pewinternet.org/PPF/r/121/report_display.asp

[2]   SCANS. (2000). Learning a living: A blueprint for high performance. In *A SCANS Report for America 2000* (p. 34). Washington, DC: U.S. Department of Labor. Retrieved from http://wdr.doleta.gov/SCANS/lal/lal.pdf

[3]   How much information? (2003). *Executive summary.* Retrieved July 18, 2006, from http://www2.sims.berkeley.edu/research/projects/how-much-info-2003/execsum.htm

Chapter V

Rethinking Cognition, Representations, and Processes in 3D Online Social Learning Environments

James G. Jones, University of North Texas, USA

Stephen C. Bronack, Appalachian State University, USA

Abstract

Three-dimensional (3D) online social environments have emerged as viable alternatives to traditional methods of creating spaces for teachers and learners to teach to and to learn from one another. Robust environments with a bias toward peer-based, network-driven learning allow learners in formal environments to make meaning in ways more similar to those used in informal and in-person settings. These new created environments do so by accounting for presence, immediacy, movement, artifacts, and multi-modal communications in ways that help learners create their own paths of knowing using peer-supported methods. In this chapter, we will review the basics of the technologies and the theoretical underpinnings that support the development of such environments, provide a framework for creating, sustaining, and considering the effectiveness of such environments, and will conclude by describing two examples of 3D virtual worlds used to support course instruction at the university level.

Introduction

Three-dimensional (3D) online social learning environments have emerged as viable alternatives to traditional methods of creating spaces for teachers and learners to teach to and to learn from one another. While games are the most prominent example of the use of a 3D graphics interface (Wikipedia, 2006), our experience and research suggests that the use of this technology in non-game settings can positively impact learning and communications among students and with their instructors (Aldrich, 2004; Jones, 2004, 2006; Jones, Morales, & Knezek, 2005; Jones & Overall, 2004). Well-designed 3D online learning environments that combine social constructivist principles with immersive gaming theory support deep cognitive learning in powerful new ways. Robust environments with a bias toward peer-based, network-driven learning allow learners in formal environments to make meaning in ways more similar to those used in informal and in-person settings. These new created environments do so by accounting for presence, immediacy, movement, artifacts, and multi-modal communications in ways that help learners create their own paths of knowing using peer-supported methods. These environments move beyond current Web and text-based methods for instructional delivery to create new Internet-based delivery methods that can facilitate new interactions, higher levels of engagement, and deeper learning.

In this chapter, we will review the basics of the technologies and the theoretical underpinnings that support the development of such environments. Then, we will provide a framework for creating, sustaining, and considering the effectiveness of such environments on the abilities of participants to use their experiences in virtual worlds to make better sense of their experiences in the real one. We will conclude by describing two examples of 3D virtual worlds used to support course instruction at the university level.

3D Online Learning Environments

3D online learning environments take elements of massively multi-player online entertainment technology and overlay selected tools to create an interface that allows students and instructors to interact and to communicate within a designed environment for the purpose of accomplishing informal or formal learning. Online environments used in games are the "convergence of two technologies: video games and high-speed Internet" (Kushner, 2004, p. 98). When an environment is built and displayed correctly, the user understands intuitively the space as displayed. For example, in an environment representing a building, users feel as though they are walking the halls of the building, or are engaged with other users in discussions, or immersed in a training situation. The user moves through and interacts with the environment using the keyboard, a mouse, or other heptic devices. As users move, the computer generates new graphics in real time to give them feedback on their position in the environment. This gives the user the feel of movement through space. Placing objects in a contextual 3D framework provides users known reference points and creates a framework for communications and interactions. Students at remote sites assume control of a representation of themselves, also called an avatar, in a shared created environment such as a school building, a park, or any other space. These highly graphical 3D interfaces allow individuals, through

Figure 1. 3D online learning environment used at the University of North Texas

their "avatar," to interact not only with the environment but also with other user "avatars" in the environment. The java-based 3D online learning environment used at the University of North Texas segments the environment into conversation areas based on physical spaces (i.e., a classroom, a meeting room, or a hallway) so that learners can move their avatars to areas for small group or private discussions. A screen-shot from the environment being used at the University of North Texas for distributed education is shown in Figure 1. These virtual worlds are persistent social worlds—spaces in which the artifacts of others help guide new learners and where users are free to move and interact as they please.

Immersive environments can range from simple instructional settings to environments created from any dataset. Created Realities Group (CRG) (2002) has created a 3D online multi-user environment that displays over 97% of the surface of Mars using NASA's Mars Orbiter Laser Altimeter (NASA, 2004). Figure 2 shows a screen shot of the summit of Olympus Mons captured from the CRG environment. Students in distributed locations are able to login, move over the virtual surface, and perform math and science exercises using actual Mars topography data. The University of North Texas in the spring of 2005 developed curriculum materials aimed at middle-school students in after school programs interested in learning math and science problems using this mars online environment (Jones & Kalinowski, in press). The materials were aligned with the Montana Educational Standards for students' knowledge, skills, and abilities. Testing with students in Montana using the materials and software has not yet taken place at the time of this writing.

Figure 2. Mars 3D environment generated in real-time based on NASA MOLA data; Olympus Mons, Top Cone (MARS_19.0_227.0) (Created Realities Group, 2002)

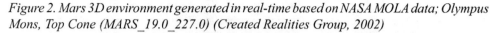

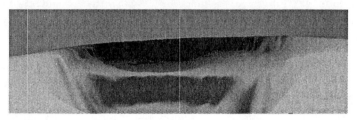

3D online learning environments are benefiting from advances in technology that earlier approaches to online learning lacked, thanks to the explosive growth of the computer enter-tainment industry. The combination of affordable consumer technologies such as personal computers and gaming consoles, widespread Internet access, and scalable server technology makes it possible for 3D online learning environments to emerge as the next generation of distributed learning technology. Multi-user online games are ubiquitous within contemporary pop culture (Steinkuehler, 2004), and emerging research suggests these games provide a complex and nuanced environment in which multi-modal social and communicative prac-tices may be developed (Gee, 2003). What is at first limited to the online environment soon moves into other forums of communications. For example, a 3D online learning environment when used to enhance a Web-based course can improve a student's interaction and discourse. Students using a 3D online learning environment showed increased daily text-based com-munications, peaking earlier in the semester, and sustaining this increase in communications longer over the semester as compared to students who only used the Web-based environment (Jones, 2006). This research will be discussed in greater detail later in the chapter.

But learning is more than downloading, and courses are more than chats. The emergence of 3D environments as viable spaces for learning is also based on the social nature of learning and the affordances such environments supply. As Palloff and Pratt (1999) note, "people and the interaction among them in the distance education environment is essential to the development of a high functioning distance education class." The key is that 3D online learning environments bring students and instructors to the front of the interaction. They share the roles of creators and consumers of knowledge and learning, thus breaking the isolated roles commonly seen in Web-based methods where instructors are subject matter experts that create and students are the consumers of that information. 3D online learning environ-ments make this possible, because the environment promotes equality of communications and interaction. In a fully interactive world that allows users to contribute content, there is no limit to what students can add to the learning environment and the learning itself.

The thing about interactive learning, however, is that you cannot just sit and ponder. At some point, learners are compelled to do something. But what can you do when you do not know what to do? How an individual behaves in an environment depends upon his/her understand-ing of the causal structure of that environment (Tenenbaum & Griffiths, 2001). A 3D online learning environment has the potential to generate structures that a user is already familiar with and can then more easily infer causation from the observation of the 3D environment as a metaphor. However, computational model structures and processes in the mind cannot adequately account for cognition in interactive learning environments alone. Lave (1988) contends that we must look at activity systems in which individuals participate in large systems. Within such systems, cognition is a complex social phenomenon that is distributed. Lave and Wenger (1991) state that the gradual transformation of an individual participant to a central member of a community through apprenticeship and increased participation is a key factor in learning. While there are numerous learning effects happening when a user is "in" the world interacting with others and the environment, the tenets of social constructiv-ism, especially the role of the expert group in providing cognitive scaffolding, play critical roles in the success of the 3D online environments.

Social Constructivism and
Online Learning Environments

Knowledge, according to social constructivists, is the artifact of decisions made by people in groups, based on their on-going interactions. In a sense, knowledge is a public record of transactions between like-minded people. It is grounded in the inquiring activities and commingled tasks through which people relate. What we each, individually, know is uncovered through the process of interacting with the world around us, and the others we find in it. And there is plenty "out there" to know, it seems. Constantly, people act based on a broad collection of assumptions—things they all seem to know to be true—that are tacit to some and mysterious to others. What differentiates those who "know" from those who do not is the process of learning that happens when one participates in a community of practice under the guidance of both more and less experienced peers.

Learning involves change brought about by experience and interaction between people and their environment. These changes manifest themselves in intellectual aptitude, cognitive strategies, motor skills, and dispositions. Some believe learning is a directly observable change in behavior—the result of conditioning by reinforcement. Others believe learning is an indirectly observable internal process where learners compare new information to existing knowledge and either build new or modify existing schemata. Social constructivists view learning as the result of neither solely intrinsic schema nor purely extrinsic motivations but, rather, as a contiguous process that exists each time people willfully interact with each other in the world around them. Any effort to develop an effective online learning environment must consider the ways in which the participants become part of a community of practice and are able to construct knowledge in a social context.

As will be discussed in the case studies presented at the end of the chapter, principles of social constructivist learning provide the foundation for the conceptual framework of the Reich College of Education at Appalachian State University. This framework provides the foundation for the students thinking about online learning environments. The conceptual framework is an evolving construct, but the underlying basis remains firmly girded in the following assumptions about learning:

- Knowledge is created and maintained through social interactions;
- Learning is participatory where students take an active role;
- Development proceeds through stages and among more- and less-experienced peers within a community of practice;
- A specific and general knowledge base emerges from learning through meaningful activity with others;
- Learners develop dispositions relative to the community of practice.

Knowledge is Social

What we know, we know together. Knowledge is situated within the communities and social interactions where it is crafted. Dewey (1897) suggests that education is both psychological and sociological, and that one cannot be considered without the other. Cognition is distributed; that is, individual thinking and problem solving are revealed through socially contextualized practices. Social constructivist learning environments provide ample opportunity for learners to interact with experts, peers, content, and activities in formal, informal, and serendipitous ways.

Learning is Participatory

Vygotsky (1978) suggests that deep learning occurs in a predictable cycle: first, on a social level and second on an individual one. Learning occurs through participation in communities of practice—loose collections of individuals with shared goals, both implicit and explicit, engaged in continuous collaborative activity. Communities of practice are generally not spontaneous, but rather develop around activity toward accomplishing tasks that matter to those involved. Communities of practice provide an important backdrop for learning because of their social nature. Social environments support the reflective thinking and complex problem solving required for learners to develop from less- to more-experienced members of the community.

Learning Leads Development

Learners develop in predictable stages and as a result of the social learning activities in which they engage. Guided by meaningful interactions with more accomplished peers and driven by the explicit expectation to engage in something useful, learners move from novice to expert over time. Learners develop from primarily externally driven reactors—appropriating the behaviors and strategies of those they believe are more knowledgeable—to more expert participants, able to organize knowledge and call upon theoretical constructs to solve contemporary problems.

Knowledge Emerges from Meaningful Activity with Others

As each community of practice evolves, their ways of thinking and the heuristics for action that emerge produce an identifiable knowledge base that is both general to the greater community and also specific to the domains that define the community. This knowledge base encompasses the shared beliefs, assumptions, and values that play a significant role in defining the communities in which learning occurs for those participating. The knowledge base frames both the public and tacit principles that guide interactivity within the environment, and also document the development of the community of practice over time.

Learning Dispositions

Each community of practice is defined by more than simply what they know or what they do. Communities of practice are defined in part by their dispositions toward that which they know and do. Dispositions serve an important role in communities of practice and, therefore, are an important component of the learning process of their members. Dispositions provide both subtle and glaring hints about what attitudes, beliefs, and values are shared by each member of a community. Dispositions shape the general nature or *ethos* of the community and, as such, form the backdrop for learning by all members within a community. Effective social constructivist learning environments accurately reflect the nature of the community in which they occur, thereby allowing new members to develop dispositions that allow each to engage in increasingly productive and useful ways.

As virtual worlds evolve into increasingly sophisticated social environments, it is important to both developers and members to recognize that as people interact within them, they are learning. Understanding the social nature of learning—and recognizing the environmental factors that impact the efficiency and effectiveness of that learning—is a critical skill. Virtual worlds are uniquely situated to serve as rich environments for engaging in communities of practice. The process of learning and the knowledge that results from the activity of these communities can provide useful insight for designers and users, alike. Environments that account for the principles of social constructivism offer users the opportunity to learn and to develop together in natural, effective ways.

Cognitive Scaffolding and
Online Learning Environments

Cognition is central to learning because it describes what we do when we think we know what we are doing. This question highlights the important role cognitive scaffolding plays in helping learners move from novice to expert thinking. Kameenue and Simmons (1999) define cognitive scaffolding as a temporary framework that allows the learner to understand the first steps in the learning process. Cognitive scaffolding has also been defined as a form of incentive or help, adapted to the student's ability level, intentionally provided to help a student perform some task (Jonassen, Mayes, & McAleese, 1993). This broader definition of cognitive scaffolding holds that learners are supported during initial, as well as later learning stages, and that initial cognitive scaffolding is not discarded, but rather integrated into the learner's primary framework of cognition. Online learning environments that incorporate 3D elements provide a valuable opportunity to promote cognitive scaffolding. Cognitive scaffolding can play an important role in improving student satisfaction and accelerating discourse within the online learning environment. The 3D environment provides a temporary framework (scaffolding) for the user to integrate into existing cognitive strategies. As learners move into new areas of learning, the environment continues to support new cognitive scaffolding for more advanced learners at a decreased level than is required by more novice learners.

The concept of cognitive scaffolding links existing theories of situated learning (Lave & Wenger, 1991), sociocultural theory (Vygotsky, 1978), Piagetian constructivism (J.S. Bruner, 1961), and cognitive apprenticeship (Brown, Collins, & Duguid, 1989) and describes the mechanisms through which such theories may be put to practice via strategies that support thinking. According to Gagne, cognitive strategies are the specific means by which people guide their intellectual functioning. They are the tools that people use for learning, synthesizing, creating, and accessing other cognitive functions required to make sense of the world and to communicate that sense to others. As we think our way through the real world each day, we develop rules and other mechanisms to help us utilize our cognitive strategies efficiently and effectively. The motif of the real-world context presented by the 3D environment combined with existing real-life rules helps virtual world learners to transfer the rules and skills learned from real-life into the 3D learning environment and then to build within that existing scaffold more quickly and easily.

In 3D online learning environments, learners and their activities are *situated*—that is, they find themselves within and as part of the constructed environment, rather than existing separately from the environment (Bredo, 1994). A learner in a 3D environment moves and interacts with the environment as an active participant, not as a viewer of a static scene. As an active participant, learners complete tasks that are helpful and useful, not forced and external. The tasks in which learners engage via situated activities are authentic—that is, they emerge from naturally occurring interactions within the environment, rather than from neatly packaged and predictably embedded external prompts. Authentic tasks engage students in their zone of proximal development (Vygotsky, 1978) through activities that may be more difficult than students can handle alone, but not so difficult that they cannot be resolved with support from peers or teachers who model the appropriate strategies.

Situated learning is a naturally occurring phenomenon when people are compelled to learn together, because it is a natural way of learning. Premack (1984) suggests, "If the adult does not take the child in tow, making him the object of pedagogy, then child will never become an adult (in competence)" (p. 33). In a 3D learning environment, the new and inexperienced typically are mentored by more experienced learners and both gain from the social interaction between the two. In more advanced online settings, groups of users work in teams to solve problems or overcome obstacles. In cognitive apprenticeship, learners work together to acquire, develop, and refine new skills in an authentic domain of activity. 3D environments can be constructed to provide authentic domain activities in a wide range of situations, many of which are inaccessible in the traditional classroom. Authentic tasks and active building of knowledge are characteristics of constructivist learning environments (Bruner, 1961, 1997; Piaget, 1972). When a learner encounters something in the 3D environment that is new or different, then the learner constructs or adds new framework to his or her understanding.

These characteristics may explain why some students feel more comfortable communicating with each other over e-mail after having used the 3D online learning environment (Jones, 2006). Even meeting only as avatars in a created reality, some students report feeling more satisfied with their communications, because they feel they have actually met with other students and the instructor via a graphical interface (Jones, 2003). Today, many massively multi-player online games (MMOG) use segments of these theories to promote game play and interaction both explicitly and implicitly among and between users and the game. The educational environments discussed within this chapter are providing basic research into the use of such environments in education and insight into the effectiveness of cognitive scaffolding as a strategy for supporting learners within.

Creating and Sustaining
Effective Learning Environments

An effective learning environment, one that the users could say fosters learning and community and the providers could say supports required learning outcomes, is only possible when the users and providers are both successful in fulfilling certain critical roles within the system as a whole. The role of the provider (schools, trainers, educational authority, instructors, etc.) is to design, develop, support, promote, and eventually migrate the learning environment. The role of the users (students, instructors, facilitators, etc.) is to communicate and interact, facilitate learning, and create community within the learning environment. The roles we discuss in this section are initial starting points for the relationships that participants might play in creating and sustaining effective learning environments. It is important to note that participants in the process might be part of one or both groups. Additionally there is no barrier to participants taking on more than one role.

For Providers

The "provider" is the group that begins the process. This could be any number of interested parties that have some stake in the development and eventual use of the learning environment. The eventual users of the environment might even be the group that begins this process. The specific roles that the provider group plays include development and implementation, production, and later migration. These areas should look familiar to anyone in software or project development, since they are based on the theories and concepts of project life-cycle management (Marchewka, 2002; Netsite, n.d.; WIPO, n.d.).

Development/Implementation

The concept of the 3D learning environment project drives both its vision and mission. The goals and desires for outcomes of the vision and mission provide the framework for the processes that follow. These fundamentals drive all the following development of requirement and design documents for the environment. During these stages the issues of who the environment is for (target audience), purpose, technological requirements for both the system and end user, and other important aspects of the system are determined. The decisions made early in the project need to be carefully considered since they will impact the final implementation of the system to be used. These decisions will then impact the users of the system and can make the difference between a successful and unsuccessful learning environment. As an example, selecting a technology that would require the users to have the most modern of computers and graphics card and broadband Internet connection might limit the initial group of users and could then jeopardize the potential of creating critical mass for the user community. How a group goes about this process will vary depending on the demands of the group and those involved. At the end of this initial stage, the learning environment is launched into production and users begin to use it for its desired purpose.

Production

After development occurs and the learning environment is launched (users are first allowed to use it outside testing), the production stage begins. Being "in production" means that users expect the system to be dependable and available on a daily basis to support their learning. The requirements and roles of the provider group in this stage are much less focused on development and much more focused on support and maintenance. The providers of the system must be able to provide support functions such as training, technical support, account management, administration, maintenance, and other like functions. These are all "mission" critical functions and roles that must be provided. Without a strong production support process in place, many issues occur that may seriously impact the potential effectiveness of the learning environment. Research suggests that new users to educational telecommunication systems can be negatively impacted by technology and training issues (Harris & Jones, 1995; Valauskas & Ertel, 1996), which, in turn, foster decreased satisfaction and reduced use of the system. Much of the success of a new learning environment hinges on the creation of a critical mass of users and over time a continual growth in use that maintains the critical mass. Ensuring users have a stable and productive experience within the learning environment is critical. Depending on the type of learning environment being developed, users of the system itself might take on significant roles related to daily operations and administration.

Migration

Migration is an important topic because any learning environment that is successful over time will be faced with the issue that technology will change and the investment of time, money, content, and community will need to be moved into a new infrastructure. While migration would seem not to impact the creation of an initially successful learning environment, it has been seen as a barrier for some to fully invest in development of content and materials for the fear that the investments could not be recovered and as a result might have caused those projects to not be as successful as they might have been. While the cost of tools and expertise to build and maintain 3D environments and related scripting/interactions is decreasing each year, the issue of updating or moving existing content between platforms is still very much in flux.

The 3D content, which we will define as those objects and resources that make up the physical 3D environment, include geometry, textures, lighting, and other information (i.e., avatars, buildings, benches, lampposts, etc.). Exchanging 3D content has the easiest path for migration at the object level. The more complicated issue to be resolved is the migration of interactions and scripting. Creating a 3D online environment consists of modeling the environment (objects, textures, relationships) and then specifying interactions and behaviors of elements within the environment. These programmed interactions take a static 3D environment and make it a dynamic system that can support situated learning and simulations. The programming also represents an additional investment in development that takes the 3D content and makes it into something much more than atmosphere that helps with immersion. The difficulty with migration of this programming between platforms is due in most part to the custom nature of the current generation of 3D online environments. Most 3D online environments have developed procedures that control these interactions, and often these procedures are tied closely to the concept and technology implementation of the application. As a result, many of the core procedures that generate a unique environment are not as portable, because they are based on libraries or other routines that are proprietary.

Migration of the programmed interactions will become less of a problem as commercial engines and middleware approaches gradually replace custom development. With more standardized tools will come the emergence of agreed upon authoring tools that will allow novices the same ability as experts to specify interaction in these 3D online environments (Hendricks, Marsden, & Blake, 2003). The emergence of future authoring tools may help resolve the issue of migrating interactions and at the same time reduce the cost of 3D environment content development and maintenance. Migration will become less of an issue in the future for providers of these new systems.

For Users

Primarily the critical roles and functions that users provide to help create a successful learning environment take place during the production (live) phase of the system. Roles and tools can be broken into the areas of discourse and interaction, course and learning facilitation, and learning community. For this discussion, we will break user functions into roles and the tools within the system that would support those roles. As noted previously, users of the environment can play more than one role. The important issue is that someone fills the role in order to have a highest probability of success.

Discourse and Interaction

Discourse and interaction is the most basic building block in the environment. Users will be using chat interfaces (text and audio) to communicate in real-time and working together to provide interactions. Discourse and interaction is happening one-to-one, one-to-many, and many-to-many. Riel (1990a) identifies several structures that lend themselves to the electronic communications medium that focus on participant roles and their needs. Based on these structures, Riel (1990b) developed an analytic framework of participant structures to compare interaction within and across computer network communities. The basic roles, based off Dr. Jones' (2001) research at UT Austin, can be broken into the basic roles of the question-asking person, the information person, and the support person, seen as follows. When these roles are provided for, meaningful discourse has the best opportunity to occur.

- **The question-asking person:** If no one asks questions, then there can be no discourse. In online real-time communication, discourse can be fragmented in open areas. One role of the learning environment is to help focus discourse onto content topics when appropriate. Questions open the flow of communications. From a simple query like, "Is anyone here?" a dialog begins. In healthy environments, all participants become question askers and are involved with the discourse.

- **The information person:** Another important role is that of information provider. This role is not necessarily assigned to the subject matter expert or instructor exclusively, but can be filled by any one or more of the participants. Information sharing can be focused, specialized, expert help, or it can be a more general forum of advice and/or consultation. In new systems that lack a critical mass of expert users, facilitators or guides can be recruited to provide this role until the general user population is more educated. In more advanced learning environments, this facilitation is provided via scripted interaction that trains new users how the environment works.

- **The support person:** As the name suggests, the support person is someone who supports the environment. In a game, this might be the game master. In an online learning environment, always having someone on-call to handle problems and issues is an important role. Many times, users will ask for help from an information person. When that fails, having a support person to contact directly can be an important factor in whether or not the environment is functioning effectively. The support person cannot be seen as a crutch, since part of the purpose of the environment is for the users to build a community of support between and among themselves. However, there will be administration and technical issues that the user popular will not be in a position to solve.

These roles might seem trivial or self-apparent, but without them, a community of active users is difficult—if not impossible—to create. Discourse and interaction are essential elements of effective learning environments. Providing simple, compelling tools users can employ to assume their social roles is a critical design factor for effective 3D learning environments. The decisions regarding communications technologies are not the only applicable ones, however. Deciding upon a model of how folks learn is also essential to creating effective learning environments.

Learning

Some believe learning is a change in behavior brought about by some external stimulus. Others believe learning is a change in the way one thinks, instigated by considered interaction with both external prompts and internal rules. Still others view learning as a social act, a continual process in which people interact with others and appropriate one another's behaviors, beliefs, and dispositions. Regardless of how one believes learning occurs, it is important for users to consider the interplay between tool and technique when creating an effective online learning environment. Later, we will describe the use of both synchronous and asynchronous learning tools to support discourse, as well as collaboration and other interactions, in several university courses. The tools facilitate sharing and conveying thoughts and concepts, and include whiteboards, overheads, group management systems, and others. The type of use and organization of the environment, however, depends on the philosophy of learning that drives the course. While much research discusses the use of 3D environments within a constructivist framework, 3D environments can support other methodologies, as well. However, it is important for designers of online learning environments to think deeply and critically about the interplay between the technology in use and the pedagogy in mind. Underlying beliefs about how people learn drives all pedagogy; and all technologies, at some level, suggest their own use. Our experience suggests that 3D learning environments are most effective when they instantiate socially-oriented, actively situated learning methods.

Whereas 3D learning environments can support any type of methodology, no environment will be effective if essential questions about learning are not carefully considered and addressed. For example, how do we define learning? Is it knowledge or skill acquired by instruction or study, alone? Also, who is involved in the process of learning? Traditionally, we think of learning as a process that requires both a teacher and a student, but perhaps this is too limited. And how does the process of learning work, exactly? It is impossible—or, at best, impractical—to observe directly the process of learning, so when we assume learning is happening, what behaviors are important to observe and to verify? Often, these include goal setting, feedback, behavior modeling, and transfer, to name a few. Finally, why does learning occur, what conditions maximize the potential for learning?

Too often, online learning is reduced to focusing on implementing a particular "learning technology" into an environment, with little regard for how the content and the message are related to the manner in which they are presented. An effective learning environment is one that supports the transmission of information by providing a context for people to communicate. The structure of an environment helps give meaning to the interactions and information constructed within it. But simply accepting structures as-is, within the environment as it is experienced, results in "surface" learning. Creating collaborative structures is deeper and requires that users go beyond just that which is present on the surface of the online environment. Fostering more mindful engagement within the learning environment is key. Learning is most likely when the users within the environment foster the appropriate motivation, activity, and interaction with peers, experts, and others necessary to offer a reasonably full and complex knowledge base upon which each learner may draw.

Community

The type of community to be built depends greatly on the type of learning environment being developed. In this section we will talk about the types of learning environments we are using to support courses at the university level. Within these systems there are two types of users that visit the system. The first is the student that is taking a course and has assigned usage as part of a course. This usage might be in the form of interaction with the system or with other students in the system. The second are users that return to the system as part of the community. While students taking courses are a constant, one of the real benefits of the technology is when an active learning community can be built. A key to this is to build in mechanisms that attract new users or retain students that have used the environment in a course. These mechanisms vary according to the available interfaces from the technology. Promotion of the environment is necessary to keep new users inflowing into the system to replace those users that leave (Butler, Sproull, Kiesler, & Kraut, 2005). At the University of North Texas, we promote the free use of the system to support student gatherings and communications. Students use the system for weekly gathering in the virtual environment and for study groups for other courses. While students do log in, we have yet to achieve enough use on campus to have a group of regulars logged in. Students normally use e-mail to arrange times to meet in the environment. At Appalachian State, users report both planned and serendipitous meetings with classmates and instructors and utilize the communication and content resources for both course and non-course interactions. Although user citizenships remain available even after a particular course has ended, it is unclear how many users remain active within the virtual world after completing their course or degree program.

User contributed content is a very attractive mechanism to gain and maintain users in the environment. As was mentioned earlier, involving users in the management and mentoring of new users to the system is valuable. People also benefit from participating in social relationships (Baym, 1999). Building a system that helps students maintain social ties with people already known off-line, as well as those first met online, is very powerful (Butler et al., 2005).

Creating the initial critical mass of users is essential to building a long-term online community. When a critical mass of users gather, the system becomes much more self-sustaining with less effort in promotion. This is because users recruit friends and other students to use the system. The more users using the system, the more opportunity there is to create new activities and interactions.

Going to College in 3D: Two Case Studies

Nearly all college students are online, and most use e-mail and IM/chat regularly. As the digital generation enters college and the workforce, the educational institutions that serve them are changing. Postsecondary enrollments are skyrocketing—and the growth is online. The U.S. Department of Education predicts new college enrollment records will be set every year during the first decade of the 21st century—reaching 17.7 million students by 2011. According to the National Center for Educational Statistics report, Distance Education at Postsecondary Education Institutions: 1997-98, half of all post-secondary institutions in the U.S. offered nearly 60,000 distance-based courses to nearly 2 million college students in 1997-1998 (Lewis, Snow, Farris, & Levin, 1999). More recently, the Pew Internet and American Life project reports that in their March-May 2002 survey, 7% of Internet users had taken a course online for college credit, and 6% had taken some other type of online course (Madden, 2003). Today, most colleges and universities offer some form of distance education (Jones, 2005). One in five institutions offers at least one completely distance-based degree and/or certification program, and two-thirds offer at least some distance-based courses. Most are offered at the undergraduate level, and public institutions are more than twice as likely as private ones to offer distance education. Postsecondary coursework in education, in particular, is moving online. Of the postsecondary institutions that offer distance-based courses, nearly one-third offer programs in education. Two-thirds of institutions that offer distance-based education indicate that increasing student access to education is their primary goal. In *Sizing Up the Opportunity: The Quality & Extent of Online Education in the U.S. in 2002 & 2003*, the Sloan Consortium notes that more than 550,000 students took *all* of their classes online in the fall 2002 semester (Allen & Seaman, 2003).

Internet- and video-based technologies are the most prevalent teaching and learning tools in distance education. Today, 90% of distance-based education uses Internet-based, asynchronous technologies as the primary mode of instruction (Jones, 2005). Fewer than half utilize synchronous methods. Interestingly, while the usage rate of video-based technologies remained steady between 1995-1996 and 1997-1998, Internet-based learning technology usage *tripled*. By the fall 2002 semester, 11% of all higher education students in the U.S. were taking online courses. Next, we describe two universities' approaches to using virtual worlds as environments for learning.

AET Zone: Creating a Social World for Learning

The instructional technology (IT) program at Appalachian State University in Boone, North Carolina has developed the program into a three-dimensional multi-user virtual world, named AET Zone. AET Zone is an innovative online medium for supporting a community of practice among distance-based students, faculty, graduates, and support staff. AET Zone adds elements of space, movement, and physical presence, along with conversational tools, artifacts, and metaphors not usually found in more traditional Web-based counterparts. Users—referred to as "citizens"—are represented by avatars and move throughout course scenes interacting with other avatars and the objects that comprise the virtual world, itself. Objects may be linked to Web pages, conversation tools, or other resources. While text-based chat is available for avatars to communicate on a large group as well as individual basis, additional chat rooms are provided for multiple small group audio discussions.

The typical student is a K-12 classroom teacher who wants to integrate technology into her curriculum or who wants to become an instructional technology specialists or chief technology officer at the district level. Most are teaching within a 100-mile radius of the university. In fact, most students do not come to campus for any classes. All required courses are offered to off-campus cohorts based in locations near their homes and/or their workplace. While the virtual world is an integral component of the program, faculty and students do meet face-to-face regularly in courses at the beginning of the program with reduced numbers and frequency of meetings as the members of a cohort gain understanding of what is expected and how to proceed during the latter stages of the program. Most courses schedule a final class session during which students present term projects and articulate their understandings; however, a handful of courses are conducted entirely online within the virtual world.

AET Zone was constructed using Activeworlds, Inc. technology (Mauz, 2001). The world is one of several within the Appalachian State University virtual "universe." The universe server is hosted by the Appalachian State University technology services team on a fully redundant server system. Citizens download a customized browser—about 3 Mb in size—that connects each directly to AET Zone. The browser has four distinct areas (Figure 3):

1. A 3D view of the world, either in first person or a third person view

2. A text-based chat that allows users to interact individually or with all who are logged on

3. A Web-based content browser that connects interactions of the user with objects in the world

Figure 3. The AET Zone Interface (3ʳᵈ Person View)

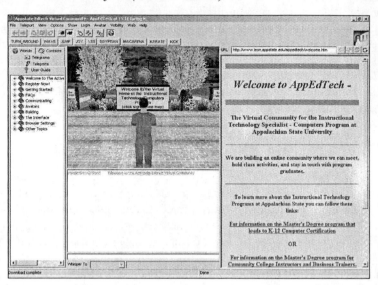

4.   A utilities space with access to help files, telegrams sent by other users, teleports (similar to bookmarks), and contacts (similar to buddies)

Students can install the AET Zone browser on any Windows computer connected to the Internet. All students in the instructional technology program are provided with access to the browser and a username and password. Broadband access is useful, but not necessary, due to the caching technique employed by the Activeworlds server. Once logged on, students

Figure 4. An overhead view of the entry area for AET Zone

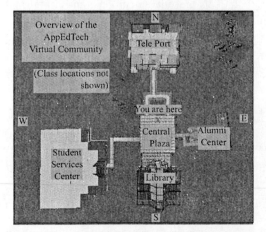

can see and interact with each other as well as with students in other courses, graduates of the program, and the instructors of the various courses.

AET Zone is comprised of many spaces (Figure 4). Behind the user, upon entry, is the library building. This AET Library is a 3D interface to the distance-based services of the physical library on campus. Students may read full-text articles from the university databases or order a book from the stacks. Students may chat directly with university research librarians. On the right side of the entry plaza is the Alumni Center building, with links to Appalachian State Alumni resources designed specifically for graduates of the instructional technology program. Straight ahead is a park. On the other side of the park is the Tele Port. Each gate within the teleport leads to a different course.

Each course within AET Zone is unique in appearance and operation according to the nature of the content and the form of interaction that is desired to meet course goals. For instance, a course on hypermedia presents students with "hypermazes," which allow students to experience hypermedia by choosing their own path through information and resources. A telecommunications course provides an opportunity to explore components of a network by walking through it, either from the Internet to the computer or vice versa. A course on Web design is organized that has physical levels through which students progress. Each level represents a set of skills encompassed by the course. Each set of skills is dependant on the skills of the previous level. A course on the integration of computer technology into instruction begins with a path around a lake. On this path, students are asked to address key questions and issues associated with the integration process. Later, a new path is opened that goes into a forest. In the forest, students are asked to build their own area (in glades set aside for the purpose) that demonstrates what they have learned in the earlier parts of the class. Also, a case-based seminar on the various issues of educational technology and organizations is set in a Roman forum (Figure 5), with teleports to a fictitious school building in which various characters present their points of view on a particular situation (Figure 6).

Figure 5. The "Forum" in the issues class

Figure 6. Getting the perspective of a group of teachers in the issues class

The organization of these areas allows students to move to them and between them in a non-linear fashion according to their needs and interests with timelines for projects, sharing (discussion, brainstorming entries, etc.), and establishing the flow of the class. All classes have discussion boards, forms for entering information to be shared with classmates for discussion, links to resources and readings, and audio chat areas where small groups can meet to discuss their projects.

The faculty in the ASU IT program has experimented with teaching multiple sections of the same class in the same virtual world environment during the same semester. Individual sections meet on different days, at different times, and are led by different instructors. Yet, all explore the same content in the same world and use the same threaded discussion board to discuss the same issues together. As each faculty member guides one or more sections of each course, each is engaged in the discussions, projects, and efforts of the entire group. Small groups form within these larger groups for various projects, assignments, discussions, and other needs. Some groups form between sections and even between classes. Occasionally, former students return to explore resources or add to the discussions. In AET Zone, participants are afforded many and frequent opportunities to interact with others who are in the same course, even if they are not in the same section of the course, with instructors from other sections of the course they are in, and with students who are at different stages of their program of study, creating a more natural and richer community in which to participate.

University of North Texas

The research at the University of North Texas (UNT) is focused on using 3D online learning environment to foster the creation of new forms of online course interaction and feedback that accelerate and increase discourse both among students and with the instructor. These online environments are showing that they also raise the satisfaction level of the students using the delivery method (Jones et al., 2004). The research has been focused on the impact that the technology provides through (a) using immersive environments that create a context for interaction, (b) cognitive scaffolding provided by the avatars and interactions, and (c) high-order communications supported by integrated voice and other collaborative tools. Unlike Appalachian State, UNT has not yet started to put content into the environment, but is examining the environment as it relates to community and interaction.

The University of North Texas uses a client/server portal-based 3D online learning environment developed by Dr. Jones' research group prior to joining the faculty at UNT (see Figure 7). Both the server and client software are written in java and allow students on Linux, Windows, or Macintosh computers to access the system for courses. The entry-level cluster system requires two servers. The first server supports database, system management, and other user applications. The second server supports user access to the cluster. Additional user servers can be added to the cluster depending on the number of simultaneous users the environment needs to support course delivery. In addition to supporting the display of the 3D environment and associated graphics and avatars, the client supports a simple set of tools that are presented within the environment to support course interaction and discourse. These tools include text, audio, overheads, whiteboard, and so forth. Additional tools can be added as needed. Students and instructors use different modes depending on their needs. Students who are uncomfortable speaking can use the text-based chat for voicing their questions in a course. The instructor can use the audio chat mode in order to provide more information than they could easily type in. Multi-modal interactions allow the system to utilize more than one mode over time to ensure that students with different learning styles are effectively reached.

In 2003, Dr. Jones began to use his 3D online learning environment with selected courses within the program of Computer Education and Cognitive Systems at UNT. He began to track message flow and later to analyze discourse in courses he taught that used both the 3D online learning environment and text-based communications. He then compared this to courses he taught that were Web-based only and those for hybrid courses that were some face-to-face and some online. For the research being presented here, no automated interac-

Figure 7. University of North Texas Online Learning Environment

tion was designed into the system. The participants in the learning environment create the discourse, interaction, and feedback. The system provides no feedback or direction to the user other than collision detection. This approach is similar to player-versus-player interaction in games, where the environment is static and the users interact with each other.

Student Satisfaction

The initial research at the University of North Texas focused on student satisfaction comparing face-to-face, Web-based, and 3D online learning environments for course delivery. Initially the attitudes toward information technology of students situated within a 3D online learning environment and students located in a traditional face-to-face classroom were compared (Jones et al., 2005). During a later semester a Web-based course and the 3D online learning environment were examined. The primary instrument used was a collection of measures gathered in the publication "Instruments for Assessing Attitudes Toward Information Technology," made available by the Institute for Integration of Technology into Teaching and Learning (Knezek & Christensen, 1997). What was of interest is that the 3D online learning environment (treatment) tracked the face-to-face course delivery (control). Students felt that the 3D online learning environment provided the same level of satisfaction and interaction as the face-to-face course. Student outcomes, based on grades, between the treatment and control were in the expected ranges and comparable to previous semesters. When the 3D online learning environment was compared to the Web-based course delivery, students felt that the 3D online learning environment provided a much richer and satisfying learning experience. A majority of students that participated in follow-up interviews indicated that this was because of the higher quality and higher fidelity of interaction they felt they had with the other students and instructor that the text-based communications did not seem to provide in their Web-based courses. The 3D online learning environment, using a similar amount of bandwidths as the Web-based course, performed at a higher level with regard to satisfaction and attitudes toward the materials and instruction for the students participating during both semesters of research.

Accelerated and Increased Text-Based Discourse

While video conferencing and other forms of high-bandwidth technology have widened the palette of communications options for distributed learning, text-based tools remain the lowest common denominator for a student population with varying levels of Internet connectivity. Web-based courses have received widespread acceptance and use for creating and supporting learning activities across disciplines within education (Hill, 2001). This is seen in the fact that more than 90% of post-secondary institutions that participated in a research study between 2002 and 2004 reported that e-mail was their primary course communications method, followed closely behind with Web pages and Web-based message boards at over 80% (Jones, 2005). The University of North Texas has been very progressive with the development of Web-based courses and now offers more Web-based courses than any other university in the region.

Dr. Jones' graduate research at the University of Texas Austin was focused on the factors involved with building high-levels of discourse and synthesis between students and mentors using text-based communications (Jones, 2001). The one pattern of interest that has emerged from the various studies is that the more message exchanges that can happen over a prolonged period of time by the participants, the better chance the participants have of attaining meaningful discourse. In his dissertation research, Dr. Jones found that participants in a facilitated message process focused on a curricula topic took between 10 and 18 weeks to reach a sustained, high-level discourse when using text-based e-mail. The participants only communicated via e-mail and never used alternate communications, like telephone, face-to-face meetings, and so forth. Even with facilitation and structuring of the initial discussion to help form successful discourse, only teams that maintained prolonged communication over 10 weeks reached meaningful discourse (Jones, 2001). Ten weeks is the better part of a long semester for most universities. This is one reason why cohorts are used, so that groups of students stay together for longer periods of time and are able to create and sustain high levels of discourse between semesters.

Courses taught at the University of North Texas take place in three modes: in-person face-to-face courses (traditional), Internet Only (no face-to-face meetings), and blended where there is a varying degree of face-to-face and Internet communications. In 2003, Dr. Jones began to track message flow and later to analyze discourse in courses taught that used each of these delivery modes. Figure 8 compares the average weekly e-mail flow per student between nine Computer Education and Cognitive Systems courses taught between 2003 and 2005 using each of the modes. Three courses were blended using an initial face-to-face class meeting, followed by 3D learning environment and e-mail exchanges to support course delivery and discourse. Three courses were blended with face-to-face meeting every two or three weeks using e-mail between class meetings. Three courses were Internet only using the university's Web-based course delivery system and tools. CECS 5100, a master's course in educational programming, used the 3D environment and e-mail. CECS 6210, a doctoral course covering theories of interactive multimedia, and CECS 5420, a Web-authoring course for educators, were taught using the face-to-face meeting every other week with e-mail. CECS 5400, a master's course in educational telecommunications, was taught using only the Web-based course delivery system. Each course was designed and taught by Dr. Jones and used the same methods and requirements for student discourse. The course sizes were between 8 and 15 students in each course. These factors allows for the comparison between the courses shown in Figure 8.

As was discussed earlier, text only communications used by the Web-based courses had student exchanges, but nothing prolonged or frequent. Initial looks at discourse revealed that students tended to answer the readings, but not move past the facilitated prompts as set in the course curriculum. The students using the 3D online learning environment showed accelerated discourse, a greater number of exchanges on average by week, and prolonged interaction via e-mail over the semester. The courses that met every other week had improved discourse, but we believe it was not as increased as the courses using the 3D online software because of the more frequent face-to-face meetings being used for high-level discussion. Blended courses are providing more feedback and structure that then allows discourse to grow in a faster manner.

The patterns of accelerated exchanges among students using a 3D online learning system are very promising. We believe that similar systems capable of providing the same types of

Figure 8. Average number of messages sent by students by week shown averaged by type of course delivery

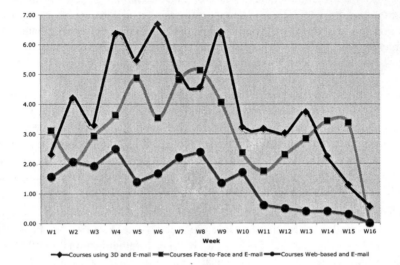

interactive fidelity to the 3D online learning system (i.e., video conference) would produce similar results. These are at least two reasons for using the 3D online learning environment over other approaches. One is an Internet bandwidth consideration, since the technology is capable of supporting users on dialup connections. The second is, that like the Web, it can be provided into every home that has an Internet connection, a computer, and a 2000 or newer graphics adapter.

What we are surmising from this data is that students have more meaningful online discourse when involved with a blended course because of discourse/cognitive scaffolding. When students and their instructor have a visual or perceived environment or structure for communication, trust is more easily accomplished that results in more frequent exchanges earlier in the semester and that then generates higher-order discourse. We are looking at doing further discourse analysis (Harris & Jones, 1995; , 1999) on this data to determine the depth and message flow of the discourse in order to build a clearer understanding of the communications.

Conclusion

Whereas virtual worlds have opened new opportunities for effective online learning, they present unique challenges, as well. For example, learners are often outside their comfort zone as they begin working within this world. Many are not comfortable in taking responsibility for their learning, in being guided rather than being told, in learning for themselves rather than attempting to please the instructor. Often, we must help our students unlearn "the ways they have learned" in the past as they explore a different paradigm of what it means to learn. Students often need encouragement to converse and to collaborate with each other and in small groups, while also fostering serendipitous meetings that serve student needs. This requires constant modeling and guidance from more experienced users. One important lesson is the freedom—and challenge—of considering student learning experiences from multiple dimensions. Many times course organization is determined by a schedule that sequences all activities. Building in a 3D world challenges us to break out of that straight-line thinking

Teaching in virtual worlds also presents several new challenges to instructors. These new types of environments require the instructor to think differently about the role of teaching, learning, content, and interaction. Such environments may be built to represent real or imagined learning spaces that may differ greatly from the traditional four-walled school classroom. No longer bound by bricks and mortar, nor time and place, instructors may create a new paradigm for instruction, for guiding and learning, and for sharing and communicating content and experiences among students who possess all levels of expertise. Instructors must think about ways students will move through a 3D space and interact with various artifacts, tools, content, and other students. They must also seek to develop learning communities in which opportunities to communicate with other students, whether with their peers or others, are a central part of the experience.

Our experiences designing 3D learning environments remind us that learning activities may not necessarily be linear and prescribed by the course designer or instructor. The process of building classes, providing services, and interacting with students in our created worlds has left us ruminating key questions about the development of virtual environments—and how they differ in ways from those we consider when designing purely Web-based courses. Designing a class in 3D causes one to think differently about class structure, representation, and processes. The 3D character of the environment, the manner in which participants interact, and the very nature of the learning activities we are attempting to foster are all impacted by the environment, the interaction, feedback, and the engagements available.

In a 3D environment, courses may be linear or more exploratory (non-linear), with activities and assignments constructed to encourage investigation and with communication tools for students and instructors to share and to learn from the results of their exploration. Courses and online interactions may also be freeform, allowing students and instructors to simply meet and dialog. Planning for user interaction and participation takes on a different character from either face-to-face classes or Web-based classes. Participants are presented with innumerable ways to experience the environment. They are not restricted to pre-determined navigation. The environment facilitates learning activities that depend on participants "meeting," planned and unplanned, in real-time.

In these courses, we are attempting to have students take on the responsibility for learning, building upon their own background and experiences, as well as developing "scaffolding" that works for them. We have learned that as each student finds his or her "voice," powerful conversations emerge that share information, resources, and creative efforts. We find that we as instructors participate in the many discussions taking place collectively and in small groups, both synchronously as well as asynchronously, throughout the environment. It is this sharing, distributing, and building of knowledge that leads to new knowledge and ultimately a different kind of learning and understanding than that often found in more traditional learning settings. Understanding how the principles of social constructivism and practical applications of cognitive scaffolding impacts online learning, will allow for the creation of richer more fulfilling educational experiences for all involved.

References

Aldrich, C. (2004). *Simulations and the future of learning: An innovative (and perhaps revolutionary) approach to e-learning.* San Francisco: Jossey-Bass/Pfeiffer.

Allen, I. E., & Seaman, J. (2003). *Sizing the opportunity: The quality and extent of online education in the United States, 2002 and 2003.* Retrieved October 10, 2005, from http://www.sloan-c.org/resources/sizing_opportunity.pdf

Baym, N. (1999). *Tune in, log on: Soaps, fandom, and online community.* Thousand Oaks, CA: Sage Publications.

Bredo, E. (1994). *Cognitivism, situated cognition, and deweyian pragmatism.* Retrieved September 15, 2005, from http://www.ed.uiuc.edu/eps/pes-yearbook/94_docs/bredo.htm

Brown, J. S., Collins, A., & Duguid, S. (1989). Situated cognition and the culture of learning. *Educational Researcher, 18*(1), 32-42.

Bruner, J. S. (1961). The act of discovery. *Harvard Educational Review, 31*(1), 21-32.

Bruner, J. S. (1997). *The process of education.* Cambridge, MA: Harvard University Press.

Butler, B., Sproull, L., Kiesler, S., & Kraut, R. (2005). Community effort in online groups: Who does the work and why? In S. Weisband & L. Atwater (Eds.), *Leadership at a distance: Interdiscplinary perspectives* (pp. 1-32). Mahwah, NJ: Lawrence Erlbaum Associates.

Created Realities Group. (2002). Retrieved January 5, 2003, from http://created-realities.com/marsonline.htm

Dewey, J. (1897). My pedagogic creed. *School Journal, 54*(3), 80.

Gee, J. P. (2003). *What videogames have to teach us about learning and literacy.* New York: Palgrave MacMillan.

Harris, J., & Jones, J. G. (1995, April). *A study of online communications among subject matter experts, teachers, and students: Message flow and functions.* Paper presented at the American Educational Research Association, San Francisco.

Harris, J. B., & Jones, J. G. (1999). A descriptive study of telementoring among students, subject matter experts, and teachers: Message flow and function patterns. *Journal of Research on Computing in Education, 32*(1), 36-53.

Hendricks, Z., Marsden, G., & Blake, E. (2003). A meta-authoring tool for specifying interactions in virtual reality environments. In J. Gain & A. Chalmers (Eds.), *Proceedings of the 2nd international conference on computer graphics, virtual reality, visualisation and interaction in Africa* (pp. 171-180). Cape Town, South Africa: ACM.

Hill, J. R. (2001). *Building community in Web-based learning environments: Strategies and techniques.* Retrieved September 20, 2002, from http://ausweb.scu.edu.au/aw01/papers/refereed/hill/paper.html

Jonassen, D. H., Mayes, T., & McAleese, R. (1993). A manifesto for a constructivist approach to technology in higher education. In T. Duffy, J. Lowyck, & D. Jonassen (Eds.), *Design environments for constructivist learning.* Heidelburg, FRG: Springer Verlag.

Jones, J. G. (2001). *A study of communications between subject matter experts and individual students in electronic mail contexts.* Unpublished doctoral dissertation, University of Texas, Austin.

Jones, J. G. (2003). Internet-based 3D graphical MOO software that supports distributed learning for both sides of the digital divide. In P. Kommers & G. Richards (Eds.), *World Conference on Educational Multimedia, Hypermedia & Telecommunications* (Vol. 2003, pp. 246-248). Honolulu, HI: Association for the Advancement of Computing in Education.

Jones, J. G. (2004). Hot topics panel: Advances in 3D image applications: Interactive and collaborative 3D online environments. In L. Schamber & C. L. Barry (Eds.), *American Society for Information Science and Technology: Managing and enhancing information: Cultures and conflicts* (Vol. 41, p. 590). Providence, RI: Information Today.

Jones, J. G. (2005). *Issues and concerns of directors of post-secondary distributed learning programs concerning online methods and technologies.* Paper presented at the American Educational Research Association, Montreal, Canada.

Jones, J. G. (2006). *Accelerating online text-based discourse via 3D online learning environments.* Paper presented at the Society for Information Technology and Teacher Education International Conference, Orlando, FL.

Jones, J. G., & Kalinowski, K. (in press). *Mars explorer! An immersive 3D expedition on the surface of the red planet.* University of North Texas.

Jones, J. G., Morales, C., & Knezek, G. (2004). Student attitudes towards an integrated 3D learning environment. In L. Cantoni & C. McLoughlin (Eds.), *World conference on educational multimedia, hypermedia & telecommunications* (Vol. 2004, pp. 1378-1382). Lugano, Switzerland: Association for the Advancement of Computing in Education.

Jones, J. G., Morales, C., & Knezek, G. A. (2005). 3D online learning environments: Examining attitudes toward information technology between students in Internet-based 3D and face-to-face classroom instruction. *Educational Media International, 42*(3), 219-236.

Jones, J. G., & Overall, T. (2004, February). *Changing logo from a single student system to a 3D online student collaboratory/participatory shared learning experience.* Paper presented at the Texas Computer Educators Association, Austin, TX.

Kameenui, E. J., & Simmons, D. (1999). *Toward successful inclusion of students with disabilities: The architecture of instruction.* Reston, VA: The Council for Exceptional Children.

Knezek, G. A., & Christensen, R. (1997). *Teacher and student attitude towards information technology questionnaire.* Retrieved July 20, 2004, from http://www.tcet.unt.edu/research/index.htm

Kushner, D. (2004, June). The wrinkled future of online gaming. *Wired, 12*(6), 98-110.

Lave, J. (1988). *Cognition in practice.* Cambridge UK: Cambridge University Press.

Lave, J., & Wenger, E. (1991). *Situated learning: Legitimate peripheral participation.* Cambridge UK: Cambridge University Press.

Lewis, L., Snow, K., Farris, E., & Levin, D. (1999). *Distance education at postsecondary education institutions: 1997-98* (No. Statistical Analysis Report NCES 2000-013): National Center for Education Statistics, U.S. Department of Education, Office of Educational Research and Improvement.

Madden, M. (2003). *America's online pursuits.* Retrieved October 10, 2005, from http://www.pewinternet.org/pdfs/PIP_Online_Pursuits_Final.PDF

Marchewka, J. T. (2002). *Information technology project management.* Hoboken, NJ: Wiley, John & Sons, Incorporated.

Mauz. (2001). *Mauz's active worlds pages.* Retrieved March 10, 2004, from http://mauz.info/awhistory.html

NASA. (2004). *Mars Orbiter Laser Altimeter (MOLA).* Retrieved January 14, 2004, from http://nssdc.gsfc.nasa.gov/database/MasterCatalog?sc=1996-062A&ex=3

Netsite. (n.d.). *Project life cycle.* Retrieved October 10, 2005, from http://www.netsite.co.uk/content-21

Palloff, R. M., & Pratt, K. (1999). *Building learning communities in cyberspace: Effective strategies for the online classroom.* San Francisco: Jossey-Bass Publishers.

Piaget, J. (1972). *The psychology of intelligence.* Totowa, NJ: Littlefield, Adams.

Premack, D. (1984). Pedagogy and aesthetics as sources of culture. In M. Gazzaniga (Ed.), *Handbook of cognitive neuroscience* (pp. 15-35). New York: Plenum.

Riel, M. (1990a). Cooperative learning across classroom in electronic learning circles. *Instructional Science, 19*(6), 445-465.

Riel, M. (1990b). Four models of educational telecommunications: Connections to the future. *Education and Computing, 5*(1989), 261-274.

Steinkuehler, C. A. (2004). *Learning in massively multiplayer online games.* Paper presented at the Sixth International Conference of the Learning Sciences, Mahwah, NJ.

Tenenbaum, J. B., & Griffiths, T. L. (2001). Structure learning in human causal induction. In T. Leen, T. Dietterich, & V. Tresp (Eds.), *Advances in neural information processing systems* (Vol. 13, pp. 59-65). Cambridge, MA: MIT Press.

Valauskas, E. J., & Ertel, M. (1996). *The Internet for teachers and school library media specialists.* New York: Neal-Schuman.

Vygotsky, L. S. (1978). *Mind in society: The development of higher psychological processes.* Cambridge, MA: Harvard University Press.

Wikipedia. (2006). *Game programmer.* Retrieved January 30, 2006, from http://en.wikipedia.org/wiki/Game_programmer

WIPO. (n.d.). *Project life cycle methodology.* Retrieved October 10, 2005, from http://www.wipo.int/it/en/projects/plc.htm

Chapter VI

E-Simulations in the Wild:
Interdisciplinary Research, Design, and Implementation

Karen Barton, University of Strathclyde, UK

Paul Maharg, University of Strathclyde, UK

Abstract

This chapter examines the relevance of research on scientific discovery learning in simulations to professional legal education simulations. There are striking similarities between the research findings from this domain, and our experience of running simulations in law in the Glasgow Graduate School of Law. However, simulation learning depends on factors that arise not only from the design of the simulation, but also from the environment of implementation. We argue that, while the paradigm of simulation research represented by many of the studies on scientific discovery learning is a valuable one for law and other disciplines, the educational effectiveness of e-simulations also depends critically on three factors: design of learning outcomes, type of simulation field, and the organization of communities of practice around and within a simulation. These factors demonstrate a fundamental need to re-configure design concepts around the potentialities of the emerging new medium in the form of a new "trading zone."

Introduction

The rise and rise of simulation as a form of entertainment is one of the Internet success stories in recent years. Massively multi-user online role-playing games (MMORPGs) have demonstrated the attraction of simulation as a form of social gaming (Castronova et al., 2003). The growth of simulation e-learning, though less developed as an industry, shows similar potential (Chapman, 2005; Gee, 2003) with one report claiming a two to three years' time-to-adoption for educational gaming applications (Horizon Report, 2005). This potential has been some time in gestation: the concept of computer-based simulation has been written about and researched for the last 20 years at least, in fields as diverse as business, mediation, engineering, and bioscience.

The value of simulations has not been lost on occasional commentators in the legal domain. One early commentator noted that simulation and gaming techniques could be used to teach problem solving; and he suggested that such techniques had potential as research and educational tools (Drobak, 1972). The first computer simulation game was used in the context of an urban legal studies program, and was built to enhance students' decision-making roles in a simulated city (Degnan & Haar, 1970). More recently, in their overview of computer simulations, Widdison, Aikenhead, and Allen (1997) observed that most educational computer simulations neglected substantive law, transactional settings, and abstract situations. The authors went on to discuss how these underdeveloped aspects might be expanded in the area of contract law (Aikenhead, Widdison, & Allen, 1999; Widdison et al., 1997). Even in these early papers there was an emphasis on the necessity for interdisciplinary work if computer simulation were to be realized as a viable form of legal education.

It is one function of this paper to explore aspects of that interdisciplinary context and its relevance to legal education—one version, as it were, of Unger's notion of expanded discourse (Unger, 1983). In the second section of the paper we briefly summarize a number of aspects of the research into what might be termed "scientific discovery learning" within the domains of science-based and medical education and draw out themes in user experiences. As we shall see, those themes revolve around the concept of the representation of reality. In a sense this should come as little surprise to anyone familiar with the literature of constructivism and project- and resource-based learning. Representation—literally, the re-presentation of reality—is a problem that surfaces in many educational approaches, including situated learning, problem- and scenario-based learning, constructivist learning, and much else (Herrington, Oliver, & Reeves, 2003; Petraglia, 1997; Shaffer, 2004). In the third section we shall briefly summarize how, on a practical level, we are dealing with these issues in a simulation environment within the GGSL. While a resolution of these issues is not possible in this chapter, in the fourth section of the paper we shall at least begin to sketch possible approaches to a number of these issues, which, on a theoretical level, address the concerns of educationalists and e-learning designers.

Representation in Simulations

The term "computer simulation," in an educational sense, is amorphous, covering a range of different applications and educational concepts. At a basic level, a computer simulation is a set of algorithms that defines a learning environment; but this tells us little about what constitutes the environment, how it is composed, how it is used, and how it affects the learning experience. For the purposes of this paper, I shall define a computer simulation in legal education as a digital environment that is a representation of aspects of legal reality, in which a user can, to a greater or lesser extent, create and manipulate data in order to learn legal procedures, concepts, and values.

There are two issues in this definition that require a little more discussion. Perhaps the key issue regarding computer simulation is that of representation. By its nature, a simulation represents some aspect of reality; but the representational relationship is a complex one. Reality can never be replicated, and therefore design involves the extrapolation from reality of aspects relevant to the educational task. *What* should the simulation simulate? *Why* should it do so, and which criteria will be applied? *How* will it do so? What we have is essentially an overlap of three distinct elements: educational intention and design (why), disciplinary content, in this case legal reality (what), and simulation reality (how). Each of them is highly complex in its own right. When overlaid, the complexity can easily spiral out of control if all three are not managed within a design environment that takes account of the relationships between the three elements.

Take for instance the relationship between educational design and what might be termed the reality of legal action and process. Paradoxical as it may seem, simulations are not a mere *mimesis* of reality. The very concept of reality of legal action involves one in choosing, shaping, and representing that reality according to educational design and intention. This relation is not causal only; it is synergistic on two levels. At a deep level, simulations can be used to critique principles and practices in law, and to raise awareness of injustices, ethical contexts, or inefficiencies in the legal system. On a more procedural level, the shape and function of a simulated transaction is determined by the shape and function of the legal process it represents, and therefore legal reality as well as educational design and intention, affects the form and content of a simulation.

The second issue is whether simulations are useful tools for learning complex concepts and values or whether their primary purpose is in the teaching and learning of merely surface procedures and tasks. In their substantial overview of the research, De Jong and van Joolin-gen (1998) make the distinction between simulations that contain "*conceptual* models" and those that are based on "*operational* models." Conceptual models focus on "principles, concepts and facts related to the 'class of' system(s) being simulated;" while operational models "include sequences of cognitive and non-cognitive operations (procedures) than can be applied to the (class of) simulated system(s)" (p. 180). As examples of the former they cite economics models, and as instances of the latter they cite radar control tasks.

The distinction between conceptual and operational models of simulations is useful for categorizing simulations. However, there are a number of problems associated with the dichotomy that is created by the distinction. First, there are always cognitive models in users' minds when they begin to use a simulation. Users always come to simulations with a schema of what they are about to do, and this is an important part of their view of both a simulation and the learning that they undertake within the simulation.

Second, professional procedures, even the merest of operational tasks, are always based on embedded concepts. It is difficult to think of any legal process, for example, that does not contain concepts or principles that are an essential, if sometimes unseen or at least inert, part of the process. It is when operational procedures break down or go wrong in some way or another that such concepts are called up and analyzed in a procedure. Eraut expressed this well when he described how the context of use affects the learning of theoretical knowledge:

It is misleading to think of knowledge as first being acquired and then later put to use. Not only does an idea get reinterpreted during use, but it may even need to be used before it can acquire any significant meaning for the user. Thus its meaning is likely to have been strongly influenced by previous contexts of use; and the idea will not be transferable to a new context without further intellectual effort. (Eraut, 1994, p. 51)

The problems encountered by de Jong and van Joolingen's attempt at formal categorization are endemic in all simulation definitions. Other examples include the distinction made by de Jong and Njoo (2000) between *transformative* and *regulative* learning processes; or Klahr, Fay, and Dunbar's (1993) theory of scientific discovery as dual search (SDDS) in two spaces, that of *hypothesis* space, where hypotheses based upon rules can be formed regarding phenomena observed, and *experiment space,* where learners perform experiments upon phenomena. Research such as this is useful in that it describes a normative model of scientific discovery, and makes this available to educationalists interested in scientific discovery. However, as Maharg (2000) has argued elsewhere, we must be cautious about the use of descriptive procedural models for prescriptive ends in learning environments. Rather, it might be helpful to examine the experience of experts and of novices, each in their communities of practice, to determine how best to shape a simulation environment and the learning that might take place there. Rather than attempt formal categorization based upon cognitive research alone, we need to consider the experience of the simulation simultaneously as designer and user. We shall see examples of later in the chapter.

One of the ways we have attempted to categorize our simulation practice in the last five years is by means of a spectrum model with, at one end, the simulation of a "bounded field" of practice, and at the other, an "open field" of practice. Adaptivity to practice, both educational practice and the field of legal practice, is the key element of this model. We would define the spectrum operationally as on a scale where users have more or less control over their actions within the simulation. The characteristics of each end of the spectrum can be summarized in Table 1.

Simulation projects that take place within a bounded field allow for less user interaction, fact-finding, or legal options. This could be a project decision by designers based on time and financial limits of the design process, or it could be a decision based on the nature of a legal transaction. Many legal transactions can be reduced to a form of document flow-chart, and it is the function of some knowledge management and risk management strategies in legal practice to create of a legal matter a process that can be streamlined within the organization. Some transactions, though, are by their nature fairly linear processes, with known correct

Table 1. Bounded—open field transactions

		Bounded field (i.e., transaction tends to...)	Open field (i.e., transaction tends to...)
1.	Learning outcomes (LOs) & assessment	Precise learning outcomes, with simulation tasks based closely on outcomes—pre-defined LOs	Bodies of evidence required to be produced to benchmark standards, but less emphasis on pre-specified outcomes
2.	Alignment with traditional learning & teaching methods	Teaching aligned with tasks and outcomes, often according to an academic structure (e.g., lecture–seminar; learning is heavily 'pushed' by curriculum structure)	Teaching provided where needed according to learners' needs, often according to a professional, just-in-time learning structure; learning is 'pulled' by learners
3.	Operational model	Linear domain procedures (e.g., predictable document chain—more operationally predictable)	More varied, open or diffuse domain procedures (e.g., transactional guidelines but no specific document chain—less operationally predictable)
4.	Student outputs	Specific documents, drafted to specific standards (e.g., initial writ; fixed or correct versions expected as student output)	Procedures that involve a variety of documentation, or documents that cannot be specified easily in advance (e.g., negotiated agreements; various versions acceptable)
5.	Resources	Resources that are tied closely to tasks and learning outcomes—highly model driven	Simulation resources that are not linked to tasks; learner needs to structure transaction through interactive querying of resources— highly learner driven

outcomes, in which a chain of correspondence is created, and the content of the chain is fairly well defined. A conveyancing transaction might be an example of this. At the other extreme are those transactions that are fluid, with variable (and equally correct) outcomes, and with no specific documentation path. A personal injury (PI) negotiation is a good example of such a transaction, where an employee's claim for compensation is negotiated by lawyers acting for the claimant on the one side, and as the insurer's solicitors on the other. There are of course strict guidelines to the performance of PI transactions in the offices of lawyers and claims handlers; but it is in the nature of the transaction that the negotiation creates of it an open field project, where at points students are not bound to follow specific actions or procedures, or produce a set of pre-defined documents.

The field metaphor has of course analogies with older, classic metaphors—Bourdieu's (1990) field, Minsky's (1975) frame, Schank and Abelson's (1977) script, Chilton's (1988) morphism, to cite but a few. The poles of the spectrum are akin to the Weberian "ideal type," which rarely exists in practical terms, but which serves to define a practice. For us, though, the metaphor helped define the nature and clarify the processes of simulation learning. It is a concept still in the process of configuration, and areas for further research will be outlined in the final section of the chapter. As we shall see in the next few sections, however, it grows from the substantial body of research into learning and simulations, not least that of scientific discovery.

Scientific Discovery Learning
Research and Legal Education

The early research on the effect of simulations upon learning presented mixed findings. Ehman and Glenn (1987) reported gains in co-operative learning skills and positive affective outcomes in social sciences. However the meta-analysis of Bangert-Drowns, Kulik, and Kulik (1985) in the domain of science education reported that simulation-based learning did not result in cognitive gains (see also Rivers & Vockell, 1987). Further results in the domain of science-based discovery learning (from where the great majority of simulation studies derive) revealed significant differences between learning from predominantly simulation environments and learning from blended simulation-tuition environments. When simulations were blended with face-to-face tutorials, assessment of students' capabilities in mastering and applying rules demonstrated higher results than if students merely attended tutorials (Rieber, Boyce, & Assad, 1990). The same proved true of simulations alone: in a study where students were given either an unsupported simulation or a tutorial, students performed worse on the simulation (Rieber & Parmley, 1995).

What counts as the measure of better or worse performance, of course, is crucial. According to Thomas and Hooper (1991), the effectiveness of learning by simulations is best measured using "application and transfer" assessments. Their view was substantiated by other studies, for example that of Shute and Glaser (1990) where learning undertaken within the simulation was compared with learning undertaken in a more formal academic setting, and no significant difference was detected. The evaluative measure used was simple rehearsal of conceptual learning.

Findings such as these have led some researchers to conclude that simulation learning is best deployed when learners are required to learn procedures—for example, the process of successful experimentation in the field of scientific discovery learning. They point to the difference between results for procedural knowledge, and those for conceptual learning, where simulations appear to be less effective in enabling learning (e.g., Mandl, Gruber, & Renkl, 1994). However other researchers show, as we shall see, that simulation learning, particularly if it is structured rather than left as a pure simulation, can enable learners to understand and transfer concepts more effectively than a traditional curriculum.

The results therefore are mixed; but further analyses of the studies in the domain of scientific discovery simulation available to us in the last 20 years do yield interesting data (for example, Lee, 1999). In the following summary (Table 2) we are indebted to the work of de Jong and van Joolingen (1998), whose fine meta-review of the research pre-1998 provided many valuable references in the area of scientific discovery learning. Post-1998 we have relied on our own summary of the research in this domain, using the same search query pattern employed by de Jong and van Joolingen.

Within the last five years, of course, the field has changed considerably. The sophistication of Web-based simulation tools and methods has grown, as has the commercial market for MMORPGs, and there are now many more educational simulation applications on the market than there were a decade ago (Brandon-Hall, 2005; Murray, Winship, Stillings, Shartar, Galton, Moore, & Bellin, 2003). There have also been a number of high-profile simulation projects that have built upon the work of educational research reviewed by de Jong and

Table 2. Summary of aspects of research into scientific discovery learning

Area of scientific discovery	Phenomenon	Authors	Brief summary of findings
Design of experiments			
1.	Confirmation bias (learners seeking to confirm, rather than question, a hypothesis)	Dunbar (1993)	Students sought for evidence to confirm their hypotheses, which prevented the formation of alternative hypotheses
2.		Quinn & Alessi (1994)	Students reluctant to use experiments to eliminate possible hypotheses
3.	Inconclusive experiments	Glaser et al. (1992)	Learners vary too many variables in an experiment, and therefore cannot come to clear conclusions
4.		Schauble, Glaser et al. (1991)	Unsuccessful learners gather insufficient data prior to forming conclusions
5.		Inefficient data gathering Kuhn et al. (1992)	Learners did not use all possible experiments before forming conclusions
6.	Experiments do not test a hypothesis	Schauble, Klopfer, & Raghavan (1991)	Learners tried to create the outcome desired, rather than using experiments to come to an understanding of the scientific model
Area of scientific discovery	Phenomenon	Authors	Brief summary of findings
7. Interpretation of data		Schauble, Glaser et al. (1991)	Successful learners identify patterns in data
8. Regulation of discovery learning	Characteristics of successful learning	Lavoie & Good (1988)	Successful learners used systematic planning and monitoring, and made more notes during learning
9.		Shute & Glaser (1990)	Successful learners were more mindful of data management
10.		Glaser et al. (1992)	Successful learners planned ahead their experiments
11.		Glaser et al. (1992)	Successful learners were persistent; but could abandon an hypothesis that proved ill-founded
12.		Charney, Reder, & Kusbit (1990)	Goal-setting was problematic for learners with low prior knowledge of the domain of knowledge

Table 2. continued

13. Simulations and instructional support	Provision of information	Berry & Broadbent (1987)	Provision of information to learners on a 'just-in-time' basis is more effective than making all information available from the start of a simulation
		Leutner (1993)	Permanently available information enabled learners to acquire domain knowledge, but information provided before the simulation was not effective
		Elshout & Veenman (1992)	Domain information provided before a simulation was not helpful during the simulation
	Information tools	Lewis, Stern, & Linn (1993)	Provided learners with an e-notation form to note phenomena, and graphing-tool, to better understand predictions
		Bodemer (2004)	Active external integration of representations, such as textual resources, can improve simulation-based learning outcomes
	Hypothesis generation tools	Shute & Glaser (1990)	Provided learners with a 'menu' of possible hypotheses
		Van Joolingen & de Jong (1991)	Provided learners with a 'scratchpad' of possible hypotheses
	Experiment design tools	Rivers & Vockell (1987)	Provided learner with experimentation 'hints' on how to carry out experiments
	Learning process tools	White & Frederiksen (1990)	A complex simulation model was introduced to students step-by-step.
		Rieber & Parmley (1995)	Learners working in a simulation with increasing control of variables scored higher than learners with full control from the start
	Planning support tools	Tabak et al. (1996)	Questions were used to help learners to set goals
		White (1984)	Simulation with games embedded in it enabled more effective learning of procedures than a pure simulation without games
		De Jong et al. (1994)	Assignments within a simulation increased learners' deep knowledge
	Monitoring tools	Schauble, Raghavan, & Glaser (1993)	Provided monitoring support for learners that included an overview of learner actions, ability to group actions together under outcomes and access to an 'expert view'

Table 2. continued

	Structuring process	White (1993)	When qualitative predictions within a simulation were measured, learners using the simulation out-performed learners using a traditional curriculum
		Njoo & de Jong (1993)	When 'qualitative insight' was measured, a group of earners whose simulation was highly structured outperformed a group working with only the simulation
		Shute & Glaser (1990)	When recall of concepts was measured, a simulation environment showed no significant difference in comparison to a traditional curriculum
		Lewis et al. (1993)	When understanding of concepts was measured, learners using a structured simulation environment to predict experiment outcomes performed better than students using a traditional curriculum
		Swaak, de Jong, & van Joolingen (2004)	Simulations are to be considered only when clear benefits of discovery are expected, and only with complex domains, sufficient learning time and freedom for students in the assignments to engage in discovery
		Zhang, Qi Chen, & Reid (2004)	Learning supports in a simulation environment should be directed towards three perspectives, interpretative, experimental and reflective, to invite meaningful, systematic, and reflective discovery learning
		Windschitl & Andre (1998)	In a study of the effect of constructivist and objectivist learning environments on student epistemological beliefs, the former enabled greater conceptual change for learners with advanced beliefs; learners with less advanced beliefs learned more from the objectivist environment
		Swaak & de Jong (2001)	One group of subjects was free to choose their own sequence while exploring the simulation environment. The sequence of a second group was largely controlled by the environment. Results showed no gain in definitional knowledge but a gain in intuitive knowledge
	Feedback	Veermans, de Jong, Wouter, & van Joolingen (2000)	Providing learners with adaptive feedback had a different and beneficial effect on the learning process compared to more traditional predefined feedback.

Table 2. continued

		Ronen & Elia-hum (2000)	Simulation was a source of constructive feedback, helping students identify and correct their misconceptions and cope with the common difficulties of relating formal representations to real circuits and vice versa

van Joolingen. As the table demonstrates, the research involves multiple disciplines. But while it is multi-disciplinary, it may not seem at first glance to be truly interdisciplinary, or capable of being applied in other disciplines. If we take the example of legal education, for instance, it may be argued that the work of de Jong and van Joolingen, sited as it is in the domain of scientific discovery learning, can have little relevance for education in this domain. Not only is the substantive area wholly different, but ways of knowing (hypothesis, experimentation, etc.) and therefore the types of simulation environments constructed by researchers appear to bear little resemblance to legal educational methods and legal epistemic norms. However there are a number of resemblances and parallels between the fields that show that the comparison is not as odd as it may first appear.

First, scientific discovery learning is fundamentally a self-directed activity within well-defined modes of procedure, as is professional legal learning, though the content of that activity differs. Second, science students are required to construct an understanding of the experimental process (and the research outlined in the table in Table 2 shows how problematic that is for students and faculty). Law students similarly are required to construct what jurists call "the theory of the case." The phrase can mean quite different things, depending on who is using it in which sub-domain of law—jurists, court practitioners, and so forth. But a common denominator is the sense of underlying legal logic, based upon either legally relevant facts, or legal sources (case law and legislation), or jurisprudential theory, or a combination thereof. The educational methods that underlie this meta-activity are similar to the learning of scientific experimental process and logic. Third, while a number of simulation tools used in scientific simulations can be inappropriate to the subject matter of law (graph interpretation, dynamically generated graphs and charts, etc.), others can be used to present the results of learner activity to the learner, and thus stimulate reflection on learning. Such use of tools is appropriate to almost all disciplines in higher education, and we shall consider some examples in the domain of law.

Perhaps most important of all, the collection of studies in Table 2 analyzes educational design issues generic to simulation environments, which are applicable to the use of simulations in all disciplines. For example, one generic concern is that simulations, particularly those built upon constructivist theoretical design, favor weak students over strong. In their study of the use of computer simulations to enhance conceptual change in commonly held alternative conceptions within science education (conceptions held of the human cardiovascular system), Windschitl and Andre (1998) investigated the role that a constructivist approach played *vis-à-vis* an objectivist approach on student epistemological beliefs. They discovered that a constructivist approach resulted in significantly greater conceptual change for some but not all alternative conceptions. More interestingly, they observed that there was a correlation between epistemological belief and conceptual change within the constructivist environment. Those students who, accordingly to Windschitl and Andre, held more advanced epistemological beliefs about cardiovascular concepts learned more within a constructivist environment; while students with less developmentally advanced beliefs learned more with an objectivist or instructivist treatment.

Windschitl and Andre do claim in their conclusions that "some evidence was obtained consistent with the view that providing learners with overly detailed procedural instructions to solve problems in a simulated environment could be deleterious to conceptual change" (p. 158). But they also discovered that learners more easily open to misconceptions regarding cardiovascular concepts learned more effectively in more highly structured, instructivist environments. Why should this be so? They suggest that the major factor may be that such students are less motivated by a constructivist environment; but they are frank enough to admit that this explanation "may not be entirely satisfactory" (p. 157). They postulate that more sophisticated students may be simply frustrated by a more highly structured learning environment, and therefore "perform poorly under such conditions" (p. 157).

These are interesting findings for the implementation of simulation environments in any discipline, including law. It may be argued that it is easier within the domain of science education to define what might be considered to be more or less advanced beliefs. While all disciplines construct and re-construct their fundamental processes, the theory of the experimental process, at the level to which it is taught to undergraduate students, is fairly well established. In legal education it may be more difficult to discern what might be more or less advanced arguments; or at least there is likely to be more debate surrounding the distinction. Nevertheless, the general conclusions that Windschitl and Andre reach are useful guidelines to simulation building for legal education. Their work demonstrates the value of an interdisciplinary approach to simulation research and applications, and the value of the research in Table 2 to legal education, which we shall demonstrate later. To do this we shall describe our own simulation environment, in use for the last five years in legal education, before describing in outline the function and content of two simulation projects within it, and then noting the parallels between our work, and the body of research in scientific discovery learning.[1]

Ardcalloch: A Simulation Environment in Professional Legal Education

The simulation environment described next was used on a postgraduate professional educational program called the Diploma in Legal Practice at the Glasgow Graduate School of Law (GGSL). The program is mandatory for all undergraduate LLB students who wish to practice as either solicitors or advocates in Scotland. It is hosted by five providers in Scotland, with a total intake of around 500 students. This year in the GGSL, approximately 280 will take the program. These students will have studied a minimum of two years of law (if they arrive *via* a fast-track graduate program) or four years (if they come, as most students do, *via* an Honours undergraduate program). They are therefore familiar with a body of academic law; and it is the function of the Diploma to introduce them to professional practice and law in practice and thus prepare them for two years of traineeship, which, if successfully completed, will result in the award of a practicing certificate.

Since 2000 at the GGSL we have been developing a range of e-learning environments for our students. Foremost among these has been a simulation environment within which students carry out legal transactions. The transactions are both a learning and an assessment zone. Simulations have often been thought to be useful professional and vocational teaching tools (Rystedt & Lindwall, 2004). While this is often assumed to be the case, the models of effective simulation construction are still imperfectly understood, as Table 2 amply demonstrates (see also Brooks, Robinson, & Lewis, 2001). Based on our reading of some of the scientific research, but more on constructivist models of learning, we constructed a fictional town on the Web, called Ardcalloch, to facilitate the legal transactions we wished our students to complete. Within this town students would play the role of solicitors. They would have virtual legal offices, be able to contact other professionals, institutions, public bodies, and so forth, to obtain information and play the role of a solicitor in practice. Other roles would be played by online tutors or facilitators who would masquerade as characters over the Web in order to communicate in role with students. Note that our aim was not to replicate reality—impossible, and not necessarily a productive educational heuristic—but to simulate aspects of it for educational purposes.

Our fictional town has a number of elements, namely the:

- Backdrop for legal transactions—what might be termed the "realia" of professional legal work. The term realia derives from archival work, and includes a vast array of objects in that domain, such as scrapbooks, newspaper clippings, advertisements, photographs, wills, bank books, account books, and so forth. We have created many such objects in the virtual town. These objects may be thought of as the surface structure of the simulation, but as we shall see, their presence and the relationship of them to their actual objects in reality contribute to the credibility and therefore the success of the simulation (van Ments, 1984).

- Characters, institutions, professional networks with which students can communicate in their transactions.

- Virtual offices within which aspects of legal transactions were replicated as they would be performed within a law firm.

- IT communicational systems embedded within the virtual community and virtual !egal offices.

The key elements of the environment are:

1.   A schematic map, interactive and zoomable, with Web sites embedded in it, and a thumbnail and pictures associated with topographical details in the town (Figure 1)

2.   A directory, organized according to business, institutions, law firms, and citizens, and consisting of several hundred items (Figure 2)

3. A history of the town, from its early medieval foundations to its 21st century revival (Figure 3)

4. Virtual law firms, consisting of a generic front page (Figure 4) and a passworded intranet (Figure 5)

Throughout the construction of the town, verisimilitude to social and urban systems was what we aimed for, not the replication of reality. As the work of Couture (2004) shows in the area of scientific discovery learning, the realia of a simulation contributes powerfully to its credibility as a learning tool. Verisimilitude, though, as Couture acknowledges, is a complex issue that goes well beyond the representation of real items. It involves the choice of which items learners will want to use in the simulation environment, the communicational networking value of the tools, their look and feel on the screen, triggers for the adaption of willing suspension of disbelief in the simulation by learners, and much else. This included a forum on the firm's intranet so that they could communicate with each other in general, and one on each transactional project page; links to the Practice Manager tutor; links to their activity log and personal log. The requirement for these types of tools is generally acknowledged in the literature—see for example Leemkuil (2003).

Clearly we had to be aware of cognitive overload during use of the environment. Feedback from the first year or so of simulation use revealed that students needed support in order to integrate their activities within the environment, and this is borne out by research. Bodemer and Ploetzner (2002), for instance, integrated different representations of reality within an environment and followed user interaction. Analysis of evaluation of such interactions showed that active integration improved learning significantly, and that structured interaction helped improve comprehension. We therefore designed an induction to the environment that included RoboDemo movies, and sandbox orientation activities that allowed the students to play and experiment in the environment before having to use it for actual learning and assessment purposes in the course proper.

The environment is under constant review, as we take account of student feedback and add and amend features of the environment. Our information about student learning is derived from three sources. The first is end-of-module student feedback, taken from feedback questionnaires, which are reviewed annually. The second is student reflective reports, which are written for a module on Practice Management, and which provide valuable insights into use of the environments within the virtual firms (Barton & Westwood, 2006). The third source is small, intensive project work on student learning (McKellar & Maharg, 2005) which has included the use of user logs and student interviews.

On one level, what we have created is a learning management system (LMS), one that is specifically developed for students who are at the professional stage of legal education. Viewed another way, it is a problem-based learning environment, one that builds an online community of educational interests, and one that is focused on legal transactions. These transactions, and the theory behind them, are the core of the environment, and as illustrations we shall give two case study examples of transactions. The first is an open field transaction, the second much more of a bounded transaction.

Figure 1. Map of Ardcalloch

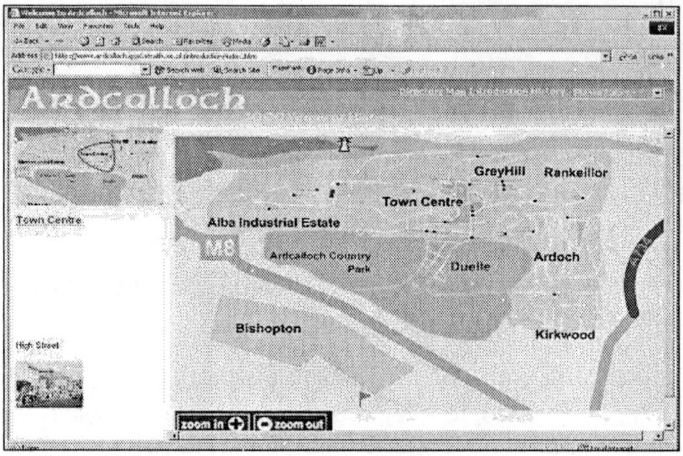

Case Studies:
Personal Injury Negotiation; Private Client

In a sense, Ardcalloch is a type of online community, but quite unlike other online communities in the normal meaning of the phrase. These have been extensively studied by anthropologists and others, such as Sherry Turkle, whose work has demonstrated the power of the Web to create online communities and sustain them from the earliest days of MUDs and

Figure 2. Ardcalloch directory

Figure 3. History of Ardcalloch; the drop-down box, top-right, gives access to seven different periods from early medieval origins to the twenty-first century

MOOs (Turkle, 1995). Of course, the power of the interaction that is present in Ardcalloch is very much restricted when compared to that of online games. Real students, playing the part of trainees in their virtual firms, can slip in and out of character quite easily, and the environment is rarely as wholly immersive as, for example MMORPGs such as EverQuest can be to sophisticated users. However, as we shall see from the feedback that they gave us, students were able to learn from the activity of "trying on" or fitting their real self into

Figure 4. Public-facing front page of a student law firm

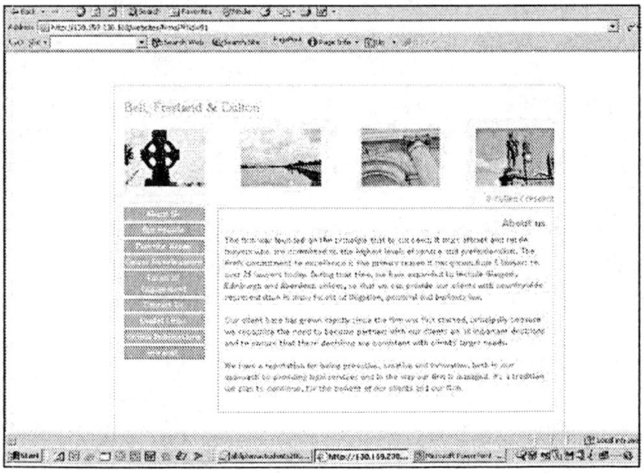

Figure 5. Student firm's intranet home page (with discussion forum — student names removed for privacy); note the tabbed links to transactions below the firm name

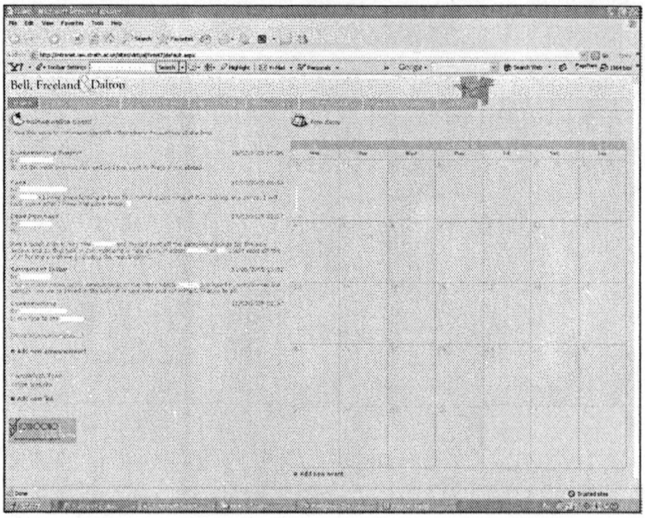

their online selves as legal professionals. This, after all, is what many of them are going to do for real in less than a year's time, and we make it clear to them that the period of the Diploma is the time for them to practice simulated roles and transactions, which will be actual in the coming few years.

Personal Injury Negotiation Project (Open Field Transaction)

The first project around which the environment was constructed was the Personal Injury Negotiation project, first implemented in 1999. This had been created three years earlier at another university as a simple e-mail negotiation between teams of students. There were no realia, no virtual community tools, and no Web-based functionality. In 1999 the first sense of an online space given to students was a Web page consisting of photomontage, later developed as a rather crude schematic map with no interactive features. We now run the project with resources that include video interviews with the client, photographs of the locus of the accident, extensive document sets with multiple sets of variables to discourage plagiarism, and a Web-based communications structure that enables students in the virtual firms to contact each other, their opposing law firm, and any institution, business, or citizen in Ardcalloch. Seven postgraduate students and Maharg feed the firms real-time communications, reacting to their queries for information. The students are trained to answer in persona, normally around 10-15 personae per transaction; and Maharg communicates with the postgraduate students *via* a discussion forum on a protected Web page of project resources.

Students are given around nine weeks to achieve a negotiated settlement of a personal injury claim (an employee injured at work). Half of the student firms represent the claimant; half are the insurer's solicitors. Each firm is required to provide four bodies of work to create the transaction: fact gathering and interpretation from Ardcalloch; legal research (online or paper-based, including topics such as contributory negligence and quantum of damages); negotiation strategy; and performance of that strategy. Each firm is assessed on the quality of the complete case file they produce.

The normal academic forms of study and communication are largely absent. Students are given no tutorials; there is no prescribed reading, no office hours for project staff, no formal examination. There is an introductory lecture, a final feedback lecture, and during the course of the project there are voluntary "surgeries," held by a practitioner-tutor, should firms wish to discuss the progress of their file. Static information in the form of an FAQ, archived discussion forums, and transactional guidelines (a week-by-week guide as to what students should be doing on the project) were available to students. All other communication with students is *via* discussion forums (one for each side of the adversarial transaction), from which they obtain information about the dynamic transactions as they developed within the simulation. The forums were thus crucial channels to tutor feedback and feed-forward. They enabled two project coordinators to comment on proposals for action by the students.

We can see this in operation if we briefly analyze the following forum postings. In the first, Sarah is unsure how to form a strategy for obtaining medical information. She sought an answer on the forum, and watching her question were around 130 other students. This is her posting, headed "Medical Records":

We have been discussing the best way to obtain medical evidence of the injury sustained by the claimant. Since the accident resulted in a hospital visit, we feel that the records made by the hospital and the GP at the time of the accident would be relevant. I notice that there has been a lot of prior discussion in past years regarding medical mandates although this seems a very detailed topic. Would it be competent for the client to obtain copies of his medical records and simply pass them onto our firm?

From the point of view of the facilitator (Maharg), this is an interesting posting. Sarah has obviously thought about the issue before posting to the forum. She has scanned the archived forum, and has a sense from them of how she might proceed. She thinks she wants to see the records, but is not entirely sure. She is also aware that obtaining mandates, writing to hospital administrators, and the like takes time and effort and understandably she wants to streamline this process, but in a way that fits with practice. She has arrived at a solution that seems to sever the Gordian knot of information retrieval at a stroke. But she is unsure if this is "competent" on several levels: can one communicate with the client in this way? And are students allowed to do this on the PI project?

Maharg's response was as follows:

This is an interesting point, Sarah. I'll deal with your ingenious solution first. It's doubtful whether the client will be in a position (either from a medical or a legal point of view) to pass on to you the information that you're seeking. He's also liable to wonder why he's pay-

ing you to represent him when he has to visit medics, come away with records, be told that these are not quite what you were looking for, and asked to go back again for more.

If your firm were to ask for medical records from hospital or doctor, the same general point about medical competence would apply. Suppose that the hard-pressed admin staff in Ard-calloch Royal sent you sheaves of your client's medical records. Which are relevant to the accident? And are you going to be able to interpret (or even decipher) medical shorthand, scribbled notes, medical jargon, etc.?

Best to request a medical report; and for that report to be focused on specific points that you want clarified as to the nature and extent of injury, and other related matters. And for that, your doctor or consultant will need your client's mandate. Don't get too involved in it: mandates can be more complicated, but they aren't in this project. Just a simple two-liner will do. Your client will return it, signed, and you can forward to whomever with a letter stating what you want.

The reply addresses the transactional issues and the project issues. The student is given advice as to the procedure to follow, and why practitioners do it this way. She is also, in the last paragraph, given directions as to how realistic the simulation is. In this respect the forum performs an interesting function on the margins of the simulations that take place in Ardcalloch. It mediates between three domains: the wholly simulated world of Ardcalloch, the reality of the Diploma as a program of study, and the reality of personal injury transactional practice. It is also an online space where students can step out of role in the simulation and get advice on what they have done, or are about to do, before they step back into the simulation again. If at first it seems shallow and superficial, the space itself, mediating between three domains of information, knowledge, and professional practice, actually performs a sophisticated educational role.

Moreover the forum follows general guidelines as to good practice, without making this too overt. We have a list of protocols for students, but the unseen protocols were there too. We encouraged students to participate, but if they did not, we assumed they were content with the information on the forum or had consulted previous forums, or had found the information they needed elsewhere, for example in practitioner journals or texts. We were content if the majority of students "lurked" on the forum. Amongst a number of summaries of this aspect of the literature, we could take Klemm's (2002) helpful synopsis, and compare it with our own practice.

Private Client (Bounded Field Transaction)

Private Client is the subject on the Diploma that deals with the winding up of a deceased client's estate, and all matters pertaining, for example, inheritance tax, trusts, and so forth. Hitherto, this subject had been assessed by four brief open-book class exams. However, this method of assessing students was unsatisfactory for three reasons. Foremost was the fact that the form of assessment was an uneasy mix of academic and professional practice. The examinations were in fact drafting activities carried out by the whole student body in an exam hall to ensure that there was no plagiarism and that the same activity was being carried out under the same conditions. The examination form of assessment was therefore used for specifically functional reasons, not because it was the best form of assessment for the subject. Secondly, students were asked to draft documents under pressure of time and often without access to the style books that they would have had to hand in the office. Finally, the academic examination structure did not produce results that were satisfactory to the practicing lawyers who taught the course. Students could gain as much as 80% and more in an examination, and yet fail the assessment because they might have made an error with the result that, in practice, the document would have been rejected either by a court administrator such as the sheriff-clerk, or by supervisors in traineeship.

For these reasons we decided to design four online assignments. Students would use the online office environment to carry out the tasks as if the work had been passed to them by a Private Client supervisor in the firm, and their tutors would take the role of supervisor in assessing their work. The fiction of the virtual firm would thus mimic the situation they would find themselves in during traineeship, and therefore be a much more appropriate assessment. Students were given two opportunities to pass each of the four assessments. If all assessments were passed the first time, the firm was awarded a merit. If one of the learning outcomes was failed at first attempt, students were given online feedback by the tutor and required to re-submit. Failure at second attempt could lead to withdrawal from the project and to presentation for a subject examination.

Table 3. Comparison of Klemm's protocols with practice on the PI project

	Klemm's anti-lurking protocols	Our practice
1.	Require participation—don't let it be optional	Lurking was acceptable to us—the forums, after all, were just one more resource for students. And if students had no questions, and no useful comments, we were happy for them to learn from others.
2.	Form learning teams	Student virtual firms were just that
3.	Make the activity interesting	Feedback from students told us the transaction was interesting and highly relevant. The degree of activity observed supported this.
4.	Don't settle for opinions only	Students asked precise questions and were given precise answers
5.	Structure the activity	Better still—students structured their own activity, based on our guidance (and the forums contributed to that set of guidance)
6.	Require a 'hand-in assignment' (deliverable)	Students required to achieve the negotiated settlement that was the end-point of the transaction.
7.	Know what you are looking for and involve yourself to make it happen	Students were clear about the aims of the forums, and two tutors answered postings on them.
8.	Peer grading	We did not use this nor do we consider it useful, given our students' inexperience in PI transactions. However next year we shall introduce self and peer grading of perceived effort (in terms of quality and quantity of effort).

Students were given instructions, and required to follow the practice that was outlined by practitioner-tutors in face-to-face weekly tutorials that supported student learning in the simulation. There were initial problems with the complexity of the document sets (effectively a different set for each of 70 firms, with variables generated and set within a SQL database structure). However feedback from students in the recent course evaluations demonstrated the effectiveness of the simulation, with at least 70% of last year's respondents agreeing that the simulated transactional assessment had enhanced their learning and was relevant and practical:

- *Assignments were excellent from a practical point of view—I would feel confident enough to complete these tasks in the office now. Our assignments were also returned promptly which was great.*

- *Assignments were a good way of bringing together knowledge obtained at tutorials. It is a practical subject and it makes sense to assess with practical assignments.*

- *Again excellent practice for traineeship.*

- *Realistic and a very reasonable form of assessment.*

- *Provided with good feedback when made mistakes with any of these assignments.*

- *Allowed us to complete them properly the second time around. Good idea that students have an opportunity to correct work as I feel that I learned more and got more from the exercise as a result.*

- *Support and advice was given by the tutor on relevant problem areas of the assignments.*

- *Very good assessments—helped understand work done in tutorials. Very useful.*

- *Good learning tool—feel I learned more doing this than just reading about it.*

- *Each of the assignments was useful as a basis for understanding how an estate would be administered and will prove helpful for practice. They also worked in well with the tutorials and the two complemented each other.*

- *It [the transaction] was very useful and practical for future work in a law firm and indeed my personal life. This was by far my favourite course.*

Discussion:
Ardcalloch and Scientific Discovery Learning

In terms of the research data on scientific discovery learning, these two case-study projects present an interesting contrast. The PI project is clearly an open-field simulation: students have much more control in determining the quantity of communications, the direction of factual and legal research, and the timing and overall shape of the transaction. The progress of the transaction is much more in their hands. The Private Client transaction, by contrast, is a bounded simulation: strict deadlines are associated with the tasks; sets of learning outcomes underpin each task; and each LO is supported by seminar and tutor-led activities.

Student performance in the PI project demonstrated many of the features of student performance in science discovery learning simulations listed in Table 2. Some firms gathered insufficient information from Ardcalloch for their case file. As one student described it in her reflective report:

Another aspect which should possibly have been covered was to get a second medical report determining the long-term prognosis for [the client] Mr. Graham. As we did not have this, we proceeded on the basis of the first report stating more or less that Mr. Graham almost had full use of his wrist back but still suffered some discomfort. We, as a group, took this to mean that Mr. Graham was suffering very little eight months on from the accident, nonetheless I feel now, reflecting back, we should have requested more information on this area.

Others focused on the wrong sort of information:

With hindsight, the condition of the equipment and the work practices of A&B DIY Ltd were in fact more important than Mr. Graham's actions leading up to the accident. Therefore next time I would insist on an independent engineer's report examining the above aspects.

Others sought to confirm their hypothesis about the accident, rather than critically examining the information they were given from a variety of sources, and from which there emerged factual contradictions that were required to be resolved. Others accepted the information given by their clients uncritically:

There was information that we failed to check (for example, we accepted Mr. Graham's word as regards his level of loss of earnings. This turned out to be false and we should have asked for a copy of his pay slips for the months proceeding and immediately after the accident). In saying this however, I do not feel it hampered our case against A&B DIY LTD as they soon pointed out our mistake as regards to Mr. Graham's pay cheque.

Others learned lessons about the importance of what they did with information they obtained, how they felt about it, and how they represented it to the opposition in a negotiation:

Our lessons for the future are not concerned with increased preparation or a more definite structure, both of which I feel we possessed, although this wasn't necessarily brought out in the negotiation. Instead I believe that confidence played a major role. We were immediately thrown by the opponent's assertions and, as such, we failed to adhere to our plan. While trying to salvage our position we did not question the other side thoroughly enough regarding the substantiation of their claim. In the future constantly seeking justification for the arguments put forward would be a prime aim. It would also be beneficial to set out the facts that can be agreed between us at the outset of the negotiation. We did not possess the confidence to rely on our other information to proceed nor did we have a back up plan in the event of our tactics being rendered useless. As a result we neglected to maintain factors previously considered to be key to negotiation. Essentially we began to panic and instead of leading we were constantly chasing to regain the initiative.

All of these learner experiences within simulations are represented in the summary of findings under "Design of experiments" in Table 2. A detailed comparison reveals a striking parallel of learning experiences in two very different disciplinary domains, brought together by the similarity in method of learning.

We found that, in our assessment of process, successful firms in the PI Negotiation project were able to identify patterns in the information they had, could assess the value of the information they had, and gaps in the information structure that were required to be filled (Schauble, Glaser, Raghavan, & Reiner, 1991). They all worked systematically—some more than others. But it was not necessarily the case that all firms who achieved good results for their clients were those who were more systematic (e.g., made more "notes to file" during the simulation—see Lavoie & Good, 1988)—there were too many other variables involved in this open field project, including the performance of the other side. However it was always the case that firms who were careless of information and process management achieved poor results (Shute & Glaser, 1990).

The findings of Charney, Reder, and Kusbit (1990)—that goal-setting was problematic for learners with low prior knowledge of the domain of knowledge—may at first glance have been true of the PI Negotiation project. Some firms confirmed that goal setting in this unusual learning environment was problematic:

The beginning of the project was somewhat daunting; I wasn't entirely clear on what we were to do. Nevertheless, I found myself really getting in to and enjoying the project as time went on.

However the predominant problem for most of our students was not one of low prior domain knowledge, as suggested by Charney et al. (1990) in their study. Our postgraduate students all had prior experience of many of the sub-domains of law that contribute to a personal injury transaction—Delict, Tax, and so forth. Rather, a significant number of firms found it problematic to transfer their knowledge of these sub-domains and apply their substantive knowledge within the context of the transaction. They also found it difficult to identify and enact at any particular stage the case management skills and legal knowledge that the project demanded:

The project was a very valuable yet very difficult assignment... The project was difficult for a range of reasons, ranging from ensuring we all met two to three times a week to agreeing the nuances of the settlement. It was complex because not only were you trying to agree with the other side but also within your group and with your client. Thus, for the very reasons the project is difficult, it is inherently valuable.

Comments such as this one demonstrated a version of the findings of Schauble, Klopfer, and Raghavan (1991)—that learners tried to create the outcome they desired in an experiment, rather than attempting to come to an understanding of the scientific experimental model. It might be said that, in wanting our students to be client-centered, and to do their best for their client, we encouraged them to do what Schauble et al. (1991) saw as a fault in learner understanding of scientific process. In this sense the scientific discovery and legal transactional approach to simulation may seem to differ considerably. And yet the difference is not so great as might first appear. After all, our simulation aims to help students come to an understanding of the complexities of the legal transaction, in much the same way as the scientific discovery process is the centre of the research detailed in de Jong and van Joolingen's (1998), and Lee's (1999) meta-analyses. For us, there is an important distance between client-*centered* approaches, and client-*led* approaches to a professional matter, and it is critical that students appreciate this in their project work. Not all did; or if they did, they found it difficulty to operationalize this insight in their relationship with their client.

The findings of the scientific discovery literature regarding information management within simulations matched our own experiences as simulation designers. We found that provision of "just-in-time" information *via* "surgery" meetings with staff and *via* the discussion forums was valuable in helping them to deal with skills-based and knowledge-based deficits (Berry & Broadbent, 1987, confirmed Rieber, 2005). We also discovered that, after the first few weeks of the project, students were unlikely to use the guidelines or the FAQ, unless directed to them by a posting on the discussion forum—in part, validating the findings of Leutner (1993) and Elshout and Veenman (1992).

All firms made use of the communication tools on their virtual firm. Least used was the calendar; most used was the drafts section in which students could store draft communications. Earlier iterations of the virtual office environment did not integrate resources well (Bodemer, 2004), and this was remedied in later iterations. In other projects within the virtual law offices, for example, Conveyancing (where students completed both sale and purchase of land) and the Virtual Court Action (in which they progressed a civil court action for payment of a debt), we provided them with banks of document styles. As ongoing research proves, careful design and integration of such tools are essential to the success of effective student learning. As Ellis, Marcus, and Taylor (2005) point out, "The benefits from case-based learning such as authenticity and active learning can be threatened if issues closely associated with qualitative variation arising from incoherence in the experience are not addressed" (p. 240).

In neither project did we provide learners with a menu or scratchpad (Shute & Glaser, 1990; van Joolingen & de Jong, 1991). Instead, we gave them hints in the PI Negotiation transaction (Rivers & Vockell, 1987), and the Private Client transaction procedure was introduced by stages in tutorials (White & Frederiksen, 1990), with tasks to perform that would increase their understanding of the process of winding up a client's estate. In this latter transaction, learners had tasks to carry out equivalent to the assignments described by de Jong, van Joolingen, Scott, de Hoog, Lapied, and Valent (1994), and students noted that they found this helpful.

As pointed out previously, the literature does show that gains can be made in "qualitative insight" or "intuitive knowledge" in simulation environments (Njoo & de Jong, 1993; Swaak, de Jong, Wouter, & van Joolingen, 2004). At no point did we use simulations specifically to support *recall* of concepts. Simulations were used to enhance knowledge of process, and procedural knowledge and skill (Lewis, Stern, & Linn, 1993; Shute & Glaser, 1990). But—and at a more profound level—the simulations gave students practice in enacting the value-system of the Scottish legal profession. Even at a simple operational level, this is il-lustrated by the extract from Sarah's posting to the discussion forum in the PI transaction quoted above; and there are many other more sophisticated examples that arose from the correspondence between firms and fictional characters.

We would agree with Swaak et al. (2004) that "clear benefits" should be communicated to students and that complex domains, sufficient learning time, and freedom for students to explore assignments are necessary to the success of simulations. We would argue, though, that there can be a variety of clear benefits, and that these are not necessarily clear to either staff or students before students start the simulation. What is important is that students understand the reasons why they undertake simulations, and the nature of the simulations, whether bounded or open. Above all, we would claim that regardless of whether the environment is, in our terms, open or bounded there are clear gains in terms of verisimilitude to transactional reality if learners are given the freedom to make errors, receive feedback, and rectify those errors. As Swaak and de Jong (2001) pointed out, freedom to explore can result in gains in intuitive knowledge learning; and when enacted in collaborative environments, such learning extends beyond the boundaries of substantive knowledge of a domain into professional knowledge, skills, attitudes, and values.

E-Simulations in the Wild: A Research Framework

Much of the work on scientific discovery learning in the 1990s was based upon a paradigm of cognitive experimental studies, often involving pre- and post-test research studies under specific and limited conditions. This work focused on the design and use of specific simulation engines within learning domains as diverse as epidemiology, programming, electrical circuits, and control theory in mechanical engineering, and in doing so it provided an essential multi-disciplinary body of research. But e-simulations also need to be studied in the wild, where the context of use is much more complex and multi-factorial. The disciplines that underlie the technical, educational, cultural, workplace, and ethical issues, to name but a few, need to converge to form what Galison (1997) terms a "trading zone." In his use of the anthropological term it denotes the ways in which different scientific communities such as physicists and engineers draw together and form creolized discourses and common languages, in which important concepts can be traded and understood. Interdisciplinary blogs such as Terranova (http://terranova.blogs.com) are one example of such a zone in the study of games and simulations, and how the zone can be a useful resource for e-simulation practitioners and researchers.

Meanwhile there are three areas for research that we would emphasize as being crucial to the design of e-simulation projects within environments such as Ardcalloch, where learning is frequently collaborative, and where it is distributed throughout the curriculum. These are the design of learning outcomes, the effect of the depth of simulation field, and the organization of communities of practice.

Design of Learning Outcomes

The use of outcomes is critical to the design of simulation learning. As Swaak et al. (2004) put it, "[f]or research and practice, this implies that simulations are to be considered only when clear benefits of discovery are expected, and only with complex domains, sufficient learning time and freedom for students in the assignments to engage in discovery" (p.225). But expected by *whom*—simulation designers, teaching staff, students? As Jonassen (2004) has pointed out, the distinction between intention and attention is important here. What designers intend learners to do within or understand from a simulation may not be what learners' attention is focused upon. This is inevitable: complete control of learner attention in any form of learning activity is impossible. Indeed, it is probably antithetical to learning processes, precisely because the designer's desire to control learning leaves little space for learners to construct their own meanings. Learning outcomes are useful in defining clear benefits; but there is a substantial body of education research on the tradition of aims, objectives, and outcomes that reveals that outcomes can also constrain learning within complex simulations and domains (Stenhouse, 1975). As we have seen from the previously discussed case studies, simulations can be open field or bounded. Learning outcomes should be aligned with the activities that learners undertake in the simulation. But they also should be derived from the transactional reality that the simulation enacts. Thus, in the PI project there are no learning outcomes. Instead, students are required to present four bodies of evidence completed to pre-specified standards in fact-gathering, legal research, negotiation strategy, and performance of strategy. The assessment criteria thus match the freedom of movement that learners have in this transaction in the simulation environment. By contrast, in Private Client the learning outcomes are much more specific and precise, directing learners to forms of drafting and writing practices that are essential for this fairly standard legal procedure. We would argue that, given the uncertain nature of the research results indicated in the research table above, both approaches to simulations are valid for learning. Critical factors are the content and procedure of the authentic legal task, the nature of the activities to be undertaken within the simulation, and the complexity of the simulation environment. Much more work is required, though, to map out the relationships of these factors, and this can be achieved by tracking learner activity within actual curricula and investigating the phenomenographical implications of this activity.

Depth of Simulation Field

The metaphor of the field references the type and extent of learner activity within the simulation. But we also need terms to describe how objects or realia are placed within that field, and how they are used by learners. Is everything there of the same importance to learners? Or is there a process of prioritisation of objects and tasks that takes place in the real world that should also be enacted in the simulation world? We therefore need to extend the shallow metaphor of open-bounded field by adding *depth* of simulation field.

The phrase comes of course from visual arts, where depth of field refers to the zone of sharpness of image within a particular field. When there is little depth of field, only the images in the foreground of an image are in focus, and the rest is indistinct. Greater depth of field allows the viewer to see more detail within the background of the image. Depth of field is critical to photography, because it is one of the focal and compositional elements that can be altered (pre-photography, painters tended to represent all detail in the painting's field as equally distinct).

We can appreciate this if we take an analogy from the field of aesthetics, and in particular the work of Roland Barthes. In describing how a photograph appears to the viewer, Barthes defined the intentional agenda of a photograph as its *studium*—for instance, a group of men wearing suits, with similar pose and attention, standing on several steps outside a hotel, all looking beyond the man in front of them who is speaking at a podium toward an audience. We treat this as the genre of conference photograph, and know it for what it is even before we notice the caption that tells us this is a photograph taken of the G8 summit in Gleneagles, in which Tony Blair gives his closing address in front of the world's leaders to the world's press (Lewis, 2005). The photograph's overt agenda is clear to us from its structure, which is part of its *studium*. But photographs can never completely control the reality beyond the lens. Incidental happenings, odd things creep into the careful structure created by the photographer. Barthes describes this as the *punctum* by which our eye is caught and held: "[a] photograph's *punctum* is that accident which pricks me, but also bruises me, is poignant to me" (Barthes, 1981, p. 27). Thus, to take the example of the photograph described above, from the formal array of figures facing forward there are two exceptions: George Bush stares not straight ahead but to the side, over at the security personnel in the mid-foreground and background, while Jacques Chirac half turns to the person on his left, Vladimir Putin, and looks to be commenting *sotto voce*. Is he really? Did the photographer intend these poses to be caught? Perhaps the most intriguing *punctum* is the small object that floats above Blair's head—is it a microphone, a camera, or a helicopter in the far distance? We cannot be sure. The process of noticing and interpreting leads us to construe the intentions of the photographer, leads us to think about contextual events around the photograph.

For designers of simulations, the problem of depth is less one of navigation and control (though of course these issues are essential for user interaction) and more of what needs to be foregrounded, structured and overt, and what can be left as background, incidental, implicit. The *studium* of a simulation, its depth of detail, needs to be carefully planned. Not everything can be shown in perfect detail. Some elements will be in focus, others out of focus, and some so indistinct that they cannot be clearly discerned at all; and this is an interpretive process that is central to learning simulations. In a real legal case, as in all professional transactions, focus of attention is a constantly shifting lens. Practitioners move between details, between documents, bringing one under scrutiny, then another, querying background information, linking evidence, drawing conclusions, making hypotheses about actions and documents, planning their own actions, and much else. They constantly vary the lens of attention to focus on different objects. It is a mark of a sophisticated simulation environment that instead of giving learners fixed objects in a field, it allows students to vary the amount of information they can acquire and allows them to vary the focus of their attention lens. This requires complex learning objects to be placed within the field, and for tasks to be designed so that students are required to vary attention, make choices, alter focus and distinguish for themselves between the important and the unimportant in a field.

There are many examples one can take of this distinction. In Ardcalloch, photographs attached to streets give a visual sense of place to the town (see Figure 1, bottom left-hand corner).

This is important for the long-term development of the project in a number of ways. First, the town becomes recognizable as a west of Scotland provincial town, perhaps around the size of Ayr, and much smaller than Glasgow (many of the photographs were taken in similar towns such as Port Glasgow, Greenock, Paisley, and were added to the map). Secondly, the map photos help to give a sense of "distributed identity" to the various districts within the town, from leafy upper-middle class suburbs to dockland slums. Thirdly, there is a synergy between environment and student projects. Clearly the environment must support the projects; but it also has the capacity to be more than the backdrop or *studium* for a transaction (Maharg, 2004; Maharg & Paliwala, 2002). Thus photographs of the locus of the accident in the PI project can be treated as background; but if opposing firms ever care to compare their photographs, they discover that they have representations of different staircases, and therefore are required to establish between them the exact location of the accident. Looking beyond law, if the town is to be used by other disciplines within the university and beyond such as architecture, engineering, planning, urban studies, social work, and the like, then the representation of place becomes important also for their students.

The distinction also applies to the design process of the simulation environment. The design of the Web pages in the Ardcalloch directory is an example of *studium* and *punctum*. As the number of Web sites grew, it became important to manage their development as mini-projects, and to consider the interface with users of the virtual environment. It was not possible for us to create a generic Web template for our town sites. In reality, commercial and institutional Web site design is really only limited by the funds available, the creative flair and, it might be added, the taste, good and bad, of the designers. It was necessary for us to create sites that gave a presence of a business or an institution to the viewer, without importing into the site all the actual functionality of a real commercial site; and so many of our sites are "brochure" sites. Some have more extensive and complex text than others—in part this is due to the enthusiasm of particular designers, and we were happy to give them relatively free rein on this within a loose framework. After all, if the Web sites in the town all had a similar look and feel, or simply dealt with matters relating to the projects, there would be no sense of realia, of the sheer randomness of reality, about the town.

There are, however, many issues associated with depth of field that require further research. Which tools would enable users to move focus efficiently between objects? How does depth of field affect the design of the simulation and the design of tasks and learning outcomes? How can we match authentic real-world depth of field to transactional contexts? There are deeper issues here, too, of research methodology and language. Depth of field, particularly in longitudinal simulations such as Ardcalloch, can only be studied using a "combination of mixed methods and design research approaches" (Rieber, 2005, p. 551). But is part of the problem that we do not possess a technical vocabulary to discuss the new environment of learning within an e-simulation? In many respects educational terms such as outcomes seem to be ill fitted to a simulation environment where open-field transactions may take place. Such environments are closer to architecture or environmental art; and it may be that as e-simulations become ever richer and more complex we shall require a new critical and aesthetic language to describe the experience of designing, working, and learning within such environments.

Organization of Communities of Practice

A simulation has the potential to be a world entire to itself. While all MMORPGs are sold on the basis of absorbing activities, of being parallel worlds that draw users into them, an educational simulation such as Ardcalloch is much less ambitious as to "flow." However, a parallel urban reality has the ability to draw around it communities of practice, drawn by similar ways of thinking, working, planning, and so forth. All such environments develop associations, habits of thought, and epistemic assumptions that derive from the professions that use it, and the designers who develop it. At least two communities are currently emerging around Ardcalloch:

Law Profession

Law students, practitioner-tutors, and the GGSL design team participate in the learning and assessment of learning that takes place in Ardcalloch. Students are thus surrounded by a community of practice that embodies distinct epistemic norms and assumptions; and it is a key part of the value of the simulations that students use it to learn what constitutes the values, attitudes, and ethics of the professional legal community in Scotland by actively participating in it. As we have seen from the research literature on scientific discovery, "intuitive knowledge" is increased when simulations are used in learning. Simulations can be used in the more complex realm of professional ethical conduct, so that students can begin to internalize the values of the profession.

But simulations can also be used to facilitate identity-change. The Diploma, like the Legal Practice course in England and Wales, is often referred to as a "bridge" program between undergraduate academic study of law and postgraduate legal practice. It is also a structure that helps students to envision not just what they will do but who they will be in the profession. This may seem to be a considerable claim for the efficacy of simulations. But research has shown that for users in simulation video games such as Sony's EverQuest their physical selves have a number of digital identities that they can take up and use as extensions of their selves (Yee, 2005). This is similar to aspects of identity-formation and use within the real world. Social psychology theories of identity within the real world such as symbolic interactionism are highly pertinent to the analysis of avatars as identity-constructs, and as such, of interest to educationalists (Goffman, 1959). In a simulation world such as Ardcalloch, learners can try out professional identities for size, and find which fits best.[2] How can we best enable learners to work within the problems and issues that arise when professional identity is first formed? Which approaches to design best enable identity change, and provide models of professional practice for learners?

Developer and User Communities

There is a growing circle of developers and academics interested in the creation of simulations within higher education. These include e-learning centers such as Futurelab, and staff within GGSL, Worcester University College, RechtenOnline Foundation, University of

Rotterdam Law Faculty, College of Law, and others. The successful implementation of the learning environment depends not just on articulation of surface project procedures, but of approaches to learning at a much deeper level. Moreover, simulation environments such as Ardcalloch cannot function well unless one considers the context of such learning environments. Viewed as an isolated artefact, its use may become problematic. But if it is planned as a piece of social software in which not only learners but designers and tutors too can examine their professional practice and improve it as part of a coherent approach to professional learning, then it becomes a much more powerful and compelling tool for learning. The question, of course, is: How can we enable this change to take place? In this respect the literature of culture change, as well as the hermeneutic and interpretive traditions, and the tradition of action research, which in the UK has been a presence in education since at least the 1970s, has much to offer the e-simulation user and design community (Gadamer, 1975; Stenhouse, 1975).

References

Aikenhead, M., Widdison, R., & Allen, T. (1999). Exploring law through computer simulation. *International Journal of Law and Information Technology, 7*(3), 191-217

Bangert-Drowns, R., Kulik, J., & Kulik, C. (1985). Effectiveness of computer-based education in secondary schools. *Journal of Computer-based Instruction, 12*(3), 59-68

Barthes, R. (1981). *Camera Lucida: Reflections on photography.* New York: Noonday.

Barton, K., & Westwood, F. (2006). From student to trainee practitioner: A study of team working as a learning experience. *Web Journal of Current Legal Issues, 2.* Retrieved July 11, 2006, from http://webjcli.ncl.ac.uk/2006/issue3/barton-westwood3.html

Berry, D. C., & Broadbent, D. E. (1987). Explanation and verbalisation in a computer-assisted search task. *The Quarterly Journal of Experimental Psychology, 39A,* 585-609

Bodemer, D., & Ploetzner, R. (2002). *Encouraging the active integration of information during learning with multiple and interactive representations.* Presented at the International Workshop on Dynamic Visualizations and Learning, Knowledge Media Research Centre, Tübingen. Retrieved July 11, 2006, from http://www.iwm-kmrc.de/workshops/visualization/bodemer.pdf

Bodemer, D. (2004). *Enhancing simulation-based learning through active external integration of representations.* Retrieved July 11, 2006, from http://www.cogsci.northwestern.edu/cogsci2004/papers/paper228.pdf

Bourdieu, P., & Passeron, J-C. (1990). *Reproduction in education, society and culture* (2nd ed.). London: Sage.

Brooks, R., Robinson, S., & Lewis, C. (2001). *Simulation. Inventory control.* New York: Palgrave.

Castronova, E. (2005). *Synthetic worlds: The business and culture of online games.* Chicago: University of Chicago Press.

Chapman, B. (2005). *Online simulations 2005: A knowledgebase of 35+ custom developers, 300+ off-the-shelf simulation courses, and 40+ simulation authoring tools.* Brandon Hall. Retrieved from www.brandonhall.com/public/publications/simkb/index.htm

Charney, D., Reder, L., & Kusbit, G. W. (1990). Goal setting and procedure selection in acquiring computer skills: A comparison of tutorials, problem-solving, and learner exploration. *Cognition and Instruction, 7*(4), 323-342

Chilton, P. (1988). *Orwellian language and the media.* London: Pluto Press.

Couture, M. (2004). Realism in the design process and credibility of a simulation-based virtual laboratory. *Journal of Computer Assisted Learning, 20*(1), 40-49.

de Jong, T., & Njoo, M. (1992). Learning and instruction with computer simulations: Learning processes involved. In E. de Corte, M. Linn, H. Mandl, & L. Verschaffel (Eds.), *Computer-based learning environments and problem solving* (pp. 411-429). Berlin: Springer-Verlag.

de Jong, T., & van Joolingen, W. R. (1998). Scientific discovery learning with computer simulations of conceptual domains. *Review of Educational Research, 68*(2), 179-201.

de Jong, T., van Joolingen, W., Scott, D., de Hoog, R., Lapied, L., & Valent, R. (1994). SMILE: System for Multimedia Integrated Simulation Learning Environments. In T. de Jong & L. Sarti (Eds.), *Design and production of multimedia and simulation-based learning material* (pp. 133-167). Dordrecht: Kluwer Academic Publishers.

Degnan, D. A., & Haar, C. M. (1970). Computer simulation in urban legal studies. *Journal of Legal Education, 23*(2), 353-265.

Drobak, J. N. (1972). Computer simulation and gaming: An interdisciplinary survey with a view toward legal applications. *Stanford Law Review, 24*(4), 712-729

Dunbar, K. (1993). Concept discovery in a scientific domain. *Cognitive Science, 17*(3), 397-434

Ehman, L. H., & Glenn, A. D. (1987). *Computer-based education in the social studies.* Bloomington, IN: Social Studies Development Center and ERIC Clearinghouse for Social Studies/Social Science Education.

Ellis, R. A., Marcus, G., & Taylor, R. (2005). Learning through inquiry: Student difficulties with online course-based materials, *Journal of Computer-assisted Learning, 21*(4), 239-252.

Elshout, J. J., & Veenman, M. V. J. (1992). Relation between intellectual ability and working method as predictors of learning. *Journal of Educational Research, 85*(3), 134-143.

Eraut, M. (1994). *Developing professional knowledge and competence.* London: The Falmer Press.

Gadamer, H-G. (1975). *Truth and method.* London: Sheed & Ward.

Galison, P. L. (1997). *Image and logic: A material culture of microphysics.* Chicago: University of Chicago Press.

Gee, J. P. (2003). *What video games have to teach us about learning and literacy.* New York: Palgrave Macmillan.

Glaser, R., Schauble, L., Raghavan, K., & Zeitz, C. (1992). Scientific reasoning across different domains. In E. de Corte, M. Linn, H. Mandl, & L. Verschaffel (Eds.), *Computer-based learning environments and problem-solving* (pp. 345-373). Berlin: Springer-Verlag.

Goffman, E. (1959). *The presentation of self in everyday life.* New York: Doubleday.

Goffman, E. (1967). *Interaction ritual: Essays on face-to-face behaviour.* New York: Doubleday Anchor.

Herrington, J., Oliver, R., & Reeves, T. C. (2003). Patterns of engagement in authentic online learning environments. *Australian Journal of Educational Technology, 19*(1), 59-71.

Jonassen, D. H. (2004). *Handbook of research on educational communications and technology* (2nd ed.). Mahwah, NJ: Lawrence Erlbaum Associates. Retrieved April 11, 2006, from http://aect-members.org/m/research_handbook.pdf

Klahr, D., Fay, A. L., & Dunbar, K. (1993). Heuristics for scientific experimentation: A developmental study. *Cognitive Psychology, 94*(1), 211-228.

Klemm, W. R. (2002). Eight ways to get students more engaged in online conferences. *The Higher Education Journal, 26*(1), 62-64.

Kuhn, D., Schauble, L., & Garcia-Mila, M. (1992). Cross-domain development of scientific reasoning. *Cognition and Instruction, 9*(4), 285-327

Lavoie, D. R., & Good, R. (1988). The nature and use of predictions skills in a biological computer simulation. *Journal of Research in Science Teaching, 25*(5), 335-60

Lee, J. (1999). Effectiveness of computer-based instructional simulation: A meta-analysis. *International Journal of Instructional Media, 26*(1), 71-85.

Leemkuil, H., de Jong, T., de Hoog, R., & Noor, C. (2003). KM QUEST: A collaborative Internet-based simulation game. *Simulation and Gaming, 34*(1), 89-111.

Leutner, D. (1993). Guided discovery learning with computer-based simulation games: Effects of adaptive and non-adaptive instructional support. *Learning and Instruction, 3*(2), 113-132

Lewis, E. L., Stern., J. L., & Linn, M. C. (1993). The effect of computer simulations on introductory thermodynamics understanding. *Educational Technology, 33*(1), 45-58.

Lewis, R. (2005). G8 in Pictures. Richard Lewis/Crown Copyright. Picture sxznumber G*255. Retrieved from http://www.g8pix.com/cgi-bin/g8

Lundquist, L. (1989). Coherence in scientific texts'. In W. Heydrich, F. Neubauer, J. S. Petofi, & E. Sozer (Eds.), *Connexity and coherence: Analysis of text and discourse* (pp. 122-149). Berlin: De Gruyter

McKellar, P., & Maharg, P. (2005). Virtual learning environments: The alternative to the box under the bed. *The Law Teacher, 39*(1), 43-56.

Maharg, P. (2000). Law, learning, technology: Reiving ower the borders. *International Review of Law, Computers, Technology, 14*(2), 155-170.

Maharg, P. (2004). Virtual communities on the Web: Transaction learning and teaching. In A. Vedder (Ed.), *Aan het werk met ICT in het academisch onderwijs—Rechten Online* (pp. 75-90). Rotterdam: Wolf Legal Publishers.

Maharg, P., & Paliwala, A. (2002). Negotiating the learning process with electronic resources. In R. Burridge, K. Hinett, A. Paliwala, & T. Varnava (Eds.), *Effective learning and teaching in law* (pp. 81-104). London: Routledge Falmer.

van Ments, M. (1984). Simulation and game structure. In D. Thatcher & J. Robinson (Eds.), *Business, Health and Nursing Education* (pp. 51-58). Loughborough: SAGSET.

Minsky, M. (1975). A framework for representing knowledge. In P. Winston (Ed.), *The psychology of computer vision* (pp. 211-277). New York: McGraw-Hill.

Murray, T., Winship, L., Stillings, N., Shartar, E., Galton, A., Moore, R., & Bellin, R. (2003). An inquiry-based simulation learning environment for the ecology of forest growth. Final Report for NSF Grant. Retrieved July 11, 2006, from http://ddc.hampshire.edu/simforest/about/SFReportSummaryTOC.pdf

Njoo, M., & de Jong, T. (1993). Supporting exploratory learning by offering structured overviews of hypotheses. In D. Towne, T. de Jong, & H. Spada (Eds.), *Simulation-based experiential learning* (pp. 207-225). Berlin: Springer-Verlag.

Petraglia, J. (1998). *Reality by design: The rhetoric and technology of authenticity in education.* Mahwah, NJ: Lawrence Erlbaum Associates.

Quinn, J., & Alessi, S. (1994). The effects of simulation complexity and hypothesis generation strategy on learning. *Journal of Research on Computing in Education, 27*(1), 75-91

Rieber, L. P. (2005). Multimedia learning in games, simulations and microworlds. In R. E. Mayer (Ed.), *The Cambridge handbook of multimedia learning* (pp. 549-568). Cambridge: Cambridge University Press.

Rieber, L. P., Boyce, M., & Assad, C. (1990). The effects of computer animation on adult learning and retrieval tasks. *Journal of Computer-based Instruction, 17*(2), 46-5.

Rieber, L. P., & Parmley, M. W. (1995). To teach or not to teach? Comparing the use of computer-based simulations in deductive versus inductive approaches to learning with adults in science. *Journal of Educational Computing Research, 14*(4), 359-374.

Rivers, R. H., & Vockell, E. (1987). Computer simulations to stimulate scientific problem solving. *Journal of Research in Science Teaching, 24*(5), 403-415

Ronen, M., & Eliahu, M. (2000). Simulation—A bridge between theory and reality: The case of electric circuits. *Journal of Computer Assisted Learning, 16*(1), 14-26.

Rystedt, H., & Lindwall, O. (2004). The interactive construction of learning foci in simulation-based learning environments: A case study of an anaesthesia course. *PsychNology Journal, 2*(2), 168-188.

Schank, R. C., & Abelson, R. P. (1977). *Scripts, plans, goals and understanding: An inquiry into human knowledge structures.* Hillsdale, NJ: Lawrence Erlbaum.

Schauble, L., Klopfer, L., & Raghavan, K. (1991). Students' transitions from an engineering to a science model of experimentation. *Journal of Research in Science Teaching, 28*(9), 859-882

Schauble, L., Glaser, R., Raghavan, K., & Reiner, M. (1991). Causal models and experimentation strategies in scientific reasoning. *The Journal of the Learning Sciences, 1*(2), 201-239

Schauble, L., Raghavan, K., & Glaser, R. (1993). The discovery and reflection notation: A graphical trace for supporting self regulation in computer-based laboratories. In S. P. Lajoie & S. J. Derry (Eds.), *Computers as cognitive tools* (pp. 319-341). Hillsdale, NJ: Lawrence Erlbaum Associates.

Shaffer, D. W. (2004). Pedagogical praxis: The professions as models for postindustrial education. *Teachers College Record, 106*(7), 1401-1421.

Shute, V. J. & Glaser, R. (1990). A large-scale evaluation of an intelligent discovery world: Smithtown. *Interactive Learning Environments, 1*(1), 51-77.

Stenhouse, L. (1975). *An introduction to curriculum research and development.* London: Heinemann.

Swaak, J., & de Jong, T. (2001). Learner vs. system control in using online support for simulation-based discovery learning. *Learning Environments Research, 4*(3), 217-241.

Swaak, J., de Jong, T., Wouter, R., & van Joolingen, R. (2004). The effects of discovery learning and expository instruction on the acquisition of definitional and intuitive knowledge. *Journal of Computer-assisted Learning, 20*(4), 225-234.

Tabak, I., Smith, B. K., Sandoval, W. A., & Reiser, B. J. (1996). Combining general and domain-specific strategic support for biological inquiry. In C. Frasson, G. Gauthier, & A. Lesgod, (Eds.), *Intelligent tutoring systems* (pp. 288-297). Berlin: Springer-Verlag.

The Horizon Report. (2005). *New Media Consortium, National Learning Infrastructure Initiative.* Retrieved July 5, 2006, from http://www.nmc.org/horizon/index.shtml

Turkle, S. (1995). *Life on the screen: Identity in the age of the Internet.* New York: Simon and Schuster.

Unger, R. (1983). The critical legal studies movement. *Harvard Law Review, 96*(7), 561-594.

van Joolingen, W. R., & de Jong, T. (1991). Supporting hypothesis generation by learners exploring an interactive computer simulation. *Instructional Science, 20*(5-6), 389-404.

Veermans, K., de Jong, T., Wouter, R., & van Joolingen, R. (2000). Promoting self-directed learning in simulation-based discovery learning environments through intelligent support. *Interactive Learning Environments, 8*(3), 229-255.

White, B. Y. (1984). Designing computer games to help physics students understand Newton's laws of motion. *Cognition and Instruction, 1*(1), 69-108.

White, B. Y., & Frederiksen, J. R. (1990). Causal model progressions as a foundation for intelligent learning environments. *Artificial Intelligence, 42*(1), 99-157.

White, B. Y. (1993). ThinkerTools: Causal models, conceptual change, and science education. *Cognition and Instruction, 10*(1), 1-10.

Widdison, R., Aikenhead, M., & Allen, T. (1997). Computer simulation in legal education. *International Journal of Law and Information Technology, 5*(3), 279-307.

Windschitl, M., & Andre, T. (1998). Using computer simulations to enhance conceptual change: The roles of constructivist instruction and student epistemological beliefs. *Journal of Research in Science Teaching, 35*(2), 145-160.

Yee, N. (2005). *The Daedalus Gateway.* The psychology of MMORPGs. Retrieved from http://ww.nickyee.com/daedalus/gateway_intro.htm

Zhang, J., Qi Chen, Y. S., & Reid, D. J. (2004). Triple scheme of learning support design for scientific discovery learning based on computer simulation: Experimental research. *Journal of Computer Assisted Learning, 20*(4), 269-282.

Endnotes

[1]   The first person plural is essential: the simulation environment of Ardcalloch is a collective effort of our academic colleagues in the GGSL, Patricia McKellar and Fiona Westwood, and the Learning Technologies Development Unit, in particular Scott Walker, development officer, and Michael Hughes, applications developer.

[2]   The simulation environment is also viewed by students with a healthy sense of irony. The sheer number of law firms within the town was the subject of comment in the Ardcalloch News, an online newspaper (written by students), who noted in a weekly column that there were more lawyers than nurses in Ardcalloch, and wondered whether this development was good for society.

Section III

What Teachers Should Know and Be Able to Do

Chapter VII

Perspectives from Multiplayer Video Gamers

Jonathan B. Beedle, University of Southern Mississippi, USA

Vivian H. Wright, University of Alabama, USA

Abstract

The purpose of this study is to determine whether multiplayer video gamers perceive that playing video games can increase higher order thinking skills such as motivation, problem-solving, communication, and creativity. Multiplayer video gaming allows participants the opportunity to collectively discuss problems with other players, find solutions, and accomplish objectives. This study was used as a barometer to determine if multiplayer gamers perceived that playing multiplayer games had educational value. This research specifically sought to verify whether multiplayer video gamers perceived that higher-order thinking skills such as motivation, communication, problem solving, and creativity were increased by playing multiplayer video games. The bulk of respondents reported that they somewhat felt there was learning occurring in all of these areas.

Gaming and Learning

Approximately six billion people around the world play computer games (King, 2002), including hundreds of thousands of people who participate in multiplayer online games. Multiplayer gaming is a term used to describe multiplayer online games (consoles and personal computers), video arcade games, and network games (both intranet and Internet). Berger (2002) indicated that most people are surprised when they find out that the video games industry is a bigger business than the film industry. According to the Entertainment Software Association (2003), the video game industry generated $6.9 billion in 2002 in the United States alone, which was up 8% from 2001. In 2000, video gaming was a $17.7 billion global industry (Lange, 2002). In 2000, the computer and video gaming industry grew at more than twice the rate of the U.S. economy (IDSA, 2002).

Most likely, gaming will continue to experience such growth. As educators, we have a responsibility to research the use of games, specifically in areas of teaching and learning. Aldrich (2004) proposed that there must be extensive learning taking place during game playing as players learn by participating and practicing until they become successful against others playing the game. This success requires gamers to learn roles, understand direction, and comprehend the complex systems within the game's structure.

The computer's artificial intelligence (AI) works as a flexible rules-based organizational mechanism to keep the game challenging to the players by presenting problems that players must solve in groups instead of solo. Players are able to construct their own meaning, relationships, character skills, and appearance in many of today's video game titles. This allows the gamer the opportunity to create and experiment with different configurations and attributes while role-playing characters that might be unlike himself or herself or any other real-life people. Role-playing allows the gamer to immerse himself or herself in a character and allows for experimentation. Video games are increasingly using greater narratives and stories to envelop characters into the storyline. Where books and video games differ is that in many video games there are communities of users who develop programs to mod or add new content and stories to games.

Previous research on video games typically focuses on negative aspects surrounding video games like aggressive behavior (Gentile, Lynch, Linder, & Walsh, 2004), violence (Thompson, 2001), and addiction (Chiu, Lee, & Huang, 2004), even though Sherry (2001) performed a meta-analysis of the video gaming literature and found only a minute relationship between hostile behavior and violent video games.

It appears that limited research has been conducted concerning gaming and its educational potential. In 1999, the independent research firm MediaScope found only 16 studies involving video gaming (Thompson, 2002). Most of the research currently available tends to focus on the negative side of games (i.e., addiction) and not on the potential educational benefits of games. According to Griffiths and Davies (2002), online games may have a larger impact on education than traditional single player games. Many online games are role-playing adventures or other teamwork-related games that require cooperation from several participants to accomplish game objectives.

A study for the Pew Internet & American Life Project (Jones, 2003) found that although some instructors and professors believe students can learn from games, 69% of those surveyed indicated they had never had an educational experience in the classroom with video, computer, or multiplayer gaming. In the same survey, one of every five student participants felt that multiplayer computer games helped them make new friends and further develop relationships. Gaming has become much more than a solitary hobby and is, instead, a social activity involving both old and new friends (Jones, 2003). This evolution of gaming into an interactive experience can potentially assist in motivating students and helping to develop problem solving, creative and communication skills.

According to Hosen, Solovey-Hosen, and Stern (2002), in order for useful learning to take place, incidental learning and peer interaction must be key elements in the educational process. Incidental learning has been identified as the foremost way language skills are developed and learned (Verspoor & Lowie, 2003). Unintended, or incidental, learning occurs through one's experiences, including mistakes, successes, and interactions with others (Marsick & Watkins, 1990).

Aldrich (2004) indicated that when learners engage with computer simulations, they become engaged in an atmosphere where they possess complete authority and are ruler supreme, such that everything within the context of the game environment is dependent on their actions. These learners become immersed in the relationships they develop within the game, and those relationships are enormously significant. Aldrich (2003) also stated that today's students need intricacy and that the traditional lecture classrooms are not providing the environments that students need for enhanced scholarship. These computer simulations provide non-linear role-playing environments where the players can immerse themselves in a stirring education environment (Squire, 2003).

The Integration of Gaming into Education

Gaming is a social activity for children, just as playing outside with others is considered a social activity (Durkin, as cited in Colman, 1999; Gros, 2003; Squire, 2003). The games children play also become the conversation of the next day in school (Colman, 1999; Greenfield, 1984; Squire, 2003). These discussions encourage new and creative ideas to be passed around at school (Colman, 1999; Squire, 2003). For example, some games can be *modded* (the code can be changed) in order to create different endings or new adventures. Modding allows participants the opportunity to become actively engaged in the learning process while constructing their own educational experience.

Some games ship with tools that allow the games to be modded easily and without any programming knowledge (Herz, 2002b). Game life can be extended through networked users who create new levels, maps, characters, and any other useful adjustments to enhance games (Herz, 2002a). All of these new aspects of a game can be uploaded to public or private online community sites like GameSpy, which records the number of times the modification has been downloaded. Console systems like the PlayStation II and the XBOX provide some content for download, but additional hardware that connects to a computer like the SharkPort for Playstation II games, and the Action Replay for the XBOX, PlayStation II, and GameCube provides user made content that is downloadable onto a memory unit and is often more up-to-date and in demand than the manufacturer's content.

Many games now provide tools that allow the user to make custom mods, so that the game has added value to the consumer. *Civilization IV* is one such game where all of the design tools used to create the single player mission are given to all game owners. One of the benefits of these tools is that anyone can turn these modules (mods) into an educational opportunity for students by creating a historic simulation, a geology experiment, or an archeological expedition without any programming skills. In fact, educators at MIT have used the *Neverwinter Nights* tools to create a historical game based on a battle in the Revolutionary War (King, 2003). Games are being released that reviewers claim are more realistic simulations of historical events, like *Battlefield 2*, which portrays the agonizing conflict of World War II.

Unfortunately, rather than using games for such creative uses, those that use computer software in educational settings typically use them for drill-and-skill activities, which are nothing more than workbook-type activities (Greenfield, 1984) and which fail to take advantage of all of the possibilities for learning through games. It is imperative that game developers, academicians, and programmers join together to create educationally sound games that are fun and that motivate students (Gee, 2003; Kirriemuir & McFarlane, 2003). According to Pivec, Dziabenko, and Shinnerl (2003), computer games motivate the gamer to manipulate various patterns and objectives in order to achieve the most desirable outcomes. These favorable outcomes come from a combination of expressive and intellectual feedback and interactions with oneself and other gamers.

The new generation of students is accustomed to fast flashing screens like those found on Music Television (MTV) and is comfortable with and exceptionally gifted at multitasking (Wiegel, 2002). Multitasking, or parallel processing, is defined by Greenfield (1984) as the processing of knowledge from more than one source concurrently. Jones (2003) found that gaming gives students multitasking opportunities and that gaming is often one of numerous activities in which a student is concurrently engaged. Gros (2003) stated that games provide a field that has the "potential for reaching, motivating, and fully involving learners" (p. 1). Games can provide motivation (Jenkins, 2003), enhance problem-solving skills (Tews, 2001), communication skills (Morton, 1998), and develop creativity through activities such as role-playing (BECTA, 2001b). According to BECTA (2001a), motivation can foster joint interactions, innovative contests, and teamwork, as well as setup a diversified but equal chance for all participants to be successful.

Motivation

Gros (2003) stated that games could potentially fully engage learners and provide motivation. However, King (2003) indicated that software companies have not embraced the educational sector as much as the entertainment side, as only 7% of the total software created for console games is educational in nature. Games can provide built-in motivation for players (Jenkins, 2003). A study conducted by Kirriemuir and McFarlane (2003) found that teachers provided motivation through use of computer games. Dawes and Dumbleton (BECTA, 2001a) found that computer games provide motivation, support teamwork, and develop cognitive abilities. Students use their intellect to solve complex problems and issues within games and try different solutions to find the best possible answer (Jenkins, 2003).

Problem-Solving

Children are initially attracted to computer games in the same way that they are drawn to certain television shows—through dynamic visual action. Children learn more information from seeing action, like television, than just by hearing descriptions, like on radio or stereo (Greenfield, 1984). The advantage that computer gaming has over both of these mediums is that it is interactive. Video games are the first interactive medium to combine video and audio components and allow the user to participate in and solve problems (Greenfield, 1984), enjoy adventures, and compete with others. When a game player becomes frustrated with being stuck on a certain level, many times he/she will stop, and come back after a period of time. Going through struggles, and then working through them, is essential if problem solving is to take place (Aldrich, 2004).

Gee adds that the real potential of computer games is to get students to think about problem solving and to analyze the complex relationships within gaming environments (*The Chronicle of Higher Education*, 2003). Multiplayer games can give teachers and instructors an opportunity to observe how students solve problems and collaborate together. According to Tews (2001), games might have more influence on behavior, problem-solving, and social management than any other medium.

Communication

Gee, as cited on *The Chronicle of Higher Education's* Web site (2003), said he sees multiplayer online gaming becoming an entertainment medium that is as well liked as intercollegiate sports. These games allow players the opportunity to not only explore new worlds, but to explore diverse new beings and to increase camaraderie with others across the globe. The importance and fun of online gaming is found, not in the technology, but with the person with whom you are communicating and collaborating (Costikyan, 1999). In other words, fun and significant collaboration happens between people not because of the elaborate interface of the game but because of the richness of the interactions (Manninen, 2003).

Multiplayer games are constantly evolving and improving because of technology that improves graphics and the speed of the game. Fifty-five percent of Americans who use the Internet now have high-speed access at home or at work, and 39% of those have high-speed access at home (Horrigan, 2004).

Other improvements flow from the creative input of those who are actually playing the games. Multiplayer games allow users to communicate and collaborate in the same game sessions synchronously. The main objective for the players in these types of games is to play with or against someone else (Manninen, 2003). Many of these games allow for in-game text chat, while XBOX Live allows gamers to use a headset and talk back and forth during a game. Others feature game message boards on the Internet. For example, many guilds, clans, or other groups from *World of Warcraft, Everquest, Tribes,* and other multiplayer video games have their own private message boards, separate from the ones provided on the game sites. Members of the guilds come together to plan strategies for battle, plan for resource gathering, devise community responsibilities, and share stories. These message boards become powerful communication tools that are beneficial to a rewarding gaming and learning experience.

Creativity

According to *A Parent's Guide to Role-Playing Games,* role-playing games tend to develop creative skills as well as allow players the chance to play leading roles and heroes, unlike movies, books, and other forms of entertainment (Hudson, 2003). Games are one of the only instruments or channels that are available to some to actually experience guilt and experiment with various actions. Games based on historical simulations allow the gamer to take on different roles as oppressor or oppressed. Many games now have multiple paths gamers can assume, and each choice has significance (Jenkins & Squire, 2003). These consequences allow the gamer to reflect on the morality of their choices. Computer games can affect all players in different ways through play, but it is important for developers to allow players to reflect and act in new ways, outside of their daily routines. Research shows that people tend to learn best when entertained and when they can use their own creative skills to attain complex goals (Carlson, 2003).

As a video game player and educational student for the past 25 years or so, my curiosity has fostered an interest in the connection between multiplayer video gaming and critical thinking skills. This study was based on a desire to better understand the feelings and perceptions of colleagues who also play multiplayer video games and to determine if they believe that these games can possibly add to traditional educational curricula through the development of motivational, collaboration, creativity, and problem-solving skills.

Description of Study

Several impetuses prompted this study. Interest in the topic by the researchers emerged from direct observations of gaming participation (and enjoyment) by colleagues, friends, and family and the perceived potential for educational value in games. The limited amount of research on how multiplayer gaming may benefit learners also pointed to a need for additional research and awareness in this area that appears to be an emerging technological trend in education. For the most part, empirical studies have focused on the negative aspects of computer gaming, like violence (Chang, 2003), anger, and obsession (Griffiths, 1998). Jayakanthan (2002) challenged teachers and game developers to analyze how computer games can be used to improve education. The authors felt that perhaps addressing how gamers perceive themselves improving their skills in areas such as communication, motivation, problem solving, higher order thinking, and creativity, would result in a contribution to the current body of research and also point to additional needed research.

For the purposes of this research, multiplayer gaming was used to describe multiplayer online games (consoles and personal computers), videogames, as well as local area network (LAN) games. While the study was concerned with *who* was playing multiplayer video and computer games, the primary goal was to investigate if the multiplayer gamers perceived that multiplayer video and computer games increased and/or promoted skills in motivation, communication, problem-solving, and creativity.

Methodology

The sample for this study was drawn from snowball, networking, or chain sampling (Bogdan & Bicklen, 1982; Meltzoff, 1999). Snowball sampling is a useful method of sampling when the population proposed to be analyzed is complex and difficult to locate (Gall, Gall, & Borg, 2003). Because the entire population of multiplayer gamers numbers in the tens of millions, the researchers could not realistically contact everyone in the population to complete this online survey.

Unfortunately, there was no readily available group of participants to study; therefore, this study began by approaching a few gaming guild and online message board members and sending e-mails to several listservs, colleagues, coworkers, and friends asking for their help in disseminating prewritten information concerning the survey. The participants were asked to refer the researchers to other associates within the multiplayer gaming community who might be willing to participate in the study (Bogdan & Bicklen, 1982). Data were collected over a six-week period. Snowball sampling provided the researchers with 346 usable responses during this time period.

Included in the e-mail were a brief description of the survey, including the purpose and the benefits of the study, and a link to the informed consent.

Those agreeing to participate completed an online survey that included questions and statements regarding demographic characteristics in the initial part and later a scale to determine personal feelings about motivation, teamwork, problem solving, and creativity, as well as statements used to determine whether these skills are perceived to be increased during game play.

The researchers assumed that the participants in the study composed a representative sample of gamers playing multiplayer games. It was further assumed that these participants provided truthful responses on the survey instrument.

The Survey

The online survey (see Appendix A) was developed by researching previous studies of gaming and other similar technology topics including distance education test assessment (Hartman, 2001), technostress studies (Weil & Rosen, 1997), and Saphore's (1999) *A Psychometric Comparison of an Electronic and Classical Survey Instrument*. The survey assessed the demographics of multiplayer gamers, their Internet usage, and their online game playing time. It also included Likert-type items regarding the gamers' perceptions of the educational benefits of playing multiplayer games. The Likert scale had responses of 1 through 6, with 1 being strongly disagree and 6 being strongly agree.

Several of the statements used negative undertones (i.e., not) in order to detect acquiescence response sets that occur when respondents support statements without regard to the actual content (Gall, Gall, & Borg, 2003). Cronbach's Coefficient Alpha test was used to indicate if there was internal consistency within each of the response sets. If the overall raw Alpha is above .70, the score is considered to be reliable (Kelley, Cronbach, Rajaratnam, & Glesertnam, 1996; Nunnaly, 1978). When Cronbach's Coefficient Alpha is high (i.e., > 70), then the set of statements or questions have high internal reliability and consistency.

Data Analyses

Demographics

More than 83% of the participants in this survey responded that they were male Caucasians with a reported mean age of 25.9. In this study, over 42% of the respondents reported they were 21-30, and almost 30% reported ages within the 10 to 20 year age group. A total of 66% of all the respondents reported household incomes in categories of $35,000 plus. The largest percentage of players (29.5%) indicated that they had completed studies at a four-year college or university, and almost 20% reported they had finished graduate or professional school. Almost 50% of the respondents reported spending more than 20 hours a week on the Internet. Approximately 40% of the respondents reported playing multiplayer games for more than 15 years, and nearly 14% played multiplayer games more than 20 hours a week.

Is Gaming Motivational?

The means and standard deviations for motivation-focused statements 12, 20, 24, 25, and 26 can be found in Table 1.

Scores for the motivation statements (12, 20, 24, 25, and 26) were above the midpoint between strongly disagree (1) and strongly agree (6). The means and standard deviations for

Table 1. Means and standard deviations of motivation-related statements

	Mean	SD
12. Encourages investigation of game's background	4.6	1.6
20. Encourages reading guide books and associated materials	4.2	1.4
24. Encourages completion of school and/or work tasks	3.8	1.6
25. Encourages learning of rules and intricacies of game	4.6	1.3
26. Encourages discussion about game strategies	4.7	1.2

Table 2. Frequencies and percentages on perceptions of the development of motivational skills in multiplayer games

Encourages investigation of game's background	Frequency	Percent
Strongly Disagree	28	8.1
Disagree	24	6.9
Somewhat Disagree	19	5.5
Somewhat Agree	44	12.7

Table 2. continued

Agree	95	27.5
Strongly Agree	136	39.3
Encourages reading guide books and associated materials		
Strongly Disagree	12	3.5
Disagree	38	11.0
Somewhat Disagree	41	11.8
Somewhat Agree	82	23.7
Agree	109	31.5
Strongly Agree	64	18.5
Encourages completion of school and/or work tasks		
Strongly Disagree	36	10.4
Disagree	46	13.3
Somewhat Disagree	60	17.3
Somewhat Agree	83	24.0
Agree	67	19.4
Strongly Agree	54	15.6
Encourages learning of rules and intricacies of game		
Strongly Disagree	9	2.6
Disagree	27	7.8
Somewhat Disagree	26	7.5
Somewhat Agree	68	19.7
Agree	106	30.6
Strongly Agree	110	31.8
Encourages discussion about game strategies		
Strongly Disagree	7	2.0
Disagree	15	4.3
Somewhat Disagree	7.2	25
Somewhat Agree	87	25.1
Agree	112	32.4
Strongly Agree	100	28.9

the perceptions of motivation skills ranged from 3.8 to 4.7 and from 1.2 to 1.6, respectively. Cronbach's Alpha was computed at .68, indicating that the motivational items cannot be used as a scale. No significant gain in the Alpha level could be achieved by the deletion of any one item. Therefore, each item was described individually using frequencies and percents (see Table 2).

Almost 74% of the respondents agreed that multiplayer games encouraged game players to read guidebooks and other related materials. Responses were more mixed with the statement

Table 3. Means and standard deviations of communication-related statements

	Mean	SD
13. Does not promote development of communication skills	3.0	1.5
16. Helps develop ability to communicate with others	3.5	1.5
22. Interaction develops interpersonal communication	3.8	1.4
28. Promotes communication with diverse individuals	4.7	1.4
33. Does not encourage communication	2.2	1.3

that indicated multiplayer games encouraged completion of schoolwork or tasks. Fifty-nine percent of the respondents agreed, while 41% disagreed with the statement. More than 82% of the respondents felt that multiplayer games motivated players to learn the intricacies and rules of the game, and more than 86% of the respondents perceived that multiplayer games encouraged discussions about strategies and planning.

Can Gaming Promote Communication?

The means and standard deviations for the communication-focused statements 13, 16, 22, 28, and 33 can be found in Table 3. Scores for all communication statements range from strongly disagree (1) to strongly agree (6). The means and standard deviations for the perceptions of communication skills ranged from 2.2 to 4.7 and from 1.3 to 1.5, respectively.

Cronbach's Alpha was computed to be .80, indicating good reliability as a scale. Deletion of item 33 would have raised the Alpha minimally to .81. Therefore, scores of all five communication statements were summed for a total communication score. The mean of the communication scale score was 17.2 with a standard deviation of 3.0. Scores ranged from 6 to 26 and were relatively normally distributed. Skewness was found to be -.62, and the kurtosis was .90. Each item was described individually using frequencies and percents before reverse coding (see Table 4).

Table 4. Frequencies and percentages on perceptions of the development of communication skills in multiplayer games

	Frequency	Percent
Does not promote development of communication skills		
Strongly Disagree	58	16.8
Disagree	107	30.9
Somewhat Disagree	65	18.8
Somewhat Agree	53	15.3
Agree	38	11.0
Strongly Agree	25	7.2

Table 4. continued

Helps develop ability to communicate with others		
Strongly Disagree	46	13.3
Disagree	47	13.6
Somewhat Disagree	68	19.7
Somewhat Agree	82	23.7
Agree	64	18.5
Strongly Agree	39	11.3
Interaction develops interpersonal communication		
Strongly Disagree	21	6.1
Disagree	52	15.0
Somewhat Disagree	56	16.2
Somewhat Agree	113	32.7
Agree	59	17.1
Strongly Agree	45	13.0
Promotes communication with diverse individuals		
Strongly Disagree	14	4.0
Disagree	25	7.2
Somewhat Disagree	24	6.9
Somewhat Agree	58	16.8
Agree	96	27.7
Strongly Agree	129	37.3
Does not encourage communication		
Strongly Disagree	133	38.4
Disagree	96	27.7
Somewhat Disagree	57	16.5
Somewhat Agree	33	9.5
Agree	20	5.8
Strongly Agree	7	2.0

The majority of respondents reported they felt that multiplayer games encouraged communication through interaction and also allowed communication with diverse individuals.

Can Gaming Promote Problem Solving?

The means and standard deviations for problem-solving-focused statements of 11, 18, 21, 23, and 30 can be found in Table 5. Scores for all problem-solving statements were above the midpoint between strongly disagree (1) and strongly agree (6). The means and standard

Table 5. Means and standard deviations of problem-solving-related statements

	Mean	SD
11. Encourages joint problem-solving	4.4	1.3
18. Encourages consideration of options and consequences	4.2	1.4
21. Promotes exposure to new ideas	4.4	1.3
23. Promotes the development of problem-solving skills	3.8	1.4
30. Encourages thinking outside of the box	3.9	1.3

deviations for the perceptions of problem-solving skills ranged from 3.8 to 4.4 and from 1.3 to 1.4, respectively.

Cronbach's Alpha was computed to be .82, indicating good reliability as a scale. The deletion of any item would not have lowered the Alpha under .82. Scores of all five problem-solving statements were summed for a total problem-solving score. The mean of the problem-solving scale score was 20.7 with a standard deviation of 5.1. Scores range from 6 to 26 and were relatively normally distributed. Skewness was found to be -.55, and the kurtosis was -.05. Each item was described individually using frequencies and percents (see Table 6).

All of the mean scores were above the median for the statements regarding problem solving. Cronbach's Alpha was computed at .82, giving the problem-solving set of statements high

Table 6. Frequencies and percentages on perceptions of the development of problem-solving skills in multiplayer games

	Frequency	Percent
Encourages joint problem-solving		
Strongly Disagree	9	2.6
Disagree	22	6.4
Somewhat Disagree	45	13.0
Somewhat Agree	103	29.8
Agree	97	28.0
Strongly Agree	70	20.2
Encourages consideration of options and consequences		
Strongly Disagree	14	4.0
Disagree	35	10.1
Somewhat Disagree	40	11.6
Somewhat Agree	94	27.2
Agree	97	28.0
Strongly Agree	66	19.1
Promotes exposure to new ideas		
Strongly Disagree	5	1.4
Disagree	38	11.0

Table 6. continued

Somewhat Disagree	34	9.8
Somewhat Agree	89	25.7
Agree	98	28.3
Strongly Agree	82	23.7
Promotes the development of problem-solving skills		
Strongly Disagree	27	7.8
Disagree	40	11.6
Somewhat Disagree	60	17.3
Somewhat Agree	106	30.6
Agree	75	21.7
Strongly Agree	38	11.0
Encourages thinking outside of the box		
Strongly Disagree	21	6.1
Disagree	29	8.4
Somewhat Disagree	66	19.1
Somewhat Agree	110	31.8
Agree	81	23.4
Strongly Agree	39	11.3

reliability as a scale. Participants in the survey reported that they felt multiplayer gaming encouraged joint problem solving, promoted exposure to new ideas, and encouraged players to consider multiple options and scenarios. Shotton (1989) pointed out that video games can increase the rate of the gamer's neural pathways thereby speeding up the decision-making processes. Often in school coursework or work assignments, people are instructed by teachers or superiors of one way to complete the task. Frequently, this recommendation is assumed to be the best choice for completing the assignment, and the student or worker is not given the chance to look for other, possibly better options and explore other avenues.

Can Gaming Promote Creativity?

The means and standard deviations for creativity-focused statements 17, 27, 29, 34, and 35 can be found in Table 7. Scores for all creativity statements were between strongly disagree (1) and strongly agree (6). The means and standard deviations for the perceptions of creativity skills ranged from 2.9 to 4.2 and from 1.4 to 1.5, respectively.

Cronbach's Alpha was computed to be .81, indicating good reliability as a scale. Deletion of item 17 would have raised the Alpha to .84. Therefore, scores of all five creativity statements were summed for a total creativity score. The mean of the creativity scale score was 17.4 with a standard deviation of 3.3. Scores range from 6 to 26 and were relatively normally dis-

Table 7. Means and standard deviations of creativity-related statements

	Mean	SD
17. Does not develop transferable creative skills	2.9	1.4
27. Inspires creativity	4.2	1.4
29. Encourages creation of artistic works	3.7	1.5
34. Promotes creation of imaginative works	3.7	1.5
35. Does not promote creative skills	3.0	1.5

tributed. Skewness was found to be -.15, and the kurtosis was -.08. Each item was described individually using frequencies and percentages before reverse coding (see Table 8).

Almost 69% of the respondents disagreed with the statement that multiplayer games do not encourage transferable creative skills, and more than 70% believed that multiplayer games inspired creativity. Over 56% of the respondents agreed that multiplayer games encouraged the creation of artistic works, but almost 44% disagreed. The largest percentage of respondents (26.9%) somewhat agreed that multiplayer games encouraged the creation of imaginative works, but 21.7% of the respondents somewhat disagreed. Only 32% of the respondents thought that multiplayer games do not promote creative skills.

Two statements in the creativity statement set were negatively drawn and included the word "not" to help protect against acquiescence response sets. There were no acquiescence response sets found in this set of statements. Reverse coding was completed on this set to determine Cronbach's Alpha, which was computed to be .81, giving the set good reliability.

Table 8. Frequencies and percentages on perceptions of the development of creativity skills in multiplayer games

	Frequency	Percent
Does not develop transferable creative skills		
Strongly Disagree	59	17.1
Disagree	102	29.5
Somewhat Disagree	76	22.0
Somewhat Agree	56	16.2
Agree	43	12.4
Strongly Agree	10	2.9
Inspires creativity		
Strongly Disagree	13	3.8
Disagree	38	11.0
Somewhat Disagree	52	15.0
Somewhat Agree	83	24.0
Agree	77	22.3

Table 8. continued

Strongly Agree	83	24.0
Encourages creation of artistic works		
Strongly Disagree	34	9.8
Disagree	47	13.6
Somewhat Disagree	68	19.7
Somewhat Agree	90	26.0
Agree	61	17.6
Strongly Agree	46	13.3
Promotes creation of imaginative works		
Strongly Disagree	24	6.9
Disagree	52	15.0
Somewhat Disagree	75	21.7
Somewhat Agree	93	26.9
Agree	68	19.7
Strongly Agree	34	9.8
Does not promote creative skills		
Strongly Disagree	68	19.7
Disagree	75	21.7
Somewhat Disagree	91	26.3
Somewhat Agree	49	14.2
Agree	33	9.5
Strongly Agree	30	8.7

Ideas for the Classroom

Video gaming, especially the multiplayer variety, allows the participant the chance to interact with both the computer AI and other players. This lets learners shroud themselves inside the game world. One possible idea for the classroom is to have educators ask students to design new worlds or attempt to recreate past events. Other groups within the classroom could then create the objectives and design rules and objectives for the class. These activities would promote basic computer skills and advanced skills such as programming, scripting, and design. Educators could help facilitate the project to ensure that all students were communicating properly, equally solving problems, developing teamwork skills, and learning to build off of each other's creativity. Motivation is the fun part, and if everyone is involved in some aspect from the evaluation, design, development, implementation, or assessment then these incidental skills should develop in ways not assessed in previous research.

Educators could use games and communication software to encourage peer discussion about game strategies, mechanics, storylines, morality, economics, or politics. Educators could also use games in teacher training and professional development (Thiagarajan &

Parker, 1999). Educators could use multiplayer games as a fun way to encourage students to spend time playing with a diverse group of students and to further multicultural studies. Multiplayer games seem to bring people from all over the world together to socialize and interact with each other.

Further studies could be conducted at gaming conventions and shows around the world and could incorporate a more qualitative approach. This would allow the researchers to verify participants' demographic information and to delve deeper into user experiences, feelings, interpretations, and motivations as they relate to multiplayer games. An inquiry into the nationality of the gamer should also be included in any future research. Gaming is an international endeavor and business, and a question regarding nationality should have been included in this questionnaire.

Conclusion and Potential

With the increase of video game sales, and the corresponding increase in the number of people playing these games (IDSA, 2002), it is of great importance to understand why multiplayer video games are being played and what educators can learn from multiplayer gamers.

Many respondents reported they at least somewhat believed multiplayer games encouraged, promoted, and inspired creative thinking. Gamers play games to have fun and to be challenged (IDSA, 2002). Games are different from movies because of the interactive experience, but many are incorporating cinematic features within these games. Creativity helps users develop characters more deeply in role-playing adventures and solve problems that are sometimes built around the uniqueness of the game's premise. Games also spur gamers to create modifications to the game such as new content, modules, characters, scripts, and items. Game developers also get many new ideas from gamers to incorporate in expansion packs and new games and encourage gamers to use the toolsets they provide to develop the games further.

Many multiplayer video games require users to utilize high-speed connections, so that most people share the same experiences during games. Low bandwidth, referred to as lag, tends to pull the other players' experiences down. For educational courses, more interactive multimedia projects can be planned if there is a greater trend toward high-speed connections.

This study should be used as a point of reference for future research into multiplayer gaming and learning. There is much that can be found within games, such as the structure, organization, dialogue, and basic programming that can benefit students in areas such as math, reading, social studies, and science. The use of video games within curricula could initially be time-consuming, especially for those educators who are not familiar with gaming. Familiarity with different genres, as well as the construction of video games, could well benefit instructors who would like to use games as part of their courses. There is much more to learn in the area of gaming research, but from this research it can be seen that there are educational benefits in areas of motivation, communication, problem-solving, teamwork, and creativity skills. To really take advantage of this medium, researchers should further study multiplayer games so that educators across the globe can take advantage of the unique educational attributes multiplayer video games can bring to the classroom.

References

Aldrich, C. (2004). *Simulations and the future of learning: An innovative (and perhaps revolutionary) approach to e-learning.* San Francisco: Pfeiffer.

BECTA. (2001a). *Computer games in education project.* Retrieved January 26, 2005, from http://www.becta.org.uk/research/research.cfm?section=1&id=2846

BECTA. (2001b). *What aspects of games may contribute to education?* Retrieved November 6, 2003, from http://www.becta.org.uk/page_documents/research/ cge/aspects.pdf

Berger, A. A. (2002). *Video games: A popular culture phenomenon.* New Brunswick: Transaction Publishers.

Bogdan, R. C., & Biklen, S. K. (1982). *Qualitative research for education: An introduction to theory and methods.* Newton, MA: Allyn & Bacon.

Carlson, S. (2003). *Can* Grand Theft Auto *inspire professors? Educators say the virtual worlds of video games help students think more broadly.* Retrieved October 16, 2003, from http://chronicle.com/prm/weekly/v49/i49/49a03101.htm

Chang, A. (2003). *Video games could be good for you.* Retrieved October 15, 2003, from http://msnbc.com/m/pt/printthis_main.asp?storyID=919010

Chiu, S., Lee, J., & Huang, D. (2004). Video game addiction in children and teenagers in Taiwan. *CyberPsychology & Behavior, 7*(5), 571-581.

Colman, A. (1999). Computer games. *Youth Studies Australia, 18*(1), 10.

Costikyan, G. (1999). *Why online games suck (and how to design ones that don't).* Retrieved November 4, 2003, from http://www.costik.com/onlinsux.html

Entertainment Software Association. (2003). *Top ten industry facts.* Retrieved October 10, 2003, from http://www.theesa.com/pressroom.html

Gall, M. D., Gall, J. P., & Borg, W. R. (2003). *Educational research: An introduction* (7th ed.). Boston: Allyn and Bacon.

Gee, J. P. (2003). *What video games have to teach us about learning and literacy.* New York: Palgrave Macmillan.

Gentile, D., Lynch, P., Linder, J., & Walsh, D. (2004). The effects of violent video game habits on adolescent hostility, aggressive behaviors, and school performance. *Journal of Adolescence, 27*(1), 5-22.

Greenfield, P. M. (1984). *Mind and media: The effects of television, video games, and computers.* Cambridge: Harvard University Press.

Griffiths, M. D. (1998). Violent video games and aggression: A review of the literature. *Aggression and Violent Behavior, 4*(2), 203-212.

Griffiths, M. D., & Davies, M. N. (2002). Excessive online computer gaming: Implications for education. *Journal of Computer Assisted Learning, 18*(3), 379-380.

Gros, B. (2003). *The impact of digital games in education.* Retrieved October 17, 2003, from http://www.firstmonday.dk/issues/issue8_7/xyzgros/

Hartman, J. A. (2001). *AFTY-R: Psychometric properties and predictive value for academic performance in online learning*. Doctoral dissertation, University of Alabama at Tuscaloosa. *Dissertation Abstracts International, 62*, 3019.

Herz, J. C. (2002a). Gaming the system: Multi-player worlds online. In L. King (Ed.), *Game on: The history and culture of videogames* (pp. 86-97). New York: Universe Publishing.

Herz, J. C. (2002b). *Gaming the system: What higher education can learn from multiplayer online worlds*. Retrieved February 11, 2004, from http://www.educause.edu/ir/library/pdf/ffpiu019.pdf

Horrigan, J. B. (2004). *Broadband penetration on the upswing: 55% of adult Internet users have broadband at home or work*. Retrieved April 24, 2004, from http://www.pewinternet.org/reports/pdfs/PIP_Broadband04.DataMemo.pdf

Hosen, R., Solovey-Hosen, D., & Stern, L. (2002). The acquisition of beliefs that promote subjective well-being. *Journal of Instructional Psychology, 29*(4), 231-244.

Hudson, C. (2003). *A parent's guide to role-playing games*. Retrieved October 16, 2003, from http://www.geocities.com/TimesSquare/Dungeon/1257/parents2.html

IDSA. (2002). *Essential facts about the computer and video game industry*. Retrieved November 6, 2003, from http://www.theesa.com/IDSABooklet.pdf

Jayakathan, R. (2002). Application of computer games in the field of education. *Electronic Library, 20*(2), 98-102.

Jenkins, H. (2003). *How should we teach kids Newtonian physics? Simple. Play computer games*. Retrieved November 4, 2003, from http://www.technologyreview.com/articles/print_version/wo_jenkins032902.asp

Jenkins, H., & Squire, K. (2003, November). Meaningful violence: How to make sense out of senseless acts. *Computer Games, 156*, 108.

Jones, S. (2003). Let the games begin: Gaming technology and entertainment among college students. Retrieved November 7, 2003, from http://www.pewinternet.org/reports/pdfs/PIP_College_Gaming_Reporta.pdf

Kelley, T., Cronbach, L., Rajaratnam, N., & Glesertnam, G. (1996). Reliability. In A. Ward, M. Murray-Ward, & H. Stoker (Eds.), *Education measurement: Origins, theories, and explications. Vol. 1: Basic concepts and theories* (pp. 245-286). Lanham, MD: University Press of America.

King, B. (2003). Educators turn to games for help. *Wired News*. Retrieved October 17, 2003, from http://www.wired.com/news/games/0,2101,59855,00.html

King, L. (2002). Introduction. In L. King (Ed.), *Game on: The history and culture of video games* (pp. 8-19). New York: Universe Publishing.

Kirriemuir, J., & McFarlane, A. (2003, November). *Use of computer games and video games in the classroom*. Paper presented at the DIGRA 2003 Conference, Level up, Holland.

Lange, A. (2002). Report from the PAL zone: European games culture. In L. King (Ed.), *Game on: The history and culture of videogames* (pp. 46-55). New York: Universe Publishing.

Manninen, T. (2003). Interaction forms and communicative actions in multiplayer games [Electronic version]. *The International Journal of Computer Game Research, 3*(1), Article 031. Retrieved November 6, 2003, from http://www.gamestudies. org/ 0301/ manninen

Marsick, V. J., & Watkins, K. (1990). *Informal and incidental learning in the workplace.* New York: Routledge.

Meltzoff, J. (1999). *Critical thinking about research: Psychology and related fields.* Washington, DC: American Psychological Association.

Morton, D. (1998). *Study sounds alarm over video game use: Isolation, helplessness, characterize the world of heavy players, study finds.* Retrieved April 24, 2004, from http://www.sfu.ca/mediapr/sfnews/1998/April2/kline.html

Nunnaly, J. (1978). *Psychometric theory.* New York: McGraw-Hill.

Pivec, M., Dziabenko, O., & Shinnerl, I. (2003, July 2-4). Aspects of game-based learning. In *Proceedings of the Third International Conference on Knowledge Management (I-KNOW '03)*, Graz, Austria (pp. 216-225). Retrieved November 11, 2003, from http://www.unigame.net/html/I-Know_GBL-2704.pdf

Saphore, R. B. (1999). A psychometric comparison of an electronic and classical survey instrument. Doctoral dissertation, University of Alabama at Tuscaloosa. *Dissertation Abstracts International, 60,* 3976.

Sherry, J. L. (2001). The effects of violent video games on aggression: A meta-analysis. *Human Communication Research, 27*(3), 409-431.

Shotton, M. (1989). *Computer addiction? A study of computer dependency.* London: Taylor and Francis.

Squire, K. (2003). Video games in education. *International Journal of Simulations and Gaming, 2*(1), 49-62.

Tews, R. R. (2001). Archetypes on acid: Video games and culture. In J. Wolf (Ed.), *The medium of the video game* (pp. 169-182). Austin: University of Texas Press.

The Chronicle of Higher Education. (2003). *Video games in the classroom.* Retrieved August 27, 2003, from http://chronicle.com/colloquylive/2003/08/video/

Thiagarajan, S., & Parker, G. (1999). *Teamwork and teamplay: Games and activities for building and training teams.* San Francisco: Jossey-Bass.

Thompson, C. (2002). Violence and the political life of videogames. In L. King (Ed.), *Game on: The history and culture of video games* (pp. 22-31). New York: Universe Publishing.

Thompson, K. (2001). Violence in E-rated video games. *Journal of the American Medical Association, 286*(5), 591-598.

Verspoor, M., & Lowie, W. (2003). Making sense of polysemous words. *Language Learning, 53*(3), 547-586.

Weigel, V. B. (2002). *Deep learning for a Digital Age: Technology's untapped potential to enrich higher education.* San Francisco: Jossey-Bass.

Weil, M. M., & Rosen, L. D. (1997). *Technology: Coping with technology @ work @ home @ play.* New York: John Wiley & Sons.

Appendix A

SURVEY

SECTION I

Please select the most appropriate answer to each question.

You must be at least 18 years of age or have your legal guardian's permission to participate in this study.

1.   Type your age in years. _____

2.   What is your gender?

      Female
      Male

3.   What is the highest level of education you completed?

      Kindergarten through 12th grade
      High school graduate or GED
      Junior, community or technical college
      Four-year college or university
      Graduate or professional school

4.   What is your annual household income?

      Under $20,000 per year
      $20,001 - $35,000 per year
      $35,001 - $50,000 per year
      $50,001 - $80,000 per year
      $80,001 or greater per year
      Don't know

5.   Which category best describes your ethnicity? Please select one.

      African-American or of African descent

      Asian-American or of Asian descent

      Caucasian or of European descent

      Hispanic-American or of Latin descent

      Native American

      Other _____

SECTION II

Please select the answer that best describes personal technology related habit. For purposes of this survey, multiplayer games refer to both video and computer games.

6.   How much time do you spend each week on the Internet? Please select one.

      0 - 5 hours

      6 - 10 hours

      11 - 15 hours

      16 - 20 hours

      More than 20 hours

7.   How long have you been playing video or computer games? Please select one.

      0 - 1 year

      2 - 5 years

      6 - 10 years

      11 - 15 years

      More than 15 years

8.   How much time do you spend each week playing multiplayer video or computer games? Please select one.

      0 - 5 hours

      6 - 10 hours

      11 - 15 hours

      16 - 20 hours

      More than 20 hours

9.   What type(s) of multiplayer games do you play? Please select all that apply.

Role-playing (i.e., Neverwinter Nights, Everquest, Star Wars Galaxies)
Strategy (i.e., Age of Empires II, Civilization III, Cossacks)
Sports (i.e., Madden, ESPN, XSN sports title)
First-Person Shooters (i.e., Quake, Doom, Halo, Rainbow 6)
Simulations (i.e., Sims, Microsoft Flight Simulator)
Card and Board (i.e., Checkers, Spades, Cribbage, Monopoly, Scrabble)
Other. Please specify. _____

10. Which platform(s) do you use to play most of your multiplayer games? Please select all that apply.

PC
Mac
XBOX
PlayStation II
Game Cube
Game Boy or Game Boy Advance
PDA
Mobile Telephone
Ngage
Dreamcast
Other _____

SECTION III

For each of the following items please select the answer that best represents how much you agree or disagree with the statement. The numbers correspond to the following responses: (1) Strongly Disagree; (2) Disagree; (3) Somewhat Disagree; (4) Somewhat Agree; (5) Agree; and (6) Strongly Agree.

11. I think that playing multiplayer games helps me learn to work with others to solve problems or accomplish goals.
Strongly Disagree   1 2 3 4 5 6   Strongly Agree

12.   I think that playing multiplayer games encourages me to look to web sites with related materials to find more information about the game's background.

Strongly Disagree   1 2 3 4 5 6   Strongly Agree

13.   I do not think that playing multiplayer games encourages me to develop my communication skills.

Strongly Disagree   1 2 3 4 5 6   Strongly Agree

14.   I think that it is easier to reach a new level or complete a mission in a multiplayer game when I am working with others.

Strongly Disagree   1 2 3 4 5 6   Strongly Agree

15.   I think I succeed at multiplayer games without cooperating with other players.

Strongly Disagree   1 2 3 4 5 6   Strongly Agree

16.   I think that my ability to express my thoughts and ideas is improved through playing multiplayer games.

Strongly Disagree   1 2 3 4 5 6   Strongly Agree

17.   I do not think that I use any of the creative skills I use in multiplayer games in my everyday life.

Strongly Disagree   1 2 3 4 5 6   Strongly Agree

18.   I think playing multiplayer games makes me think about options and their consequences in order to be successful.

Strongly Disagree   1 2 3 4 5 6   Strongly Agree

19.   I think playing with others in multiplayer games makes it easier for me to collaborate with peers at work or school.

Strongly Disagree   1 2 3 4 5 6   Strongly Agree

20.   I think that the competition of multiplayer games encourages me to try harder to succeed at the game, including seeking hints in guidebooks or other sources.

Strongly Disagree   1 2 3 4 5 6   Strongly Agree

21.   I think that multiplayer games expose me to ideas and approaches to problems that are different from my own ideas and approaches.

Strongly Disagree   1 2 3 4 5 6   Strongly Agree

22.   I think that interacting with others in multiplayer games helps me develop my ability to communicate with others.

Strongly Disagree   1 2 3 4 5 6   Strongly Agree

23.   I think that I learn how to solve problems through playing multiplayer games.

Strongly Disagree   1 2 3 4 5 6   Strongly Agree

24.   I think that my desire to have free time in which to play multiplayer games motivates me to complete tasks at work or school.

Strongly Disagree   1 2 3 4 5 6   Strongly Agree

25.   I think that I am enthusiastic about learning the rules of controls of a multiplayer game when I first begin to play.

Strongly Disagree   1 2 3 4 5 6   Strongly Agree

26.   I think that playing multiplayer games encourages me to talk with other players about game strategies.

Strongly Disagree   1 2 3 4 5 6   Strongly Agree

27.   I think that the imagination shown by the graphics and stories within multiplayer games inspires my own creativity.

Strongly Disagree   1 2 3 4 5 6   Strongly Agree

28.   I think that playing multiplayer games provides me the opportunity to communicate with a diverse group of individuals.

Strongly Disagree   1 2 3 4 5 6   Strongly Agree

29.   I think the authors, coders, and designers of multiplayer games inspire me to create artistic works.

Strongly Disagree   1 2 3 4 5 6 Strongly Agree

30.   I think that the situations encountered in multiplayer games force me to think outside my comfort zone to find solutions.

Strongly Disagree   1 2 3 4 5 6   Strongly Agree

31.   I think multiplayer games are isolating.
      Strongly Disagree   1 2 3 4 5 6   Strongly Agree

32.   I think that I am successful if I can help another player succeed within the multiplayer game.
      Strongly Disagree   1 2 3 4 5 6   Strongly Agree

33.   I think that communication with others is rare during multiplayer games.
      Strongly Disagree   1 2 3 4 5 6   Strongly Agree

34.   I think that multiplayer games lead me to create my own imaginative works.
      Strongly Disagree   1 2 3 4 5 6   Strongly Agree

35.   I do not think that playing multiplayer games has any effect on my creative skills.
      Strongly Disagree   1 2 3 4 5 6   Strongly Agree

36.   How do you think games can benefit education? _____
      _____
      _____
      _____

37.   How did you hear about this study? _____

Chapter VIII

Gamer Teachers

David Gibson, CurveShift.com, USA

William Halverson, SimSchool, USA

Eric Riedel, Walden University, USA

Abstract

The divergence between the generation of people who grew up before versus after computer games became ubiquitous—a new kind of digital divide—is characterized by differences in thinking patterns, perceptions about the world, approaches to challenges, evaluation of risks, and expectations about leading and interacting with other people. Some argue that because of these sorts of differences, students of today have new expectations about learning, which suggests that we need new approaches to teaching and gamer teachers (the pun is intended). This chapter outlines a potential framework for research on teaching that understands and uses the power of computer games and simulations to improve student achievement. Along the way, we raise new research questions, which we hope that you and others will help answer.

Introduction

The terms "games generation" (Prensky, 2001a) and "gamer generation" (Beck & Wade, 2004) have recently captured the idea that a group of people born after 1970 are learning something—and learning it differently—by playing computer games. The term also implies that there are other generations—like the baby boomers born in the 1950s—who differ from the gamers and who are situated across a gap defined by digital game playing.

In our research and development of simSchool—a Web-based game designed to improve teaching skills—we began to wonder if today's preservice students (tomorrow's teachers) are more like boomers or gamers? Did they play games as kids? Do they still play? What do they think about the potential of teaching with games? Are they ready to teach with them?

In this chapter, we raise and give initial possible answers to questions like these, organized by four primary questions. What are the concerns of critics of educational games and simulations; are those concerns well founded, and is there a generational gap in attitudes about those concerns? How is the landscape of future teachers changing because of the impact of games and simulations on learners? To what extent do the people now becoming teachers share experiences, perceptions, and attitudes with the rest of their "gamer generation?" How can researchers approach the task of understanding teachers of the game generation?

The Concerns

Why not teach with games and simulations? Many of the concerns about playing games "instead of doing schoolwork" result from a mental model that having fun and learning are mutually exclusive. Why not say playing games "are a form of schoolwork?" There are several possible answers that have been called upon by critics of mass media in each era as first film, radio, television, computers, and now video and computer games have been introduced and their educational value assessed (Wartella & Jennings, 2000).

- The new technology takes time away from other things.
- It does not work any better than other teaching techniques.
- It has potentially harmful side effects, especially exposing young minds to commercialism, sex, and violence.

Games, in particular, are the number one use of home computers by kids over the age of eight (Becker, 2000). Are parents and teachers taking best advantage of them? Is it possible that, like technology in general, games can not only help children learn things *better*; they can help them learn *better things*? To believe in this possibility, people have to get over their reasonable fears of the influence of media.

Roots of the Fear of Games

Before the gamer generation was born (prior to 1970), research on the effects of media on children was well underway with film and television. It seems likely that this early research, which demonstrated media's potential influence on children's aggression and violence, has left a negative reverberation in the public mind about games. Some game makers are not helping the situation of course, producing violent and sexually explicit games, which gives politicians an easy target and creates grist for sensational "news" mills. But if research on games and simulations follows the path taken by research on other media, the evidence will begin to mount in favor of its positive potential.

The Center on Media and Child Health of Children's Hospital of Boston has recently prepared a report for the Kaiser Family Foundation titled "The Effects of Electronic Media on Children Ages Zero to Six: A History of Research" (KFF, 2005). The emphasis in this literature is plain to see; mass media takes valuable time and attention away from healthy pursuits, is capable of prompting violence, encourages antisocial behavior, and is a bad influence on the minds of the young. It exposes them to commercials, sexual themes, and promotes passive couch-potato behavior. The reverberation of the early generation of studies is still ringing.

The early research on the effects of media on socialization and cognitive development became focused during the years when television began to air educational programs designed for young children. Social learning theory (Bandura & Walters, 1963) influenced the earliest research efforts. Social cognitive theory that emerged later characterized learning "as a triadic, dynamic, and reciprocal interaction of personal factors, behavior, and the environment" in which most behavior is learned "vicariously" (USF, 2005). This cognitive framework equally supports both positive and negative effects of media such as games, and we will return to it later to develop a framework for research on gamer teachers.

The media studies of the 1960s found that young children reproduced specific acts of aggression they observed on film, when the film aggressors were either rewarded or not punished and the children were placed in a situation with an immediate opportunity to display aggression. For example, some children immediately after viewing violent films, were given dolls to play with in which pressing a bar caused one doll to hit another (Lovaas, 1961). Children who had viewed violent impressions pressed the bar more than children who had not. Other young children heard negative comments by an experimenter while watching films with aggressive acts, and were then found to be inhibited only by the experimenter's presence, which influenced them to be less likely to show aggressive behavior than children who had heard neutral or positive comments (Hicks, 1968).

With the advent of *Sesame Street* in 1969, the next two decades witnessed an explosion of research reports by the Children's Television Workshop, some of which, perhaps influenced by the agenda of the sponsored research, "demonstrated that TV could be a powerful teacher of academic and social skills" (KFF, 2005, p. 3). However, research on media violence and other negative effects continued to mount, including studies that produced evidence of desensitization to violence (Cline, Croft, & Courrier, 1973) and lowering of grades and contributing to antisocial behavior (Burton, Calonico, & McSeveney, 1979). A few studies began to explore cognitive differences in various age groups, while staying focused on the media's potential negative effects on children. For example, one study found that much larger percentages of fifth and eighth graders included motives in their evaluations of aggressive films than did kindergarteners (Collins, Berndt, & Hess, 1974), and another showed that older students were more likely than the younger children to be inhibited by an experimenter's negative comments (Grusec, 1973). These sorts of studies implied that younger children were more impressionable and less able to filter or evaluate the negative effects of media on their behavior.

It is not difficult to see that the research evidence indicating negative effects of mass media and the inappropriateness of exposing children of certain ages to such influences has in part been translated into attitudes about computer video games. One early study specifically found no differences between the ill effects of watching TV and playing video games on aggression or pro-social behavior (Silvern & Williamson, 1987).

But research evidence of the 1970s and 1980s also began to broaden from its roots in studies of violence and aggression. Pro-social results, for example, were found for particular shows like *Mister Rogers* and *Sesame Street*. And an unexpected additional cognitive effect was discovered. Children who watched while playing with toys paid half as much attention but had similar comprehension gains to children who only watched (Lorch, Anderson, & Levin, 1979), suggesting cognitive mechanisms of distributed and strategic attention.

As computer and video game use by children appeared in the late 1980s and 1990s, a small body evidence of a positive potential for media continued to gather. Children who used developmentally appropriate software showed improved intelligence test scores, non-verbal skills, dexterity, and long-term memory. And at the same time, creativity was reduced among children who used non-developmentally appropriate software (Haugland, 1992).

By 2000 it was understandably clear that abundant, unmonitored access to television and home computers uses up time at the expense of other activities, thereby putting children at risk. But at the same time, playing computer games had the potential to build literacy by enhancing children's ability to read and visualize images in three-dimensional space and track multiple images simultaneously (Subrahmanyam, Kraut, Greenfield, & Gross, 2000). The limited evidence also indicated that home computer use might be linked to slightly better academic performance. And various studies have shown that computers can facilitate social interaction and cooperation, friendship formation, and constructive group play (Chen, 1985).

Thus with the recent introduction of games and simulations in education, we might expect a similar line of research developing as it has with other media. Proponents will tout the educational benefits for children, while opponents will voice fears about exposure to inappropriate commercial, sexual, and violent content. The opponents' problem of the use of time taken up by the new media will result in conclusions that monitored use and educational purposes are preferred in order to avoid harmful effects on a child's physical, social, and psychological development. As the research on games and simulations matures, study will turn to the effects on children's knowledge of the world, attitudes, values, and moral conduct. The greatly enhanced interactivity of network-based uses of the technology will be found to enable both greatly enriched learning as well as increased risk of harm.

To garner the maximum benefit of games and simulations for learning, the social cognitive theory suggests that well-aligned relationships need to exist among the kind of game, the kind of child, and the kind of situation that brings the three together. To design and use games with these relationships in mind, schools need teachers who see the value of teaching with games and simulations and who have the skills to construct the best alignments for learning. No matter what generation they come from, we call them "gamer teachers." But the question arises, are today's newest teachers more likely to turn to games and simulations as teaching devices than their older counterparts? Is there a "gamer gap" in the teaching profession?

Characteristics of the Gamer Generation

The fundamental idea about the gamer generation is that because they have grown up playing with computers, they are digital natives, compared to the rest of the digital immigrants who were born before 1970 (Prensky, 2001b). The premise is that they have developed into different kinds of thinkers; their cognitive styles have been shaped by ubiquitous access to computers and games. How does this notion fit with modern ideas from cognitive theories of learning, and what exactly are the changes?

Cognitive research has shown that learning is facilitated when four fundamental characteristics are present: (1) active engagement with content (knowledge centered), (2) participation in groups (community centered), (3) frequent interaction and feedback (assessment centered), and (4) personally relevant connections to real world contexts (learner centered) (Bransford, Brown, & Cocking, 2000). These ideas about how to situate learning experiences for maxi-

Table 1. Gamer cognitive styles—Prensky's list

On a scale of 1 to 5, how do you think and learn best?	
1. Twitch Speed vs. conventional speed 1 2 3 4 5	1—High speed reactions motivate/excite you 5 – You would rather take your time on things
2. Parallel vs. linear processing 1 2 3 4 5	1—You like several things going on at once 5—You prefer to deal with one thing at a time
3. Graphics vs. text first 1 2 3 4 5	1—You learn by seeing, finding patterns 5—You read directions before trying things
4. Random access vs. step-by-step 1 2 3 4 5	1—Bouncing around is fine, you have a hyperlinked mind 5—Step 3 has to come only after step 1 and 2
5. Connected vs. standalone 1 2 3 4 5	1—You would like to have three Web windows open, IM your friends, and talk on the phone while working 5—You would rather take a book to a quiet place to work alone
6. Active vs. passive 1 2 3 4 5	1—You act first, then ask 5—You watch for a while before deciding what to do
7. Play vs. work 1 2 3 4 5	1—You fool around to make gains 5—You work hard to make gains
8. Payoff vs. patience 1 2 3 4 5	1—You need to know immediately if something is working or not 5—You appreciate "delayed gratification"

Table 1. continued

9. Fantasy vs. reality 1 2 3 4 5	1—You are drawn to make-believe situations 5—You are drawn to today's news and discussions
10. Technology as friend vs. foe 1 2 3 4 5	1—You cannot imagine learning or working without a lot of technology in hand 5—You use technology when it is necessary, but probably have forgotten how to do a few things since the last time you used it

mum effectiveness are a close fit with how games work. How people learn = how games work. We display this relationship in a synthesis model in Table 2.

Beyond the promising context of games and simulations as environments for learning, has the ubiquitous presence of games since the 1970s actually changed the way a generation thinks? Prensky (2001a) lists 10 cognitive style changes he has observed in the games generation, all of which raise new challenges for education (Table 1). Where do current and future teachers stand within these styles as learners? How does their stance affect their approach to teaching and recognition of learners' individual needs? Take a minute to assess your own learning style on "Prensky's List."

Whether or not a teacher exhibits characteristics that approach "1" in the Prensky List scale, a good proportion of their students probably do. So research on teaching needs to begin to document how instructional design and classroom practice takes advantage of these principles. Whether it's the middle of a game or not, is a student experiencing learning that is fast-pace, multi-channel, visually stimulating, option-rich, collaborative, active, fun, with rapid and focused feedback, self-fulfilling, and technologically advanced? How does the future teacher think these things fit into the design of learning environments? How are teacher preparation programs, and then induction and support programs gearing up to provide training so that teachers can deliver on these characteristics?

Expanding on the theme of the changed learner, Beck and Wade (2004) elaborate on the characteristics of gamers with the following:

- Gamers expect to be in direct control of the situation. Games are responsive to you. You decide "what course or scenario to experience; and what tools, competitors, and abilities to work with" (p. 65).
- Because the audio-visual inputs are focused within the screen, and create a kind of "consumer theater," gamers opt for attention-intensity, and have learned to quiet external chatter so they can think and react.

- Games reward technical skills, especially the ability to automate effective actions and "think strategically in a chaotic world" (p. 69).

- Gamers have spent hours "rapidly analyzing new situations, interacting with characters that don't really know, and solving problems quickly and independently" (p. 80).

- They have "highly developed teamwork skills and a strong desire to be part of a team" (p. 82).

- They are "motivated by skill, competition, rewards, and the sensory excitement of swimming in dynamic data" (p.96).

- They have "somehow accumulated experience beyond their years" (p.128).

- They see "digital environments as simply additional parts of the everyday world" (p. 130).

Table 2. Gamer teacher instructional design skill requirements that help people learn

Learner Centered	Knowledge Centered
Allow the student to choose what course or scenario to experience; and what tools, competitors, and abilities to work with.	Ask for pattern recognition instead of data classification; provide hyperlinked content and referencing.
Create a kind of "consumer theater." Create experiences that maintain a fast pace and exploit the facility of twitch speed.	Present knowledge to be consumed in small bits, usually just before you need it.
Facilitate self-fulfillment through learning; have fun with titles and recognition.	Feed more information, in simultaneous multiple channels; provide content redundancy and ubiquitous access to content.
Play is serious work; achievement, winning and beating competitors is both fun and hard work; develop game interfaces for serious business.	Design for doing; expect users to dive in and make mistakes as they learn by using.
Community Centered	**Assessment Centered**
Facilitate community and cooperative or collaborative work; develop capabilities in managing communications and group work processes.	Give instant feedback and shower rewards and punishments now, not later.
Design spaces for informal relationships and assume that there will be a lot of learning from peers.	Use and expect visual data analysis and visual intelligence.
Provide ubiquitous global community access with high-speed, high-end equipment.	Provide feedback on strategic as well as technical skills.
	Develop measures of the users ability to analyze new situations, interact with uncertain characters, and solve problems quickly and independently.

Table 3. Characteristics of respondents

		Median Age	% Male	N
Under 34 years—the Gamer Generation	Non-Gamer	22	15.6%	96
	Gamer	22	23.2%	112
Over 34 years—the Boomers	Non-Gamer	40	6.7%	15
	Gamer	36	20.0%	5

- Gaming has created a new learning style…one that
  - Aggressively ignores formal instruction,
  - Leans on trial and error,
  - Includes lots of learning from peers,
  - Sees that knowledge can be consumed in small bits, usually just before you need it.

It is time to revisit general instructional design with the above features in mind so that the new generation of teachers knows how to evaluate, select, and use games and simulations within a research-based framework that combines recent cognitive theories with observations of today's students.

We offer a synthesis (Table 2), which is structured around the four categories developed by Bransford and others, with details supplied by Prensky, Beck, Wade and others.

Gamer Teachers

Does the new generation of teachers resemble the picture of the gamer generation? Do their attitudes align with the above framework for how people learn through games and simulations? Do they know how to provide learning experiences like the previous profile—with or without games and simulations?

To begin to develop answers about the extent to which new teachers share experiences, perceptions, and attitudes with the rest of their generation, we recently surveyed 228 preservice students and divided the group by age and game playing experience (Table 3).

Those surveyed were mostly inexperienced future teachers, 80% of whom were white females. In the age range of 20 to 23 year old students, females outnumbered males by 3 to 10 times. Higher percentages of the males (68% compared to 35% of the females) mentioned secondary licensing in their goals, and higher percentages of the females (77% to 55% of the males) mentioned elementary in their licensing goals. The vast majority had little teaching experience; 74% had observed two or more weeks of classrooms, while less than 10% had been in a classroom for a term or more.

Attitudes About Importance of Games and Simulations

Sixty-five percent of the respondents noted that games and simulations could be an important (46%) or very important (19%) learning tool. Only 7% felt that they were a little important or not important at all; and 28% ambivalently said games could be a "somewhat important" learning tool. Females were more positive (70%) than males (53%), who in turn were more ambivalent than negative about the matter. There was no discernable generation gap in the recognition of the potential importance of games and simulations as learning tools.

Before College, Gamer Teachers Outplay Boomers, and Strategy Games Rule

Respondents under 34 years of age reported 2.21 games played before college, while those over 34 years reported a mean of 0.90 games (t=4.04, p < .01). A small percentage of respondents (19.8%) did not report any games at all.

Respondents were asked about the game they played the most out of the ones listed. Strategy games were the most frequently reported, although this proportion is based mainly on one game—Oregon Trail—which accounts for 44 out of 54 mentions. No other single game is mentioned nearly as frequently. Respondents reported playing this game a median of three hours and a mean of 3.9 hours per week.

After College, Game Playing Declines, and Shifts from Strategy to Recreation

When asked about games played during or after college (adult), they reported far fewer games, with a mean of 1.09 and median of 1.00 games. Again, there was a difference by age with respondents under 34 years reporting a mean of 1.18 games and respondents 34 years and older reporting a mean of 0.55 games (t=2.057, p < .05). Nearly half of the respondents (47.7%) did not report any games.

Using Prensky's (2001) classification of computer games, no particular game stood out after college. The most frequently mentioned individual game was Solitaire, accounting for 12 of 32 mentions in the Sports/Card game category. Respondents reported playing their most frequently played adult game a mean of 3.7 hours per week and a median of 2.0 hours per week. The lesson for educators seems to be that games and simulations for learning are best employed while people are in the "learning mode" because once they start "working" games become a pastime.

There was a surprisingly strong pattern of association, however, with the number of games played before college being strongly related to the number of games played during or after college (Spearman Rho correlation = .60). Gamers before and during college stay gamers after college, lending credence to the notion that gamers (including gamer teachers) do indeed think, work, and play differently than non-gamers.

Table 4. Differences in learning styles between gamers and non-gamers under 34 years of age (* p < .05 statistically significant difference based on Mann-Whitney U Test)

		A. Being involved in a new, concrete experience (e.g., labs, field work).	B. Observing others or reflecting on my own experience (e.g., logs, journals).	C. Creating theories to explain my observations (e.g., lectures, papers, analogies).	D. Applying theories to problems or decisions (e.g., homework, case studies).
Not helpful at all	Non-Gamer	0.0%	1.0%	1.0%	0.0%
	Gamer	0.0%	1.8%	1.8%	0.9%
Slightly helpful	Non-Gamer	4.2%	6.3%	17.7%	10.4%
	Gamer	1.8%	4.5%	9.8%	8.9%
Somewhat helpful	Non-Gamer	11.6%	18.8%	41.7%	34.4%
	Gamer	2.7%	16.1%	42.0%	30.4%
Helpful	Non-Gamer	33.7%	42.7%	17.1%	35.4%
	Gamer	33.9%	40.2%	37.5%	33.9%
Very helpful	Non-Gamer	50.0%	31.3%	12.5%	19.8%
	Gamer	61.6%	37.5%	8.9%	25.9%
Mean Score	Non-Gamer	4.31*	3.97	3.32	3.65
	Gamer	4.55*	4.07	3.42	3.75

Gamer Teachers' Learning Style Ranks Concrete Experiences Significantly Higher

Our survey asked about Kolb's four learning styles, as expressed by Hartman (1995). They included concrete experience, reflective observation, abstract conceptualization, and active experimentation. Gamers ranked concrete experiences (e.g., labs, field work) significantly higher than non-gamers in helpfulness for learning (Mann-Whitney U Test $Z=-2.081$, $p < .05$). Gamers did not differ from other gamers in how they rated other learning activities (Table 4).

Being Daring, Creative, and Imaginative Matters More to Gamer Teachers

Respondents were asked to rate a set of 18 instrumental values taken from Rokeach's Value Survey. A series of chi-squares on the proportion naming each value first revealed that the gamers differed from non-gamers in naming "imaginative" as the highest rank value (p < .05, one-tailed based on Fisher's Exact Test). Four point five percent of gamers ranked this value highest, while none of the non-gamers did so (Table 5). In addition, when we look at the percentage of gamers versus non-gamers who listed an item first, another pattern emerges, which is consistent with observations of others (Aldrich, 2005; Beck & Wade, 2004; Prensky, 2001b). We see that gamers and non-gamers tended to favor different values.

Gamers tended to favor values such as:

- Imaginative
- Cheerful
- Broadminded
- Courageous
- Independent

Table 5. Gamers and non-gamers differ in values (* Fisher's Exact Significance (one-sided) p < .05)

Rokeach Values	Non-gamers	Gamers	% Difference
imaginative	0.00% *	4.50% *	4.50%
cheerful	2.10%	6.30%	4.20%
broadminded	8.30%	11.60%	3.30%
courageous	2.10%	4.50%	2.40%
independent	2.10%	4.50%	2.40%
logical	0.00%	1.80%	1.80%
intellectual	1.00%	2.70%	1.70%
capable	2.10%	3.60%	1.50%
polite	1.00%	1.80%	0.80%
forgiving	0.00%	0.00%	0.00%
obedient	0.00%	0.00%	0.00%
self-controlled	0.00%	0.00%	0.00%
clean	1.00%	0.00%	-1.00%
ambitious	15.60%	14.30%	-1.30%
helpful	2.10%	0.00%	-2.10%
responsible	12.50%	9.80%	-2.70%
loving	16.70%	11.60%	-5.10%
honest	31.30%	23.20%	-8.10%

Non-gamers tended to favor values such as:

*   Honest
*   Loving
*   Responsible
*   Helpful

Gamer Teachers Value Individualization and Customization

Respondents were asked in an open-ended question, "In your opinion, what are the three most effective things a teacher can do to help his or her students learn? Briefly explain why you think each would be effective." They were then offered three blanks to name a teaching strategy. These were coded into one of five types of responses: vary teaching (e.g. use different teaching styles); socio-emotional characteristics of the learning environment (e.g. be available to the students and show them compassion and respect); active learning (e.g. allow for student questions and make sure to listen to their inputs and concerns); teacher skills and effectiveness (e.g. be knowledgeable and organized); and customization and individualization (e.g. understand the students' individualized needs). Forty point two percent of gamers named customization and individualization as a teaching strategy at least once, while only 26.0 percent of non-gamers did so (X=4.627, p=.037). Gamers and non-gamers did not differ at a statistically significant level in how often they named any other teaching strategy (Table 6).

Summary

Preliminary evidence points to a few key differences in values and attitudes about teaching and learning held by gamer teachers compared to non-gamer teachers. These values align well with what observers have been saying about the gamer generation. In addition, many

Table 6. Proportion naming teaching strategy at least once (* p < .05 based on Pearson Chi-Square)

Teaching Strategy	Non-Gamers	Gamers
Vary teaching	26.0%	29.5%
Socio-emotional characteristics of learning environment	59.4%	65.2%
Active learning	20.8%	23.2%
Teacher skills and effectiveness	62.5%	55.4%
Customization and individualization	26.0%*	40.2%*

of the requirements for the gamer generation's preferences for learning are recognized by cognitive research on how people learn and are made available for learning through the characteristics inherent in games and simulations. It seems natural to expect that "gamer teachers," if trained and supported in using games and simulations in teaching, will be able to make strong connections with their students and provide them with highly compatible and effective learning experiences.

The research on teaching with games and simulations should pay attention to the values and attitude of the teacher concerning games and simulations in order to more fully understand the context of implementation. We should also expect to see a natural rise of games and simulations in teaching as the gamer generation teachers become established and the research mounts in favor of the positive potential of games for providing rich learning experiences that are well-matched to student learning characteristics. It would behoove programs that train future teachers to incorporate games and simulations not only because they are essential tools of the modern teacher, but because they match the learning characteristics of a significant proportion of the new generation of teachers as well as their students.

References

Aldrich, C. (2005). *Learning by doing: The essential guide to simulations, computer games, and pedagogy in e-learning and other educational experiences*. San Francisco, CA: Jossey-Bass.

Bandura, A., & Walters, R. (1963). *Social learning and personality development*. New York: Holt, Rinehart, and Winston.

Beck, J., & Wade, M. (2004). *Got game: How the gamer generation is reshaping business forever*. Boston: Harvard Business School Press.

Becker, H. (2000). Who's wired and who's not: Children's access to and use of computer technology. *Children and Computer Technology, 10*(2), 44-75.

Bransford, J., Brown, A., & Cocking, R. (Eds.). (2000). *How people learn: Brain, mind, experience and school*. Washington, DC: National Academy Press.

Burton, S., Calonico, J., & McSeveney, D. (1979). Effects of preschool television watching on first-grade children. *Journal of Communication, 29*(3), 164-170.

Chen, M. (1985). A macro focus on microcomputers: Eight utilization and effects issues. In M. Chen & W. Paisley (Eds.), *Children and microcomputers: Research on the newest medium* (pp. 37-58). Beverly Hills, CA: Sage Publications.

Cline, V., Croft, R., & Courrier, S. (1973). Desensitization of children to television violence. *Journal of Personality & Social Psychology, 27*(3), 360-365.

Collins, W., Berndt, T., & Hess, V. (1974). Observational learning of motives and consequences for television aggression: A developmental study. *Child Development, 45*(3), 799-802.

Grusec, J. (1973). Effects of co-observer evaluations on imitation: A developmental study. *Developmental Psychology, 8*(1), 73.

Hartman, V. (1995). Teaching and learning style preferences: Transitions through technology. *Virginia Community College Association Journal, 9*(2), 18-20.

Haugland, S. (1992). The effect of computer software on preschool children's developmental gains. *Journal of Computing in Childhood Education, 3*(1), 15-30.

Hicks, D. (1968). Effects of co-observer's sanctions and adult presence on imitative aggression. *Child Development, 39*(1), 303-309.

KFF. (2005). *The effects of electronic media on children ages zero to six: A history of research.* Report prepared for the Henry J. Kaiser Family Foundation by the Center on Media and Child Health, Children's Hospital, Boston. Retrieved July 1, 2006, from http://www.kaisernetwork.org

Lorch, E., Anderson, D., & Levin, S. (1979). The relationship of visual attention to children's comprehension of television. *Child Development, 50*(3), 722-727.

Lovaas, O. (1961). Effect of exposure to symbolic response times. *Journal of Experimental Child Psychology, 66*(32), 37-44.

Prensky, M. (2001a). *Digital game-based learning.* New York: McGraw-Hill.

Prensky, M. (2001b). Digital natives, digital immigrants. *On the Horizon, 9*(5), 1-6. Retrieved July 1, 2006, from http://www.twitchspeed.com

Silvern, S., & Williamson, P. (1987). The effects of video game play on young children's aggression, fantasy, and prosocial behavior. *Journal of Applied Developmental Psychology, 8*(4), 453-462.

Subrahmanyam, K., Kraut, R., Greenfield, P., & Gross, E. (2000). The impact of home computer use on children's activities and development. *Children and Computer Technology, 10*(2), 123-144.

USF. (2005). *Social cognitive theory.* Retrieved July 1, 2006, from http://www.med.usf.edu/~kmbrown/Social_Cognitive_Theory_Overview.htm

Wartella, E., & Jennings, N. (2000). Children and computers: New technology—Old concerns. *Children and Computer Technology, 10*(2), 31-41.

Chapter IX

Developing an Online Classroom Simulation to Support a Pre-Service Teacher Education Program

Brian Ferry, University of Wollongong, Australia

Lisa Kervin, University of Wollongong, Australia

Abstract

Evaluations of our pre-service teacher education program identified a need to provide more classroom-based experience for our students. This motivated us to embark on the journey of developing an online classroom simulation. The establishment of a team and the different areas of expertise we brought to the project resulted in a theoretically sound response to this challenge. In this chapter, we share some of our insights from our experiences over the past three years working on this project. In particular, we focus on the key stages in the development of the software, the roles we assumed, and the lessons we learned.

Rationale for Designing a Classroom Simulation

Having spent some time working with James Gee in the United States of America, Cambourne, and Turbill, two of our team members bought The SIMS™. This was one of the many computer games that Gee had discussed that engages the user in ways that involve deep level cognitive and linguistic skills. On the long flight back to Australia, while playing with the simulation, Cambourne had the idea that it would be great to create a simulated classroom that could be used by our pre-service teachers.

Once back at the University of Wollongong, a team was established to prepare a submission for funding to the Australian Research Council. The team proposed that the development of a classroom-based simulation would support both our pre-service teachers and the pre-service teacher programs in three key ways.

Firstly, it acknowledged that the work of a teacher is very complex and one that requires complex decision making. Danielson's (1996) research showed that classroom teachers can make over 3,000 nontrivial decisions each day, and these findings pose serious challenges to pre-service teacher education. The development of a simulated classroom would provide an avenue to support pre-service teachers to think like a teacher and participate in making "typical" classroom decisions.

Secondly, recent reviews into teacher education identified that many university courses failed to help pre-service teachers make meaningful and clear links between the theory of teacher education and the practicalities of the classroom. Batten, Griffin, and Ainley (1991, as cited in DEST, 2002, p. 104) suggested that the challenge for teacher educators is "…in helping students to make stronger links between theory and practice." The use of a simulation was identified by the team as one way to support pre-service teachers in making these connections while working within a "virtual" classroom.

Finally, the team concurred that the development of a simulation would provide pre-service teachers with an additional classroom-based experience. Like many institutions, we have limitations on how often our pre-service teachers can visit "real" classrooms. Indeed, the cost of the practicum experience, school availability, and university course requirements place limits on access. Ramsay's (2000) review of teacher education in New South Wales strongly recommended that pre-service teachers receive quality classroom-based experience supervised by an accredited teacher mentor; however, the provision of more extensive classroom-based experience does not guarantee quality experience. Darling-Hammond (1999) and Ramsay (2000) both conceded that school-based practical experience often consists of a series of isolated, decontextualized lessons prepared and implemented according to the requirements of the supervising teacher and at worst can be an unsupported and disillusioning experience.

Establishing a Simulation Team

The team Ferry, Cambourne, Turbill, Hedberg, and Jonassen worked together throughout 2001 to formulate the initial proposal for funding to support the development of a classroom-based simulation. Each of these initial team members had significant expertise to bring to this initial phase. Each team member was an educator with experience in both the primary and tertiary classrooms. In addition, each team member brought both national and international recognition to the team within their respective areas of expertise, Cambourne and Turbill within literacy education and Ferry, Hedberg, and Jonassen within technology and education. This team put together an application for the Australian Research Council (ARC), which was successful and provided $190, 000 funding for the project for a duration of three years.

Throughout the following six months, members of this team met each week to discuss and plan how to begin the development of the simulation. Considerable time was spent on the purpose of the simulation, how it might be used, and who would be its audience. Since Cambourne and Turbill had spent many hours in classrooms observing effective literacy classrooms, it was decided to draw on these data. Ferry and Hedberg focussed us on how such data could be used in a "virtual classroom." Once we had decided on a class (kindergarten), a scenario (teaching literacy through a focus on days of the week), and some key principles that we wanted embedded in the simulation (e.g., decisions about classroom organization, behavior management strategies, diversity, forcing students to reflect on the decisions they had to make), we were ready to get started on creating the simulation. It was time to find a project manager. Kervin, who had almost completed her doctoral studies and had recent experience as a primary classroom teacher, joined the team and began to work with the team to plan and begin preliminary developments of the simulation software.

Critical to the development of the simulation was the Faculty of Education's internationally renowned Educational Media Lab. Our team now included a computer programmer and a graphic designer who worked closely with the Project Manager to begin the development of the software needed for the simulation.

Two research students from the Faculty of Education have also worked within the project. Puglisi's (2004) research titled "An investigation of the role of an online simulation in supporting the development of the pedagogy of pre-service teachers" provided significant insight into the way that pre-service teachers interacted with the first prototype version of the software. Carrington's (2005) research provided insight into the decision-making processes employed by pre-service teachers as they engaged with the fourth prototype of the simulation.

The Process of Developing Prototype Software

Upon reflection, there are a number of key processes we have engaged with to this point to get the software to the stage it is at. The simulation software reported on in this chapter has been under construction since mid-way through 2003. At this time (2006), prototype version number 5 is being developed. A description of the processes we engaged with through the development of each prototype version follows. Each of these processes will be described, and time spent and approximate budget on each of these activities will be indicated.

Step 1: Planning the Simulation

Time Spent	Approximate Budget
9 months	$5,000 Teaching relief

During the planning of the software, two distinct activities were engaged with by team members and were shared and explored among the team as possible options for the development of the software. Each of these will be described further.

The Development of "Inputs" and "Outputs" to Guide the User

During the planning process, Stella™ was actively explored as a possible architecture for the simulation. It was acknowledged at this time that software tools such as Stella™ could be used to create simulations, and it became apparent that many simulations do make use of programs like Stella™ to develop outputs that reflect the inputs from the user to support student understanding of that particular system. Such a framework was developed within Stella™ to reflect the way that classrooms operate and was used to model how teacher, student, and lesson inputs interacted to effect key classroom elements such as student engagement, intellectual quality, productive conversations, and artefacts. A possible output of this process is represented by the interface and graphical output shown in Figure 1. It shows how the different components of the lesson, those represented along the top of the graph, are sustained throughout this period of time. This relates to Jonassen's (1993, p. 21) notion of "contextualizing the instruction."

Figure 1. User interface and output from the original model

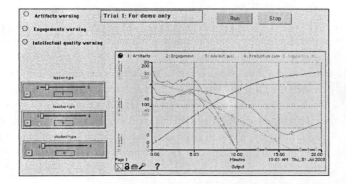

This model has not been used in the prototype versions of the software to date, but they did serve to focus the research teams' ideas around the relationships among key variables.

The Development of "Story" to Guide the User

Team members also began to explore the notion of teacher narrative in order to design teacher-created scripts. Pre-service teacher education often presents "abstract" knowledge, removed from the reality of the classroom. When in the classroom, teachers are called upon to integrate and apply this knowledge with what they do in the classroom, incorporating this into their "narrative of experience"—"this process of weaving abstract theory into a narrative of learning from experience generates an embodied living theory of practice" (McNiff & Whitehead, 2000, p. 38). We began to construct our own narratives with the focus on teaching "the days of the week" in a kindergarten classroom. We drew upon our own classroom teaching experiences and the data we had collected from the many teachers we had observed and documented. Each of us worked on "…fitting the data together so that the story achieves coherence" (Clandinin & Connelly, 1998, p. 170).

Our challenge in the development of our narratives was to capture the practical knowledge within these stories as we drew upon our own experiences and from those of the teachers we have observed in our research. The stories we developed supported the "vicarious experience" of the teaching accounts we were drawing upon as they typically emphasized time, place and person, and the relationships among these (Stake, 1995, p. 87). Discovering and making explicit the knowledge embedded in these stories then provided us with a framework to showcase and explore the reality of a kindergarten classroom. As we continually shared our drafts within the team we were able to draw upon those who had technological expertise to plan how this could "look" in the simulation. The sharing of our individual narratives within our team highlighted the differences and similarities between our experiences and allowed the three "perspectives" to come together. This then enabled us to highlight issues around classroom organization and classroom management along with four key teaching episodes that could be incorporated within the simulation. Barth (2001) acknowledges, "…with written words come the innermost secrets of schools" (p. 66). Capturing this in the simulation would allow pre-service teachers to be both exposed to and able to interact with the richness of these experiences.

We were confronted with the question of how to best learn from these stories, how to analyze them, how to keep the teacher voices intact, and most importantly how to get others with limited classroom experience to interact with these. The narratives that we had composed were interwoven into each other and one story—a teacher-created script—with many different options evolved. This teacher-created script then became the framework for the flow of the learning and teaching of literacy practices within the virtual kindergarten classroom to be focused on in the simulation. We had used narrative as a way of reflecting upon our experiences and viewpoints to communicate what we know about classroom-based literacy experiences.

Figure 2. Basic flow of the simulation

Step 2: Using the Teacher-Created Script to Shape Prototype Version 1 of the Software

Time Spent	Approximate budget
12 months	$100,000 Project Manager, Teaching relief, Programming, Graphic Design

The developed teacher-created script provided us with an emerging framework that we could use to structure the virtual classroom contained within the simulation. For the purposes of this script, the teacher was given a name, "Sharon." We then modelled the simulation around this teacher and what the possibilities were for her in this virtual kindergarten classroom. This enabled us to identify a basic flow for the simulation, represented in Figure 2.

This basic flow coupled with the teacher-created script assisted us in identifying key decision points for the user. From this process, we were able to identify some distinct "cycles" to incorporate within the simulation software.

Management cycles	Teaching and learning cycles
1. The organization of the classroom	5. Sequencing episode
2. The start of the day	6. Modelled reading episode
3. The late arrival of a student	7. Modelled writing episode
4. Random decisions	8. Retell of a familiar story episode

These "cycles" were expanded upon in terms of student updates and support material (in the form of excerpts from core textbooks, Department of Education and Training Web links, and additional reading material) to ensure that the user was both informed and supported in his or her decision-making.

What follows are three excerpts from this script along with an example of associated screens from Prototype Version 1 developed for each within the simulation. An example for each of the focus areas of the simulation—classroom organization, classroom management, and organizing the teaching and learning experiences—is provided. Each example is discussed in order to demonstrate how the teacher-created script provided the framework for the concepts within the "virtual classroom." These three examples highlight the way that the key issues of the organization of teaching and learning experiences, classroom organization, and classroom management issues have been addressed within the creation of this virtual classroom through the use of the teacher-created script.

Classroom Organization

The furniture comprises student-sized tables and chairs, which are arranged in "islands" at various locations in the room. The room was dominated by six "islands" of two tables each, (placed back to back), with four chairs at each "island." It means that at each island two pairs of students face each other across the width of two tables. Slightly behind these islands is another comprising a couple of hexagonal tables back to back with a some chairs on opposite sides. This "island" served as a workspace.

Along the wall opposite the entrance to the classroom there is a range of furniture, which serves different purposes. There is one large un-recessed cupboard that contains craft and art supplies. This is jammed up close to a series of tote-tray cupboards that poke out into the center of the classroom at right angles to the wall. Another row of tote tray shelves continues to about half way along the wall. Each of these has a student's name card attached near the top of the opening. Students seemed to make a beeline for these shelves to unload the contents of their school bags and to find materials they know they will use during the course of the morning session. A large electric heater and some shelves for teacher's books and materials fill the rest of the space along this wall. (Excerpt 1 from teacher-created script)

This description from excerpt 1 of the teacher-created script encapsulates one classroom layout the user is presented with. Our classroom experiences and observations revealed to us the importance of the way the classroom is organized for the learning experiences. We therefore decided to provide options as to what this could look like in a kindergarten classroom, and we scripted the possible consequences of different choices. In particular, we focused on the horseshoe and table groups layouts. To draw the attention of the users to this we built in the option for the user to select a classroom layout. Figure 3 illustrates the options available to the user—two typical classroom layouts we have observed used in

Figure 3. Classroom organization screen from the simulation (Prototype 1)

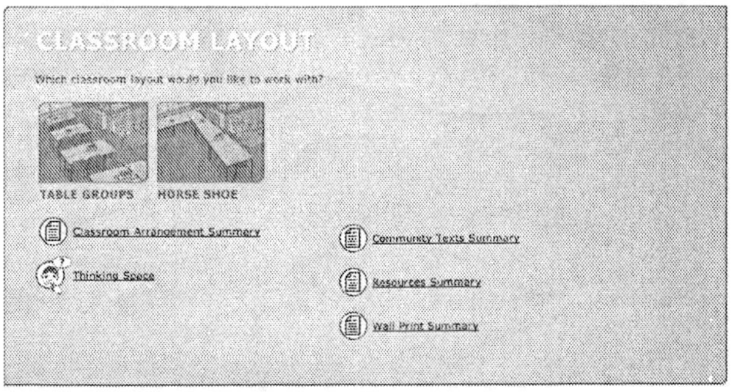

classrooms. Additional reference material is provided to enable the user to engage with the considerations that need to be made by the teacher.

Classroom Management

9:32 am: *The kids are finished packing up and putting things away and, except for two girls, all are seated in the WCF position, looking at Sharon who is sitting on the teacher's chair.*

Harley asks Sharon something, which is drowned out by the last few getting ready.

She focuses her gaze on the couple who are still not fully settled and who are still carrying out an audible conversation and says:

"Hands in laps, close your lips; you two were talking at the wrong time and I couldn't hear Harley. Most of you were a lot better than yesterday but there are still some children having a big chat. When you come to the floor you must sit with lips closed and hands in lap". (Excerpt 2 from teacher-created script)

Excerpt 2 begins to identify some possible classroom management issues to be included within the simulation. The screen captured in Figure 4 identifies some of these issues the teacher is faced with. Again, additional information is provided for the user to peruse in the form of a "classroom management summary." Subsequent decisions follow this screen where the user has to make decisions about how they will address classroom management issues that they are presented with in this simulated classroom.

Three targeted students were presented to the user that needed to be monitored throughout the simulation. These targeted students were developed by the team and were representative of three of the most difficult students we felt our pre-service teachers could come across

Figure 4: Classroom management screen from the simulation (Prototype 1)

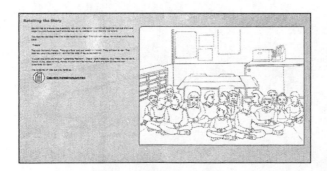

Figure 5. Sample of student update within sequencing cycle according to NSW Pedagogy Model (Prototype 1)

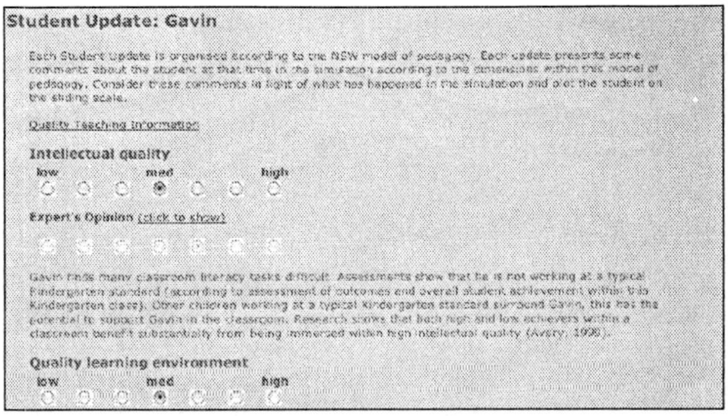

in schools. These three students remained constant throughout the simulation, and the user could view the impact of their decisions upon these students throughout the running time of the simulation. These updates are referred to as "student updates." Initially at these points a sliding scale was available for the user to plot the expected performance of the targeted students as identified in the NSW model of pedagogy. Written feedback was also presented according to these criteria so users can compare their predictions to that of a panel of experts. Once the user has made his or her predictions the user is able to select a button titled "see what the experts think." At this time, they will be presented with the plotting of an "expert" for that student at that time. Figure 5 shows an example of the teacher's thinking about the sequencing episode and predictions about how "Gavin" will respond to this. The user is able to employ sliding scales to plot his or her expectations of student outcomes at this point to each criterion. The user can then compare his or her expectations with those of experts (will be superimposed over the output displayed).

Random decisions are interspersed within the teaching cycles of the simulation. These were programmed to occur within certain cycles and are designed to expose the user to some

Figure 6. Teaching and learning decision screen from simulation (Prototype 1)

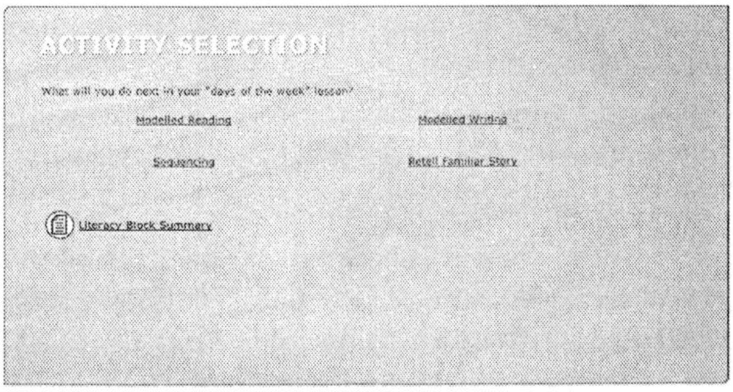

typical teaching interruptions and will impact upon the running of the simulation. These decisions include a knock at the door, a student arriving late, and a student needing to leave the classroom to go to the toilet. At each of these points, different options are available to the user, each of which has the potential to impact the users direction throughout the rest of the simulation.

Teaching and Learning

Like most modern infant school teachers in local schools, Sharon organizes her literacy teaching time using "Blocks" and "Episodes."

A " Literacy Block" is typically 90 minutes → two hours in length and usually occurs in the first or morning session of school each day (e.g between 9:00am and 11:00 am)

This "Literacy Block" is divided by Sharon into a series of shorter sessions, which she refers to as "Episodes"

Episodes are Units of teaching-learning behavior that the teachers purposely plans and runs for the purpose of creating opportunities for her students to learn the skills of reading and writing.

These vary in time from 10 minutes to 20 minutes. (Excerpt 3 from teacher-created script)

Excerpt 3 demonstrates this teacher's organization of teaching and learning experiences according to a "literacy block." The screen capture from the simulation represented in Figure 6 demonstrates how this teacher-created script has been used. The user is presented with a situation where they have to select possible teaching "episodes" for the kindergarten class. An additional link is available to additional reading material about a "literacy block."

The episodes captured in Figure 6 were drawn from the components within the teacher-created script. In this version of the software, users were required to select one of the four available "episode" options and follow that cycle through to its completion before selecting a follow-on episode.

The Development and Incorporation of an Embedded Tool

An interactive tool, referred to as the "thinking space," was designed for incorporation throughout the simulation. In the development of this, we acknowledged that while pre-service teacher reflection is crucial to professional understanding, it is not a natural process for our students to engage with. As such, we needed some way to "scaffold" them in articulating their understandings. The "thinking space" presents three key questions developed to promote thoughtful decision making among the simulation users. The help screen shown

Figure 7. The thinking space (Prototype 1)

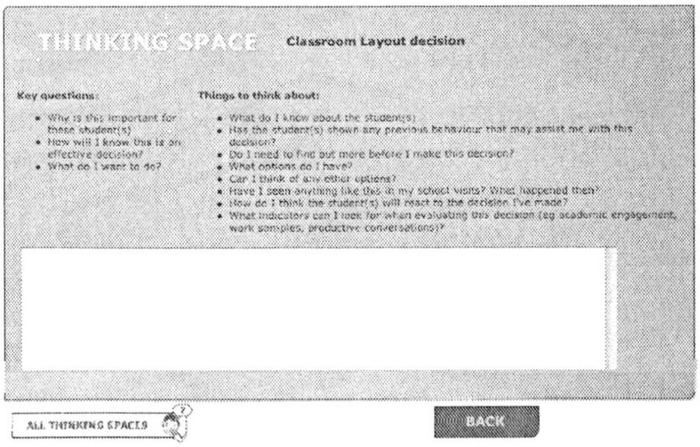

on the right hand side, which offers prompts and additional things for the user to consider, supports these key questions. The design of the "thinking space" as incorporated within the initial simulation prototype is shown in Figure 7.

The "thinking space" tool in the first prototype of the software was designed to appear at decisive points throughout the running time of the simulation. This tool is a space for the user to plan and justify new decisions, and to reflect upon the consequences of previous decisions. The user types reflections and thoughts into the blank space and can save notes. The user is able to retrieve and review their previous decisions and thoughts throughout the duration of the simulation. The user is able to revisit previous spaces and add to comments previously made.

Step 3: Trial of the Simulation Software

Time Spent	Approximate Budget
2 months	$10,000 Project Manager, Teaching relief, programming

Our first trial of the simulation was conducted in the first semester of 2004 with a cohort of 24 pre-service teachers. These pre-service teachers were enrolled in their first session of the Bachelor of Teaching program. The participants engaged with the simulation software for two 90-minute sessions over a two-week period. During the introductory session the group was broken in to two sub-groups of 12, and each sub-group spent 90 minutes familiarizing themselves with the simulation. In these sessions, three researchers took field notes. The users were videotaped, and audio recorders were placed randomly on computer workstations to capture dialogue between the users. Each member of this cohort was provided access to the simulation via a CD copy after this introductory session. Another 90-minute session was held with these participants the following week where they once again engaged with

Figure 8. Teaching and learning decisions

Reading	Writing	Language Activities
Retell of a familiar story	Constructing a text around that day's name and weather	Sequencing activity
Modelled reading using the names of the days of the week on individual cards	Innovation on a poem	Handwriting task
Modelled reading using a calendar	Recount of previous week	Poetry activity
Modelled reading using a poem	Creation of a daily schedule	Search for the days of the week in community texts

the simulation with the researchers present. Twenty-one of the users gave the researchers permission to download and analyze their personal thinking space entries. These data were analyzed, and a purposive sample of four users were then interviewed. The interviews were audio-recorded, transcribed, and analyzed.

This trial identified that the simulation appeared to support them with issues around classroom organization, classroom management, and the organization of teaching and learning experiences. The data collected in this trial indicated that while the participants were immersed in the virtual classroom created from the script, these pre-service teachers engaged in processes of connecting experiences, problem solving, critiquing the simulation teacher, and reflective practice.

In addition, the interaction of the students with the simulation software identified a number of implications for the design features of the simulation that needed further investigation. In particular, the students noted the need for consistent navigation throughout the software, the ability to save and re-enter the software, the need for increased teaching and learning options, and decision points. At this time, collaboration occurred again among the team members to prioritize the identified areas and further refine the software.

Figure 9. Simulation design features (Prototype 2)

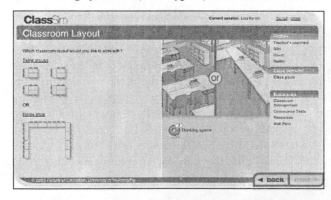

Step 4: Refining the Software

Time Spent	Approximate Budget
9 months	$60,000 Project Manager, Programming, Graphic Designs

A consistent theme in the recommendations from the pre-service teachers that trialed the software in 2004 was the need for increased options within the simulation software, particularly with regard to the teaching and learning experiences available. The initial teacher-created script provided three main episodes for the user to engage with. The process of creating this script had provided the research team with a way to combine classroom-based teaching experience with classroom-based research. Kervin engaged with several visits to kindergarten classrooms to collect additional data on how teachers' engaged children with the concept of the "days of the week" in literacy experiences and used this data in connection with her own classroom experience to write additional "episodes" to incorporate within the simulation. These scripts were drafted and shared with classroom teachers and faculty members.

This process resulted in a range of possible episodes for the user to select from. The different options available to the user are represented in Figure 8. While these "episodes" are primarily concerned with the organization of teaching and learning experiences, there are elements of classroom management contained within each, adding to the depth of the simulated classroom experience.

In addition, the navigation within the simulation was streamlined to ensure consistency across the pages. In particular, the location of key information about the classroom was available to the user on the right hand side of each page. Also, the "thinking space" was able to be accessed from each page providing the user with the opportunity to engage with this tool at times selected by them, rather than the decisive points we had previously indicated in the earlier version. Figure 9 presents a typical page within the simulation demonstrating these design features.

Also, the student update pages were reviewed according to feedback from the users. Initially these were organized according the New South Wales Model of Pedagogy (Department of

Figure 10. Student update for Gavin (Prototype 2)

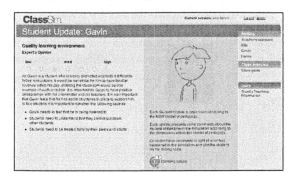

Figure 11. Student work sample

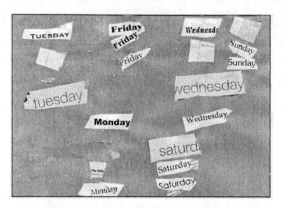

Education and Training, 2003) where the user had to plot the targeted students according to their perception of the students at that time in the simulation. Upon reflection, we realized that this task was too difficult for our typical first year student. The team's review of this tool revealed that this information needed to be represented in a more meaningful format for the users. A series of images representing how each targeted student might "look" at different times were developed, with different images imported on these pages to provide the user with a visual reminder of that student. The New South Wales Model of Pedagogy was also incorporated within these pages, this time with commentary and plotting provided for the user. These changes are represented in the screen capture in Figure 10.

Step 4: Authenticating the Virtual Kindergarten Experiences

Time Spent	Approximate Budget
6 months	$10,000 Project Manager

At this time the simulation software was shared informally with a variety of different groups. The project was reported on in the period of 2003 to the beginning of 2005 at five national conferences and two international conferences. Feedback was used to guide the re-development of the software. In addition, fourth year students (some of whom were employed as beginning teachers) at the University of Wollongong were given opportunity to engage with the software and provide comment and recommendations.

At the end of 2004 Kervin with Carrington worked with two kindergarten teachers in local primary schools on a number of occasions. During these visits, Kervin and Carrington in collaboration with the kindergarten teachers taught each of the scripted episodes. This was done to further refine the scripts presented to the users throughout the simulation and to also collect work samples from the kindergarten students to add depth and authenticity to the simulated experiences. This process stimulated significant discussion between two "actual" classroom teachers and two researchers that could be shared with the wider project team and implemented into the simulation software.

The work samples that were collected from the kindergarten classrooms were analyzed by members of the research team and sorted according to how the three-targeted students may have responded to the tasks within the simulated episodes. These were built into the next version of the simulation to provide users with an indication of how these different children were coping at different times. Figure 11 provides an example of a work sample nominated for Harley.

Step 5: Trial of the Software

Time Spent	Approximate Budget
3 months	$5,000 Project Manager, Teaching relief, programming

As significant changes had occurred with the infrastructure of the simulation, a pilot study was conducted with a cohort of 24 first year students enrolled in an alternate mode of the Bachelor of Teaching degree at the University of Wollongong. This trial was conducted in order to ensure that the basic running features of the simulation were working and to identify and respond to any navigational issues before the next trial.

In April 2005, 186 first year students enrolled in the Bachelor of Teaching degree at the University engaged with the fourth version of the simulation prototype. Each student worked with the simulation for two 60-minute sessions within the context of a core subject titled Curriculum and Pedagogy 1. A purposive sample of students was identified before use of the simulation, and these participants were interviewed before using the software. Throughout the two lab sessions, three researchers observed participants; audio and video recordings were also made during this time. Entries into the thinking spaces were downloaded and analyzed. Each of the participants was interviewed after these sessions using researcher field notes and thinking space entries as stimulated recall to guide the dialogue between a researcher and the participant.

In May 2006, we will trial prototype version 5 of the software with the new cohort of first year students. This version will incorporate many new design features (such as audio, increased options, and an increased number of virtual students to impact upon the user's experience). At this stage, the research design for this trial is still being planned.

Challenges and Problems for the Project

Originally, the proposal for the project was to develop a simulation. While this remained the final goal, what we have been able to achieve with the money and time available for the project is not as interactive as we had initially hoped. The software that we have developed has a strong theoretical base as it draws upon significant research and classroom-based experience. However, we acknowledge that it is more of a "walk-through" of a classroom with some interactivity rather than an actual simulation. Each prototype version has revealed numerous things that we could do in order to make it more interactive; however, these have had to be prioritized according to available expertise, financial, and time constraints.

The ever-increasing size of the research team involved with the project was at times difficult to manage. At different stages throughout the project, team members had increased or decreased input into the developed software according to areas of expertise. A conscious effort has been made throughout the duration of the project to consistently involve team members and acknowledge areas of expertise.

Lessons from the Field

In hindsight, we spent time throughout this project exploring avenues that were not necessarily used in the prototypes that were developed. While this may be seen as a waste of time, we found that these "tangents" did serve to focus the team on what it was we wanted to encapsulate in the software we ultimately produce.

The number involved in our project team enabled us to have a wide range of expertise at hand to support the development of prototype software. Each team member made a valuable contribution to the project and needed time to be "heard" by others. The employment of someone to oversee this process and manage the team members was crucial to the cohesiveness of the project over its duration.

Future Directions for the Team

Our experiences with the cohorts of pre-service teachers who have trialled the different prototypes have showed that the simulation design has the potential to engage pre-service teachers in deep thinking about the work of teachers and how this may look in a classroom environment. Many users, in their interaction with the software, have demonstrated that the simulation supports them in linking their school-based experiences and the theory presented in their pre-service teacher education training to classroom practice. Responses from students include: use of the simulation assisted her to "put things into perspective," "…it was the closest thing to actually being in a classroom that I have experienced at university. It gave me something that was really tangible," and "the simulation helped me understand that the work of a teacher is complex." Comments like these motivate the team to keep exploring simulation as a way to support pre-service teacher education programs.

References

Barth, R. S. (1990). *Improving schools from within: teachers, parents and principals can make the difference.* San Francisco: Jossey-Bass Publishers.

Clandinin, D. J., & Connelly, F. M. (1998). Personal experience methods. In N. K. Denzin & Y. S. Lincoln (Eds.), *Collecting and interpreting qualitative materials* (pp. 150-178). Thousand Oaks, CA: Sage Publications.

Danielson, C. (1996). *Enhancing professional practice: A framework for teaching.* Alexandria, VA: Association for Supervision and Curriculum Development.

Darling-Hammond, L. (1999). Teacher education: Rethinking practice and policy. *Unicorn, 25*(1), 31-48.

Department of Education, Science and Training. (2002). *An ethic of care: Effective programmes for beginning teachers.* Sydney: Commonwealth of Australia.

Department of Education and Training (2003). *Quality teaching in NSW public schools: Discussion paper.* Sydney: Professional Support and Curriculum Directorate.

Jonassen, D. H., & Grabowski, B. L. (1993). *Handbook of individual differences, learning and instruction.* Hillsdale, NJ: Lawrence Erlbaum Associates, Publishers.

McNiff, J., accompanied by Whitehead, J. (2000). *Action research in organisations.* London: Routledge Studies in Human Resource Development.

Ramsey, G. (2000). *Quality matters revitalising teaching: Critical times, critical choices. Report of the Review of Teacher Education in NSW.* Sydney: NSW Department of Education and Training.

Puglisi, S. (2004). *An investigation of the role of an online simulation in supporting the development of the pedagogy of pre-service teachers.* Unpublished master's thesis, University of Wollongong, Australia.

Stake, R. E. (1995). *The art of case study research.* Thousand Oaks, CA: Sage Publications.

Chapter X

Lessons Learned Modeling "Connecting Teaching and Learning"

Gerald R. Girod, Western Oregon University, USA

Mark Girod, Western Oregon University, USA

Jeff Denton, Western Oregon University, USA

Abstract

While designing a Web-based simulation to provide practice for teacher education students as they sought to master the complex skills expected of them as they produce work samples, the authors learned eight important lessons during the development of Cook School District. Work samples are a methodology for helping students learn to analyze their teaching by seeking connections between their work and student achievement. Cook School District serves as a site where teacher candidates begin the arduous process of learning to determine which strategies of instruction and assessment will result in greater student growth. The four years required to develop the simulation brought home eight lessons, often painfully acquired, that are shared with readers.

Introduction

Learning and teaching are not inherently linked. Much learning takes place without teaching, and indeed much teaching takes place without learning. (Wenger, 1998)

Many of us know too well the experience of sitting in a classroom listening to a lecture and having only a vague idea of the intended learning outcomes. Wenger's quote conjures images of the fluent professor behind the lectern dispensing information with little regard to student learning. Unfortunately, in the minds of many teachers, learning is the onus of the student, while teaching is what the teacher does. Though it may seem obvious that these two acts should be related, all too often, they are not. This chapter describes a project in which we diligently sought to connect teaching and learning in the minds of our teacher preparation candidates.

Perhaps more than ever before, student learning and the teaching that facilitates it are at the fore of conversations in education. Increasing societal diversity, economic instability, high stakes testing, and teacher shortages are significant factors driving this focus on student learning. Teacher preparation becomes, inexorably, central to the debate.

Research is clear that good teachers help students learn (Sanders & Horn, 1998). The question becomes, how do we prepare good teachers—teachers who can systematically establish connections between their actions and the learning of all students? This quest is an essential goal of teacher preparation and is at the heart of our chapter.

Current Context of Teacher Education

Heightened by the No Child Left Behind legislation, pressures for increased student achievement have dominated policy and practice conversations in pK-12 schooling. Teacher preparation has not been immune to this pressure, as teacher effectiveness has been targeted as a direct route to increasing student performance. As a result, the teacher preparation community is working harder than ever to prepare teachers who can affect learning in all students. Cochran-Smith and Fries (2005) have characterized this shift as one from thinking about teacher preparation as a knowledge problem (emphasis on analyzing teacher knowledge and problem solving) to one of a policy problem (emphasis on constructing policies and practices that analyze and make decisions about teacher effectiveness). The result has been a convergence of attention upon teachers and their abilities to teach in ways that facilitate the learning of all students. This "connecting teaching and learning" (Girod, 2002) has become galvanized through policy. For example, one standard that must be met for the accreditation of teacher preparation programs (see National Council for Accreditation of Teacher Education, 2001) calls for prospective teachers to "advance learning" (Elliott, 2004, p. 5), and teacher educators across the country are struggling to meet that call.

Teacher Work Sample Methodology as a Means to Demonstrate Teacher Effectiveness

One increasingly popular solution to this challenge has been the employment of teacher work sample methodology (TWSM). Developed 30 years ago at Western Oregon University, TWSM has been expanded upon and disseminated widely by, most importantly, the Renaissance Partnership for Improving Teacher Quality (see http://fp.uni.edu/itq/). TWSM is a framework or model for thinking systematically about the connections between teacher actions and student learning. This "connecting teaching and learning" is demonstrated through the construction of a teacher work sample (TWS). A TWS has several components including: (1) a description of the school, classroom, and community setting; (2) the targets for learning mapped to local, state, and national goals and benchmarks for student learning; (3) a series of lesson plans designed to move all students toward these learning targets; (4) a pre-assessment used to determine the prior skills, knowledge, and interests of the students; (5) a description of the modifications or individualizations necessary to ensure that all students reach the learning targets; (6) a post-assessment and data analysis section examining individual student learning, and; (7) reflections on teacher effectiveness and teacher professional development needs. As each of these products are constructed and represented together, they make-up a TWS. However, these products are not the goal of the process of teacher work sample methodology.

The goal of TWSM is for teacher candidates to gain skillfulness in several critical areas that will, when employed together in the work sample process, improve connections between teacher actions and student learning. These areas of critical skillfulness include: (1) analysis of the context in which teaching and learning will occur; (2) selection of content to be learned that is important and developmentally appropriate for the learners; (3) selection of pedagogical strategies appropriate for moving students toward these learning targets; (4) the ability to modify or individualize curriculum, instruction, and assessments in ways that allow all learners to be as successful as possible; (5) the ability to use assessment to support student learning rather than only to measure it; (6) the ability to employ each of these skills in ways that are aligned with one another—to best support learning, and; (7) the ability to reflect analytically and thoughtfully about the "value added" by the teacher. TWSM is the means to utilize these areas of skillfulness to effectively connect teaching and learning—as evidenced by the production of a TWS. In other words, the seven components of a high quality TWS (i.e. description of the school, classroom, and community setting) demonstrate skillfulness in each of the seven areas described above (i.e., analysis of the context in which teaching and learning will occur).

It is with these goals in mind that our work in helping prospective teachers practice insightfully connecting teaching and learning through the *Cook School District* simulation is situated. Before describing *Cook School District,* it is necessary to contrast the nature of different practice experiences provided by simulations for teacher education. The section on "Modeling an Experience or a Procedure" illustrates one such difference.

Modeling an Experience or a Procedure

Within the field of teacher preparation, two kinds of simulations currently seem common. First, is an *experience-based* simulation, where developers provide users an activity where widely divergent activities mark the product. A single user in an experience-based simulation may undergo instructional experiences not replicated by any other user. Experience-based simulations, residing inside non-linear curriculum outcomes and sequences, provide an exercise that is idiosyncratic from one user to the next.[1]

The second type of simulation is *outcome-based*, where users are to acquire skillfulness with clearly specified knowledge and/or procedures. Users are taught, provided practice, and receive feedback on their efforts to master the intended outcomes. The instructional experiences with this type of outcome are quite similar from one user to the next. *Cook School District* is an outcome-based simulation. Applications of this kind in other fields include typing programs, individualized mathematics tutorials, flight simulators, and applications commonly referred to as computer assisted instruction (CAI). In these applications, users move through the curriculum in an often lock step, linear fashion allowing for clear articulation of intended outcomes. More than 40 years ago, Kersh (1963) developed an outcome-based simulation called *Mr. Land's Classroom* that taught teacher candidates 11 principles to help them acquire classroom management skills.

This chapter describes the lessons the authors learned while producing the outcome-based simulation, *Cook School District*. The experiences we encountered during our developmental efforts will be of interest to those whose work parallels ours, though those working with experience-based simulations will find several of our experiences informative as well.

Our Simulation Setting

Cook School District is a Web-based, interactive system allowing students to practice the skills necessary in the design and implementation of a teacher work sample. The purpose of a TWS is to serve as a demonstration of a prospective teacher's skill in connecting teaching and learning. *Cook School District* simulates pupil learning that results from instructional strategy choices made by users. In other words, *Cook School District* invites users to decide how they wish to instruct a group of students about whom they are provided familial and scholastic information. The user designs an instructional treatment, and the computer identifies the outcome for each simulated pupil. The simulation has, then, an independent (treatment) and dependent (outcome) structure. The relationship between these variables is represented visually below and elaborated upon in the text that follows.

Figure 1. Variables within the Cook simulation algorithm for generating student responses

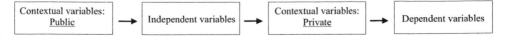

Independent Variables

The independent variables include six elements candidate users manipulate as they design their instruction (see Table 1). The users' descriptions of each variable become part of the interactions within an algorithm utilized to develop behavior patterns for the simulated students. For example, "curriculum area" is one of the independent variables. Real-world students respond differently to different curriculum areas (i.e. mathematics, art, language

Table 1. Independent variables within the achievement algorithm

Independent Variables	Specific Elements
Test sequence	Pretest, formative, post-test
Item type	Oral, written, performance, or constructed
Curriculum area	Math, science, art, health, wood shop, and so forth
Instructional strategy (see Figure 1)	Independent assessment, group assessment, group work assigned, independent information gathering, independent problem solving and explanation, discussing, practice provided, lecturing/explaining, modeling or models provided, homework assigned (see Figure 1)
Domain and level (see Figure 2)	Attitude—topical and self-confidence; Cognitive—remember, understand, apply, analyze, evaluate, and create; Physical—simple and complex.

Figure 2. Screen shot of the Instructional Strategies page

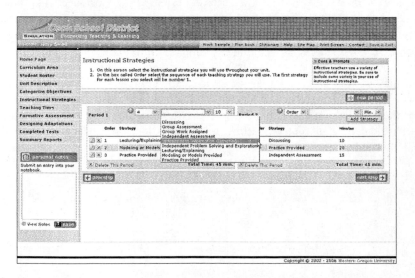

Figure 3. Screen shot of the Categorize Objectives page

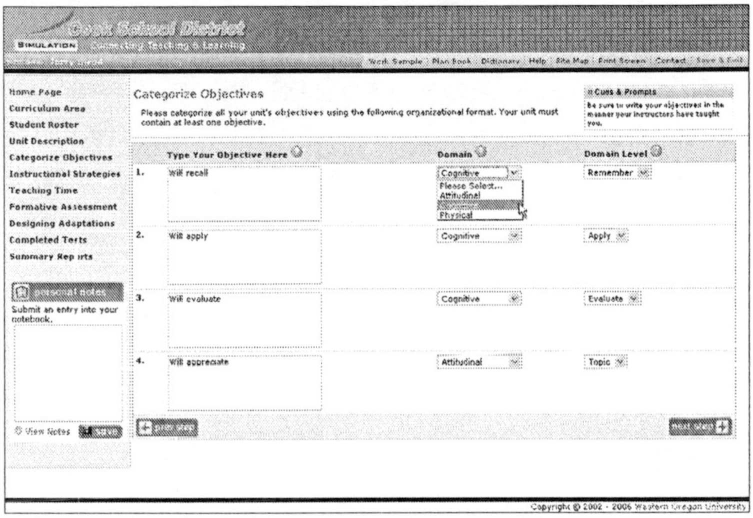

arts). The simulated students respond differently to subject areas they enjoy versus those they approach with limited enthusiasm. The specific components of the six independent variables are shown in Table 1. Users of the simulation select from the specific elements list (Table 1) descriptions of their decisions regarding the independent variables. As an example, a candidate may choose from three different options (pretest, formative, or post-test) for the test sequence independent variable.

Contextual Variables

The contextual variables include two types—public and private. The public variables are those made known to the candidate user and employed in guiding instructional design decisions. These public contextual variables include information such as:

- Parents'/guardians' names, addresses, and occupations;

- Siblings—number of siblings and student's birth order;

- Health and behavioral reports from previous years;

- Academic records such as attendance, grades from previous years, standardized test performance, current class schedule, special program inclusion (i.e. special education services), if any, and teacher comments;

- Activities—athletic, special activities, and membership in leadership/service groups sponsored by the school; and,

- Teacher/counselor comments—intended to be similar to those shared in a teachers' lounge.

Figure 4. Screen shot of the Student Roster page

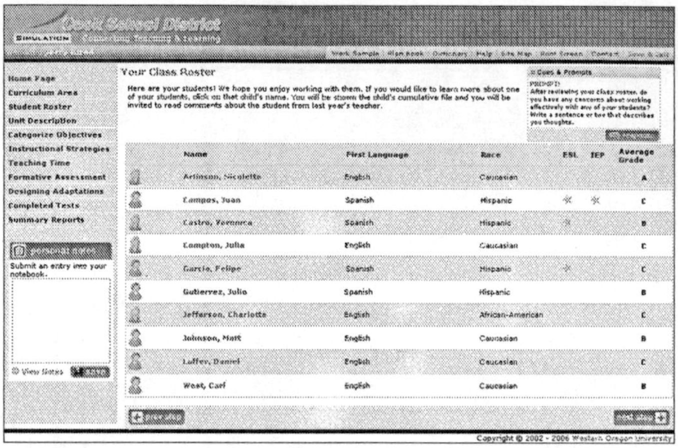

Figure 5. Screen shot showing public contextual file data for one simulated student

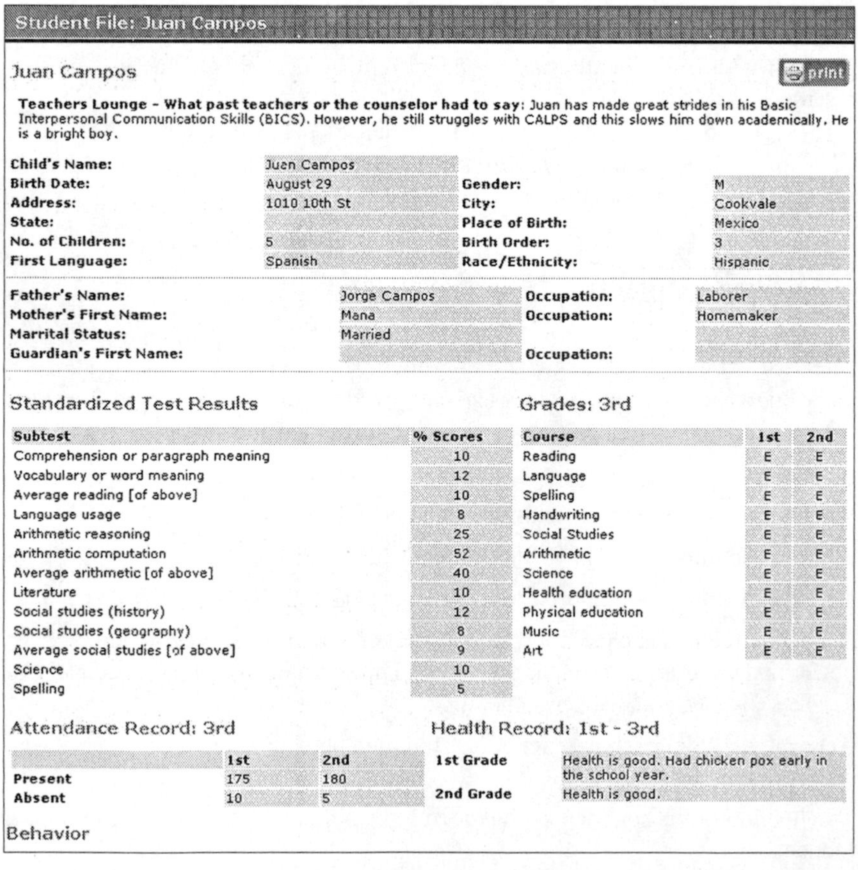

Student File: Juan Campos

Juan Campos

print

Teachers Lounge - What past teachers or the counselor had to say: Juan has made great strides in his Basic Interpersonal Communication Skills (BICS). However, he still struggles with CALPS and this slows him down academically. He is a bright boy.

Child's Name:	Juan Campos		
Birth Date:	August 29	**Gender:**	M
Address:	1010 10th St	**City:**	Cookvale
State:		**Place of Birth:**	Mexico
No. of Children:	5	**Birth Order:**	3
First Language:	Spanish	**Race/Ethnicity:**	Hispanic

Father's Name:	Jorge Campos	**Occupation:**	Laborer
Mother's First Name:	Mana	**Occupation:**	Homemaker
Marrital Status:	Married		
Guardian's First Name:		**Occupation:**	

Standardized Test Results

Subtest	% Scores
Comprehension or paragraph meaning	10
Vocabulary or word meaning	12
Average reading [of above]	10
Language usage	8
Arithmetic reasoning	25
Arithmetic computation	52
Average arithmetic [of above]	40
Literature	10
Social studies (history)	12
Social studies (geography)	8
Average social studies [of above]	9
Science	10
Spelling	5

Grades: 3rd

Course	1st	2nd
Reading	E	E
Language	E	E
Spelling	E	E
Handwriting	E	E
Social Studies	E	E
Arithmetic	E	E
Science	E	E
Health education	E	E
Physical education	E	E
Music	E	E
Art	E	E

Attendance Record: 3rd

	1st	2nd
Present	175	180
Absent	10	5

Health Record: 1st - 3rd

1st Grade	Health is good. Had chicken pox early in the school year.
2nd Grade	Health is good.

Behavior

The public contextual variables are presented to give the teacher candidate user an overview of factors that might be expected to influence how students will perform in class (see Figures 3 and 4).

The private contextual variables are those that bear directly on the simulated students' academic and on-task performance. Each of the nearly 200 simulated students is based on a real person and was described by an author who knew the student well. The simulated students were described by the author in terms of how they would respond to each of the specific elements that correspond to the six independent variables. The authors were asked to state the range of success expected when each of the specific elements was encountered by the simulated student. For example, authors were asked, for Item Type, the score range a specific pupil would have to each of the assessment choices. The simulated student Robert, who is very shy and very bright, has an achievement score range in the private file that is lower for an oral performance assessment item than for a written assessment item.

Dependent Variables

Dependent variables within *Cook* are of two kinds—achievement scores and on-task responses. Both scores are influenced by the candidate's use of the independent variables. The manner in which these variables interact, support or mitigate one another, and yield individual student achievement and on-task behavior is computed using the simulation's algorithm. The algorithm is a complex mathematic formula that weights each of the variables to produce a potential outcome range. Random numbers generated are compared to this outcome range and then converted to right or wrong answers or on/off task behaviors. The exact interaction of the variables within the simulation is based on the experience of the author with the real student who was described for the simulation. An understanding of empirical research developed around human learning guided development of the algorithm, but authors of the simulated students recounted performances of real people rather than a generalized population of students as would be found in a literature review. It was not the intent to perfectly model how learning and engagement unfold in classrooms (as if that is possible) but rather to provide a picture or suggestion of reality—real enough to allow teacher education faculty to draw logical decisions and inferences about teacher candidate effectiveness in connecting teaching and learning. The simulation designers and previous users agreed that reality is modeled sufficiently well to effectively practice important skills.

Using the system and variables just described, *Cook School District* was designed to provide teacher candidates a place to practice TWSM skills as they learn to design the TWS components. Because the TWS skills and components are incredibly complex, teacher candidates need a chance to practice them in a protected setting where they receive feedback. In such a setting, teacher candidates would neither harm their future students nor would they be precluded from "trying their hand" with new and even innovative instructional ideas.

To allow as much flexibility and accessibility as possible, *Cook School District* was designed as a Web-based simulation. The goals for the format of the simulation included providing teacher candidates a setting where:

- Sufficient reality was provided that candidates would believe the instructional activity helpful to the attainment of their professional goals;

- Candidates could try out new ideas and receive feedback regarding pupil achievement and on-task behavior;

- Candidates could access the simulation at a time convenient to their schedules;

- Teacher education faculty could use the simulation to provide additional practice without assigning the candidate to another practicum, and;

- Teacher education faculty could use the simulation in their college class settings to model and discuss professional skills.

As we strove to develop a simulation that met the above goals, we learned many lessons. From our lengthy and continuing discovery of good and bad design solutions, we selected eight lessons we learned—often the hard way. We hope our errors and eventual insights will be of help to readers.

Lessons Learned

Lesson #1: Decide Whether to "Approach" or "Mimic" Reality

One of the illusions we had to dispel when introducing the simulation to faculty users was *Cook School District* is not a space designed for student users to try out their lessons before they actually employed them in real classrooms with real pupils. Though they certainly could do this, it was never our intention to give users a preview of how their lessons might work in the real world. The *Cook* simulation was designed as a practice space, not a testing arena.[2]

Because of its role as a practice space, the *Cook* simulation provides more guidance or "clues for success" than many other simulations. This is an advantage over a real-world teaching setting, where prospective teachers rarely receive any feedback about how to work more effectively with students. Aldrich (2005) provides a useful analysis of this issue by describing successful simulations as needing either high fidelity with the real world and low pedagogical guidance *or* low fidelity and high levels of pedagogical guidance. Knowing that we simply could not simulate very high levels of fidelity with teaching and learning in the real world, but that effective practice was still the major goal of the simulation, it became necessary to provide intensive instruction within the *Cook* simulation.

Initially, we struggled a bit trying to decide how much information we needed to provide users as they practiced TWS components and skills. For example, some on our design team wanted to provide three-dimensional figures to furnish users information about whether pupils were on-task during the work sample instruction. Because we were not making an effort to teach users to differentiate on-task from off-task behaviors, the need to provide visual signals was not necessary. We would have spent an enormous amount of time trying to decide how to portray, visually only, whether a pupil was on-task. While doing all that work we would not be advancing toward teaching the goals of connecting teaching and learning through the use of teacher work sample methodology. We chose, therefore, to (a) focus on TWS skills and components by (b) providing more pedagogical guidance while (c) maintaining a low-fidelity product. We concluded we needed to portray classrooms well enough that the *feedback candidates received was perceived as being useful in gaining professional content and skills*. High fidelity adds seductive details that, in our opinion, may have shifted the focus away from the central objectives of the simulation.

Lesson #2: Be Clear About Which Skills to Include—and Exclude

There are components of a work sample we excluded from *Cook School District*. Within a TWS it is expected teacher candidates will, for example, reflect upon their teaching performance and pupil performance to think about what needs to be done next time to improve the work sample *and* what the candidate needs to do to further develop missing or ineffective professional skills. We do provide information necessary to allow candidates to look for patterns between their plans and performance and pupil achievement, *but* we have no way to provide a controlled practice and feedback setting for users around that skill. Teacher preparation faculty could certainly provide feedback around making those connections—but we could not. Our support materials for the simulation encourage faculty users to engage students in becoming reflective practitioners—but our simulation does not provide feedback regarding this goal. We excluded reflection as a skill included in the simulation though student users are provided information necessary to perform the reflective components of a work sample (i.e. reflecting on student achievement and engagement data).

We knew if the simulation was to be useful to teacher education faculty we had to include practice opportunities for the following TWS skills:

- Selecting outcomes aligned to pupil needs;
- Categorizing outcomes by domain and domain level;
- Selecting instructional strategies aligned with the outcomes and pupil needs;
- Deciding whether homework would be expected;
- Designing assessments aligned with the outcomes and pupil needs;
- Designing adaptations aligned with pupil needs;
- Analyzing assessment data; and
- Analyzing on-task data.

We were very precise in stating for faculty users exactly which content and skills they could expect to find within *Cook School District*.

As faculty users thought more creatively about the simulation, they often proposed using it to teach other components of their teacher preparation curriculum. We now tell faculty users the simulation is not intended to be a practice and feedback device for topics such as:

- Classroom management and discipline;
- Recognizing when students are off-task;
- Supporting teaching and learning for social justice;
- Developing professional leadership skills; or
- Enhancing candidates' computer literacy skills.

Cook School District is a practice and feedback setting where candidates learn the content and skills associated with teacher work sampling. We think we do a good job with that task but make no claims beyond that to other teacher preparation components.

Lesson #3: Clearly Specify the Sophistication Level Anticipated of the Users

Because of our experience teaching candidates seeking an initial teaching license, often as undergraduates, we developed *Cook School District* with that audience in mind. However, as other teacher educators began to employ the simulation, they sometimes used it with experienced practicing teachers to focus their attention on a task like "designing adaptations," a skill many general education veteran teachers were not taught when they attended their initial preparation program.

Despite our care in planning and designing user materials, we often failed to anticipate the level of sophistication necessary to use the simulation effectively. For example, in early pilot testing of the *Cook* simulation, we asked pre-service teachers new to their preparation program to engage in use of the simulation. Though the organization of the simulation seemed to make sense to them, as did the general tasks they were asked to complete, we failed to anticipate which conceptual understandings and language patterns were necessary for full and successful use of the simulation. For example, students sometimes could not find a teaching strategy in our list they had learned in their preparation programs. We were required to provide much clearer guidelines for the introduction and use of the simulation with those students in mind.

We developed user guides, including activities and materials for both faculty and candidate users. *It became clear that we needed to specify for whom the guides were intended — novices or veterans **and** those who taught them.* Recently, we have begun to devise guides for veteran teachers and those who teach them.

We now design user outcomes and activities that distinguish between novice and veteran teachers around common topics like lesson planning, designing assessments, selecting adaptations, and analyzing learning gain data. As users become more experienced in the craft of teaching, they are able to use the simulation to help them increase the sophistication of their skills in even the most basic tasks.

Figure 6. Screen shots of the various support features including personal notes, cues, and prompts response box

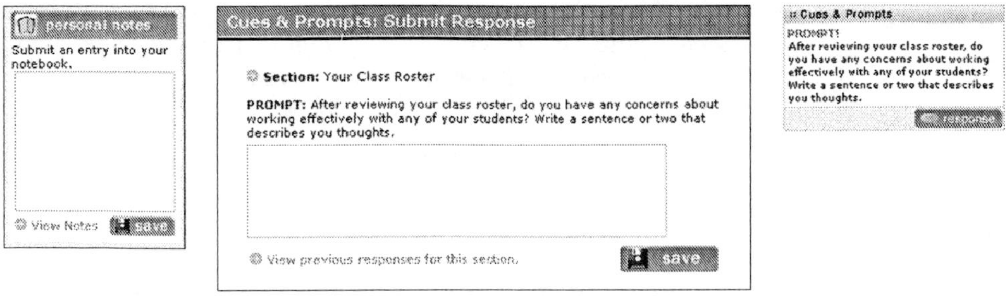

Lesson #4: Account for Both Faculty and Student Usage Preferences

The further we moved into the design of the simulation, the more apparent it became that candidate and faculty users had many more agenda than we anticipated. For example, faculty wanted help introducing content around TWSs while we intended to only provide a practice space. To help faculty users, we provided prompt screens to encourage candidate users to think more critically about their decisions while using the simulation. In other words, we provided questions and information a seasoned veteran of teacher education, such as we authors, would employ (see Figure 5). Because we were not sure, however, all faculty users would want that kind of support, we built into the simulation the option of choosing whether candidates would see any prompts or they would see them only the first time or two through the simulation. We also provided faculty instructional help—but only if they wanted it.

Faculty can also control the *Cook School District* environment in which their candidates will work. Faculty can select the size of the class, the racial composition of the class, the frequency of special education and English language learners, and the demandingness of the students. In other words, faculty can determine the degree of complexity the roster of simulated students will represent. For example, one faculty user reduced the Cook School District student population to five to ensure that each of his teacher candidates would have

Figure 7. Screen shot illustrating the "hover" feature over the key word "objective"

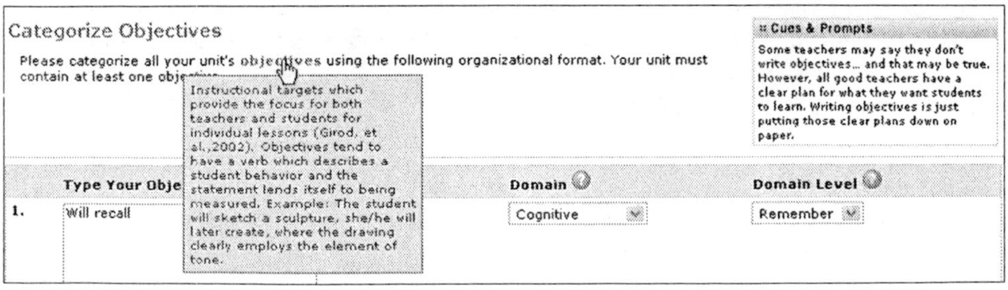

the same students in his or her simulated classroom. The teacher candidates elected to teach these five students in a variety of subject matter areas (mathematics, science, foreign language, art, physical education) using a variety of instructional strategies (lecture, group work, independent seat work). Using this common student roster, the goal became one of examining each of the five simulated students carefully to determine their individual strengths and weaknesses. This activity modeled the process of individual student analysis useful for all teachers as well as the value of collaborative analysis of student learning.

Some candidate users wanted to see more examples or synonyms or wanted reminders about how the step they were working on related to a previous activity. To help, we provided three supports—(1) prompts and reminders, (2) a format for recording their lesson plans, and (3) a spot for them to record notes or reminders to themselves. The *prompts and reminders* included invitations to see examples of "acceptable" user responses, requirements to explain one's decisions (see Figure 6), and/or suggestions or hints about how to think about a concept or teaching/learning issue. As users selected the goals and strategies for their TWS, a record of their decisions was recorded into a *plan book* that they could revisit at any time to review or modify their decisions. Particularly when reading about the simulated students in their "classrooms," candidates often wanted to jot *notes* about student traits they needed to recall. Additionally, when providing synonyms for terms, we used a "hover" feature over concepts like a teaching strategy (see Figure 7). If the candidate hovers the cursor over a strategy, synonyms or examples appear on the screen to help clarify what the strategy entails. In each case, however, candidates can ignore or not employ those options. *We designed the simulation to allow faculty and student users to employ it in a way most consistent with the way they wanted it configured.*

Lesson #5: Simulating Human Learning Requires a Carefully Tested Algorithm

Cook School District portrays simulated students responses to candidates' instructional decisions. It is a heroic endeavor though it describes only a few human learning patterns. In this way, *Cook School District* attempts to describe the "black box" of human learning and its causation. While flirting with hubris, our efforts turned out more positively than we hoped. Candidate users found the scores we provided were similar to what they expected and, typically, they seemed satisfied.

To generate those learning scores, the developers of *Cook School District* devised an algorithm to guide the computer in selecting scores for each simulated student on each item the candidate constructed. We found it necessary to bench-test the algorithm with many types of outcomes and many types of assessment strategies we constructed before we were able to judge the algorithm as providing realistic scores. We then gathered response patterns from candidate-designed assessments to compare against our bench-test data. (We also had to test the other half of the algorithm to decide whether it realistically portrayed on-task behavior patterns.) Those tests provided early data, and so far it appears the algorithm is describing human behavior well.

An interesting side note is candidate users who are "gamers" often want to know how to go about "winning" the simulation. After we explained that each instructional and assessment strategy will help some simulated students but create a barrier for others, the gamers began to understand their task was to enhance learning for all though they would never attain "100% of the students learning 100% of the outcomes."[3] Teacher candidates invariably noted that such outcomes, though disappointing, seemed to match their understanding of today's classrooms. *Describing learning within the simulation required us to portray learning as realistically as possible though there would always be non-human quirks in the data.* The algorithm that determines the outcomes variables is represented broadly in Figure 2.

Lesson #6: Remove Barriers to Enhance Use by a Wide Audience

When we first began design of the simulation, we thought of it as an instructional device for local purposes only. Within a short time, as teacher education colleagues remarked on its utility at regional and national conferences, the marketability of *Cook School District* became apparent. For example, as we have described earlier, we thought our users would be novice rather than veteran teachers. As practicing teachers became part of our audience we were faced with devising a new set of user descriptions.

Teacher education tends to embed into preparation programs local terminology and local expectations for candidates. Nationally, though, there are conceptual and language similarities across all institutions whether they are public or private, secular or faith-based. We needed to remove from the simulation any references to our local region—in terms of curriculum guides, agencies, and even descriptions of the schools the simulated student attended and where they were born. We needed to develop the simulation so preparation program faculty in Delaware or Alaska could use the simulation without needing to modify it. *With widespread usage as our goal, it became necessary to deal with the issues of variances of language used within the profession itself.* For example, some teacher preparation programs describe learning outcomes as goals and objectives, while others describe them as targets for learning. It became necessary to add supports within the simulation to help users negotiate these language differences. The task became one where *Cook School District* was developed so users around the country, rural or urban, could employ the simulation—so long as they were providing practice for teacher work sample skills.

Lesson #7: Evaluation of the Product Must be Encompassing (Recursive and Thorough)

When we first thought about designing an evaluation of the use of, and outcomes attained via the simulation, we thought only in terms of the impact of the additional practice using *Cook* on the quality of teacher work samples candidates prepared. The longer we worked with the simulation and listened to our teacher education colleagues, the more fully we came to appreciate the breadth necessary to establish the impact, if any, of the simulation. We needed to focus on the broad range of elements implicit in product improvement not just determining the simulation's influence on candidate performance. We needed to stop thinking only as researchers and broaden our evaluation scope to include service and usage documentation. Following are some of the questions we devised, across time, to guide our evaluations.

For candidate users versus those who did not experience the simulation, what differences exist in terms of:

- Attitudes about teacher work sampling
- Attitudes about the utility of this simulation
- Attitudes about simulations in general
- Observed skillfulness in designing plans for instruction
- Observed skillfulness in designing plans for assessment
- Observed skillfulness in designing adaptations
- Observed skillfulness in interpreting learning gains
- Observed skillfulness in connecting teaching and learning—developing plausible hypotheses as to the relationship between instructional decisions and achievement or on-task behavior

For faculty users, how did they typically view their experience with the simulation in terms of:

- Attitudes held about teacher work sampling
- Attitudes held about the benefits of this simulation
- Attitudes held about simulations in general
- Types of instructional activities undertaken with the simulation
- Types of feedback provided while using the simulation
- Number of trials with the simulation
- Types of controls employed while using the simulation—see lesson #4
- Amount of class time devoted to use of the simulation
- Position in the curriculum sequence the simulation took as teacher work samples were taught

As we began to gather data from faculty and candidates we found the more information we collected the better we came to understand user perceptions and usage patterns. *Asking evaluative questions helped us improve our product and our service to our users along with verifying its beneficial impact on prospective teachers.*

Lesson #8: Support Materials Need to Receive Developmental Attention

The excitement of designing a Web-based simulation is often tempered by the need to update the support materials. For *Cook School District* we developed and made available to users:

- A student user guide
- A faculty user guide
- Scoring rubrics for evaluating the construction of work sample components
- Attitudinal assessment items
- Example work samples
- Dictionary of terms within the simulation
- Site map
- Example context description for the simulated school district — Cookvale USA
- Help screens
- Response prompts

But every time we made a change in the simulation, the support materials also needed to be changed. It was not long before definitions were out of date, the site map was incomplete, and the terminology in the scoring rubrics did not match the concepts discussed on the screens of the simulation. All those constant revisions wore on the staff and required more discipline than did the creative tasks of devising new ways to improve the simulation. But candidate and faculty users felt alienated when they could not get the help they needed from the source and support documents we provided them. *We learned to provide time and structure in our work period to ensure the support materials were up-to-date and aligned with the simulation.* Prior planning in this regard is essential for simulation developers.

Conclusion

We are sure these lessons are similar to the experiences of others who have designed Web-based simulations, but they are lessons learned too often the hard way. We found our work important to our colleagues, their teacher candidates, and us. Because of that, we have enough courage to tell stories about our failures. We hope our lessons learned will help readers increase their efficiency and success.

References

Aldrich, C. (2005). *Learning by doing: The essential guide to simulations, computer games, and pedagogy in e-learning and other educational experiences*. San Francisco: Jossey-Bass.

Cochran-Smith, M., & Fries, K. (2005). Paradigms and politics: Researching teacher education in changing times. In M. Cochran-Smith & K. Zeichner (Eds.), *Studying teacher education: The report of the AERA panel on research and teacher education* (pp. 69-110). Mahwah, NJ: Lawrence Erlbaum.

Elliott, E. (2004). Student learning in NCATE accreditation. *Quality Teaching, 13*(1). Washington, DC: National Council for the Accreditation of Teacher Education.

Girod, G. (Ed.). (2002). *Connecting teaching and learning*. Washington, DC: American Association of Colleges for Teacher Education.

Kersh, B. Y. (1963). *Classroom simulation: A new dimension in teacher education*. (Final report, NDEA, project #886). Monmouth, OR: Teaching Research Division.

National Council for Accreditation of Teacher Education. (2001). *Professional standards for the accreditation of schools, colleges, and departments of education*. Washington, DC: Author.

Sanders, W., & Horn, S. (1998). Research findings from the Tennessee Value-Added Assessment System (TVAAS) database: Implications for educational evaluation and research. *Journal of Personnel Evaluation in Education, 12*(3), 247-256.

Wenger, E. (1999). *Communities of practice: Learning, meaning, and identity*. Cambridge, UK: Cambridge University Press.

Endnotes

[1]   Other experience-based applications include simulated dissections and the popular Sim series such as SimFarm, SimCity, and SimCoaster. Though much learning may occur, the outcomes are more difficult to define as the user controls the manner in which the application is employed.

[2]   Cook could certainly be used to test how types of students (boys, TAG, IEP) might respond to different teaching and learning conditions, but we have done no research, nor do we intend to do any, testing the similarity of our simulated students to those of real students.

[3]   An example we have used elsewhere is this one. If one chose to use an oral assessment, where students answered questions publicly, a pupil who found difficulty writing would likely be advantaged. But a student who was very shy probably would be hindered by an oral exam. Almost every instructional or assessment strategy will help some but hinder others.

Chapter XI

Educational Theory Into Practice Software (ETIPS)

Sara Dexter, University of Virginia, USA

Abstract

The ETIPS software is a Web-based learning environment that delivers cases that allow educators to practice instructional decision making. Here I recount its development but mainly emphasize the two key concepts that were central to our design process. The first was the Conceptual Assessment Framework, an evidentiary reasoning and design perspective that helped us to focus on which key attributes to build into the software and cases. The second concept is described as extreme programming, which is an iterative approach to software programming based upon user stories and rapid prototyping. The story of developing the ETIPS cases illustrates the need to know very clearly what the point is of the educational experience you are creating and to design software where form follows function.

Introduction

In this chapter, I recount the important aspects of the creation of the ETIPS software and its cases but mainly emphasize the two key concepts that were central to our design process. The first was the *Conceptual Assessment Framework*, developed by Mislevy, Steinberg, Almond, Haertel, and Penuel (2001); this framework helped us to focus on which key attributes to build into the software and cases. The second concept is described as extreme programming (Beck & Fowler, 2000), which is an iterative approach to software programming based upon user stories and rapid prototyping.

The story of developing the ETIPS cases illustrates the need to know very clearly what the point is of the educational experience you are creating and to design software where form follows function. The first generation of ETIPS cases was created with existing case-authoring software; halfway through this four-year project our team realized that this software constrained the sort of learning experience we wanted the cases to provide. During the project's third year we began to create from scratch software for a second generation of cases and an interface that brought to fruition our case-based pedagogical approach. We used the *Conceptual Assessment Framework* (Mislevy et al., 2001) to guide the development and refinement of each user story for the software; this helped us to connect form to function in the second generation of software and to recognize how our case-based pedagogy could be used with other topic areas as well. Thus, a side benefit of using these conceptual approaches was that we increased our product's sustainability through broader user bases, potential co-authoring partnerships, and licensing.

Educational Purpose of the Cases

The purpose of the ETIPS project was to create teacher education cases that were learning exercises about educational technology integration and implementation. The primary audience for our cases was pre-service teacher education classes on either educational technology or pedagogical methods. Key premises upon which we based the software for our second generation of cases were that teaching is decision making—and decision making is a process that can be taught and requires practice in order to learn—and that instructional decisions are guided by schemas, or mental models.

The cases allowed students studying to be teachers to practice making instructional decisions about educational technology use in classrooms and schools using the Educational Technology Integration and Implementation Principles as a schema, or the basis of a schema, for those decisions. By providing instructors nine virtual yet realistic schools among which to choose to set these decision-making exercises in it allowed them to give their students multiple practice opportunities to see how these principles can guide instructional decision making about technology integration and implementation in a variety of school contexts.

The six principles summarize what research suggests are the conditions that should be present in order for educational technology integration and implementation to be effective (Dexter, 2002). The first three educational technology principles focus on integration, meaning teachers' instructional decision-making process when considering the use of educational technology resources in their classrooms. Discussion of these principles develops the premise that a teacher must act as an instructional designer and plan for the use of the technology to support student learning.

- **Principle 1:** Learning outcomes drive the selection of technology.
- **Principle 2:** Technology use provides added value to teaching and learning.
- **Principle 3:** Technology assists in the assessment of the learning outcomes.

The last three educational technology principles focus on the implementation of technology at the school level—that is, how a school setting can create a supportive context that provides teachers with the necessary access to technology, technical and instructional support, and a positive climate for professional collaboration about educational technology tools.

- **Principle 4:** Ready access to supported, managed hardware/software resources is provided.
- **Principle 5:** Professional development is targeted at successful technology integration.
- **Principle 6:** Professional community enhances technology integration and implementation.

Unique Features of the ETIPS Case Method

ETIPS stands for Educational Theory into Practice Software. It is a Web-based learning environment in which students complete cases that are set in a K-12 school and focus on an educational theory. Unlike text-based cases, which are read in a linear fashion and emphasize the multiplicity of perspectives inherent in an event that is often told in chronological fashion, cases in ETIPS present learners with a scenario in which they need to make an instructional decision, and require them to select which information they think they will need to make that decision. The case is an opportunity to practice reasoning with a guiding theory that relates to the case topic and to develop an understanding of how the different school contexts in which the cases are set might influence how that theory is applied in practice.

This case approach emphasizes learners' metacognition—their thinking about their thinking—through a software feature called a PlanMap. The PlanMap asks students to check off what information they think they will need to make the decision posed in the scenario (see Figure 1); if they return to their PlanMap during the case, they will see that these choices are noted with a checkmark (see Figure 2). As students look at information in the case—and their choices are not limited to only what they checked while planning their search—the software records what they access and uses a different icon to record it on their PlanMap; in addition, experts' recommendations of which key items should be considered are indicated with yellow highlighting. Thus, the PlanMap provides feedback to the learners on their

Figure 1. The PlanMap page view initially explains to students the purpose of the PlanMap, and asks them to click in the box next to each category of case information they think will be necessary to access in order to complete the case

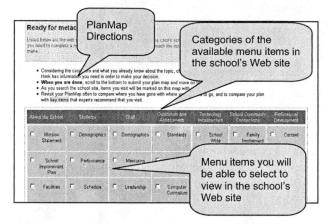

planned and actual progress as well as an in-progress check of their approach as compared to experts'.

Another formative assessment tool in ETIPS is automated essay scoring, which students can use to get feedback on their decision; this feedback is in the form of a predicted score of their short answer responses against a rubric before they submit it to their instructor for a final grade (see Figure 3). The automated essay scoring engine software compares the student's response to other essays, which were scored by humans against the same rubric, predicts

Figure 2. This close up of a PlanMap from a case in progress shows how checkmarks indicate items the user planned to visit; green arrows indicate what case information the user has viewed so far, and yellow highlighting shows which pieces of information experts deem as key for making a decision such as the case requires

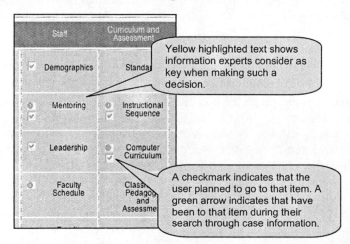

Figure 3. On the submit answer page, students can chose to save their work as a draft, use the automated essay scoring feature, or submit their response to their instructor as a final answer

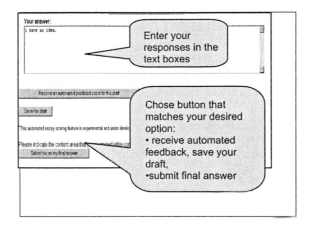

which score a student is most likely to receive, and presents it and the scoring criteria to them. In addition, if students have not yet been to the case information items that experts consider to be key, it suggests they review that information.

Figure 4. The automated essay scoring engine shows the student their predicted score for that answer, the rubric criteria, and suggests any of the case's information items they should also take into consideration

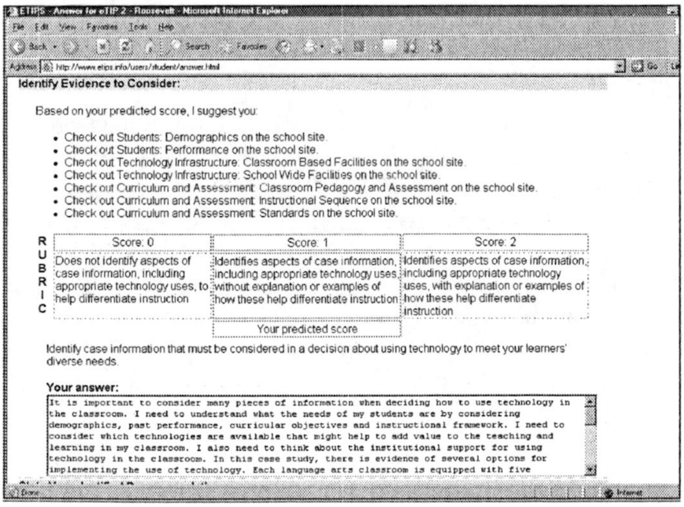

ETIPS Project Team Members

The ETIPS project was funded by a grant from the US Department of Education through its Preparing Tomorrow's Teachers to Use Technology (PT3) initiative. A majority of the grants were made to colleges of education; consortiums were encouraged, and awardees were required to include a project evaluator to collect data for performance feedback. The initial ETIPS team represented a strategic alliance among the project lead, which was a college of education at a major research university, a software development lab based at a similar type of institution, and a non-profit organization with extensive experience developing software and delivering professional development. Toward the end of the second year of the project, when the project director decided to create from scratch the software that was the basis for the second generation of cases, the software development lab agreed to bow out of the partnership.

At the lead university the team included the half-time project director, who had educational technology and teacher education expertise, a full-time project coordinator and two half-time graduate assistants who wrote case content and supported our test-bed of faculty members and their students, and a half-time project evaluator. At the non-profit organization there were two part-time collaborators who brought extensive assessment experience to the project as well as a software programming company with whom they had successfully worked and that we hired on an hourly basis.

Project Challenges

The major challenge that the project faced was articulating clearly the pedagogical purpose of the case-based learning experience we wanted to provide to learners. Because at the outset of the project we began to create cases using the software developed previously by the university-based software development lab in our consortium we initially assumed the learning experience functions inherent in that software. While aspects of the resulting learning experience worked well for this audience and these topics, other aspects were not well suited to practicing instructional decision making.

The first generation of cases was based upon the case approach pioneered by the IMMEX Software Development Lab at UCLA (Stevens, 1991). The IMMEX approach posed a problem to the learner and presented him or her with a menu-driven approach to selecting information necessary in order to solve it. The problem had a right answer, which—after having looked through sufficient case information—the user would select from a multiple-choice format. IMMEX software allowed case designers to elect to limit how much information the users could select through a points system. This rewarded learners who understood the correct problem solving approach and could recognize what information to seek out and how to interpret it because they could use the least number of points to determine the correct answer choice. The software tracked their information choices and graphically portrayed the sequence of their choices and the time spent at each using IMMEX's proprietary SearchPath Map. The SearchPath Map was designed to show learners' strategic responses to solving the problem. Each labeled icon on a SearchPath Map represents one menu item; the lines connecting the icons illustrate the path a student took in trying to solve the challenge presented in the case. Lines lead from the upper left-hand corner of an icon to the middle of the icon of the next menu item that was accessed. In this way, the SearchPath Map also illustrates the order in which students visited menu items.

The map on the left represents that the student explored many menu items and thus made a rather complete search of the problem space. The performance of the student at right shows only two general areas of the problem space were explored, indicating they do not have a firm grasp of the concepts underlying the problem that was presented

The IMMEX developers applied neural network analysis to determine the most common problem-solving approaches used by students who selected correct and incorrect answers, and to infer the likely student misconceptions that would lead to their taking such paths (Stevens, Johnson, & Soller, 2005; Stevens, Wand, & Lopo, 1996).

At the outset of the ETIPS project it appeared that the major change to IMMEX that would be required to create cases about technology integration and implementation for pre-service teachers would be to allow for short answer responses. Adding a text box for responses was easy, but soon our test-bed faculty members wanted online modules for scoring essays, recording the scores, and then reporting them to students. We also saw that the instructional decision making exercise at the core of the ETIPS cases did not have a right or wrong answer and that scoring was a key point of the analysis of IMMEX cases. Further, students' searches through case information did not result in predictable, categorizable sequences that the SearchPath maps could help illustrate. Consequently, our test-bed instructors reported that they often did not use the maps with students, which reduced the case experience's potential for helping students become aware of their schema for their instructional decision making about technology integration.

User performances and faculty feedback made clear to the project leadership team which aspects of the emerging vision of the ETIPS case-based pedagogy were not compatible with the IMMEX software's features, and so we redirected a significant portion of the project's budget away from this partner and to the programming company associated with the non-profit organization. This mid-course redesign was thus a challenge to the project's budget, timeline, and consortium partner relationships.

In retrospect, the initial design of the ETIPS cases in the IMMEX software served as a fast way to create a prototype and proof of concept for an online case-based pedagogy that was focused on student reasoning and decision making. The downside to this rapid start-up was that by using an existing software to author the cases it let us skip over what we now would argue is an essential step of creating educational games or simulations: articulating what you want to learn about the student's knowledge and skills, and determining what tasks in the game or simulation will elicit that information.

The data we collected through the evaluation component of the project reinforced the project director's impressions that there were discontinuities between our users' intended and actual experiences with the cases. The evaluation process enabled us to attend in a rigorous way to our test-bed faculty members' experiences with the cases as an instructional resource and whether or not their students learned what we wanted them to learn about the case's use.

At the time project leaders decided to create our own ETIPS software some project leadership team members had been reading about assessment design, namely the Conceptual

Table 1. Timeline for key development steps of ETIPS

Timeline	Key steps
2003	**Project Year Two**
April	Software development planning meeting with Green River
May	Consultations with Mislevy on Conceptual Assessment Framework Test-bed faculty meeting at end of Year 1 of generation 1 cases' use
June	Programming commences
July	Review of key elements in ETIPS engine with project leadership team
August	Alpha testing with students and faculty, usability expert's review
September	Programming meeting and beta testing with one test-bed faculty member's students
October	Planning for more responsive feedback to students on their case performance User interface planning for incorporating cases on multiple topics Co-authoring of cases on new topics begins with selected organizations Graphic re-design of interfaces for public part of site, post log-in, and cases
November	Programmer's meeting to develop PlanMap feature Systematic data collection on students' reaction to automated essay scoring
December	Begin discussion with publisher about bundling cases with book
2004	**Project Year Three**
January	New Web site interfaces deployed PlanMap deployed
March	Usability testing of new interfaces with faculty and students
May	Section 508 compliance review
July	Revise navigation scheme per users' and 508 report input
September	Implement revisions Design better feedback on answer to students per results from student data
October	Begin controlled experiments with students to determine impact of a student's use of the automated essay scorer on his or her essay's quality
2005	**Project Year Four**
February	Begin controlled experiments with students to determine impact of a student's use of the PlanMap on his or her essay's quality
June	Improve performance of automated essay scorer

Assessment Framework developed by Robert Mislevy and his colleagues. Applying this framework forced us to articulate what we wanted the cases to help the user learn, and what task we would create in order to elicit that knowledge and skills, and then how to interpret and report their performance data. Through this process we determined how our software could be thought of as a general case-based pedagogy where the virtual schools could serve as the settings for cases on a variety of topics. We then began to think of ETIPS as standing for Educational Theory into Practice Software and that the Educational Technology Integration and Implementation Principles, for which the acronym was originally coined, would be just one topic about which we would offer cases. We enlisted two other organizations, chosen because of their large member bases and project leaders' connections to them, as co-authors of cases about urban teaching and digital equity.

At the outset of designing the software that would anchor the second generation of cases, the software programming company the project leaders hired (Green River; see http://green-river.org), asked us to read *Extreme Programming* (Beck & Fowler, 2000) and to take that approach to our development work together. From the project leadership team's perspective as a client, this is a user-centered design process that is articulated through descriptions of desired functionalities called user stories that are then checked out through usability testing and revised accordingly. Thus it was congruent with our on-going evaluation process.

Table 1 recounts the timeline of the key steps during the development of the ETIPS software that anchored the second generation of the cases.

The overall budget allocated for the software development, as well as the domain name and hosting costs, over this two-year process was approximately $450,000. The personnel costs for the project director and coordinator and graduate students at the lead institution and the team members at the non-profit organization were approximately $640,000. Additional costs were incurred for travel to project meetings and for dissemination and co-authoring work that was undertaken. All the personnel costs given are for the entire life of the grant; during the first two years this went mostly for case topic conceptualization and case authoring work and in the latter two years it was for test-bed member implementation support, co-authoring, and dissemination efforts. The portion of the budget allocated for the evaluation work was approximately $210,000. In addition, the direct cost for the training and travel to project meetings for the test-bed faculty members' was approximately $80,000.

Lessons to Pass Along to Others

Games and simulations produced for educational purposes in effect serve as a sort of formative, and perhaps summative, assessment. That is, they allow the user to practice doing something that is based upon some key premises that guide the operational rules of the game or simulation. It is likely that through his or her performance the software indicates, among other things, how well the user understands those key premises. From the outset, the ETIPS project leaders knew we wanted the cases to be an opportunity to practice instructional decision making while keeping an educational technology integration and implementation principle in mind. But when designing the specifics of the software—especially what feedback we could give to the learner during the case—Mislevy et al.'s (2001) Conceptual

Assessment Framework helped us to work more efficiently, as well as with confidence since this framework draws upon contemporary learning and assessment theory.

The National Academy of Sciences report *How People Learn: Brain, Mind, Experience and School*, (Bransford, 1999) suggested that effective learning environments, among other things, are assessment-centered in the sense of providing multiple opportunities to make students' thinking visible so they can receive feedback and be given chances to revise and to learn about their own learning. The companion National Academy of Sciences report, *Knowing What Students Know: The Science and Design of Educational Assessment* (Pellegrino, Chudowsky, & Glaser, 2001), addresses principles of assessment design for learning situations aligned with the findings reported in *How People Learn*. According to Pellegrino et al. (2001), central to assessment is reasoning from evidence generated through a process consisting of three points: "a model of how students represent knowledge and develop competence in the subject domain, tasks or situations that allow one to observe students' performance, and an interpretation method for drawing inferences from the performance evidence thus obtained" (p. 2). Mislevy et al. (2001) incorporate these same three points into their Conceptual Assessment Framework by specifying it consists of a student model, task model, and an evidence model.

Almond, Steinberg, and Mislevy (2002) write that the student model is "the knowledge, skills, and abilities…to measure for each participant" (p. 35); the task model includes "the presentation material to be presented to the user…[and] a description of the work products that will be returned as a result of user interaction with the task" (p.24); and the evidence model acts as a bridge between the student and task models in that it describes how to analyze the evidence called for by the task model and so as to assess the student's understanding.

In writing about assessment designers, Mislevy et al. (2001) and Pellegrino et al. (2001) assert that networks, new media, and new methodologies have much to offer us in the way of support and enhancement of assessment but that technology has the potential to lure designers into creating complex tasks where substantial amounts of data are collected without any plan for analyzing how it can combine as an assessment of learner progress. To guard against this, Mislevy and colleagues (2001; Almond et al., 2002) promote using evidentiary reasoning and a design perspective during the development of instruction and assessment materials so that the focus remains on construct definition, forms of evidence in keeping with the construct, and the creation of tasks that would produce such evidence.

Extreme programming is an approach to programming developed by Beck and Fowler (2000) that describes how a team of software programmers works together with the client to efficiently create reliable code. Its creators describe it more as a set of values and disciplined approach than a strict set of steps. From our programmer's use of it and the project director's and other team leaders' experience designing ETIPS, this strategic approach was excellent for letting the design of a case-based pedagogy emerge. This included the focus on developing an overall metaphor to illuminate what you are creating and then expressing distinct aspects of functionality in user stories that are coded, reviewed by the client and users, and then revised as needed.

Extreme programming demands a lot of communication between the client and the programmers, often on a quick-turnaround basis. Further, to the degree the design process is driven by user testing, this requires advance planning for data collection, analysis, and reporting so that the code revisions can occur on a timeline that meets deadlines. Our team used a wiki to record our user stories and record notes from project meetings. The project director and programmers used a trouble ticket system to record the priority of the various user stories, recorded one per ticket, and their timelines and related communication. Working with the project evaluator, the project director and coordinator arranged for data collection from faculty and student users as needed. We also consulted experts on the usability of our site, including our compliance with disabled users' needs as specified Section 508 of the Rehabilitation Act.

Considering the Conceptual Assessment Framework during the design phase and following the approach advocated in *Extreme Programming* to bring that design into code can help creators of games and simulations work efficiently toward the educational purpose of their work. More importantly, it will encourage the development of assessment-centered learning environments, which we know will aid learning.

What is Next For Our Team

At the time of this writing the project has about six months of funding left and so in addition to refining all features and user interfaces and support materials, we are focused on creating a revenue stream that will ensure the sustainability of our work. Over the last year we explored various models for generating income from the use of the cases. We have decided upon three related strategies.

The first is to consider the functionality of the software and the case-based pedagogy it supports as a separate product that can be marketed to developers of educational cases on various topic areas. Developers would pay to license the ETIPS engine, and any income could help to improve the software. This strategy involved setting up working arrangements with a company that is focused on marketing the ETIPS engine as well as other educational software.

A second strategy is that we will work with the membership networks and organizations that inspired the cases that we authored on additional topics. They, in turn, may promote the use of these cases to their members, who may then purchase access to the cases.

The third, and most promising, strategy pertains to just the ETIPS cases on technology integration and implementation. The project director and a long-time test-bed faculty member are writing a series of books on technology integration in secondary science, mathematics, social studies, and English language arts. The educational technology integration and implementation principles serve as an organizational framework for the books; in the chapters about each of the six principles the online ETIPS cases are presented as homework exercises that learners complete to practice applying the main idea from that chapter. With this strategy the student who purchase the book is then very likely to purchase access to the cases, through an e-commerce functionality we have added. This model of students assuming responsibility for the costs of the educational materials associated with a class is familiar to students and faculty alike, and also allows our development team to leverage the publishing company's expertise in marketing, selling, and distributing the books, and their inherent relationship to some of the ETIPS cases.

References

Almond, R. G., Steinberg, L. S., & Mislevy, R. J. (2002). Enhancing the design and delivery of assessment systems: A four-process architecture. *Journal of Technology, Learning, and Assessment,* 5. Retrieved from http://www.jtla.org

Beck, K., & Fowler, M. (2000). *Extreme programming explained.* Boston: Addison-Wesley.

Bransford, J. D., Brown, A. L., & Cocking, R. R. (1999). *How people learn: Brain, mind, experience, and school.* Committee on Developments in the Science of Learning with additional material from the Committee on Learning Research and Educational Practice, National Research Council. Washington, D.C.: National Academy Press. Retrieved May 24, 2002, from http://www.nap.edu/html/howpeople1/

Dexter, S. (2002). eTIPS-Educational technology integration and implementation principles. In P. Rodgers (Ed.), *Designing instruction for technology-enhanced learning* (pp.56-70). Hershey, PA: Idea Group Publishing.

Mislevy, R. J., Steinberg, L. S., Almond, R. G., Haertel, G. D., & Penuel, W. B. (2001). *Leverage points for improving educational assessment* (Tech. Rep. No. 534). Retrieved from http://cse.ucla.edu/CRESST/Summary/534.htm

Pellegrino, J., Chudowsky, N., & Glaser, R. (2001). *Knowing what students know.* Washington, DC: National Academy Press.

Stevens, R. H. (1991). Search path mapping: A versatile approach for visualizing problem-solving behavior. *Academic Medicine, 66*(9), S72-S75.

Stevens, R., Johnson, D., & Soller, A., (2005). Probabilities and predictions: Modeling the development of scientific problem solving skills. *Cell biology education, 4*(1), 42-57.

Stevens, R., Wang, P., & Lopo, A. (1996). Artificial neural networks can distinguish novice and expert strategies during complex problem-solving. *JAMIA, 3*(2), 131-138.

Section IV

Using Real Space in Digital Games and Simulations

Chapter XII

Pervasive Game Design as an Architectural Teaching and Research Method

Steffen P. Walz, Swiss Federal Institute of Technology (ETH) Zurich, Switzerland

Odilo Schoch, Swiss Federal Institute of Technology (ETH) Zurich, Switzerland

Abstract

Today and in the future, architectural students must be prepared for designing both physical and adaptive, computer-integrated, that is, "hybrid reality" spaces. The question is: How do we easily and effectively convey architecturally relevant theories and practices of pervasive computing in teaching? In this paper, we present an instructional model that is a possible answer. During a semester-long design class, we supervised an interdisciplinary group of architecture and computer science students who worked together on a serious pervasive game prototype, which we will refer to as "ETHGame." The class culminated in a two-week intensive workshop and a presentation before school executives involved in strategic e-learning projects. The resulting interactive prototype takes advantage of our university's extensive wireless local area network infrastructure (> 250 access points), allowing for player geo-positioning, location-based learning and servicing, as well as mediated communication. ETHGame transforms the school's campus into a knowledge space, with key locations issuing position dependent and position relevant questions to players. ETHGame involves participants in an academic quiz by the way of a given university place, rewarding them for collaborating both face-to-face and online. The game helps players build a collective academic and spatiotemporal identity whilst being immersed in a sentient environment. Thus, in this chapter we introduce serious pervasive game design as a novel design, research, and teaching paradigm for Computer Aided Architectural Design (CAAD), as well as an e-learning design strategy.

Introduction

Increasingly, information and knowledge technologies pervade our physical environments—they are being woven into the very fabric of everyday life. Objects, devices, services, and people that surround us as well as the spaces that we inhabit over time are becoming digitally and wirelessly networked. Furthermore, our activities are becoming mediated by these technologies, often in a location-based manner. For example, museums use location-based information to offer guided tours of exhibits; credit card purchases routinely record the location as well as other aspects of transactions; and cell phones and handheld computers find the nearest and strongest links for networking. This third wave of computing is commonly referred to as "pervasive computing," and it deeply impacts how we design "sentient" spaces and resulting social situations now and in the future.

Pervasive Computing and CAAD: Games as Teaching Methods and Results

Architecture and Computer Aided Architectural Design (CAAD) in particular should reflect pervasive computing as a new field of interest through innovative research and teaching. We believe this field to be as important as other CAAD education cornerstones such as history, design, structure, or finance. In order to address this challenge, we have gathered a multidisciplinary team of architects, game designers, social anthropologists, and computer scientists at our chair. During the winter semester 2004/2005, this team has carried out a studio course culminating in an intensive two-week project together with 10 students of architecture and computer science, two women and eight men. The class has concerned the detailed conceptualization and prototypical design of a location-based "serious pervasive game," which we will refer to as "ETHGame."

Pervasive gaming integrates the technical approaches of computer gaming with emerging mobile interfaces, wireless and digital networks, and positioning technologies. By the way of this integration, game experiences are introduced that combine both virtual and physical game elements in computer-integrated environments (Figure 1). We define serious pervasive games as computer integrated games that conduce to purposes other than entertainment, for example, learning, security, building/environment administration, and management (http://www.seriousgames.org, 2005). In this kind of game scenario, players engage in an artificial conflict in a sentient, computer-integrated environment, resulting in a quantifiable outcome, which serves an end beyond the means of mere gameplay fun.

Figure 1. Gameplay situation: A player enters a sentient location, carrying a tablet PC

In earlier CAAD teaching, games and their level editors have been used to let students explore virtual and, often, utopian realities taking place within the constraints of the computer display (Engeli, 2002). Today, pervasive games allow students of architecture to explore their roles as architects who design not only passive space or displayed surface, but also physically based interactivity, dramaturgy, emotion, and social experiences over time. Yet in order to use games as a teaching vehicle, students must first learn how to design them.

The theme of a serious game can be learning—although it should be mentioned that, beyond this notion, we subscribe to Koster (2005), who argues that virtually all games are learning experiences, by their nature. So by designing such a serious game, students learn hands on how they can help others to learn. Fullerton, Swain, and Hoffman (2004) provide an excellent step-by-step workshop on how to develop game ideas from scratch. We have used their guidance and had students, over the period of the design studio class, increasingly detail their vision from pen & paper models over to prototype board games to a final soft- and hardware prototype.

Combined with the faculty's goal to solidly teach future architects concerning various aspects of building design, we did and do understand serious game design as a promising method to convey the technological principles of pervasive computing. Choosing this applied teaching method, we intend to lower the psychological barrier for architects to comprehend a complex and mostly invisible, embedded technological concept (Weiser, 1991).

Specifics of Serious Pervasive Game Design for CAAD

In contrast to most computer games and computer game design, pervasive game design takes into account the architectural "genius loci" of the physical "game board," including its everyday utilizations. These utilizations can be mapped with the help of social science techniques, for example ethnography, field observations, or interviews. Additionally, in our class, architectural drafting techniques were used to approximate location qualities such as spatial uniqueness, iconography, and atmosphere. Consequently, we have introduced students of our class to these techniques through lectures and exercises. The social science design techniques mentioned previously are even more important when the goal of a game is serious and when this project, in addition, intervenes in the public sphere, as does ETHGame.

Other academic and corporate institutions have developed a variety of pervasive games. We summarized these examples and introduced them to the students. This method follows the school's tradition in teaching architectural design by referencing and analyzing comparable projects. In our case, references included, for example, the mapping of the classic computer game *Pac Man* onto a real-world setting (retrieved February 15, 2006, from http://www. pacmanhattan.com); a smaller scale, social and collaborative location-based campus game developed at our sister university EPF Lausanne (retrieved February 15, 2006, from http:// craftsrv1.epfl.ch/research/catchbob/); and a hybrid hunting experience (retrieved February 15, 2006, from http://www.blasttheory.co.uk/bt/work_cysmn.html). Walz (2005), another of our references, describes a pioneering serious pervasive multiplayer game from the year 2002, which is documented in full detail at http://www.madcountdown.de (retrieved February 15, 2006). In the latter experiment, trust and mistrust were examined during an emergency bomb threat situation involving a saboteur amongst the crisis squad. Other experiments at our university have included, for example, a biofeedback game that allows one to direct computer-integrated building functionalities such as light control by the way of playfully manipulating one's own heart rate variability as well as skin conductivity (retrieved February 15, 2006, from http://www.building-ip.ethz.ch/education/Biofeedback).

Pervasive Game Design as a CAAD Teaching and Research Paradigm

When we understand pervasive games as systems of excitement and education in hybrid space-time, then learning to design these kinds of games becomes the act of understanding how to design for both learning and interacting with synchronously physical and virtual architectures. This is why we believe that serious game design—turned pervasive—can serve as a novel design research and teaching paradigm for technologized architecture. As an exemplary application of this paradigm, we describe the planning and implementation of our ETHGame course, its results, its documentation, and a number of future research issues in the following sections.

Instructional Organization of the Design Studio

In the following subsections, we outline the instructional and structural organization of the ETHGame design class from the planning phase until the final presentation.

Goals of the Design Studio

For the students taking the ETHGame class, we defined the objectives to (a) design a campus-wide game concept that would focus on online and face-to-face interaction; (b) incorporate geo-linking between physical locations and players; and (c) allow for interaction between players by the way of physical locations. We consider this approach a model for creating sentient architecture augmented with digitally stored knowledge, in that certain locations are being overlaid with an interactive "narrative character" that is only recognizable with the help of digital media and wirelessly networked hardware. Ideally, these enhanced locations become a player's play partner rather than a functional enclosure made out of passive walls. This way, our students become aware that pervasive games help built architecture to be experiential, emotive, space-time based, and entertaining. Furthermore, students also learn that mapping knowledge onto computer-integrated buildings results in novel approaches of drafting spatial qualities. Digital media defines these qualities, and digital devices such as mobile computers or media walls make them accessible. The resulting services are usually invisible, yet they have a huge impact on the perception of space through its overlaid information. In our exemplary class, we defined these spaces to be "knowledge spaces." From this perspective, physical architecture turns into a dynamic learning space and serves to connect people with a site's past, present, and future narrative.

Initially being a side aspect for the design studio, the ETH Zurich's 150th anniversary in 2005 turned out to be an ideal content database—the academic knowledge of the sites ("loci")

Figure 2. ETHGame map interface, indicating loci names and the player's geo-position

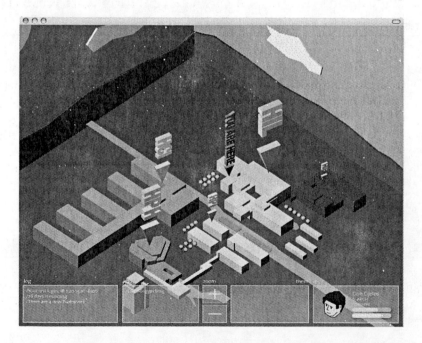

themselves would deliver information the spaces would be augmented with. During its 15 decades of evolution, countless generations of students and professors "wrote" small and big stories related to given loci, and therefore, left invisible traces in history that—in review—can be accessed through the ETHGame and its knowledge spaces. Figure 2 depicts an exemplary ETHGame interface that displays a map of the ETH Hönggerberg campus, a number of these loci, and the current player position.

Curriculum and Structure

Topics taught during the weekly three-hour long class included (pervasive) game design fundamentals, ethnographic methods, digital building interaction, media architecture, as well as wireless and mobile application design. We have met these demands with the help of our multidisciplinary teaching team, and individuals whose expertise we either sought, or who we invited for teaching.

With the help of spatial categories already known to architectural students, we exemplified pervasive game design techniques, increasing scale week by week. We used spatial categories such as artefact, one's own body, room, level, building, campus, and city. Each of these categories demands differing, though related, design approaches. In succession, students homeworked miniature pervasive games, addressing these spatial categories as their game platform. Didactically, it was a success to introduce architectural students to two new fields—pervasive computing and game design—based on pre-existing, agreed on architectural vocabulary. This method proved to be one of the key elements to our planned process, pushing the class at high speed.

Our learning-by-doing approach (Dewey, 1916) has helped to successfully convey the technical issues of pervasive computing. We also included lectures on formal and dramaturgical game design vocabulary and elements to the course, applying the techniques Fullerton et al. (2004) suggest. Besides this input, the course featured site-specific history research and pervasive technology lectures, as well as exercises in ethnographic observation of people's behaviors across the campus, next to spatial analyses of playgrounds, and game play flowcharting.

By analyzing campus locations, students identified the locations' specific "stories." These analyses led to a game design in which players and specific locations can communicate through the player's mobile computer. Moreover, we also offered programming sessions wherein students learned how to work with a custom "building intelligence" middleware (Strehlke, Ochsendorf, & Bahr, 2004). Additionally, during the beginning of the semester, two game design researchers—Jussi Holpainen (Nokia Research Center, Tampere, Finland) and Dr. Staffan Björk (Chalmers University Gothenburg, Sweden)—held a one-week voluntary workshop about "Game Design Patterns" in order to deepen the serious game design skill set.

Jointly, students and design studio supervisors settled on a basic game design concept by the end of the semester, after student groups had pitched concept ideas against each other. Game designer Jochen Hamma—chair of the Frankfurt/Main chapter of the International Game Developers Association (IGDA)—then visited us for a daylong intermediate game design review. This workshop provided valuable feedback concerning our results up to that point, as well as tips for how to carry on. At the same time, it strengthened the group feeling.

During the academic vacation period, students and professors finalized a core concept as well as an early, stable game prototype during a two-week intensive workshop that took place at the university. This workshop—we call it a "compact phase"—enabled students to concentrate daylong on the prototype in comparison to the timeslot during normal semester weeks. The workshop culminated in a presentation before e-learning specialists we had invited beforehand.

During the compact phase, we divided the participants into sub-groups, each responsible for a certain game development aspect, for example game design, prototyping, marketing, and so forth. Each group had to deliver its work packages in time to meet the production schedule, which the faculty had worked out in the role of "game producers."

Ongoing and outside of class lectures, tutorials, and the workshop, we also organized a se-mester-long lecture series entitled "CAAD:Perspektive: The Architecture of Games," giving insight into possible interfaces between CAAD and game design. These lectures were open to all students of the faculty. In total, we believe that the students of our class were introduced to serious pervasive game design quite intensely throughout the design studio process.

Class Twiki: Realtime Web Collaboration Tool for Successful Group Organization

A Twiki is special instance of an open source collaborative "wikiwiki" Web site, which mul-tiple site visitors can edit in real time through an Internet browser. Wikis offer a framework for easy, fast, and seamless documentation, teaching, monitoring, and communication. At the ETH Zurich's chair for CAAD, we have been using this handy tool widely for a couple of years, asking new students to learn how to work with it, too. Our large ETHGame Twiki Web site can be explored at http://wiki.arch.ethz.ch/twiki/bin/view/Game0405 (retrieved February 15, 2006).

Especially during the intensive workshop, the class Twiki proved to be an efficient platform for students to exchange ideas, organize, and update themselves concerning the overall progress of group and subgroups. Additionally, the ETHGame Twiki enabled the professors to supervise and monitor each student's working process. In return, the whole of the process as well as each student's results have been documented visibly and lastingly. We have found that the extensive usage of Twikis initiates both the usage of media, as well as competitive transparency, and group spirit.

Final ETHGame Feasibility Study, Concept, and Early Prototype

In the following section, we present the final core concept of the ETHGame, as well as an early prototype we finalized during our two-week intensive workshop: At http://wiki.arch.ethz.ch/twiki/bin/view/Game0405/ETHGameSessionFinal (retrieved February 15, 2006), you can download the complete feasibility study. On this Web site, you will also find an interface demo, movies exemplifying the ETHGame, as well as Java files you may want to integrate into your own serious pervasive game endeavour.

ETHGame Summary

The ETHGame prototype game is a location-based question and answer quiz-like experience in physical space, linking mobile computing and computer-integrated buildings. The game takes place on the whole of the city wide school campus, involving a virtually unlimited number of student and faculty players, and about 250 wireless LAN (WLAN) ETH Zurich access points. These access points represent interactive locations and their locative narratives. The game serves as a vehicle for transmitting and querying knowledge about the individual location's narrative. Thus, each physical location serves as a game locus and interface for the game, and the combination of locations serves as a seamless cross-campus playground. The pervasive environment of the building sites connects players and the game system. The final game is playable on campus with any mobile or stationary computer and a valid school network account. Upon physically entering a predefined knowledge space with a mobile device, the game locus will ask players location-dependent questions concerning general and technical, school related topics. Figure 3 illustrates an exemplary application interface for the locus "Baumensa," *engl.* "cafeteria of the architectural department." The locus has certain characteristics such as being "moody" during certain times. We achieve this by the way of parametric authoring of the locus; because we may change the interactive behavior of a given space, we may modify the current use of certain locations. For example, and de-

Figure 3. ETHGame main application interface, including dragable chat client

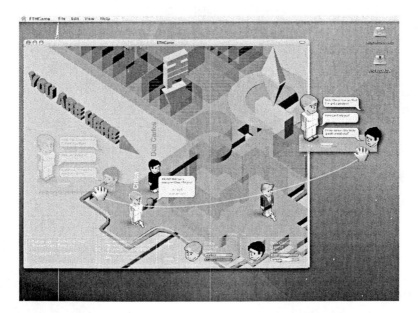

pending on the game state, currently unused spaces may become key spots for the player to achieve higher scores. Still, these attractive loci have to be identified by the player, because our knowledge spaces and their narratives are camouflaged by their conventional, pre-existing design. Theoretically, a permanent use of the game might influence both the use and the physical design of certain spaces. We assume that this form of puppet mastering computer integrated spaces, and, as a result, puppet mastering players, is becoming a defining issue in future architectural design.

Throughout the class, we were amazed that students had problems realizing that WLAN access point radio clouds describe blurred spatial areas, although this had been an immediate output of our initial WLAN based geo-positioning prototype, which had been tested in our

Figure 4. Sketches of departmental avatars and their level up instances

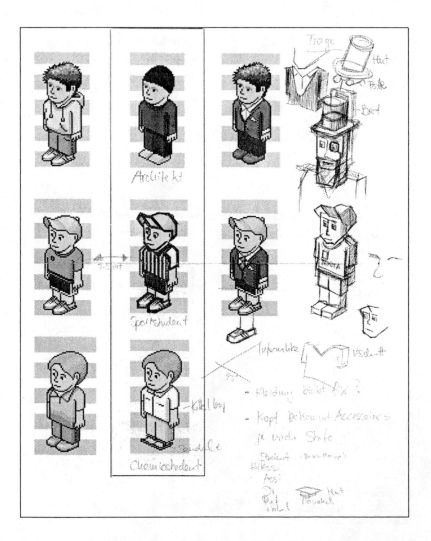

departmental building. Our students, it seems, were not yet able to leave behind the classical perception of space—they did not grasp *the stylistic potential of hybrid reality*.

For the player, ETHGame's gameplay foresees role-playing an avatar that has to collect points by answering loci questions. Starting out as a "freshman," the player tries to become the one and only Nobel Prize winner by climbing the virtual hierarchy of the game. Once a player reaches the level of a "professor," he or she keeps collecting points to ensure victory. Only one player can win the ETHGame "Nobel Prize" upon correctly answering the last question of the game. If a previous question has not been answered to a locus's satisfaction, a player has to consult with another player in proximity and solve the puzzle cooperatively. Game high scores are displayed on a public high score board. Players may also swap points for coffee discounts in the school's cafeterias.

The game's story underlines the social and collaborative, yet competitive learning nature of the experience in an ironic fashion: "The professors of the ETH Zurich conduct an experiment where physical rooms of knowledge take over the lecturer's teaching role. Meanwhile, the professors can devote themselves to their research. By ascending game levels through cooperation, answering questions (together with other players) and collecting credit points, a player can win the game and be awarded with the ETHGame's Nobel Prize." (excerpt from our feasibility study). Once implemented, the game—which is supposed to last for six weeks—could change the curriculum as the physical rooms take over the lecturer's teaching. In consequence, one impact might be that "real" professors may skip teaching (as it is suggested by the game), and concentrate on their research, for real.

Functional Specifications of the ETHGame

After having downloaded the game application onto a notebook computer equipped with a WLAN card, players choose a nickname, register with the game, and log into it. Each player receives a school department dependent avatar. For each school department, there is a male and a female "freshman" avatar, which changes over time and according to a player's level up success. Figure 4 shows exemplary avatar level up hierarchies for an architectural, a sport's, and a chemistry avatar; obviously, the graphic design has been inspired by the isometric online world of http://www.habbohotel.com (retrieved February 15, 2006).

By the way of departmental avatars, players easily recognize another player's background, which may help them in case they are seeking specific knowledge for answering locus questions. Figure 5 flowcharts how the game—as a whole—works conceptually from the player's perspective.

Our game's credit point system adjusts to the player and depends on a location's IT and WLAN infrastructure, as well as on the overall game service availability, so that players from smaller departments and only a few access points should not be at a disadvantage. On the other hand, we are rewarding courageous and enthusiastic players who explore other buildings and departments. Eventually, the game rewards those players who cooperate with another player when answering a question. This way, the game supports social interaction and community building, while remaining balanced with a competitive goal of winning the one and only ETHGame Nobel Prize.

Figure 5. Functional flowchart specifications of the ETHGame concept

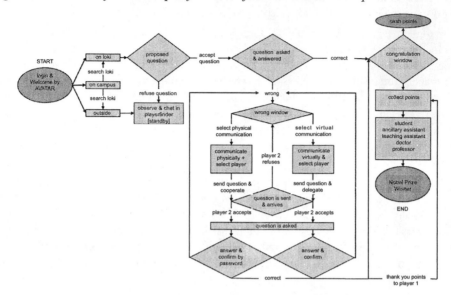

Technical Specifications of the ETHGame

To our knowledge, the wireless infrastructure at our university is Europe's largest wireless local area network, with over 250 access points up and running. Usually, the school's community uses these access points as Internet connection gates for mobile computers. The ETHGame prototype uses this infrastructure to geo-locate single clients—the players—in a building by measuring the signal strength of the receivable access points.

We have found that an exact positioning with a triangulation of all building access points is currently impossible. As a solution for locating a client at a game locus, we have defined the condition to receive the signal of two or more specified access points (see Figure 6). For player-to-player communication, a messaging tool makes up another core function of the ETHGame.

In this article, we will not go into details regarding other prototype components we have programmed or planned, such as using Java for implementing the game logic.

In total, our technical findings strongly influenced the design of the gameplay and created student awareness concerning the generally strong impact of technical limitations to any given design.

Miscellaneous Specifications

Other groups of our team have worked on specifying marketing, sponsoring, and the research sustainability aspects of the ETHGame. Future research associated with the ETHGame

Figure 6. Schematic section through a building; WLAN clouds from different access points (AP) generate blurred reception areas

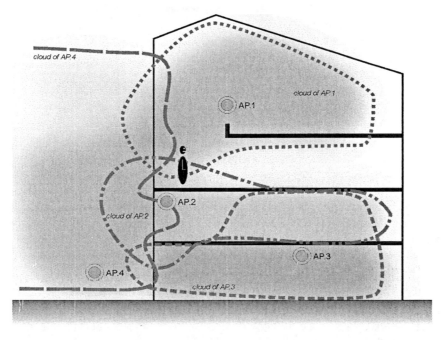

could encompass questions concerning location-based interactive site maps; geo-positioning tools; site identity authoring tools; visitor information applications; a spatial annotation framework; or departmental messaging services.

Design Studio Post Mortem

For purposes of wrapping up the class, we required each participating student to deliver a written documentation of their specific role within the prototyping team after the prototype had been officially presented to the ETH Zurich's e-learning strategists. On basis of this deliverable, and on basis of their overall performance, their contributions to the group product, and the quality of their individual task fulfilment, we graded students.

Conclusion

By using pervasive game design as a teaching and prototyping method for architectural students, we have created an architectural framework for effectively empowering the player experience within a large-scale computer-integrated environment. Hands on, students have learned how passive architecture can turn into an interacting organism and adaptive surrounding. In addition, students have learned that designing fun experiences is a serious fun experience in itself.

The methods and techniques we have been applying in our course allow a perception of space and time from the point of pervasive and wirelessly networked computing. Students have assessed the possibilities and limitations of designing an adaptive building scenario that supports location- and game-based learning. In addition, students have addressed issues of digitally connected location-based services, and location-based gaming. Another result of the design studio approach shows that students have started to include pervasive computing into their skill set as an additional, yet fundamental architectural design element.

As pervasively computed buildings are steadily becoming reality, the applied teaching method of our design studio introduces both a pragmatic design tool, and a scantly developed formal design field. In future courses, we aim at developing pervasive computing authoring and scripting tools and templates for easy prototyping and authoring, as well as for exciting and playful forms of location-based services in sentient environments. We will continue to study pervasive e-learning at our chair theoretically and practically, also in combination with projects such as our university's "Building IP—Lecture hall of the future" project (retrieved February 15, 2006, from http.//www.building-ip.ethz.ch), as well as the Blue-C immersive video technology endeavour (see http://blue-c-ii.ethz.ch [retrieved February 15, 2006].)

With the ETHGame design studio, we have successfully introduced a novel design paradigm to the fields of CAAD and game design—serious pervasive game design. We have also shown that pervasive game-based learning opens up interesting opportunities to the e-learning research community, the building industry, as well as the serious games and, eventually, the surveillance and process management industry.

Acknowledgments

The authors would like to thank game designer Jochen Hamma/Fantastic Realms, for his valuable input, as well as the ETH Zurich's central computer services and mobile communication staff. The research presented herein has been partially funded by the Swiss National Fund NCCR Mobile Information and Communication Systems (MICS), and the ETHWorld project Building IP.

References

Strehlke, K., Ochsendorf, M., & Bahr, U. (2004). Generative interfaces and scenarios for intelligent architecture—A framework for computer integrated buildings. In *Proceedings of the Generative Art Conference 2004, Milan*. Retrieved February 15, 2006, from http://www.generativeart.com/papersGA2004/13.htm

Björk, S., & Holopainen, J. (2005). *Patterns in game design*. Hingham, MA: Charles River Media.

Dewey, J. (1916). *Democracy and education. An introduction to the philosophy of education*. New York: The Macmillan Company.

Engeli, M. (2003, December 13). Levelsbyarchitects. In J. C. Hubers, M. van Veen, C. Kievid, & R. Siemerink. (Eds.), *Gamesetandmatch. Proceedings of the GSM Conference* (pp. 51-59). TU Delft: publikatiebureau Bouwkunde.

Fullerton, T., Swain, C., & Hoffman, S. (2004). *Game design workshop. Designing, prototyping, and playtesting games*. Gilroy, CA: CMP Books.

Koster, R. (2005). *A theory of fun for game design*. Scottsdale, AZ: Paraglyph Press.

Ochsendorf, M., & Strehlke, K. (2004, May/June). Internetgesteuerter projektionsraum in der ETH Zürich: Rote Hölle. *Intelligente Architektur, 46*(Mai/Juni), 45-49.

Salen, K., and Zimmermann, E. (2003). *Rules of play. Game design fundamentals*. Cambridge, MA: The MIT Press.

Weiser, M. (1991). The computer for the 21st century. *Scientific American, 265*(3), 66-75.

Walz, S. P. (2005). Constituents of hybrid reality: Cultural anthropological elaborations and a serious game design experiment merging mobility, media, and computing. In G. M. Buurman (Ed.), *Total interaction. Theory and practice of a new paradigm for the design disciplines* (pp. 122-141). Basel: Birkhäuser.

Chapter XIII

Reliving History with "Reliving the Revolution":
Designing Augmented Reality Games to Teach the Critical Thinking of History

Karen Schrier, MIT, USA

Abstract

Students need to learn the critical thinking of history, yet they rarely have opportunities to authentically simulate historic inquiry. Research has suggested the pedagogical potential for using augmented reality (AR) games—location-based games that use wireless handheld devices such as PDAs to provide virtual game information in a physical environment. The novel AR game, Reliving the Revolution (RtR), was created as a model for studying how AR games can engage students in interpretive, collaborative, and problem-solving activities. In this chapter, the game is introduced, and main results of the initial iterative tests are discussed, including what went wrong and how the game was redesigned to better support deeper engagement and historical thinking and learning.

Introduction

There may be at least two versions to every story, but how do you determine the truth when both sides have valid, but differing, perspectives? Active participants in a democracy must be able to question sources, seek out and manage differing viewpoints, and develop their own interpretations of the information they receive. Social problems do not have one clear solution; rather they require the complex consideration of multiple possibilities, prior knowledge sets, and rubrics (Brush & Saye, 2005). Likewise, historians weigh evidence and decide to emphasize the particular perspectives that they feel are the best representations of the past. K-12 social studies students typically receive a litany of facts, events, names, along with one master narrative; they are rarely encouraged to empathize with alternate views or question the so-called authoritative versions of history. Teaching as though there is only one right way to view history is problematic because students are not practicing the skills necessary for historic inquiry (Hoge, 2003), and also because they are not learning how to unravel the complexity of social problems, nor evaluate the world as an engaged citizen. In this chapter, I present a new augmented reality game, Reliving the Revolution (RtR), as a model for teaching historic inquiry and critical thinking, and for considering how to design engaging educational games. RtR is not envisioned as a standalone educational solution, but as an activity supported by a teacher or mentor, and integrated into a broader history curriculum that incorporates experiential learning, teamwork, and critical thinking skills.

Overview of RtR

What better way to prepare students for skills essential to democratic engagement than by immersing them in a time when these democratic values were being questioned? RtR takes place in Lexington, Massachusetts—the site of the Battle of Lexington, which precipitated the American Revolution—and enables participants to simulate the activities of a historian. The game functions as a virtual analogue to the Battle and a practice field for historical methodology; it encourages the collection and analysis of evidence, the testing of hypotheses, and formulation of conclusions, in the site where this evidence was first generated. Thus, the participants learn about a specific historic place and time, as well as the context for what occurred there, and construct their own views of the past, while considering alternative views of history (see Figure 3 for a detailed list of pedagogical goals).

The participants' primary goal in RtR is to reconstruct the events of April 19, 1775 and decide who they think fired the first shot that initiated the Battle of Lexington. To do this, participants walk around present-day Lexington Common and encounter the physical buildings and sites involved in the Battle of Lexington. They also use a personal digital assistant (PDA) to "interact" with virtual historic figures and gather virtual testimonials, evidence, and items, all triggered by Global Positioning Software (GPS) depending on their specific location. For example, when a player approaches the Buckman Tavern (Figure 1), a historical personality such as Paul Revere appears on the PDA and provides his story of the events at Lexington. These virtual historic figures, also called non-playing characters (NPCs), provide a testimonial (and often a document) based on what they think happened before and during the Battle (see Figure 5).

The participants play the game in pairs and as one of four historic roles: Prince Estabrook (African-American slave/Minuteman soldier); John Robbins (free/Minuteman soldier); Ann Hulton (Loyalist/townsperson); Philip Howe (Regular [British] soldier). These participants collect differing evidence based on their historic role in the game; for example, an NPC like Captain John Parker, the leader of the Minutemen, provides very different evidence to a fellow Minuteman soldier than to the female townsperson or the British soldier roles. The game also has two time periods: Time 1 in the game simulates the moment before the

Figure 1. Image of Buckman Tavern in Lexington, Massachusetts

Figure 2. Schematic of RtR; The participants first collect evidence during Time 1 and Time 2, and then compare evidence with other roles during the debate

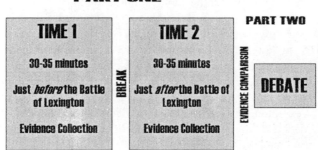

Figure 3. Summary of pedagogical goals for RtR, based on history education standards and John Hoge's description of historic inquiry (Hoge 2003). The letters next to the goals are referenced throughout the chapter.

(a) Acquire a Meaningful Understanding of Key Historical Themes and People
(1) Understand better the people and leaders involved in the Battle of Lexington and the American Revolution [a1]
(2) Become more aware of the social, economic, geographic, and political context surrounding the Battle of Lexington and the American Revolution [a2]
(3) Learn more about a local historic site and how it functioned in the past. [a3]
(b) Build Knowledge of the Methods and Limitations of History
(1) Question sources and authorial intent of evidence; identify biases in evidence [b1]
(2) Create hypotheses, and draw inferences and conclusions based on historical evidence [b2]
(3) Consider the limits of historical methods and representations of the past [b3]
(c) Confront Multiple Perspectives and Mainstream Interpretations of the Past
(1) Understand and critique master narratives of the Revolutionary War, the Battle of Lexington and history in general [c1]
(2) View, seek out, consider and manage multiple views of the Battle of Lexington and other historic moments [c2]
(3) Reflect on ones' own perspective on the past and recreations of events [c3]

Battle has begun, and Time 2 simulates the moment immediately after the Battle ends (see Figure 2 for a schematic of the game). The NPCs provide different information in Time 1 and Time 2, and there is a short game break between the two time periods. Then, after the participants gather information in Time 1 and 2, they collaboratively compare their evidence, share hypotheses, and debate who they think fired the first shot.

Augmented Reality (AR) Games for Education?

The development of RtR stems in part from two recent educational initiatives. First, there have been reforms in history standards to include "doing history" activities—such as evidence investigation and validation, exposure to multiple historical views, and narrative creation—and educators are beginning to search for new ways to teach critical thinking as it relates to the study of history (International Society for Technology in Education, 1998;

National Center for History, 1994). Simultaneously, video games are gaining increased acceptance as educational tools and supplements to classroom curricula, and wireless handheld devices such as PDAs are becoming more ubiquitous in the classroom because of their low cost, flexibility, accessibility, wireless capability, portability, and ease of use (Dede, 2004; Dieterle, 2005; Klopfer, Squire, & Jenkins, 2003). Although PDAs are the primary devices discussed in this chapter, cell phones should also be studied as potential platforms for educational games, especially because of their already high penetration in the student population. Thus, I wanted to explore the possibility for using augmented reality games for history education

Augmented reality (AR) games are gaming environments that integrate virtual, location-specific media within the physical world. To play an AR game, participants might use GPS-enabled PDAs or other wireless handheld devices to access virtual information that has been previously mapped to specific locations. For example, a game designer could pre-program information to appear at specific GPS coordinates, or embed information in a specific location that only can be retrieved by reading an RFID (radio frequency ID) tag. In an AR game, participants can use their PDA to interact with real-world objects or receive data about a particular spot in the physical environs. A building or historic site can suddenly become a game board, and statues or doors can provide virtual clues or act as portals in the context of the game.

Thus, AR games may potentially allow students to "do history" situated in a real-world context, rather than passively learn historical "facts" in a classroom. This reflects Brown, Collins, and Duguid's "situated learning" paradigm, in that the "concept" of history remains married to the activity and culture (1989). AR games may also further encourage collaborative learning because the portability of the devices encourages physical and social interaction, and, for example, the sharing of ideas and collaborative decision-making. Moreover, AR games may motivate those with the increasingly prevalent neo-millennial learning style—learners who favor more experiential, reflective, mentored and collaborative learning, nonlinear expressions of ideas, and individualized learning experiences (Dede, 2005).

AR games, however, do not necessarily support learning, collaboration, imagination, or interest. How do we design educational AR games that are deeply engaging and motivating, while also incorporating history pedagogy? How do we use AR games to teach students to consider both the holistic and microscopic, to negotiate multiple viewpoints, evaluate diverse opinions, and, more broadly, to be more democratically engaged?

In the next sections, I provide an overview of the design process of RtR and then explore in more detail nine elements of the game, and how these elements support the game's pedagogical objectives and provide deeper immersion in the game world as well as the historic moment of the Battle of Lexington.

Designing RtR

One of the major challenges in designing RtR, and in educational games in general, is incorporating learning goals into the game play: "Play which is not removed from a learning experience, but inherent to it" (Squire, Jenkins, & The Games-To-Teach Team, 2003, p. 19). How do we embed learning within the game in a way that does not water down the educational content or disengage the player from the fun of playing a game (Thomas, 2003)? Even more challenging, perhaps, is how you do all of this with a limited budget ($0), limited resources (just myself), and limited time (less than a year).

The simple answer is that I created the game by taking on multiple roles: designer, writer, researcher, tester, and educator. I am not a historian, nor do I have specialized knowledge of the Battle of Lexington, so I immersed myself in the town of Lexington and its lore. The game content—including the testimonials, documents, and game item descriptions were a mix of artistry and historic precision. I needed to balance pedagogical, practical, design, historical, and dramatic concerns to create an engaging experience that was based on accurate portrayals of the viewpoints on the Battle.

I also studied current AR games and considered how to translate them to a historical setting. MIT's Teacher Education laboratory has developed and tested four AR games, each of which invites participants to solve scientific problems from within an authentic practice field. One, "Environmental Detectives," is an outdoor AR game where participants work in teams to analyze a virtual oil spill that occurred on the actual MIT campus. The participants navigate a physical location and use a PDA to "interact" with pre-scripted virtual experts and gather information on the toxicity of various predetermined locations around campus (Klopfer, Squire, & Jenkins, 2002). In "Oubreak@MIT," an indoor AR game, participants work in teams to investigate a simulated disease outbreak on the MIT campus. To investigate the disease, participants use handhelds to interview virtual people in specific rooms around MIT's campus, obtain and analyze virtual samples, and medicate and quarantine players who might be "infected" with a disease. Similarly, in "River City AR," a handheld game based on Dede's MUVE (a multi-user virtual environment where participants can interact with digital artifacts in a 3-D, networked environment), participants investigate a potential biological epidemic in an outdoor portion of MIT's campus. A team of participants with distinct roles must work together and interact with virtual characters to examine a simulated spread of disease.

MIT's Teacher Education Laboratory created a prototype of their AR game editor system, which enables designers like me to modify "River City AR" and create a GPS-enabled, location-based, role-playing AR game with little programming. RtR served as a test case for their in-progress editor system, and future versions have since been used to design other educational AR games.

Iterative Design

In creating RtR, I used an iterative design process, which Eric Zimmerman (2003, p. 176) explains as "a design methodology based on a cyclic process of prototyping, testing, analyzing, and refining a work in progress." With an iterative process, Zimmerman continues, the product or game develops through a meaningful dialogue between the designers and the audience or participants. This means constantly testing and reassessing the game using actual participants, observing their play and asking targeted questions, redesigning the game, and then testing it out again.

I began prototyping elements of the game play a full year before finally testing the full-scale game. For the full-scale tests, I ran two phases of trials. The Pilot study included two trials with a mix of graduate students and educators. Following these results, I did an extensive redesign of the game and then conducted another trial of the game (the Redesign trial), which involved eight individuals, ranging in age from 13 to 17, all attending local and regional high schools. The Pilot and Redesign trials included pre- and post-game surveys on game play, attitudes toward history, and knowledge of the Revolutionary War; videotaped and in-person observations of participants' level of engagement in the game; and a content analysis of the debate, game discussions, and notes. Please see Figure 4 for a comparison of the main game elements in the Pilot and Redesign trials.

Results and Findings

In this section, I present the major results from the Pilot and Redesign trials of the game. In doing so, I describe some of the initial problems with "Reliving the Revolution," and how I redesigned the game to better support engagement and learning, as well as the results of these changes. In what follows, brackets referencing Figure 3 are used to match the game's findings to the original desired learning outcomes. For example, [b2] references the goal: "Create hypotheses, and draw inferences and conclusions based on historical evidence." Hopefully others will find these helpful as suggestions for how to think about creating engaging educational AR games.

Overall Results

The results of my initial and iterative tests suggest that an AR game such as RtR, if designed appropriately, can engage learners in a historic moment and place, and in the practice of history. RtR motivated discovery and enthusiasm; reflection, collaboration, and teamwork; problem solving, interpretation, and analysis; and the consideration of alternative views of history. The participants enjoyed being in the actual site of the Battle of Lexington—the PDAs afforded them the opportunity to integrate virtual information with a real-world context. The game felt novel and authentic, and the participants felt as though they were imbued with a special responsibility to solve an important "history mystery." They took this "serious game" very seriously—they embraced its challenges and critically immersed themselves in the game as such. Accordingly, the participants acted in their historic roles, roles as game players, and roles as learners. By trying on these new identities, striving for a common goal, and collaborating with others, the participants were more open to consider new perspectives, re-evaluate their beliefs and values, and create bridges among them (Gee, 2003). Finally, RtR encouraged the participants to reflect on their interpretations of the event, but also to think more deeply about their preconceived notions about the Battle of Lexington and history in general. The participants began to take their more multifaceted conceptualization of the American Revolution and relate limitations in historical understanding to other situations and even global social issues.

Figure 4. Summary of game elements for the pilot study and redesign study

	PILOT	REDESIGN
Locative technology	GPS	GPS
Game infrastructure	XML/.NET (RiverCityAR Engine)	XML/.NET (RiverCityAR Engine)
Instructions?	In-person instructions by educator	In-person instructions by educator
# of time periods	Two	Two
Linearity?	Nonlinear	Nonlinear with more direction (built-in check points)
Goal	Who fired the first shot at the Battle of Lexington?	Who fired the first shot and two mini-goals for each role
# of roles played	One out of four	One out of four
Pairs?	Play one role as a pair	Play one role as a pair
Collaborative?	During evidence collection, in pairs; during debate as a group	More inter- and intra-pair collaboration throughout
Length of game	~80 min + debate	~80 min + debate
Game play	Search for location-based NPCs and game items triggered by GPS; interview NPCs and gather documents and items	Search for location-based NPCs and game items triggered by GPS; interview NPCs and gather documents and items

Goals and Motivations

Overall, the participants were enthusiastic about the primary goal (who fired the first shot?), and it seemed to motivate their actions throughout the game, structure their navigation of the evidence, and draw them further into the game world. One participant noted that this goal helped orient the way she read and used the evidence, and how she managed a vast amount of game content [a1, a2], saying that "When you have a goal to figure out, you look more." Her involvement in the game world was more targeted because she had this specific goal in mind.

It was sometimes difficult, however, for participants to balance the extensive game information with the requirements of the game play, including the game's goal:

I loved the detail, but I was overwhelmed by it. I wanted to take more time to let it sink in... To me it was a push and pull between getting immersed in the detail, and needing to remember to look around me. ... But on the other hand, that is also what makes it rich, because the richness of detail delivers the message that you want—that this is a complex thing, there are lots of points of view, and there was a ton of stuff going on [during the Battle of Lexington].

This comment also points to the difficulty as a game designer in finding a delicate balance between discovery and familiarity. RtR needs to provide enough novelty and a diversity of viewpoints to engage the participants and fit with my educational objectives, but it also needs to imbue participants with a sense of accomplishment. It needs to always be offering new tidbits of data, while also enabling participants to quickly grasp the bigger historic picture of this shared game world, no matter which order the participants actually navigate the game.

Thus, to further direct the participants' navigation of the game and provide more checkpoints in which to measure game progress, I redesigned the game to include smaller objectives—in the form of role-specific secret missions or mini-objectives—which helped the participants break down and compartmentalize the larger historic problem. Explained one participant, the "secret missions kinda orient you to figure out a certain thing." Echoing this, one participant thought that the question of "who fired the first shot" was too broad, and felt that even more secret missions would make the game "more definite." Moreover, to complete the secret missions, participants needed to rely on a piece of information only gathered by a different historic role, so participants were more motivated to collaborate with other groups. These mini-objectives, such as naming the spies in the town, or finding out what was in Paul Revere's trunk, also helped the participants piece together the events at Lexington and address the broader question of who fired the first shot. Tackling the primary goal was initially very unwieldy; but after investigating the mini-questions, the participants became more comfortable with their evidence, and were better able to back up their claims, and provide counter arguments to other participants' information [b1, b2].

Game Play Constraints

In any game, it is important for the participant to know how it ends, how success is measured, and what qualifies as "being done." In "RtR," the evidence collection period ends when the time runs out, and then the entire game finishes during the debate when the participants agree upon a commonly understood story of the Battle of Lexington and who they think fired the first shot. Thus, it was essential to communicate the time constraints to the participants and ensure that they understood these limitations [b3]. A few participants felt that verbal communication of the time limit was not enough; they also needed visual reminders of the time constraint to motivate them, particularly because they were not competing against each other, but against the clock. Future iterations of this game should have a countdown clock incorporated into the interface of the game or a different visual or audio reminder of time running out.

No participant can possibly gather all the available historic evidence in the time allotted. This constraint helped the participants better appreciate the limits of interpreting the past without all the possible evidence, a key learning objective of the game [b3]. Likewise, during the debate period, many participants acknowledged holes in their data or the need for specific material that would help them feel more confident in their conclusions. For example, one Redesign study participant said the following during the game debate:

How do we know for sure? I feel like we don't have enough evidence. Even with all of us finding different stuff, finding different things, pieces of evidence, how do we know who fired the first shot? Of course if you are loyal to British ... you are going to say, 'Oh the Minutemen fired the first shot' and if you are loyal to America and you are fighting the British, you are going to say, 'the British fired the first shot.' So how do you know?

As the participants began to reflect on their ability to construct valid narratives of the past, they also grappled with current political issues, and how these issues would be later reflected in the history books [c1, c2]. Said one participant:

In America, we have American textbooks and they are written by Americans, so of course you always get that portrayal of the British as being the bad guys and I'm sure the British kids when they learn about this, it's completely different. ... The same with Iraq, people are going to, in years to come when we read about that in textbooks, it is going to be different.

Such a critique on history construction stemmed in part from the *lack* of constraints in this game: participants were liberated from focusing on the single point of view that is often present in textbooks. I carefully devised the game's content to incorporate multiple, alternative views of the past instead of one restrictive master narrative; and I encouraged the participants to create their own interpretations of the past. This freed the participants to try on others' perspectives of past and current moments, and consider how their own cultural and socioeconomic status affects their point of view [c3].

Collaboration and Social Interaction

Almost all of the participants enjoyed playing the game with a partner because they could share ideas and tasks, engage in mini-debates, remember information better, practice decision-making skills, and reflect more deeply on the evidence they gathered. For example, one participant noted that she liked playing with a participant because she "could exchange ideas, notes, plan what to do next," while another participant noted that, "It was fun to play with others, one, to have someone to help with the handheld/taking notes, and two, just to have someone to bounce ideas/theories off." Because the game play and collaboration necessitated dialogue and the sharing of evidence, the participants needed to reflect on the evidence and their interpretations, formulate and offer hypotheses, and collectively decide on next steps—all activities related to developing critical thinking, collaborative, and problem solving skills [b1, b2].

During both the evidence collection and debate periods of RtR, the four roles can share information. The relatively compact area of the Lexington Common, coupled with the mobility of the handheld, allowed for physical interactions and the verbal exchanges of evidence among the various roles. Participants in different roles could ask each other for advice, share discoveries, and make connections based on serendipitous exchanges. The mini-objectives in the secret missions also further enhanced inter-role collaboration.

Not only did the participants become more deeply invested in the game because of the interdependence of roles and sharing of responsibilities, but also they were engaged in the game play; enthusiastic about its content; and retained, learned, and even taught each other its historical information.

Role-Playing

In each trial, a pair of participants played one of four historic roles during the game. Based on their role, they received distinct information from the NPCs and accessed unique descriptions of game items. This meant that they received slightly biased accounts of the Battle of Lexington, depending on their historic role. In general, the inclusion of the roles further engaged the participant in a historic moment, and also the game play, because they instilled them with the responsibility of seeing Lexington through the eyes of another.

My challenge was designing the game to ensure that the participants were appropriately immersed in their roles, despite the technical limitations of the game system. First, I was restricted by the River City AR game system because although the participants could receive information from NPCs, they could not actively interact with NPCs *in* their roles. In other words, the participants could not *play* their role except with each other. This made it difficult to emphasize each participant's unique role in the game, as they could not fully test out their new identities. Therefore, I needed to design the game content ahead of time and use language, tone, and style to reinforce to the participants the characteristics of their historic role.

The initial results were mixed. Some of the Pilot study participants commented that during the game they forgot they were playing a historic role, and felt as though they were instead applying a perspective as a filter on the information they were receiving. Other participants, however, felt that the roles were very dynamic, and felt that having a role helped them better understand alternative perspectives on the Battle. For example, one participant stated that it helped him realize "that you cannot just take one point of view when trying to understand and re-creating historical events." Another said it was "interesting to learn the different characters' reactions to the players' roles;" similarly, another participant felt that having a role was "engaging, I felt like I got a lot of information from other characters." Some participants expressed a personal allegiance to the perspective of their historic role, and tended to credit evidence that supported their views. Moreover, during the debate period, when offering evidence to support an argument, each participant considered their role as integral in their analysis and estimation of each piece of evidence [b1, b2].

The participants felt more invested because they had experienced the moment of April 19, 1775 from a distinct point of view, and had gathered evidence accordingly [a1]. They were also more motivated to fulfill the requirements of the game because they had developed loyalty to other game participants and to their role; they relied on each other to interpret evidence or find the next hot spot. Furthermore, sharing a role with a partner provided a point of commonality, compelling them to work more closely together and initiate dialogue for the evidence they gathered. And because pairs needed to compare and corroborate evidence with other pairs, they had to collaborate and collectively seek out other perspectives [c2].

In the redesign of the game, I further incorporated the benefits and limits of each historic role into the game play. For example, the Prince Estabrook role was not able to talk to as many historic figures; however, he was privy to certain testimonials, which emphasized his status as well as his role as a game character. I also created role-specific tasks (the mini-objectives, described previously), in addition to the main objective of figuring out who fired the first shot, to make the roles even more interdependent. Finally, I provided to each participant a physical nametag with the name of the role and type of role to again emphasize that they were playing a role and that this affected their game play.

Integration of Physical and Virtual Worlds

The integration of text and images with the physical world of Lexington seemed to help the participants absorb, categorize, remember, and recall the information, and supported multimodal learning styles. The overlap between the physical and virtual seemed to motivate and direct the navigation of the historical content, while encouraging deeper inspection of the physical environment [a1, a3]. When the virtual information supported what was being seen in the environment, it seemed more valid. For example, when participants read John Parker's testimonial and saw that it was echoed on a small monument on the Lexington Common, they regarded it as more reliable [b1, b2].

The interplay among the real, the virtual, and one's own imagination also created location-based mini-stories, which further engaged the participants in the overall "story" of Lexington. Said one participant:

My favorite part of the game was when I found out that John Harrington had been shot in the game. It was neat because you met someone on the street who told you that [he was dead] and then you ran into his wife who was like 'Oh my god.' And then you passed his house and you looked at the house and it has the actual plaque saying that this is where John Harrington died in his wife's arms and it corresponded to the story. And then you saw John Harrington, who was dead and didn't have anything to say, and it felt like the process of discovering.

Thus, participants could access and interact with these spontaneous mini-stories, which were amalgams of physical and virtual narrative threads. This further strengthened the connection between the real and virtual worlds, and also helped the participants to construct rich narratives about their game experience, leading to greater retention of information and enjoyment of the game.

For example, one participant in the Redesign trial explains why he felt that this game helped him learn about the Revolutionary War better than a traditional history classroom:

I re-learned U.S. History One, which is what I took sophomore year of high school, and it was a total waste of my time. And I just re-learned it in three hours,...this recapped it and I re-learned it and now I know more about history... the pictures, and the items [helped make it clearer].

The richness and variety of the game content, coupled with the ability to explore a physical site, contributed to the participants' interpretive dialogue throughout the game, and especially during the debate period, where they provided detailed arguments and in-depth syntheses of information [b1, b2]. The location-anchored historic data quickly became tangible building blocks with which to construct and share a narrative of Lexington with others.

By combining a present-day physical environment with a virtual historic moment, RtR enabled a deeper exploration of the historic site of Lexington, Massachusetts, while effectively conveying the Battle of Lexington from diverse and reflective perspectives. The interplay between the physical and virtual deepened the participants' engagement with both worlds, while also creating unique connections.

Reflection and Debate

In RtR, after gathering evidence for an hour, the participants all come together to collectively debate what they think happened in Lexington in 1775. This debate period is an important extension of the learning because a major pedagogical goal of the game is that participants are not just gathering material, but using it: sifting through it, analyzing it, applying it, talking about it, and showing where they retrieved it. Also important was providing time so that the participants could reflect on their process to solidify new knowledge and further integrate historic methodology and concepts. The debate period was also a motivating factor for the participants in the game, because it further compelled them to learn their roles, thoroughly and intelligently gather evidence, and interact with the game world. It was an important impetus for the participants, because they knew they would have to share their findings and lessons learned with the group later, and that the other participants would rely on them for knowledge.

In each of the trials, the participants created unique hypotheses and interpretations of the material; constructed counter arguments; and worked fluidly among multimodal texts. Participants were constantly referencing and questioning evidence—sharing it verbally and physically showing it to each other on their handhelds. They would read aloud pieces of testimonials and offer hypotheses or counter-arguments based on these stories or documents [b2, c2]. When providing evidence, they considered the source of the evidence, as well as their own historic role and his/her relationships with the NPCs [b2, c3]. Each participant seemed fully invested in trying to determine who fired the first shot at Lexington's battle based on their evidence, and each trial of the game had a distinct final conclusion based on the consensus of the group [c1].

Although the participants were able to grapple with a large amount of information, they sometimes needed targeted questions and suggestions to guide their debate, encourage reflection, or properly contextualize their evidence. The participants needed scaffolding to support their visit to this "practice field" and the incorporation of new epistemic frames, tools, and concepts. This further expresses the need for an instructor or mentor to direct learning in the game and that multimedia platforms are not replacements for teachers.

The debate and collaborative decision-making during the game seemed beneficial to strengthening the participants' understanding of history, their application of critical thinking skills, and reflection on historical inquiry, but it also made "RtR" sometimes feel less like a "game."

One participant in the Pilot study noted that while she loved the collaborative aspect, she felt like, since there was no competition *per se,* "we're all going to just come together and see what we got anyway." Thus, it did not feel as pressing to gather everything, or to digest all the evidence, since there would be time for sharing later. In the Redesign study, I further emphasized that the participants, and their concomitant roles, were dependent on each other to gather more information or solve the mini-objectives, and this seemed to increase the participants' motivation to collect and interpret evidence.

Overall, the debate period enabled the participants to retrace their steps; review and apply the game's historic content; and practice teamwork, hypothesis formation, and analytical skills. Moreover, it gave the participants an opportunity to reflect on their own processes of evidence appraisal and history construction, and relate their game experiences to others.

Nonlinearity and Control

The nonlinear structure of the game, which allows the participants to interact with historic figures and access their stories in any order, evokes temporal simultaneity—which I hoped would underscore the idea of multiple truths and possibilities. In other words, the self-guided navigation of the game and open availability of the stories further suggests that one view is not necessarily more correct than another. In the trials, the participants considered alternative perspectives of the Battle of Lexington, for example, said one participant, "I learned about all the different sides. Normally you would just think of the American soldiers and the British soldiers, slaves, the wives, … the Minutemen, there are people frustrated here for personal reasons, patriotic reasons … You get a sense of the different roles of that time period." Furthermore, the game's nonlinearity also more closely mimics the work of a historian. No historian has a set linear path in which to gather evidence; s/he must navigate a vast archive of historical information and create his/her own version of the past.

Figure 5. Screenshot of a virtual historic figure (NPC); participants can click on "interview" to receive a testimonial from Paul Revere

Some participants, however, desired a more linear game. They felt that because the game was open-ended, it did not feel as goal-oriented. They were unsure of their status in the game as they navigated it because there was little feedback on whether they were gathering enough evidence or finding enough historic figures. Some felt that there were too many choices at once and they wanted more of a progression of events.

In the Redesign, I established new mini-objectives as role-specific secret missions (as described previously). These objectives functioned as checkpoints that helped direct the participants' navigation of the content. Interestingly, the Redesign trial participants especially did not seem overwhelmed or frustrated, but thrived in the nonlinear environment because they liked to "figure something out for [themselves]." These participants enjoyed having agency or control over how they navigated the game world, perhaps because these younger participants appreciated the opportunity to transgress boundaries during learning, since traditional education is usually highly structured (Gee, 2003). For example, one participant liked that in this game, the results were not pre-established and she needed to create the "game ending" herself. Through a self-directed construction of her learning, she was able to delve more deeply into the historic moment, as well as the game itself. She said, "in [this game] you had to put it together, you had to research and then figure something out for yourself. It wasn't like a set [answer] like 'you have to click on this conclusion now.' You have to come up with whatever." Having the responsibility to perform motivated her to complete the game and engage in its world (Oblinger, 2004), but then to also question what she received, and devise her own, novel interpretation of the past [b2, c1, c2]. A nonlinear world with well-placed boundaries and sufficient direction seemed to support the pedagogical objectives of encouraging alternative views of history, and also engaged participants by enabling them to have enough control over their game experience to encourage them to use their critical thinking skills as well as their imagination.

Figure 6. Screenshot of a testimonial from Margaret Winship, a virtual historic figure (NPC), found in the time period before the Battle of Lexington

Mobility and Discovery

Most participants felt that the ability to wander around the site of Lexington and discover information at particular sites was one of their favorite aspects of the game. One participant noted that walking around made the game "more engaging and more interactive," and another said that the best part of the game was "getting to know a physical site. To me that is the excitement of the game." [a3]

Being outside in a group playing a game and exploring a site together also facilitated more social interactions, which the participants felt added to their enjoyment of the experience. The physical nature of the handheld game may also have increased the game's collaborative potential—being close together and crossing each other's paths encouraged the participants to interact socially.

This game was especially appealing to kinesthetic learning styles. Many participants found particular pleasure in moving around the Lexington site and discovering information embedded in the environment, especially as opposed to sitting in the classroom and being taught the same information, as exemplified by the following exchange:

Participant 1: *Yeah, if we sat in a classroom and did this and I would walk away and be like "Yeah, okay."*

Participant 2: *But when you are actually moving around to do it … I think it's definitely more interesting to do it this way than to sit in the classroom.*

In addition, the novelty of watching the PDA suddenly present an NPC or game item "mimicked the process of discovery," as one participant commented. Another participant noted that, "the thing we had the most fun with on our team was 'oh we're getting closer, oh we found one,' the wandering and finding" of the hot spots, which contributed to greater engagement in the game, and thus, increased curiosity about its content.

Authenticity

Integral to simulating and teaching history is the creation of an authentic learning environment for practicing historical methodology. In RtR, the participants were in the place where the Battle of Lexington occurred; they were viewing the real historic buildings and structures mentioned in many testimonials; and they were reading detailed personal accounts of the Battle from actual historic figures—all of which provided a distinct and immersive experience of the historic moment. This feeling of authenticity underscored all of the game's activities, and strengthened the connection between game play and historical methodology. Said one participant, "[The game] put you in the real place where everything happened. It gave you the real, actual people who were there, like the names and their opinions." [a1, a2] In RtR, participants are evaluating "real" evidence in a "real" place, and attacking a "real" question based on a "real" battle, which encouraged them to practice and apply critical thinking skills. Almost every participant enjoyed being at the site of Lexington because they felt that it "made history more real" and gave them a better sense of the "history of the site." [a3]

The ability to apply historical inquiry skills in an actual historical site also added to the authenticity of the game's tasks, their desire to complete them and learn from them, and their willingness to apply this learning to other similar tasks in the future. The participants consistently treated the historical evidence they gathered as valid, and made informed hypotheses, partially because they viewed the historical problem of trying to understand who fired the first shot as authentic. Moreover, the genuineness of their experience further engaged them in the historic moment of the Battle of Lexington, and also in historical methodology and construction. They felt responsible for deciding who fired the first shot, so they were more passionate about playing the game. They felt like historians; therefore, they took the game's tasks more seriously and performed the related critical thinking skills more rigorously.

Design Summary

The following is a list of recommendations for educational AR games (and games in general), as derived from my process of simultaneously designing RtR to meet my pedagogical objectives and engage the participant.

- **Goals:** Participants need feedback and "checkpoints" throughout the game, so include both large overarching goals as well as smaller mini-objectives. The large ones guide the game play to the ending and help set boundaries, while the smaller ones can heighten their sense of engagement, responsibility, and accomplishment, and help make the primary one more manageable.

- **Constraints:** Provide necessary constraints (and reminders of constraints) to motivate game play, particularly in non-competitive games. Also, consider well-timed or well-placed open-endedness in the game play to encourage participants to experiment with new ideas or identities.

- **Collaboration:** Enable social interaction by placing participants in groups, teams, or roles and creating tasks that require discussion, debate, or the sharing of resources. Also, provide distinct game content or game play to various teams or pairs, encouraging them to exchange information or allocate responsibilities.

- **Roles:** Include roles to further engage the participants in the game's content, and also increase their investment in the game. Provide distinct information, responsibilities, and goals to each role to create more interdependence among participants and heighten motivation.

- **Integration of Physical and Virtual Worlds:** Consider how the real world and virtual information can interact to spark unique connections, enhance learning, and further engage the participants in both the game site and its educational content. Think about how the interplay between the real, the virtual, and one's imagination can create powerful stories and help participants more fully integrate new knowledge.

- **Reflection and Application:** Provide time in the game not only to absorb information, but to apply it in ways that enhance the game's pedagogical goals. Allow time for reflection; while there should be periods of novelty and discovery, there should also be periods that simply strengthen connections to the new material.

- **Control and Navigation:** Find ways to enable the participant to personalize his/her experience and feel a sense of agency over one's game destiny, while also creating supportive boundaries and checkpoints so that participants are not too overwhelmed. Respect the participant as an equal—encourage them to make their own decisions, test rules, and guide their own game play. Enable unexpected permutations and juxtapositions, as you will never be able to design for every possible scenario.

- **Mobility:** Particularly in AR and location-based games, find ways to motivate a deeper discovery of a physical site, while also encouraging a "directed wandering." Consider how mobility and physical interactions can support greater collaboration, and more serendipitous social exchanges.

- **Authenticity:** Think about how to create a game environment that appropriately mimics or simulates the processes you want to teach. Provide real data, evidence, sources, names, places, and people when you can, and think of the game as a "practice field" where students can actually perform skills or tasks.

Next Steps

As I continue to refine RtR, larger questions of choice emerge—how we balance practical, artistic, pedagogical, and historical considerations to create such a game—and what that means for how we represent a historic moment. Taking it to the next level: how do we encourage the metacognition of these educational games, and enable kids to assess a game's implications for conveying history and historical thinking? My response would be to encourage students to create their own mobile games, and to reflect on their own game design decisions. Using these general principles as guides, they could choose a local and/or personally meaningful site; work together to research historic figures and write testimonials; outline and experiment with the game's play; and then analyze how these choices affect and reflect our understanding of history. By becoming creators of the medium, they will be even better able to evaluate critically their own and others' assumptions about history. These learners can then take their newly prismatic eye and apply it to other disciplines—to identify biases in newspapers, consider authorial intent in an essay, privilege information on one Web page versus another, and incorporate other perspectives in a debate.

Activities such as RtR are essential for further study because they can potentially engage learners not only as participants in a game, but also as more active participants in society. As Jefferson suggested during America's infancy, history is integral to citizenship (Carpenter, 2004)—and this has become more important as America becomes more economically, socially, and culturally varied. By understanding the past, people can better evaluate the future; by listening to multiple perspectives, people are more empowered to appreciate a situation, and better equipped to defend their freedoms (Carpenter, 2004).

Acknowledgments

The author would like to thank Eric Klopfer and Judy Perry and the rest of the MIT Teacher Education laboratory, as well as Henry Jenkins, Chris Dede, Edward Dieterle, Brian Jacobson, Edward Barrett, and Steven and Janet Schrier, for their advice and mentorship.

References

Brush, T., & Saye, J. (2005). *The effects of multimedia-supported problem-based historical inquiry on student engagement, empathy, and assumptions about history*. Paper presented at the 2005 AERA, Montreal, Canada.

Carpenter, J. J. (2004). Jefferson's views on education: Implications for today's social studies. *The Social Studies, 95*(4), 140-146.

Dede, C. (2004). Enabling distributed-learning communities via emerging technologies. In *Proceedings of the 2004 Conference of the Society for Information Technology in Teacher Education (SITE)* (pp. 3-12). Charlottesville, VA: American Association for Computers in Education.

Dede, C. (2005). Planning for "neomillennial" learning styles: Implications for investments in technology and faculty. In J. Oblinger & D. Oblinger (Eds.), *Educating the net generation* (pp. 226-247). Boulder, CO: EDUCAUSE Publishers.

Dieterle, E. (2005). *Handheld devices for ubiquitous learning and analyzing*. Paper presented at the 2005 NECC, Philadelphia, PA.

Gee, J. (2003). *What video games have to teach us about learning and literacy.* New York, NY: Palgrave MacMillan.

Hoge, J. (2003). Teaching history for citizenship in the elementary school, *ERIC Clearinghouse for Social Studies/Social Science Education.* Bloomington, IN: ERIC Digest.

International Society for Technology in Education (ISTE), (1998). National educational technology standards (NETS). Retrieved from cnets.iste.org/currstands/cstands-ss_ii.html

Klopfer, E., Squire, K., & Jenkins, H. (2002). *Environmental detectives: PDAs as a window into a virtual simulated world.* Paper presented at the IEEE International Workshop on Wireless and Mobile Technologies in Education (WMTE'02) (p. 95).

Klopfer, E., Squire, K., & Jenkins, H. (2003). *Augmented reality simulations on handheld computers*. Paper presented at the 2003 AERA, Chicago, IL.

Liss, A. (2002). Review: Whose America? Culture wars in the public schools. *Social Education, 68*(3), 238.

National Center for History in the Schools, UCLA. (1994). *Standard 4: Historical research capabilities*. Retrieved from http://nchs.ucla.edu/standards/thinking5-12-4.html

Squire, K., Jenkins, H., & the Games-To-Teach Team. (2003, September-October). Designing educational games: Design principles from the games-to-teach project. *Educational Technology, 43*(5), 17-23.

Thomas, S., Schott, G., & Kambouri, M. (2003). Designing for learning or designing for fun? Setting usability guidelines for mobile educational games. In *Proceedings of MLEARN 2003, Learning with Mobile Devices,* London.

Zimmerman, E. (2003). Play as research. In B. Laurel (Ed.), *Design research: Methods and perspectives* (pp. 176-184). Cambridge, MA: MIT Press.

Section V

Embedding Assessment in Games and Simulations

Chapter XIV

Building Artificially Intelligent Learning Games

Richard Van Eck, University of North Dakota, USA

The biggest thing limiting games in education in my view is the lack of good artificial intelligence to generate good and believable conversations and interactions ... We need games with expert systems built into characters and the interactions players can engage in with the environment. We need our best artificial tutoring systems built inside games, as well ... Then we will get games where the line between education and entertainment is truly erased.
(James Gee, 2003)

Abstract

The idea of digital game-based learning (DGBL) is gaining acceptance among researchers, game designers, educators, parents, and students alike. Building new educational games that meet educational goals without sacrificing what makes games engaging remains largely unrealized, however. If we are to build the next generation of learning games, we must recognize that while digital games might be new, the theory and technologies we need to create DGBL has been evolving in multiple disciplines for the last 30 years. This chapter will describe an approach, based on theories and technologies in education, instructional design, artificial intelligence, and cognitive psychology, that will help us build intelligent learning games (ILGs).

Introduction

The learning potential of games has been discussed in the popular press and academic journals since at least the mid-60s with the advent of simulation games in the social sciences. Yet games and learning have also always been viewed by many with a healthy dose of skepticism. One of the reasons for this has always been the dichotomization of play versus work, in which play is seen as frivolous entertainment and therefore the opposite of work and learning. This popular belief has begun to change, however, in part thanks to the efforts of scholars and researchers who have studied games and learning and published in the mainstream press (e.g., Gee, 2004; Johnson, 2005; Prensky, 2000; Reiber, 1996). Some 200 academics interested in developing and using games for learning have attended at the Game Developers Conference each year since 2002, and hundreds of academics are conducting game studies, designing games, and/or finding ways to integrate commercial games into the classroom (Foreman, 2004). This has been in part spurred by the tremendous growth in the games industry, which is currently estimated to be a $10 billion industry (eSchool News, 2005). This, of course, is in turn driven by the growing number of people who are playing games, and they are not all net gen-ers. The Entertainment Software Association (ESA) reports that 75% of heads of household play computer games, and that 62% of game players are over 18 with a mean age of 30. This increase in the game industry and number of games has, most recently, led to an increase in the number of colleges offering game design programs, which will further break down barriers to the acceptance of games and learning.

But even as games become more mainstream and the idea of games as a learning medium gains acceptance, the promise of learning games remains largely unrealized. Although the edutainment industry (initial attempts at learning games) has grown in sales over the years, it has not revolutionized learning nor experienced the explosive growth originally predicted. The combination of the adaptive and tireless nature of computer-based instruction with both entertainment and authentic problem solving should have produced a host of games that teach all learners at their own pace. So where are these games?

One reason for the dearth of these games may be that the dominant paradigms in education and the gaming industry are too different to allow for good synergies. The world of education is focused on providing the best path for learners to get from novice to expert in different domains. Content is thus privileged over experience. The game world, in contrast, is focused on providing a rewarding, interactive experience. Content is secondary to experience and is willingly sacrificed for game play when and where needed. In the cases of edutainment titles, these worlds often clash, with educators developing content (often linear, hierarchical, and instructivist) without regard to experience, and game developers building interactive environments (often non-linear and player-driven) without regard to the content or instruction. It is this culture clash that has led to titles in which game play is interrupted by long bouts of reading and drill and practice, and/or where game play is used as a reward for slogging through such instruction. In these edutainment titles, the game and the content are rarely if ever integrated. Seymour Papert (1998) refers to these as Shavian Reversals, which is a term from genetics indicating an offspring that has inherited the worst characteristics of both parents. As expected, these titles have rarely been financially success-ful, making game companies leery of anything that smacks of education. Game developers often believe that "whenever you add an instructional designer, they suck the fun out" of the game (Prensky, 2004).

While there has been some progress made through initiatives like the Serious Games initia-tive, the games-to-teach project at MIT, and the Education Arcade, which focus on games that teach content in the context in which it is demonstrated (e.g., Carnegie Mellon's *HazMat* project, Chris Dede's *River City* project, Education Arcade's *Revolution* history game, and Muzzy Lane's commercial game *The Calm and The Storm*), blending instructional content and games remains a significant challenge for the field.

Part of the reason for this is that the field is too young to have many established research methods and theoretical models for game design, let alone instructional games (e.g., Pearce, 2004; Prensky, 2001; Smith & Mann, 2002). What we need is to establish new models for developing learning games that account for the strengths of both the educational and game worlds. To do this, we must recognize that while games may be a new phenomenon, the tools and theory we need to forge these new models exists already in multiple fields and domains; we have just not yet examined them to see what each can contribute to the new field of digital game-based learning (DGBL). The reason for the failures of many edutain-ment titles was that the model of instruction, direct instruction, was not compatible with the game environments. But there are theories and instructional strategies in education and other fields that are compatible with (and indeed, used by) games. We need to examine games for their underlying strengths and weaknesses, and look to the fields of education, psychology, and to theories of narrative and storytelling to find compatible methods of instruction and learning.

For example, instructional designers have recognized for years that different types of learning require different instructional strategies and approaches. Gagné's seminal book, the *Condi-tions of Learning*, first published in 1965, distinguishes between five types or varieties of learning: motor skills, attitudes, cognitive strategies, verbal information, and intellectual skills. He further breaks intellectual skills into five sub-types: problem solving, rules, de-fined concepts, concrete concepts, and discriminations (presented in order of complexity from most to least). All of these varieties of learning require different types of instructional events and strategies. While this may seem to be common sense, teachers who fail to make this distinction have a tendency to treat all instruction the same way, and to use the same activities and strategies for all types of learning.

We face a similar situation now with games; there is a tendency to discuss all games as if they were the same. In fact the several different game genres (see Table 1), each with its own strategies and approaches, require different approaches as well. It follows that we must understand how these different game taxonomies and their attendant strategies align with learning taxonomies and strategies so that we can begin to match learning and games without sacrificing playability or learning. Table 1 provides an example taxonomy of game types (based on Bates, 2002) and learning taxonomies presented together to facilitate exploring

Table 1. Matrix of Game and Learning Taxonomies (Source: R. N. Van Eck and J. Gikas, 2006, used with permission)

Taxonomy of Games	Explanation of Genre	Gagne's Intellectual Skills
Action	Keeps the player moving and involved at all times. Primary skills are eye/hand coordination and quick reflexes. Deep thinking is generally not required.	Defined Concepts Concrete Concepts
Role Playing	Revolves around characters, story and combat and takes place in large, expansive worlds. Usually collaborative, often online.	*Problem Solving* Rules Defined Concepts Concrete Concepts
Adventure	Story based on exploration and puzzle solving where the player is the protagonist. Player must determine best path through storyline and obstacles on own or with others.	Problem Solving Rules Defined Concepts Concrete Concepts
Strategy	Emphasize strategy and theory, often in recreations of historical or other human events.	Problem Solving Rules Defined Concepts Concrete Concepts
Simulations	Simulation of processes, events, or phenomenon. Emphasis on realistic representation.	*Problem Solving* Rules Defined Concepts Concrete Concepts
Sports	Allows players to play simulated sports activity.	Problem Solving * Rules* Defined Concepts* Concrete Concepts*
Fighting Games	Players engage in combat individually or in teams. Story is present but ancillary to fighting skills.	Rules* Defined Concepts* Concrete Concepts*

*Notes: * Within limited domains—assumes content and game fantasy are integrated (endogenous fantasy); Italic: Taxonomic level partially addressed and/or may require facilitation, guidance, and/or debriefing to fully address taxonomic level.*

where synergy exists at the intersection of both fields. These kinds of tools are only possible if we draw upon multiple fields such as instructional design, education, and games.

This chapter will focus on an approach for developing DGBL that maximizes the potentials for both learning and entertainment by drawing upon established fields including psychology (artificial intelligence, pedagogical agents, and intelligent tutoring systems), English (narrative and storytelling), and education (instructional design). Blending such disparate fields and approaches with games is not simply a matter of combination. Any instructional content we hope to integrate with games must be compatible with the underlying pedagogy and assumptions of games, or the learning will remain a separate construct and ruin the game experience. So we must also examine games for the pedagogical principles they employ in the learning that naturally takes place.

In this chapter, I will begin by outlining four principles of learning inherent in digital games:

- Play theory, cycles of learning, and engagement;
- Problem-based learning; situated cognition and learning;
- Question-asking, cognitive disequilibrium, and
- Scaffolding.

I will then discuss how pedagogical agents and intelligent tutoring systems, modified by the four game principles and by narrative, can be combined for use in designing intelligent learning games (ILGs).

Assumptions

What Is The Purpose of This Chapter?

This chapter is not a prescriptive method for developing DGBL, nor is it intended to provide specific guidance for integrating games into the curriculum. It is a preliminary outline of the ideas and approaches from which a model could be developed for developing intelligent learning games. It is written assuming little background knowledge and in a manner that is accessible to anyone. Those who are involved (or who wish to become so) with the design and development of serious games will hopefully find it most relevant.

How Is This Chapter Organized?

The order in which I address the different theories and research areas that underlie the proposed model for intelligent learning games should not be taken as an indication of the relative importance of each area. Rather, topics are presented in the order in which they address pertinent questions in the design of serious games. This progression reflects the natural progression of questions and answers (at least mine, and hopefully the reader's) one goes through when considering how best to design truly engaging and effective learning games. In this sense, topics are addressed in terms of their importance in answering the most salient questions during each stage of this process. As with most such endeavors, the answers to each question inevitably lead to other questions, which must also be addressed.

What Do I Mean By Games?

I postulated earlier that not all games are alike, and castigated those use "game" as a universal term. I can hardly proceed with this chapter, then, without clarifying what I mean by "games." First, I am speaking only of computer or console games. Within the world of computer and console games, this chapter builds a model for designing DGBL by focusing on adventure games with multiple characters. Adventure games have, in my opinion, the greatest potential for addressing all levels of the learning taxonomy.

Adventure games are situated in environments that are generally immersive, allow (and even require) exploration, are driven by narrative and story, and often require hypothesis formulation, testing, revision, and re-testing. These kinds of strategies are conducive both to adventure game play and to problem solving. Adventure games thus address all levels of the learning taxonomy, and in particular focus on the highest levels. Problem solving skills (also sometimes referred to by educators and parents as critical thinking skills) are among the most highly desired goals in education, but they are typically among the most difficult to address in any instructional medium. Adventure games are well aligned with existing pedagogical theories such as situated cognition and learning (e.g., Brown, Collins, & Duguid, 1989; Lave & Wenger, 1991), anchored instruction (e.g., Bransford, Sherwood, Hasselbring, Kinzere, & Williams, 1990; CGTV, 1990, 1993, 1996) and discovery-based learning (e.g., Bruner, 1960), all of which have been shown to promote problem-solving skills.

The use of multiple characters is key as well, whether those characters are driven by humans or artificial intelligence, as they allow for the social nature of learning and working with others that more closely reflects how we demonstrate knowledge in the "real world." In contrast to the way learning appears in many classrooms, in the real world we rarely work independently on problems. Rather, we work with others either formally in teams or informally as colleagues because knowledge and skills are distributed rather than concentrated in one person or position.

While today's learners, as digital natives (Prensky, 2001), may learn differently from previous generations and thus expect and prefer different strategies and approaches, this by itself is not enough to justify the expense and difficulty of developing high-quality DGBL. The ratio of learning to effort/expense must be favorable to justify the use of games in learning. Adventure games, because they embody problem-based learning, have the potential to not only promote problem solving and critical thinking but to do so while teaching content at all other levels, which given the difficulty of addressing these goals, makes their use justified. However, precisely because of their complexity, they are resource intensive to develop, and thus require more planning and effort. This makes the need for theoretical frameworks and development models most critical for this type of DGBL.

Finally, adventure games require discourse and narrative as part of the game world. Adventure computer games are narrative-based problem-solving activities in which the storyline drives the actions of the player and the movement through the game through a continuous cycle of hypothesis formation, action, and feedback. Narrative and storytelling, I will argue, is the oldest form of instruction, and therefore one of the most powerful instructional strategies available to us. Narrative theory also provides guidance for how we can blend the "narratives" of games and learning technologies like pedagogical agents (PAs) and intelligent tutoring systems (ITSs). This represents the kind of intersection and alignment of powerful learning and game play strategies that we must explore if we are to create great DGBL instead of Shavian Reversals.

Pedagogical Principles in Games

Principle 1: Games Employ Play Theory, Cycles of Learning, and Engagement

Games are effective not because of what they are, but because of what they embody. One could argue that play is the dominant feature of games (e.g., Pearce, 2004). I will argue later that games, when viewed as narrative texts, also illuminate the concept of play and learning. Researchers like Crawford (1982), Gee (2004), Lepper and Chabay (1985), Papert (1998), and Rieber (1996) point out that play is a primary socialization and learning mechanism common to all human cultures and many animal species. Play theory says that play is the most effective instructional technique. This conclusion is based largely on the observation that we learn more in the first years of life than we do in any other corresponding time in our lives (Lepper & Chabay, 1985). The play of young animals as they are growing up is the means by which the most important life skills are naturally learned. "Games are thus the most ancient and time-honored vehicle for education" (Crawford, 1982, Chapter 2). Only mammals and birds engage in play, indicating that the role of play in fostering higher learning is critical (Crawford, 1982). Rieber (1996) says research in "anthropology, psychology, and education indicates that play is an important mediator for learning and socialization throughout life" (p. 44) and that, "Having children play games to learn is simply asking them to do what comes naturally… However, playing a game successfully can require extensive critical thinking and problem-solving skills" (p. 52).

The problem, according to play theorists, is that at some point in our development, play is replaced by work, which may account for poor motivation in schools today. "Work is respectable, play is not" (Rieber, 1996, p. 43), and so our school and work lives are dominated by work instead of play. Proponents of play theory, in contrast, say play and work can be synonymous when work is its own reward (Rieber, 1996).

According to Brian Sutton-Smith (1997), there are seven kinds of play:

1. **Play as progress:** Purpose of play is to learn something useful.

2. **Play as fate:** Gambling and games of chance.

3. **Play as power:** Winners and losers.

4. **Play as identity:** When play serves to confirm the identity and power of those playing.

5. **Play as the imaginary:** Improvisation, imagination.

6. **Play as self:** Solitary play activities like solitaire.

7. **Play as frivolous:** The intrinsic worth of the experience is of primary concern (pp. 9-11).

So we can see that play is just as complex a concept as are games or learning. It seems logical to expect, then, that different kinds of play will support different kinds of learning and be appropriate for different learners. Computer adventure games seem to most closely reflect type five, although there are certainly elements of types two through four as well. Type one might also be said to come into play with DGBL since games provide constant feedback regarding progress, and because players are focused on making progress within the game. Key to this aspect of play, however, is that what is being learned in the game is that which is required to "solve" the game; one does not *usually* pursue a game to learn something. The question of how different types of play interact with learning outcomes and individual differences is an important one for DGBL designers to answer.

One of the key aspects of play that makes it so effective is interaction. It is not possible to be passive during play; play always requires some form of input or response on the part of each person. Play in its most free-form sense (e.g., kids in a backyard) appears to be uncon-strained, but in fact is guided by rules and goals. These rules may not be fixed ahead of time, and indeed may change frequently during play, but they demand and constrain actions on the part of each player; anyone who does not "play by the rules" will suffer consequences (in the game, socially, or both). Likewise, there is a constant cycle of action and reaction that occurs in play, although the pace and frequency may vary. We take turns in board games, at bat, or on offense and defense. We roll dice, spin spinners, act, and respond to others who act. Thus play requires active participation by all involved, both physical (during your turn) and mental (during other players' turns). Players are always either acting or preparing to act. Likewise, every act results in feedback, usually contiguous to the action. This constant cycle of action, feedback, and reaction according to the constraints of the rules is in large part what underlies the effectiveness of the learning process (play) in digital games.

Not surprisingly, the active interaction cycle also helps account for the high engagement in digital games. We know that learners who are engaged (e.g., those who formulate and ask questions, make predictions, practice and demonstrate what they are learning, incorporate feedback, monitor their learning) tend to learn the most. The characteristics, or events, that occur during this kind of engaged learning are key to designing instruction that is effective and engaging. Gagné (2005), after examining the literature on cognitive psychology, learn-ing, and education in 1968, derived nine principles, or events, of instruction that unify the external events of instruction with the internal events of information processing:

1.   Gaining attention

2.   Informing the learner of the objective

3.   Stimulating recall of prerequisite learned capabilities

4.   Presenting the stimulus material

5.   Providing learning guidance

6.   Eliciting performance

7.   Providing feedback about performance correctness

8.   Assessing the performance

9.   Enhancing retention and transfer

These events remain one of the most significant contributions to instructional design today, and are widely used to ensure effective instruction. Each one of these events is designed to promote the learner's active engagement and metacognition. In particular, events 4 through 7 mirror the cyclic process of active interaction described in play, and in fact make up the bulk of activities in effective instruction.

Many who look at Gagné's nine events for the first time immediately dismiss them (and all instructional design) as inappropriate for the design of learning games. The perception is that the nine events might run like this:

1. Hey! Listen up, students.

2. You are going to learn the following information during this lesson (insert objectives here).

3. Remember what we studied last week?

4. (Insert long-winded content here).

5. You can remember this best if you make up a story about it for yourself.

6. What did I just say about (content from 4 here)?

7. That's (right or wrong), and here's why. You should study the things you missed. Read Chapter 15.

8. Take this test.

9. Any time you come across (content here), you should remember that it shares these common principles (insert principles here), and so you will always be able to apply (content here) when you learn about other (content here).

Obviously, this would be stultifying dull, either as a game or formal instruction. But this is a misinterpretation that needs to be corrected. These events are not a prescriptive list of actions to be employed one at a time, one right after the other, or just once during instruction. In other words, these are not strategies; they are events. Any good designer of instruction attends to these events, but does so through a variety of strategies. Each of Gagne's events can be achieved in much more subtle, recursive, and engaging ways. In fact, *every single one of these events* occurs naturally in games. Table 2 presents the nine events again along with typical examples for each event in games.

So the first principle of learning in games is that all learning must adhere to the tenets of play, and be subservient to the game play.

Principle 2: Games Employ Problem-Based Learning

Problem-based learning is "an instructional approach that organizes the curriculum around loosely structured problems that students attempt to solve by using knowledge and skills from several disciplines or subject areas" (Collins & O'Brien, 2003, pp. 282-283). Problem-based learning is effective in promoting greater comprehension because it serves as a vehicle for discovery of concepts and rules, as well as a means of learning how to think about and apply that knowledge to solve the kinds of problems learners are likely to encounter later (Delisle, 1997). Problem solving is also the highest level of learning we can strive for. Gagné, Wager,

Table 2. Gagné's Nine Events of Instruction and Examples from Games (Source: R. N. Van Eck, 2006, used with permission)

Instructional Event	Examples from Games
Gain attention	Motion, cut scenes, noise, music, character speech, health meters, attacks, death
Inform of objective	Documentation for the game, introductory movies, cut scenes, character speech, obstacles that limit movement or interaction
Stimulating recall	Environmental cues (e.g., in Laura Croft: Tomb Raider, ledges that look like those trained on in the earlier tutorial), obstacles (search for solutions involves recalling solutions and events from earlier in the game)
Present stimulus	All of the above (characters, environment, objects, puzzles and obstacles, conversation) arranged according to goals of game
Provide guidance	Cut scenes, non-player character (NPC) or player character (PC) speech, hint books, cheats and walkthroughs, friends, partial solutions to puzzles (pressing on the wall makes it rumble, but it does not open). Also, much comes from the learner themselves as they process what has occurred in the game, but the arrangement of the actors and objects in the environment and the structure of the story itself also provide implicit guidance
Elicit performance	Players cannot progress through the game without demonstrating what they know or think they know—all knowledge is demonstrated within the confines of the game narrative and structure.
Provide feedback	Character speech, sounds, motion, etc., Player gets past the obstacle or achieves the goal, or does not. Every action has immediate feedback, even if that feedback is that nothing happens.
Assess performance	Movement through the game IS assessment. Nothing is learned that is not also demonstrated.
Enhance retention	Things learned early in games are brought back in different, often more complex forms later. Players know that what they learn will be relevant in the short and long term.

Golas, and Keller (2005) discuss five different varieties of learning: verbal information (facts, labels and name, propositions), attitudes (a person's affective stance toward something, measured by their choices), motor skills (coordinated physical movements), cognitive strategies (strategies for enhancing and monitoring one's own learning process), and intellectual skills (those skills used for solving problems and for learning rules and concepts).

Each of the varieties of learning is distinct, and requires its own kinds of instructional events, strategies, and approaches. For example, learning to hit a baseball is both a motor skill (the mechanics of the swing) and intellectual skill (knowing the rules for positioning the bat, when to start the swing, using different swings for different pitches, and knowing what to do at different ball and strike counts). The motor skill portions can be best taught through guided practice and modeling. The intellectual skills parts can be taught out of context, without modeling, using traditional forms of direct instruction, guided discovery, and so forth. One cannot hit a baseball without both aspects, however, and one cannot learn either aspect effectively without using the appropriate instructional strategies.

In addition to separating learning into these five varieties, Gagné et al. (2005) describe how intellectual skills themselves are comprised of different kinds of skills (see Table 3), at the top of which lies problem solving. Each level of intellectual skill requires as pre-requisites, the skill below it. Thus to solve a problem, one must be able to combine rules learned previously to form more complex rules that can solve a novel problem. For instance, a customs official in India must determine whether to let people into the country according to many different criteria, including citizenship, passports, visas, lists from Interpol, and so forth. Each person may meet different criteria to varying degrees, and the agent must decide based on dozens of rules whether that person meets the criteria for admission to the country. In order to solve novel customs entry problems using all of the different rules, the agent must have mastered the defined and concrete concepts that comprise the building blocks of those rules. For instance, it is not possible to know the rule that, "U.S. citizens must have a passport in order to enter other countries" (one of the many rules the agent must use to solve the problem of entry) without also knowing that "a citizen is anyone who was born or nationalized in the country in question" (defined concept) and what a U.S. passport looks like (concrete concept). Finally, to be able to know what a U.S. passport looks like, the agent must also be able to tell the difference between the many things that determine what a U.S. passport is, including at its most basic level, the ability to tell whether blue differs from other colors (a discrimination). This illustrates how problem-based learning of necessity requires the full range of intellectual skills in learning.

If you refer back to Table 1, you will see that many games reach the problem-solving level. One could argue that every game in fact is a form of problem solving, and varies from other games primarily in the complexity and type of problem, and the requisite solution strategies required to win.

According to Jonassen (2002), there are two critical attributes of a problem. First, all problems have at their heart some goal, and the fact that we don't know how to get to the goal without generating new knowledge makes it a problem (Jonassen refers to this first

Table 3. Gagné's Taxonomy of Intellectual Skills (Source: R. N. Van Eck ©2006, used with permission)

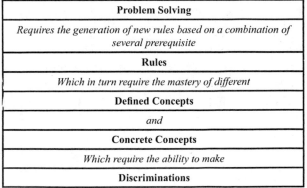

Problem Solving
Requires the generation of new rules based on a combination of several prerequisite
Rules
Which in turn require the mastery of different
Defined Concepts
and
Concrete Concepts
Which require the ability to make
Discriminations

attribute as the unknown). Second, there is some kind of value to the problem-solver that is inherent in finding a solution to the problem. Likewise, problem solving is also comprised of two stages, in which we formulate a representation of the problem for ourselves (called the problem space), and then we work within that representation to change and modify it in an attempt to find the solution (the unknown).

One of the keys to the effectiveness of problem solving as an instructional strategy is the process of goal setting. To solve a problem, one is initially given a goal, which is then internalized. In order to achieve that goal, the learner must formulate sub-goals related to identifying what is known and unknown, strategies for acquiring what is unknown, a process for testing and revising hypotheses, and so forth. Immediate and short-term goals such as these promote more *effective* learning and cognitive development in general, as well as self-efficacy *about* learning (Bandura, 1997).

One of the most popular strategies for solving problems is to make "moves" that appear to reduce the gap between where we are now (the current problem space) and where we want to be (the goal state). The strategy works in some problems, but is counter-productive at times in others (e.g., the tower of Hanoi, http://www.mazeworks.com/hanoi/, and missionaries and cannibals http://www.plastelina.net/games/game2.html), where moves that appear to increase the gap between the problem state and the goal state must be made first in order to solve the problem. It is for this and other reasons that problem solving is considered domain specific and cannot be taught as abstract rules or principles, instead requiring multiple practice opportunities in multiple domains (Larkin, 1989). Games can be a great vehicle for this repeated, multidisciplinary problem-solving practice.

Games always have a goal, which some might argue makes them problem solving by default. From the marketing and promotion of games to the documentation that accompanies them, the goal of the game is made the focus. Consider the box panel description of a recent Game of the Year Award Winner, *The Longest Journey*:

Between science and magic, between order and chaos, between Stark and Arcadia, there is an ancient balance. For thousands of years, this balance has weighted the scales of the cosmos evenly, ensuring harmony between the twin worlds. But now, in an age of great turmoil, chaos threatens to turn the scales and bring our most terrifying dreams to life. The Guardian of the balance has abandoned his throne... the armies of the Vanguard are advancing... a storm is coming... and the fate of the worlds is in the hands of one person: April, a Shifter. April's future is shrouded in a veil of mystery, and the journey ahead is treacherous and winding. A journey not only through twin worlds, but into her own heart and soul.

There is clearly an unknown here, which is how the player character April will achieve this balance between science and magic, order and chaos, Stark and Arcadia. Just as clearly, we have no way at this time of knowing really what any of this means, nor of any strategies we might already possess to achieve the goal. Despite this, many people (10, 873 in the first month of its release, and more than 50,000 the next year) felt that this was a problem whose solution held value for them.

Like problem solving in other venues, playing a game requires us to formulate a problem space for both the overall goal of the game (e.g., to help April maintain this balance) and the subordinate problems along the way (often numbering in the hundreds for adventure games). Two key points are clear. First, just about everything one does in an adventure game is problem solving—there is very little "down" time. Second, we rarely have any of the prerequisite knowledge needed to solve the problem. This is the strength of both games and of problem-based learning. The problem (and a game is a complex problem made up of multiple problems) itself guides the learning, and serves as the impetus and vehicle for learning all of the subordinate intellectual skills (rules, concepts, and discriminations).

Consider Gagné et al.'s (2005) description of the conditions of learning needed for problem solving. Learner "performance requires the invention and use of a complex rule to achieve the solution of a problem novel to the individual. When the higher order rule has been generated, it should also be possible for the learner to demonstrate its use in other physically different but formally similar situations" (p. 73). Game players will immediately recognize this as part of what one does during a game.

For example, consider the following scenario from the game *Mysterious Island*. I am stranded on an island with only a few items, among them, a satellite phone with a built-in encyclopedia. Unfortunately, it is out of power and I do not have access to electricity. I know that my phone needs power to work and that an outlet is needed to charge it (prerequisite rules). I also know that I have an inventory with some items in it and, if I have played any game before, know that things I have found will be useful in some way during the game (cognitive strategy and a rule). Later, in a laboratory in a cave, I find instructions on how to build a battery out of common objects, some of which I have already located on the island. Rather than recharging the battery I have, I have found a way to replace that battery. I combine the required objects in my inventory by dragging and dropping them onto each other to build a battery that provides minimal power (enough to activate the encyclopedia on my phone, which will help me solve other problems in the game). I have combined several rules in the game, some of which I knew (phones and batteries) and some of which I had to learn (how to make a battery, alternate ways to power my phone, and how to combine things in inventory). These rules have helped me formulate a new complex rule: information can be found (on the island or in my phone) that can help guide me as I combine useless things into things that will help me solve problems. This new rule will help me later in the game (many times). For instance, I have to heal a monkey I find by researching common antibiotics, combining items I find on the island to make them, and administering them to the monkey who gets better (a reward of its own) and later helps me get past other puzzles.

These examples are typical of the literally hundreds of instances of problem solving in many complex adventure games. So according to the performance requirement outlined by Gagné et al., performance in the game is indicative of problem solving.

Gagne et al (2005) then go on to list six external conditions, or characteristics of the instruction, that are required of the students to support problem-solving in traditional instruction: (1) be confronted with novel (new to the learner) problems for which they have the requisite rules; (2) apply problem solving strategies (there is no direct instruction involved); (3) receive feedback; (4) be encouraged to reflect on the solution; (5) be provided with practice on similar problems to encourage transfer; and (6) engage in problem-solving that is facilitated by collaborative group work. If games were instructional applications of problem solving, we would then expect these attributes to be present in some form or fashion in the game as well.

From the *Mysterious Island* scenario described earlier, one can see that conditions one, two, three, and five are all present. Condition one because I was presented with a novel problem, although I do not have the requisite rules (yet) for solving it. Condition two is satisfied because the game does not provide direct instruction for solving the problem (although it does provide direct instruction for a rule, building a battery, that will be requisite for solving the problem). Condition two lists several other requirements as part of the condition. Among these are that instructors should make sure that students should monitor their own progress, identify ineffective strategies and irrelevant rules, select appropriate rules, and should provide just enough assistance and guidance for the learner to accomplish things they could not do autonomously. All of these things occur during game play, although whether the learner is responsible themselves or the game provides them varies.

Condition three is satisfied because my phone works or does not, my battery parts assemble or do not, and so forth. Condition four is satisfied because knowing that what I learn and demonstrate on this problem (and what I have learned already) may be useful for the solution of other problems, I am encouraged to reflect on my actions. The game requires reflection on the part of the player, and if they are unable or unwilling to do it, they will not learn as much, nor succeed as quickly than if they do reflect and learn during play. Condition six—collaborative problem solving—is not typically present in games, although the massively multiplayer online role playing games (MMORPGs) embody the concept, as we'll discover later in the discussion of pedagogical agents and intelligent tutoring systems.

In addition to the instructional benefits of problem-based learning, DGBL that embodies problem solving is cost effective. Building truly intelligent learning games will require significant human and financial resources, both time and money, which is most justifiable if the results address the highest levels of learning, often the hardest and thus least frequently addressed in public education. Further, problem solving, because it requires all the lower level intellectual skills as well, is necessarily complex and offers the greatest potential for integrating large amounts of content. In other words, it has the best educational cost to benefit ratio because we can use it to address large parts of the curriculum.

So our second pedagogical principle of learning in games is that learning is problem-based, and involves solving problems that are used to structure additional learning of prerequisite skills.

Principle 3: Games Embody Situated Cognition

Another reason that games are effective is because the learning takes place within a meaningful context; what you must learn is directly related to the environment in which you learn it, and is thus not only relevant but also applied and practiced within that context. Most research has shown that congruence of learning and performance contexts promotes performance (Anderson, 1995), and changes in context decrease what is recalled from prior sessions (Bower, 1981, 1987; Clark, Milberg, & Ross, 1983; Smith, Glenberg, & Bjork, 1978).

Context effects can be partially explained by a theory called "encoding specificity." According to Begg and White (1985) congruence between the encoding and recall contexts will improve recall. These context effects have been demonstrated using a variety of modalities, including textual, verbal, visual, and emotional. Learning in games is "encoded" within the context of the problem(s) being solved in the game.

Just as real-world contexts for mood can impact performance, real world and/or meaningful contexts for learning can improve performance as well. Gildea, Miller, and Wrutenberg (1990) found that embedding newly defined words in a story line and supplementing them with visual context information enhanced learning the words. The story context produced good performance on vocabulary learning, although not as good as the story context with pictures, which in turn was surpassed by those who received the story context, pictures, and solicited help in the form of illustrative sentences. These and similar results have led researchers like Griffin (1995) to call for the embedding of material in a complex environment (like games) to make it more meaningful, which will in turn lead to improved learning and performance.

These learning context principles are at the heart of what researchers like Brown et al. (1989), and later Bransford, Sherwood, et al. (1990) and the Cognition and Technology Group at Vanderbilt (1992a, 1992b, 1992c) identify as situated cognition. Situated learning, the practical application of situated cognition to formal learning, arises out of a movement in cognitive studies in the 1970s that began to study human cognition in the contexts in which they naturally occur (Cohen & Siegel, 1991; Graesser & Magliano, 1991). Situated learning holds that learning is effective to the degree that it is embedded in a meaningful context (e.g., Choi, 1995; Choi & Hannafin, 1995).

Games make perhaps the best use of both context and situated cognition of all other instructional media outside of actual apprenticeship. They do this within the context of Gagne's nine-events of instruction as well, employing each of them regularly, recursively, and contiguously to the action. The goal of the game (the unknown) drives every aspect of the game, from the nature of each puzzle or obstacle to the learner actions and the constraints thereof. Almost no learning takes place out of the context of the game; no learning is unrelated to what is currently going on in the game; and no learning advances you through the game unless it is demonstrated. Even when game players seek assistance from friends and hint books, the learning is contextualized to the game world.

Because the context of the game world and the learning that takes place are perfectly aligned, it follows that any instruction we attempt to embed in a game must do the same, which thus becomes our third principle: games embody situated cognition.

Principle 4: Games Encourage Question Asking Through Cognitive Disequilibrium and Scaffolding

Researchers have claimed that tutoring can increase learning performance by as much as two standard deviations over traditional instruction, a phenomenon often referred to as Bloom's 2-sigma effect (Bloom, 1984). The reason for this, many say, is that the instruction is individualized (content, strategies, media, and pace of learning are customized according to the student's knowledge, skills, abilities, and preferences). Individualizing instruction is much more practical when teaching under a one-to-one (as with tutoring) than it is under a 25-to-1 (as with traditional classroom-based instruction) student-teacher ratio.

Another reason tutoring is so effective is that it promotes question asking (Graesser & Person, 1994), which is critical to the learning process. Unfortunately, in most classrooms, question asking is rarely done (Otero & Graesser, 2001). The typical student asks only six to eight questions per hour (Graesser, Wiemer-Hastings, K., Wiemer-Hastings, P., Kreuz, & Tutoring Research Group, 1999), for example, and most of those are shallow (e.g., Graesser & Person, 1994). According to Otero and Graesser (2001), the research not only shows that question asking is key to comprehension, problem solving, reasoning, and other cognitive activities, it also shows that students who are trained to ask good questions become better learners. In fact, one finds that question asking in one form or another is a part of most effective learning strategies. For instance, problem-based learning requires that students formulate questions as part of the process. The problem is presented, and students are expected to formulate their own questions to guide their acquisition of the knowledge needed to solve that problem (Delisle, 1997).

Questions are also key to the process of self-regulation and metacognition (mental self-reflection, awareness, and regulation) in learning. The best learners are those who are constantly making predictions and asking themselves questions about what they are learning (e.g., Do I understand that? How does that relate to what I already know? What does this mean? How can I best understand and remember this?). Asking such questions activates prior knowledge structures, or schemas, and promotes better learning. Because schemas are in effect networks of propositions and declarative knowledge, asking questions promotes more complex and refined schemas because questions help emphasize, refine, and build the relationships between and among propositions. Research has shown that one of the differences between experts and novices is the depth and complexity of the schemas and mental models they hold in a given subject (e.g., Bransford, Brown, & Cocking, 1999).

Related to the idea of schemas and mental models are Piaget's theories of assimilation and accommodation. Piaget believed that when confronted with new world knowledge, the learner has two options. The learner can integrate that knowledge into what is already known and believed (a schema for how the world works in relation to the new knowledge). Piaget referred to this as assimilation, and it requires the least effort of the two approaches. One can think of this as walking down a shopping aisle at the grocery store and filling your cart with bread, milk, eggs, and canned goods (new world knowledge). Each item is easily placed in the cart (your mental model, schema, or propositional network). With assimilation, we attempt to fit new, often complex information into existing slots or categories by simplifying or re-conceptualizing it to match what we already know. Imagine, however, that you then find an elephant. The cart cannot possibly hold the elephant, and the cart will have to change drastically for you to be able to accommodate the elephant (the new knowledge). Accommodation requires much more effort than assimilation, including replacing or reconstructing existing ideas. With accommodation, we must modify our existing model of the world to accommodate new information that does not fit into an existing slot or category. Accommodation occurs in order to deal with the problem of holding contradictory beliefs, a state that Piaget referred to as cognitive disequilibrium. Piaget believed that intellectual maturation was dependent upon cycles of assimilation and accommodation, and that cognitive disequilibrium was the key to the process.

Piaget was concerned primarily with children's development, and knowledge construction for children necessarily involves a great deal of accommodation. This is because their existing models are ill formed and weak, driven as they are by limited experience with the world. As we mature, we spend more time in assimilation than accommodation, because our mature mental models are more robust, having been tested and modified over many years and many encounters with new information. One might erroneously conclude that accommodation and cognitive disequilibrium are most relevant in the early years of development, and less so during our adult years.

However, it is important to recognize that just as children have weak models due to lack of exposure in general, adults as novices in a new domain of knowledge or experience share the same characteristics. Thus one can think of development both in terms of maturation and in terms of expertise in a given domain. The design of any learning endeavor, including DGBL, in which novices are moving toward expertise by necessity, must attend to cognitive disequilibrium, accommodation, and assimilation.

Question asking and assimilation and accommodation are also closely related to metacognition and self-regulation in learning. The more the learner is responsible for in the learning process, the deeper and more efficient their learning will be. This is the same principle behind what Vygotsky (1962, 1978) called the zone of proximal development and scaffolding. The essence of these concepts is that there are some activities (physical or mental) that are completely within the ability of the learner to accomplish on their own. Alternatively, there are some things that are completely beyond the ability of the learner to accomplish regardless of whatever assistance might be given them. Somewhere in between these two extremes lie tasks that the learner is capable of doing with some assistance, often from adults or more competent peers, or in the case of games, from role-playing characters, hints, and responsive interactive features of the game space. Vygotsky believed that this area, or zone, was where learning occurred. More importantly, he believed that the most effective learning would occur when students were in the upper ranges of this zone of proximal development (ZPD). In other words, educators should strive to provide just *enough* assistance and guidance to allow the learner to progress, but no more. This supports the concept that by maximizing the role of the learner in acquiring knowledge, we maximize learning. Vygotsky called this minimal assistance the "scaffolding" for its metaphoric relation to the role it plays in building and supporting learning.

Scaffolding also theoretically promotes cognitive self-efficacy, the learner's perceived competence in learning within specific domains. Because learners in the ZPD are continually accomplishing things that would normally be beyond their abilities, their perception of their own abilities in regards to the learning will also improve (Bandura, 1997). This is important because cognitive self-efficacy (beliefs about one's competence and ability) improves learning *independently* of metacognitive abilities (the ability to monitor their own learning and select and use appropriate cognitive strategies) (Bandura, 1997). When consistent and accurate feedback is available to increasingly confident learners, they will regularly set goals near the upper limit of their zone of ability in an effort to monitor and ensure their own progress (Bandura, 1991; Bandura & Cervone, 1983, as cited in Bandura, 1997).

Games embody the processes of cognitive disequilibrium, accommodation, and scaffolding. Interacting with a game requires a constant cycle of asking questions, and forming, testing, and revising hypotheses. This cyclic learning process happens rapidly and frequently during the game, with immediate feedback. The extent to which games foil expectations (create cognitive disequilibrium) without exceeding the capacity of the player to succeed (going beyond the zone of proximal development), determines to a large extent whether they are engaging.

Games also often provide hints to help advance the game, either directly (through characters or game hints) or indirectly (the wall rumbles but does not move when pressed, indicating you have found a secret door, but it is locked). Hints serve as scaffolding for new learning, and have been shown to facilitate the active construction of knowledge (e.g., Graesser, Person, & Magliano, 1995; Lepper, Aspinwall, Mumme, & Chabay, 1990; Merrill, Reiser, Ranney, & Trafton, 1992). Far from interrupting the game, hints are sought out by players, who populate message boards and Web sites with questions, and who purchase not solution books, but hint books. Players instinctively seek out the least amount of help necessary to advance them through the game, intuitively implementing a scaffolding approach to keep themselves in the ZPD. Making this guidance and scaffolding process a more regulated feature of the game would lessen the extra steps players must now take outside the game environment to get assistance. Indeed, many games provide these kinds of resources through lists of questions the player can choose from when speaking with a character in the game, or through agents in the game who can provide limited hints.

The Problem of Integration

We have seen that traditional approaches to direct instruction are incompatible with games. The result of ignoring this incompatibility during the early years of edutainment development led to what Papert (1998) called Shavian Reversals, which in turn led many to conclude that games and education cannot be merged. However, we now also see four principles of learning in games that are tied to established educational and instructional learning theories. These principles can provide relevant guidance as a new generation of DGBL designers strives to find ways to develop new games for learning.

There are several questions that we must answer in our quest to integrate instructional events, strategies and subject area content into games, some driven by the principles outlined earlier in this chapter, and some that are driven by practical reality. These questions will guide and inform the balance of this chapter:

1.   What mechanisms exist in other fields that can be used to present content within a game in a way that is compatible with the game and game principles?

2.   What mechanisms exist in other fields that can support the principles of scaffolding, question asking, and problem solving?

3.   How must these mechanisms be modified according to the principles outlined here and other theories or approaches?

4.   How, assuming we can answer the first three, can we make sure that intelligent learning games are extensible to multiple problems and domains, and ensure that any content expert can generate content for these games without "sucking the fun out" of them?

These questions are addressed in the following sections. The answer to question one, I believe, lies in pedagogical agents. The answer to question two lies in the field of artificial intelligence and Intelligent Tutoring Systems. The answer to question three lies in the principles I have outlined earlier and in the area of narrative in games and learning. The answer to question four lies in the use of a form of electronic performance support system (EPSS) called authoring tools.

Pedagogical Agents

One of the problems we face when attempting to bring learning content into a game is that the content is often at odds with the game world, storyline, or structure of the game. While it may be realistic to say that a character in a game who does not know something can go to the library or return to headquarters for training, such strategies are assumed to take place off camera. If we instead force the player to wade through electronic texts or a tutorial, we have interrupted the game, or what Csikszentmihalyi (1990) calls flow—the optimal learning state that occurs when learners (or game players) are immersed in an activity to the extent that they lose track of time and the outside world. Flow is the ultimate goal of any game designer and educator, and anything that interrupts it should be avoided. Often, designers will use PDAs and tablets as tools within the game context to help deliver information. Such devices partially satisfy Principle 3 (situated cognition and learning), but they cannot be used extensively without violating Principle 1 (play theory, a continuous cycle of learner input and feedback, engagement), and making it difficult to address Principle 4 (question asking, cognitive disequilibrium, and scaffolding), at least in the same manner that games do.

One partial solution to this problem lies in an area of study in cognitive psychology and instructional design called pedagogical agents. Pedagogical agents are typically used in computer-based instructional environments where learners interact with a computer-based character to get advice, feedback, or instruction. Pedagogical agents can look like humans, animals, inanimate objects, or fantastic creatures (e.g., genies or space aliens). The increasing research on the use of pedagogical agents in learning environments (e.g., Baylor, 2000; Baylor & Kim, 2005; Baylor & Ryu, 2003; Graesser, VanLehn, Jordan, Rose, & Harter, 2001; Johnson, 2004; Lester, Converse, Kahler, Barlow, Stone, & Bhoga, 1997; Moreno, 2004; Moreno, Mayer, Spires, & Lester, 2001) presents a rich resource to draw on for the use of agents in games. Perhaps the most well known (though not most effective) agent is "Clippy," the paperclip character in *Microsoft Word*. The idea is that he/she pops up with information that might be helpful to the person working with a word-processing document at the time. Clippy takes on a persona that is tied to the context in which he/she appears. A paperclip, after all, is a highly recognized part of an office that is relevant to printed documents. By embedding help systems in pedagogical agents, we provide social aspects of learning when humans cannot be present, and we do so without violating the environmental context. These animated pedagogical agents can take on different roles, or persona, in computer-based instruction, including assistant, pedagogical expert/mentor, learning companion (Baylor, 2001), and motivators (Baylor & Kim, 2005), making them ideal candidates for these same roles in intelligent learning games (ILGs).

Likewise, then, a pedagogical agent in a game allows us to provide the instructional content within a game, without having to resort to decidedly non-game-like methods such as stopping to read a manual, or using a built-in tutorial. Actions like those just described do not fool game players—they know they have been asked to leave the game world for that of the classroom. Agents in games can provide the necessary content in the context of any of several different roles or personas within the game including as co-investigators, mentors, team members, or peers with content knowledge.

However, using pedagogical agents merely trades one problem for another; how do we best use agents to deliver content and provide learning guidance in a game? Agents are compatible with the situated cognition nature of games (Principle 3), but though ostensibly part of the game play are not in and of themselves part of the constant cycle of learner input and feedback (Principle 1), nor are they by themselves part of the problem solving, question asking, cognitive disequilibrium, or scaffolding of learning that occurs in games (Principles 2 and 4). It does no good to simply replace the PDA in a game with a human tutor who delivers the content in a tutorial approach, which would clearly not be part of the game, and might be much more irritating. Research has shown that people treat pedagogical agents the same way they treat humans in terms of their expectations and responses (Reeves & Nass, 1996). As a player, I am not expecting an online tutorial to act like a human, so while it may be annoying, I am at least getting what I expect. A character who comes up to me as part of the game, however, and instead of answering questions in a forthright manner begins to quiz me, evades my direct questions, and provides long didactic statements is likely to receive the same response I would give to a co-worker who did the same thing.

Just as importantly, an agent who behaved this way would clearly not be a part of the game world, regardless of the role he or she held in the game. Every character in a game (including the player) is guided entirely by the goals and sub-goals in the game. Non-player characters (NPCs), characters controlled entirely by the game, never step "out of character"; all their actions take place within the context of their roles and the narrative structure of the game. The player, likewise, is guided entirely by her or his desire to solve the game, again within the narrative structure of the game.

Pedagogical agents in and of themselves do not entirely solve the problem of content integration and instructional guidance in games, because most current agents (there are none in games as of this writing) utilize the same instructional approaches that doom edutainment titles—dull, boring monologues. What is needed to bring agents into games is an approach that more closely reflects the natural exchange of information among characters and players in the game world. When only one character or entity in a game has the content knowledge, the learning will of necessity interrupt the game flow as the player interacts with that one person. And while much can be done to keep the style of instruction thematically connected to the game in such cases, there is no getting around the fact that you have just spent 20 minutes (or more!) talking to someone to learn something to move on in a game.

So it is not enough for a pedagogical agent to be merely thematically tied to the game (e.g., a trainer within the game world); the agent must be a character who is engaged in advancing the goals and story of the game world according to the same motivations and constraints as other characters in the game. They must present any instructional content as contiguously as possible to the events in the game that require the application of that content. What we need to integrate agents into games, then, is a pedagogical approach that is compatible with this constant cycle of player action and game feedback, the "conversation" between player and game.

There is an established pedagogical technology that can address Principles 1, 2, and 4, and because it has already been combined with pedagogical agents, potentially can address Principle 3 as well. Intelligent tutoring systems (ITSs) have been around for more than 30 years, and engage the learner in problem-solving tutoring conversations with frequent student contributions and feedback. Moreover, they do this through natural language processing (so the learner can say anything they want and the system will respond appropriately) and recently, with pedagogical agents acting as the tutors.

Intelligent Tutoring Systems

ITSs are computer-based applications that engage learners in a tutoring dialog to help them construct knowledge in a given domain. The system attempts to get the student to articulate knowledge about a given topic, and provides feedback and structured guidance (e.g., hints, prompts, etc.) through conversational "turns." ITSs have been around for more than 30 years, but have essentially remained unchanged from the three features proposed by Hartley and Sleeman (1973): the Expert Model, Student Model, and Tutor. The expert model is the component of the tutoring system that contains all that an expert in the domain knows. This component can be thought of as a recognized expert in the field or a definitive textbook on the subject.

The expert model represents not only the content of the tutoring system, but also the model for how that content organized. The dual representation comes from the fact that experts not only know a lot about the given content, they *organize* what they know in ways that are efficient. Learning theorists refer to these organizations as schemas, mental models, or propositional networks. One way to think about the role of organization of knowledge is to think about a spreadsheet with multiple columns of data. One could sort the data by any column, and the information would in each case be equivalent, but the ordering would allow different patterns and meanings to become more visible.

Experts have very well-developed schemas and mental models for what they know, developed through assimilation and accommodation over a long period of experience with the domain, with multiple connections and relationships between concepts. Learning theorists suggest that it is therefore not enough for a learner to know only *what* an expert knows, but to also know it in the same *way* that an expert knows it. In other words, we want the student's mental model of the domain to eventually approximate the mental model of an expert.

The expert model thus approximates both the content knowledge and the structure or organization of that knowledge. The tutoring system then uses the expert model as a source of knowledge and structure for that information. The goal of the system is to reduce the disparity between the expert model and what the learner knows. Of course, the system does not have direct access to what the student knows, and so it must develop a representation during the tutoring session by tracking what the student says that is correct, incorrect, or irrelevant, during the tutoring conversation. This representation is called the student model. Each time the student articulates something, the system compares what was said to what it knows about the structure and content of the domain (the expert model) and determines how closely the two are aligned. It then modifies the student model to reflect its best guess about what the student knows, and selects the best pedagogical response that it believes will reduce the gap between the student model and the expert model, while maintaining the principle of scaffolding.

The means by which the system makes these pedagogical decisions is called the tutor. Through a series of different pedagogical and conversation moves, the tutor provides feedback to the student based on what it gets from the expert model and on the underlying pedagogical approach used by the system. Tutors generally operate under the assumption that the best learning occurs when the student contributes the most to the tutoring dialog (similar to our earlier discussion of self-regulation, efficacy, problem-solving, and scaffolding). Accordingly, the tutor tries to get the learner to articulate as much as possible without any assistance. As the learner hits the limit of his or her knowledge and either is unable to contribute anything further or begins to make errors, the tutor provides corrective feedback, but again just enough to get the learner to be able to contribute more to the tutoring conversation.

There are many examples of ITSs (e.g., PACT, Andes, Atlas, Why Tutor, Why2, LISP, Smithtown, Sherlock, Stat Lady, Geometry Tutor, *AutoTutor*) that have been shown to be effective in teaching computer literacy (Graesser et al., 1999), algebra, geometry, computer languages (Anderson, Boyle, & Reiser, 1995; Bonar & Cunningham, 1988; Koedinger, Anderson, Hadley, & Mark, 1997, Schofield & Evans-Rhodes, 1989), physics (Gertner & VanLehn, 2000; Graesser et al., 1999; VanLehn, 1996), and remediating misconceptions (Stevens & Collins, 1977). In all cases, the tutors result in learning gains, reduction of instructional time, or both. Research shows that human tutors result in a .4 to 2.3 SD gain in learning over traditional classroom instruction (Graesser et al., 2001). ITSs, on the other hand, result in a .3 to 1.0 SD increase in learning (Corbett, Anderson, Graesser, Koedinger, & VanLehn, 1999). So while ITSs are not as good as humans are in all cases, they produce reliable and significant learning gains when they are used.

As mentioned earlier, ITSs are effective in part because they embody Vygotsky's concept of scaffolding and the zone of proximal development (Principle 4) and in part because they require constant input from the learners and promote a frequent cycle of response and feedback (Principle 1). One other reason that tutoring is effective is that it employs problem-based learning (Principle 2). ITSs specify complex problems that require application and synthesis of lower-level skill and facts. Rather than presenting information in direct instruction fashion, the system presents a complex problem that the student and system work together to solve, with the system pushing the student to do as much of the work as possible, and providing guidance when and if needed.

To illustrate how ITSs manage this process, it may be helpful to examine a typical problem scenario used by an actual ITS, *AutoTutor*. This has the added advantage of illustrating an ITS that has already integrated a human-like pedagogical agent (in this case, a 3D talking head), illustrating that integrating an ITS into a game is not *much* more complicated than integrating a pedagogical agent into a game.

AutoTutor was developed by the Institute for Intelligent Systems' Tutoring Research Group at the University of Memphis. *AutoTutor* uses a talking head agent to engage in a tutoring dialog with the learner. The agent uses gestures, facial expression, and synthesized speech. In a typical tutoring episode, *AutoTutor* presents a tutoring problem to the learner. The expert model has been defined for the system by an expert in the given domain (e.g., physics). A typical problem might be as follows:

Suppose a runner is running in a straight line at constant speed, and the runner throws a pumpkin straight up. Where will the pumpkin land? Explain your answer.

The learner responds by typing his or her response, although the capability for speech recognition exists as well. As soon as the learner responds in any way, several things happen in the background. While the specifics of this process are very complex, they can be characterized adequately by discussing them in more general terms (see Graesser, Person, & Harter, 2000; Graesser et al., 2001 for more detailed descriptions). *AutoTutor* examines the student answer and compares it to expected good and bad answers that have been pre-specified by an expert. The goal is for the student to articulate an "ideal answer" that encompasses not just the correct response, but also an elaboration of the logic of that response, drawing upon relevant concepts, principles, and rules of, in this case, physics. However, this comparison is not a simple matching process, but a sophisticated set of computations. *AutoTutor* first takes the learners response and runs it through a language module (syntactic parser) to decompose the utterance into its component elements and to categorize it as an assertion, question, metacognitive comment, and so forth. Latent semantic analysis (LSA) is then used to compare the student response to a whole host of possible responses using sophisticated mathematical computations to determine the likelihood of a match. Based on the type of response returned by the parser and the LSA result, *AutoTutor* does one of several things. If the response is a question, *AutoTutor* either provides the answer from a corpus of knowledge, for example, the electronic text of a physics textbook, (if the student prompted the agent with a domain related question), indicates yes or no (in response to a question that is right or wrong), or provides the one of several other possible responses based on the learner's request (repeats the questions, clarifies a point) or the appropriate tutoring move (prompts the learner to elaborate, provides a hint, etc.).

As the learner articulate parts of the answer, *AutoTutor* updates the student model accordingly, and adjusts the dialog to address areas the student has not yet articulated. In this process, *AutoTutor* uses a series of hints, prompts, and assertions to get the learner to contribute as much as possible (scaffolding). This behavior is based on existing research on tutoring and the dialog moves that are made by novice and expert tutors.

So ITSs provide a pedagogical approach that is compatible with learning in games because they promote the continuous cycle of student response and feedback (Principle 1), embody problem-based learning (Principle 2), emphasize learner contributions and promote question asking (Principle 4), and employ naturalistic conversation and dialog, all of which games do naturally. Because ITSs have already been combined with human-like agents (e.g., *AutoTutor*), and because many people support blending ITSs with agents in games (e.g., Laird, 1999) and immersive environments (e.g., Ravenscroft & Matheson, 2002; Rickel, Marsella, Gratch, Hill, Traum, & Swartout, 2002; Shute & Psotka, 1996), ITSs represent an ideal way of bringing content and instructional guidance into a game according to Principle 3 as well. One can easily imagine the architecture running in the background to govern the dialog of the characters within the game during relevant portions of a game, and lying dormant during portions of the game where the game AI is dominant.

But once again we find that we have traded old questions for new. The models of dialog in tutoring are only marginally more naturalistic than are didactic tutorials or lectures. Their purpose is still quite obviously to teach content, which as a goal outside the game in which they reside, will always feel like a separate endeavor. Players would quickly become irritated with an agent who continually responded with suggestions for them to think more about the material, or who gave them hints and prompts instead of direct information relevant to solving the problem at hand. These are effective moves and strategies in learning environments, but are incompatible as formulated for game environments and the characters within them. Also, tutoring dialogs are designed to take place in one-to-one environments, but games require the learner to interact with multiple characters and in many places—rarely does the player stay in one place or interact with one person for any length of time. No matter how natural or integrated an agent is in a game, if the learner must interact with that character for long periods of time, it will be difficult to maintain the integrity of the game.

What is needed is a way to re-conceptualize the dialog structure to account for the game environment. One way to do this is to study how this kind of tutoring dialog could be adapted to include multiple agents (all connected to the ITS) in the game, and to determine how traditional tutoring dialog structure could be modified to take place during shorter interchanges, and in a more distributed (among agents and within the game environment itself) fashion. To understand how we might begin to do this, we can study how narrative and discourse are structured in both ITSs and in games to see where they align and how they could potentially be modified in ITSs to allow for a more seamless integration in intelligent learning games.

Narrative

"…If you're going to tell a story, you must not only master what storytellers in other media already know, you must also learn to adapt that knowledge to games" (Bates, 2001, on the prevalence of story elements in modern games).

There are three reasons we should attend to narrative in our design of intelligent learning games. First, narrative is among the most effective learning strategies and may in fact be at the heart of all effective learning. Second, narrative is arguably the dominant feature of games when they are conceptualized as texts that are read and co-constructed through player interaction. Third, narrative psychology studies how people makes sense of inanimate and animate objects. Games, and the characters within them (including agent/ITSs) straddle the world between animate and inanimate objects, and can thus be informed by attention to narrative psychology principles.

Narrative as a Learning Strategy

Narrative is among the oldest forms of learning, predating the written word. Oral histories and traditions were the only means of education for the approximately 7,000 years prior to the first written language by the Sumarians in 3,200 B.C., and the written language preserved much of this tradition in narrative form from then on. Narrative still drives much of what we do outside of learning environments as well, with books, television, and film remaining among the most popular forms of information organization and sharing. The prevalence of narrative as a strategy for learning makes it perhaps the most powerful and accessible instructional strategy available. Narrative itself is simply a structure for organizing information (by theme, chronology, etc.). As such, it is a powerful means of organizing knowledge while preserving the relationships between ideas and concepts; conditions well suited to higher-order learning such as problem solving and the attendant processes of assimilation and accommodation.

We have already seen how problem-based learning, one of the most effective means of learning, involves the generation of questions and predictions (themselves effective learning and metacognitive strategies) and a running narrative of proposed strategies for acquiring new information, assessment of progress (e.g., dead ends versus effective strategies), and reflection on the solution once achieved.

We have also seen how self-efficacy influences performance. Perhaps even more than with problem solving, self-efficacy is closely related to narrative. It is, in effect, the story we tell ourselves about our abilities and place in the world of knowledge (I am a good learner; I am a poor learner; I cannot do math). As such, it is a part of the larger narrative we construct for ourselves about who we are in the world, what our place is, how we have gotten to where we are, and where we hope to go. Narrative is at the heart of all knowledge, not just as a learning strategy, but also as a *way* of knowing. For example, what is science but the story of how the universe and we came to be, backed up by observation and experimental data? A lack of attention to narrative is what accounts for our inability to relate to current agents; "observers have difficulty understanding them narratively" (Sengers, 2004).

Narrative in Games

David Braben, president of Frontier Developments and creator of the seminal game *Elite* and the popular *Rollercoaster Tycoon 3*, believes that storytelling and emotions are the biggest missing element in games, and will be what game designers will be working on in the future (Braben, 2002). Phoebe Sengers (2004) argues that the "juice" missing in current agent technology (what makes them "soul-less") is narrative. These sentiments are representative of the importance game designers and educators place on the use of narrative in games and DGBL (for more on this topic, see a recent collection of essays on the subject called *First Person: New Media as Story, Performance, and Game*, edited by Noah Wardrip-Fruin and Pat Harrigan, and published in 2004 by MIT press).

There is a seamless dialog, or discourse (albeit non-verbal), that exists between learner and game, in which the learner poses hundreds, if not thousands, of questions, hypotheses, and statements about the game (that is probably a door; something on the other side is worth seeing; there may be somebody around that corner; I bet I can pick up something I need here, back at the shop). As the player acts on and tests these questions and beliefs, the game immediately and consistently provides answers in the form of feedback (this does not move when you push it; it is locked; there was somebody around the corner and he just shot you; you now have a pry bar that can be used here). It is impossible for the game to progress without constant action on the part of the player.

Contrast this with traditional direct instructional methods like the lecture, textbook reading, watching video, and so forth, which are often characterized by long stretches of content "delivery" without response and feedback from learners. This is not to say that direct instruction does NOT require learner interaction. In fact, of course, any instructional designer will build in opportunities to elicit responses from the learners and provide feedback, and indeed the most effective learning (direct instruction or not) occurs when the learner is contributing questions, restating knowledge, and getting feedback. However, when there are large amounts of "information" that are part of the instruction, the opportunities for student contributions are limited and generally not spontaneous (i.e., the instructor elicits student responses directly).

In contrast, games automatically demand player input and do so frequently. Perhaps more importantly, most student contributions are self-initiated, rather than elicited. This is much more closely aligned with the principles of constructivism. Constructivist views of learning hold that we create meaning (knowledge) through our interactions with ideas, content, people, and so forth. The meaning derived through this interaction will differ from person to person based on that person's individual characteristics (e.g., their prior knowledge, beliefs, attitudes, sensory abilities, etc.) and the characteristics of the content or ideas or people they are interacting with. Thus, knowledge is not static, but fluid and highly dependent on contexts and individual differences. With games, then, we can conceptualize the experience as being co-constructed by the player and the game. James Gee discussed this co-construction of the game world and story in an online colloquy in 2003: "A game is an intricately designed world that encourages certain sorts of actions, values, and interactions. At the same time, the player co-designs the game's world by the actions and decisions the player takes. The player brings the world alive and in open-ended games every player ends up with a different world and having played a different game." Other game researchers echo this interpretation of games as a co-constructed narrative (e.g., Sengers, 2004). Anything that interrupts this conversation, if you will, will interrupt the game flow.

Adventure games rely perhaps the most heavily of all game genres on the use of traditional conceptions of narrative: narrative in the sense of the back-story of the game, the actual story generated through computations based on the interaction of player and game, and the running narrative players create for themselves as they consider how they will approach the game at any given moment. Just as narrative is essential to adventure games, narrative is also a powerful instructional strategy. All learning is, in one sense, a running narrative. A learner's journey from novice to expert in a domain is a kind of narrative; the running metacognitive commentary learners maintain about what they know, what they are learning, and how the things they learn relate to each other is a kind of narrative; the assessments we require of learners are a narrative both of the right answer and the rationale for it.

There are some in the gaming community who question whether interactivity and narrative are compatible goals in games (Bates, 2001; Jenkins, 2004), arguing that the needs of learner control, flexibility of game flow, and immediacy of response do not allow for the traditional components of a linear narrative. But narrative is much more complex than a simple linear definition implies. Games, as a new form of media, are also a new form of narrative, as Henry Jenkins (2004) argues in his excellent treatment of this issue in "Game Design as Narrative Architecture."

"One gets rid of narrative as a framework for thinking about games only at one's own risk" (2004, p. 119). Designers should think less of themselves as storytellers than as narrative architects: designers of narrative story spaces and environments. The game serves as a frame for a story that is co-authored by the interaction of player and game. "One can imagine games taking their place within a larger narrative system with story information communicated through books, film, television, comics, and other media, each doing what it does best" (Jenkins, 2004, p. 124). It takes only a small stretch to imagine instructional content as one of those other channels, even within the game environment itself. Jenkins refers to this as the concept of embedded narrative, where "comprehension is an active process by which viewers assemble and make hypotheses about likely narrative developments on the basis of information drawn from textual cues and clues" (p. 126). Instructional content as "embedded narrative" has obvious application to problem solving and learning in games, as does his assertion that such stories are not chronological and linear, but more a body of information distributed across the game environment, as might be the case with the interplay of agents, content, game space, and learning described earlier. In fact, some argue (e.g., Pearce, 2004) that game narrative is by definition incomplete: "It must be in order to leave room for the player to bring it to fruition" (p. 146). Here again we find further evidence for the requirement of learner/player participation in game, which we have already seen is a critical element in problem-based learning and perhaps all instructional methodologies.

Narrative Psychology, Socially Situated Agents, & Games

Narrative is critical also in helping us determine how to integrate agent-based ITSs into games. Narrative tools like plot structure, character development, dialog, and conversation will help us ensure that agent-ITSs are subservient to the game problems and goals, are realistic and compatible with other NPCs, and interact with other NPCs and the player in appropriate and believable ways. The field of narrative psychology accounts for how we make sense of animate objects in the world. Inanimate objects we understand in terms of cause and effect rules, whereas an animate object "is made comprehensible, not by figuring out its physical laws, but by structuring it into narrative or 'stories'" (Sengers, 1999, page 3). Because human-like agents and NPCs in games straddle both the animate and inanimate world they will be understood by game players as animate characters and woven into the story learners create through their interaction with the game. Accordingly, we have to attend to making these characters as human and natural to the story and game space as possible, rather than the "fragmented, depersonalized, lifeless, and incomprehensible" pedagogical agents that currently exist (Sengers, 2004, page 95).

So what will socially situated agent/ITSs look like in games? We can find part of the answer in an examination of problem solving in the real world. In our everyday lives, we rarely interact with just one person when seeking assistance. To be sure, we will seek out someone with expertise in the area for which we need assistance, but that person will differ by area. Accordingly, we should not have just one agent/ITS in the game who provides all assistance. Knowledge should be distributed among multiple agents in the game, just as it is in the real world. Additionally, although we seek out different experts when needed, this is not the only reason we seek those people out. We interact with people differently depending on the context and nature of our daily lives; sometimes as friends, colleagues, lunch mates, superiors, significant others, and so forth. Our human-like agents should have as many roles as those we work with on a day-to-day basis, and interact with us accordingly. Their roles should change with the social context they are in at the time game players interact with them.

Finally, the nature of problem solving is often a collaborative effort involving our seeking help and advice from many sources, both to gather the information needed as well as to help with the problem-solving strategies. Sometimes the people we interact with have the knowledge we need; sometimes they have strategies for getting that knowledge. This too should guide our design of agent/ITSs in games. We should seek assistance from multiple characters and they should seek assistance from us; sometimes we will have information that is needed, and sometimes they will have it. This is not to say that all characters in the game should be intelligent or even on our side; just that our instruction should come from multiple sources, and in a form that is consistent with human interactions and naturalistic problem solving. Sengers (2004) calls this "socially situated AI," and makes a convincing argument for how we can design more natural agents by attending to several factors, the foremost of which is that the social and culture environment in which the agent is situated. By extension, the agent then should be "socially" aware of the game environment, the other agents and NPCs, and the player, through her or his interactions with the game.

Authoring Tools

Authoring tools are the final key to implementing the process of designing intelligent learning games. Because game designers are generally unfamiliar with the educational aspects outlined here, and the educators are generally unfamiliar with game design, we need ways for non-game designers (e.g., content experts and instructional designers) to generate content for games so that we are not asking game designers to be instructors, nor instructional designers to be game developers. And we need to find ways to make this process scalable and portable, so that when appropriate, multiple learning games can be created and modified by modifying the content and connecting it to the game. What is needed is authoring tools that support both designers and educators as they develop DGBL, tools that embed the knowledge from both sides in their very structure.

The *Greenwood Dictionary of Education* defines an authoring tool as, "A software application designed for use by a non-computer expert to create computer programs... Authoring tools are designed to be used by individuals without substantial programming knowledge or skills" (2003, p. 33).

Authoring tools are a kind of expert system, and as such are closely connected with the evolution of artificial intelligence as a field. Expert systems were initially conceptualized as computation tools that represent an expert's knowledge in a given domain. As such, they are similar to the expert module of an ITS. However, their purpose as expert systems was to support, augment, or in some cases replace human decision-making (Shute, 1985). Authoring tools grew out of a desire to automate the *creation* of expert systems, which initially were very difficult to create. The idea was to create tools that would allow a subject matter expert (SME) with little or no knowledge of the programming requirements for building a system (or even how a system worked) to generate the content needed by an expert system through simplified computer interface.

ITS developers faced a similar problem recently, as we now do with intelligent learning games. Ideally, a game should act as a shell, which can become a number of intelligent learning games in multiple domains through the creation and specification of new problems and content areas. This is necessary both for reasons of cost of development, and because we need to be able to have experts generate content without having to know how to program games. The authoring tools should translate what the expert knows into something that will be compatible with the game and intelligent agent architecture we embed in it. If not, intelligent learning games will not only be too expensive to develop, but will engender an expertise/content bottleneck that precludes their widespread application. This approach maximizes both what game designers know about games and what experts and educators know about instruction, without asking either to develop expertise in the other domain.

It is important to realize that the authoring tool serves to translate what an expert knows (content knowledge) into the pedagogical framework that has been established for bringing content into a game through agent/ITSs. Neither the subject matter expert nor the game designers must know anything about each other's domains. In order to understand what authoring tools are and how they will impact DGBL as outlined in this chapter, it may help to see how a development team faced and solved a similar problem in the development of *AutoTutor* (the ITS described earlier).

One of the chief challenges in the ITS enterprise has been building authoring tools for developing new content. For example, it initially took a little under three months to develop an *AutoTutor* version on a new topic. This was far too slow a process and relied on too limited a resource pool (those with knowledge of the inner working of *AutoTutor*) for widespread adoptions and diffusion of this learning technology. We needed to find a way to increase the number of people who could generate the content needed by learning technologies like *AutoTutor*. This is the same resource and expertise bottleneck we will face with building ILGs.

In the case of *AutoTutor*, the curriculum scripts (content) were written for the benefit of the tutoring system, not for the end user, and their development was driven by computational needs rather than human factors. The result was that they were complex and difficult to understand for those who were not privy to their development and the relation of their components to the various components of the tutoring system itself. Faced, as we were then, with the prospect of dissemination to educators in all domains and educational levels, we had to decide now how to map what the system needed in the form of these scripts to what SMEs know about content and instructional preferences. This is the same chasm we must bridge between the worlds of game design and the educational and psychological principles and applications outlined in this chapter; how will we support those with expertise on one side or the other as they develop ILGs?

One way to build this bridge between what an expert in one domain knows and what the learning technology needs lies in Electronic Performance Support Systems (EPSS). This term was first coined by Gloria Gery (1991) in her book by the same name. She defined an EPSS as:

An integrated electronic environment that is available to and easily accessible by each employee and is structured to provide immediate, individualized online access to the full range of information, software, guidance, advice and assistance, data, images, tools, and assessment and monitoring systems to permit job performance with minimal support and intervention by others. (p. 6)

EPSSs are usually knowledge management or decision-making support systems, but their definition and purpose has grown over time. Bill Miller (1996) broadens their definition:

An electronic performance support system is any computer software program or component that improves employee performance by either reducing the complexity or number of steps required to perform a task (process simplification), providing the performance information an employee needs to perform a task, or providing a decision support system that enables an employee to identify the action that is appropriate for a particular set of conditions.

The *AutoTutor Script Authoring Tool* (*ASAT*) was the first prototype of such a tool for use with *AutoTutor*. This system adopts a coaching methodology and language that is familiar to subject matter experts to help guide them as they develop the type of content needed by the system. The pedagogy and vagaries of the system (i.e., tutoring, hints, prompts, and scripting tags) are hidden, and are instead embedded in the tool itself. The end result is that an expert in some subject area is supported by the tool as they develop content appropriate for the system. Once we have established models for blending the different principles, approaches, and technologies outlined in this chapter, we can embed those models into authoring tools to support those who would develop the content for the new generation of digital learning games.

This also yields the solution to the problem of scalability, since more people can develop the content for the games, more quickly. Perhaps more importantly, authoring tools also open the door for generating a single game environment with dozens of scenarios for learning without having to redesign the entire game each time our learning goals change, although significant challenges face us in accomplishing this.

Summary

This chapter began by examining games for existing principles that can help guide the integration of instructional content with games. Through this process, the chapter identified the following four principles:

1. Games employ play theory, cycles of learning, & engagement
2. Games employ problem-based learning
3. Games embody situated cognition & learning
4. Games encourage question-asking through cognitive disequilibrium and scaffolding

Any attempt to build content into games that hopes to avoid Shavian Reversals must adhere to these principles. From there, I discussed research, theory, and technologies from other disciplines (artificial intelligence, psychology, English, and instructional design) that I believe can help us build intelligent learning games. The structure of this discussion was guided by the following questions:

1. What mechanisms exist in other fields that can be used to present content within a game in a way that is compatible with the game?
2. What mechanisms exist in other fields that can support the principles of scaffolding, question-asking, and problem solving?

3.   How must these mechanisms be modified according to the principles outlined here and other theories or approaches?

4.   How, assuming we can answer the first three, can we make sure that intelligent learning games are extensible to multiple problems and domains, and ensure that any content expert can generate content for these games without "sucking the fun out" of them?

The answer to each of these questions, is that pedagogical agents can serve as vehicles for instructional guidance and co-construction of knowledge within the game, adhering as they potentially do to the situated nature of agents in the context of the game world, but that they must be guided by a pedagogy that reflects the problem-solving and "conversational" nature of player/learner and game interaction. Intelligent tutoring systems, by virtue of their use of tutoring dialogs, problem-solving, continuous learner-system interaction, and emphasis on self-regulation and scaffolding, can provide this pedagogical approach. Because ITSs have already been combined with pedagogical agent technology (e.g., *AutoTutor*), models already exist for how the two technologies can be combined for use in intelligent learning games.

Neither ITSs nor pedagogical agents are yet suitable for integration into games, however, because they ignore important aspects of play and social/culturally situated agents. The field of narrative, and in particular narrative psychology provides clues to how these systems must be modified, including socially situated AI (Sengers, 2004), and dialogs that are suitable for the distributed kinds of problem-solving strategies we employ in the "real" world.

Finally, authoring tools allow us to constrain the input of subject matter experts to fit the new pedagogical model for intelligent learning games created through the approaches outlined here. This allows game designers to design games, SMEs to design content, and authoring tools to design the learning. This process maximizes quality, minimizes costs, and ensures more widespread application of intelligent learning games across domains and populations.

There is a big difference, of course, between describing the process of blending all these technologies and actually getting them to work together. None of these approaches are perfectly suited for integration with games without modification. We need to find ways to modify ITSs so that the tutoring is done in a distributed manner, with conversational turns occurring between player-agent, agent-agent, and perhaps even multiple agents within each conversational turn. We need to explore discourse models that are appropriate to team and group interaction, rather than the typical tutoring dyad of tutor and student, and to examine how question asking and problem solving are done in group situations. These models will in turn drive and constrain the design of the ITSs and the agents.

Finally, our authoring tools will need to reflect the needs of all of these elements as well as the manner in which the agents and content are connected to the game engines (no small feat itself). By looking to these established models and approaches rather than reinventing the wheel, however, we are well on the road to developing a new model for integrating learning into games that draws from decades of proven techniques in learning while staying true to the power and nature of games. While the map is not the journey, it is nonetheless the pre-requisite to planning and taking that journey.

References

Abdullah, M. H. (2001). *Self-directed learning.* ERIC Digest (ED459458). ERIC Clearing-house on Reading English and Communications. Retrieved December 18, 2005, from http://ericdigests.org/2002-3/self.htm

Anderson, J. R. (1995). *Cognitive psychology and its implications* (4th ed.). New York: W. H. Freeman.

Anderson, J. R., Boyle, C. B., & Reiser, B. J. (1985). Intelligent tutoring systems. *Science, 228,* 456-462.

Bandura, A. (1997). *Self-efficacy: The exercise of control.* New York: W. H. Freeman and Company.

Bates, B. (2001). *Story: Writing skills for game developers.* Presentation at the Game Developers Conference, San Jose, CA, March 20-24. Retrieved October 5, from http://www.gdconf.com/archives/2001/index.htm

Bates, B. (2002). *Game design: The art and business of creating games.* Indianapolis, IN: Prima Tech.

Baylor, A. (2000). Beyond butlers: Intelligent agents as mentors. *Journal of Educational Computing Research, 22*(4), 373-382.

Baylor, A. (2001). Permutations of control: Cognitive consideration for agent-based learning environments. *Journal of Interactive Learning Research, 12*(4), 403-425.

Baylor, A. L., & Kim, Y. (2005). Simulating instructional roles through pedagogical agents. *International Journal of Artificial Intelligence in Education, 15*(1), 95-115.

Baylor, A., & Ryu, J. (2003). Does the presence of image and animation enhance pedagogical agent persona? *Journal of Educational Computing Research, 28*(4), 373-395.

Begg, I., & White, P. (1985). Encoding specificity in interpersonal communication. *Canadian Journal of Psychology, 39*(1), 70-87.

Berlyne, D. E. (1960). *Conflict, arousal and curiosity.* New York: McGraw-Hill.

Bloom, B. S. (1984). The 2-sigma problem: The search for methods of group instruction as effective as one-to-one tutoring. *Educational Researcher, 13*(6), 4-16.

Bonar, J., & Cunningham, R. (1988). Bridge: An intelligent tutor for thinking about programming. In J. Self (Ed.), *Artificial intelligence and human learning* (pp. 391-409). London: Chapman and Hall Computing.

Bower, G. H. (1981). Mood and memory. *American Psychologist, 36*(2), 129-148.

Bower, G. H. (1987). Commentary on mood and memory. *Behavior Research Therapy, 25*(6), 443-455.

Braben, D. (2002, March 21-23). *Another five years from now: Future technologies.* Presented at the Game Developers Conference, San Jose, CA. Retrieved October 5, 2005, from http://www.frontier.co.uk/press/articles/gdc2002-5yrsfromnow.ppt

Bransford, J. D., Brown, A. L., & Cocking, R. R. (1999). *How people learn: Brain, mind, experience, and school.* Washington, DC: National Academy Press.

Bransford, J. D., Sherwook, R. D., Hasselbring, T. S., Kinzere, C. K., & Williams, S. M. (1990). Anchored instruction: Why we need it and how technology can help. In D. Nix & R. Spiro (Eds.), *Cognition, education and multimedia: Exploring ideas in high technology* (pp. 115-141). Hillsdale, NJ: Erlbaum Associates.

Brown, J. S., Collins, A., & Duguid, P. (1989). Situated cognition and the culture of learning. *Educational Researcher, 18*(1), 32-42.

Bruner, J. S. (1960). *The process of education.* Cambridge, MA: Harvard University Press.

Choi, J. I. (1995). The effects of contextualization and complexity of situation on mathematics problem-solving and attitudes. (Doctoral dissertation, Florida State University, 1995). *Dissertation Abstracts International, 56*(10), 3884A. (UMI Microform No. 9605031)

Choi, J. I., & Hannafin, M. (1995). Situated cognition and learning environments: Roles, structures, and implications for design. *Educational Technology Research and Development, 43*(2), 53-69.

Clark, M. S., Milberg, S., & Ross, J. (1983, December). Arousal cues arousal-related material in memory: Implications for understanding effects of mood on memory. *Journal of Verbal Learning and Verbal Behavior, 22*, 633-649.

Cognition and Technology Group at Vanderbilt. (1990). Anchored instruction and its relationship to situated cognition. *Educational Researcher, 10*(6), 2-10.

Cognition and Technology Group at Vanderbilt. (1993). Anchored instruction and situated cognition revisited. *Educational Technology, 33*(3), 52-70.

Cognition and Technology Group at Vanderbilt. (1996). Multimedia environments for enhancing learning in mathematics. In S. Vosniadou, E. De Corte, R. Glaser, & H. Mandl (Eds.), *International perspectives on the design of technology-supported learning environments* (pp. 285-305). Mahwah, NJ: Erlbaum.

Cohen, R., & Siegel, A. W. (1991). A context for context: Toward an analysis of context and development. In R. Cohen & A. W. Siegel (Eds.), *Context and development* (pp. 3-23). Hillsdale, NJ: Erlbaum.

Collins, J. W., & O'Brien, N. P. (Eds). (2003). *Greenwood dictionary of education.* Westport, CT: Greenwood.

Corbett, A., Anderson, J., Graesser, A., Koedinger, K., & VanLehn, K. (1999). Third generation computer tutors: Learn from or ignore human tutors? In *Proceedings of the 1999 Conference of Computer-Human Interaction*, (pp. 85-86). New York: Association of Computing Machinery.

Crawford, C. (1982). *The art of computer game design.* Out-of-print book. Retrieved December 20, 2005, from http://www.vancouver.wsu.edu/fac/peabody//game-book/Coverpage.html

Csikszentmihalyi, M. (1990). *Flow: The psychology of optimum experience.* New York: Harper Perennial.

Decker, K. A., & Ware, H. W. (2001). *Elementary teacher planning time: Teacher use; parent perception.* Paper presented at the Annual Meeting of the American Educational Research Association, Seattle, WA. April 10-14, 2001). Eric Document Reproduction

Services (ED46324). Retrieved from http://www.eric.ed.gov/ERICDocs/data/eric-docs2/content_storage_01/0000000b/80/0d/d4/aa.pdf

Dillon, J. T. (1988). *Questioning and teaching: A manual of practice*. London: Croom Helm.

Duffrin, E. (no date). *Direct instruction making waves*. Retrieved December 15, 2005, from http://www.catalyst-chicago.org/arch/09-96/096main.htm#Critique

eSchool News. (2005). *$10B gaming field inspires new curricula*. September 30, 2005. Retrieved October 1, 2005, from http://www.eschoolnews.com/news/showStoryts.cfm?ArticleID=5896

Festinger, L. (1957). *A theory of cognitive dissonance*. Stanford, CA: Stanford University.

Foreman, J. (2004). Video game studies and the emerging instructional revolution. *Innovate Journal of Online Education, 1*(1), 1.

Gagne, R. M., Wager, W. W., Golas, K. C., & Keller, J. M. (2005). *Principles of instructional design (5th ed.)*. Belmont, CA: Wadsworth/Thomson Learning.

Gery, G. (1991). *Electronic performance support systems*. Tolland, MA: Gery Associates.

Gee, J. P. (2003). *Video games in the classroom?* Colloquy live, The Chronicle of Higher Education, August 27, 2pm ET. Retrieved October 5, 2005, from http://chronicle.com/colloquylive/2003/08/video/

Gee, J. P. (2004). *What video games have to teach us about learning and literacy*. New York: Palgrave-MacMillan.

Gertner, A., & VanLehn, K. (2000). Andes: A Coached problem solving environment for physics. In G. Gauthier, C. Frasson, & K. VanLehn (Eds.), *Intelligent Tutoring Systems: 5th International Conference* (pp. 133-142). Berlin: Springer.

Gildea, P. M., Miller, G. A., & Wrutenberg, C. L. (1990). Contextual enrichment by video-disc. In D. Nix & R. Spiro (Eds.), *Cognition, education, and multimedia* (pp. 1-29). Hillsdale, NJ: Erlbaum.

Graesser, A. C., & Magliano, J. P. (1991). Context and cognition. In R. Cohen & A. W. Siegel (Eds.), *Context and development* (pp. 57-76). Hillsdale, NJ: Erlbaum.

Graesser, A. C., & McMahen, C. L. (1993). Anomalous information triggers questions when adults solve quantitative problems and comprehend stories. *Journal of Educational Psychology, 85*(1), 136-151.

Graesser, A. C., & Person, N. K. (1994). Question asking during tutoring. *American Educational Research Journal, 31*(1), 104-137.

Graesser, A. C., Person, N., & Harter, D. (2000). Teaching tactics and dialog in *AutoTutor*. *International Journal of Artificial Intelligence in Education, 12*(3), 257-279.

Graesser, A. C., Person, N. K., & Magliano, J. P. (1995). Collaborative dialogue patterns in naturalistic one-on-one tutoring. *Applied Cognitive Psychology 9*(4), 495-522.

Graesser, A. C., VanLehn, K., Rose, C., Jordan, P., & Harter, D. (2001). Intelligent tutoring systems with conversational dialogue. *AI Magazine, 22*(4), 39-50.

Graesser, A. C., Wiemer-Hastings, K., Wiemer-Hastings, P., Kreuz, R., & Tutoring Research Group. (1999). AutoTutor: A simulation of a human tutor. *Journal of Cognitive Systems Research, 1*(1), 35-51.

Hartley, R., & Sleeman, D. H. (1973). Towards more intelligent teaching systems. *International Journal of Man-Machine Studies, 5*, 215-236.

Hu, X., Mathews, E., Graesser, A. C., & Susarla, S. (2002). EBOOK.EXE: A desktop authoring tool for HURAA. In M. Driscoll & T. C. Reeves (Eds.), *Proceedings of E-Learn 2002* (pp. 471-476). Montreal, Canada: AACE Press.

Jenkins, H. (2004). Game design as narrative architecture. In N. Wardrip-Fruin & P. Harrigan (Eds.), *First person: New media as story, performance, game* (pp. 118-130). Cambridge, MA: MIT.

Johnson, S. (2005). *Everything bad is good for you*. New York: Penguin Group.

Johnson, W. L. (2004). *Motivational effects of socially intelligent pedagogical agents*. Paper presented at the annual meeting of the American Educational Research Association, San Diego, CA.

Jonassen, D. H. (2002). Integration of problem solving into instructional design. In R. A. Reiser & J. V. Dempsey (Eds.), *Trends and issues in instructional design & technology* (pp. 107-120). Upper Saddle River, NJ: Merrill Prentice Hall.

Koedinger, K. R., Anderson, J. R., Hadley, W. H., & Mark, M. A. (1997). Intelligent tutoring goes to school in the big city. *International Journal of Artificial Intelligence in Education, 8*, 30-43.

Larkin, J. H. (1989). What kind of knowledge transfers? In L. B. Resnick (Ed.), *Knowing, learning, and instruction: Essays in honor of Robert Glaser* (pp. 283-305). Hillsdale, NJ: Erlbaum.

Larochelle, M., & Bednarz, N. (1998). Constructivism and education: Beyond epistemological correctness. In M. Larochelle, N. Bednarz, & J. Garrison (Eds.), *Constructivism and education* (pp. 3-20). New York: Cambridge University.

Lave, J., & Wenger, E. (1991). *Situated learning: Legitimate peripheral participation*. Cambridge, MA: Cambridge University Press.

Lepper, M. R., Aspinwall, L. G., Mumme, D. L., & Chabay, R. W. (1990). Self-perception and social-perception processes in tutoring: Subtle social control strategies of expert tutors. In J. M. Olson & M. P. Zanna (Eds.), *Self-Inference Processes: The Ontario Symposium* (Vol. 6, pp. 217-237). Hillsdale, NJ: Erlbaum.

Lepper, M. R., & Chabay, R. W. (1985). Intrinsic motivation and instruction: Conflicting views on the role of motivational processes in computer-based education. *Educational Psychologist, 20*(4), 217-230.

Lester, J. C., Converse, S. A., Kahler, S. E., Barlow, S. T., Stone, B. A., & Bhoga, R. S. (1997). The Persona Effect: Affective impact of animated pedagogical agents. *Association of Computing Machinery*. Retrieved June 12, 2001, from http://www.acm.org/sigchi/chi97/proceedings/paper/j1.htm

Macías, M., & Castells, P. (2001, December 18-20). Authoring tool for building adaptive learning guidance systems on the Web. In J. Liu, P. C. Yuen, C. H. Li, J. K.-Y. Ng, & T. Ishida (Eds.), *The Proceedings of the Sixth International Computer Science Conference on Active Media Technology (AMT'01)*, Hong Kong (pp. 268-278). London: Springer-Verlag.

Merrill, D., Reiser, B., Ranney, M., & Trafton, J. (1992). Effective tutoring techniques: A comparison of human tutors and intelligent tutoring systems. *The Journal of Learning Sciences, 2*(3), 277-305.

Miller, B. (1996). *EPSS: Expanding the perspective.* Retrieved February 19, 2003, from http://www.pcd-innovations.com/infosite/define.htm

Moreno, R. (2004). *Agent-based methods for multimedia learning environments: What works and why?* Paper presented at the Annual Meeting of the American Educational Research Association, San Diego, CA.

Moreno, R., Mayer, R., Spires, H. A., & Lester, J. C. (2001). The case for social agency in computer-based teaching: Do students learn more deeply when they interact with animated pedagogical agents? *Cognition and Instruction, 19*(2), 177-213.

Murray, T. (1998). Authoring knowledge-based tutors: Tools for content, instructional strategy, student model, and interface design. *Journal of the Learning Sciences, 7*(1), 5-64.

Murray, T., Blessing, S., & Ainsworth, S. (2003). *Authoring tools for advanced technology learning environments.* Norwell, MA: Kluwer.

Otero, J., & Graesser, A. C. (2001). PREG: Elements of a model of question asking. *Cognition & Instruction 19*(2), 143-17.

Papert, S. (1998, June). Does easy do it? Children, games, and learning. *Game Developer*, 87-88.

Pearce, C. (2004). Towards a game theory of game. In N. Wardrip-Fruin & P. Harrigan (Eds.), *First person: New media as story, performance, game* (pp 143-153). Cambridge: MIT.

Phillips, D. C. (1995). The good, the bad, and the ugly: The many faces of constructivism. *Educational Researcher, 24*(7), 5-12.

Prensky, M. (2000). *Digital game-based learning.* New York: McGraw-Hill.

Prensky, M. (2004, July 13). *Future predictions: Trends in virtual education. What does the future hold?* Department of Education Secretary's NCLB eLearning Summit: Increasing options through e-Learning, Orlando, FL. Retrieved October 5, 2005, from http://www.nclbtechsummits.org/summit2/presentations/5.3.Prensky.pdf

Ravenscroft, A., & Matheson, M. P. (2002). Developing and evaluating dialogue games for collaborative e-learning. *Journal of Computer Assisted Learning, 18*(1), 93-101.

Reeves, B., & Nass, C. (1996). *The media equation: How people treat computers, television, and new media like real people and places.* New York: Cambridge University Press.

Rickel, J., Marsella, S., Gratch, J., Hill, R., Traum, D., & Swartout, W. (2002). Toward a new generation of virtual humans for interactive experiences. *IEEE Intelligent Systems, 17*(4), 32-37.

Rieber, L. P. (1996). Seriously considering play: Designing interactive learning environments based on the blending of microworlds, simulations, and games. *Educational Technology Research and Development, 44*(2), 43-58. Retrieved from http://it.coe.uga.edu/~lrieber/play.html

Schofield, J. W., & Evans-Rhodes, D. (1989). Artificial intelligence in the classroom. In D. Bierman, J. Greuker, & J. Sandberg (Eds.), *Artificial intelligence and education: Synthesis and reflection* (pp. 238-243). Springfield, VA: IOS.

Sengers, P. (1999). Narrative intelligence. In K. Dautenhahn (Ed.), *Human cognition and social agent technology* (pp. 1-26). Philadelphia: John Benjamins.

Sengers, P. (2004). Schizophrenia and narrative in artificial agents. In N. Wardrip-Fruin & P. Harrigan (Eds.), *First person: New media as story, performance, game* (pp. 95-116). Cambridge: MIT

Shute, V. (1985). Artificial intelligence. In T. Husen & T. Neville Postlethwaite (Eds.), *The international encyclopedia of education* (pp. 333-340). Oxford, UK: Pergamon.

Shute, V. J., & Psotka, J. (1996). Intelligent tutoring systems: Past, present and future. In D. Jonassen (Ed.), *Handbook of research on educational communications and technology* (pp. 570-600). New York: Simon and Schuster.

Smith, L., & Mann, S. (2002, July). Playing the game: A model for gameness in interactive game based learning. In S. Mann (Ed.), *Proceedings of the 15th Annual NACCQ*, Hamilton, New Zealand. Dunedin, NZ: Wickliffe.

Smith, S. M., Glenberg, A., & Bjork, R. A. (1978). Environmental context and human memory. *Memory and Cognition, 6*(4), 342-353.

Stevens, A., & Collins, A. (1977). The goal structure of a Socratic tutor. In *Proceedings of the National ACM Conference* (pp. 256-263). New York: ACM.

Susarla, S. C., Adcock, A. B., Van Eck, R. N., & Moreno, K. N. (2003, November). Authoring for *AutoTutor*: Adding a new dimension to an intelligent tutoring system. In G. Richards (Ed.), *Proceedings of the World Conference on E-Learning in Corporate, Government & Higher Education 2003*, Phoenix, AZ. Chesapeake, VA: AACE.

Susarla, S., Adcock, A., Van Eck, R., Moreno, K., & Graesser, A. C. (2003). Development and evaluation of a lesson authoring tool for *AutoTutor*. In V. Aleven, U. Hoppe, J. Kay, R. Mizoguchi, H. Pain, F. Verdejo, et al. (Eds.), *AIED 2003 Supplemental Proceedings* (pp. 378-387). Sydney, Australia: University of Sydney School of Information Technologies.

Sutton-Smith, B. (1997). *The ambiguity of play*. Cambridge, MA: Harvard University Press.

Toole, J., & Heift, T. (2002). The tutor assistant: An authoring system for a Web-based intelligent language tutor. *Computer Assisted Language Learning, 15*(4), 373-386.

VanLehn, K. (1996). Conceptual and metalearning during coached problem solving. In C. Frasson, G. Gauthier, & A. Lesgold (Eds.), *Proceedings of the Third Intelligent Tutoring Systems Conference* (pp. 29-47). Berlin: Springer-Verlag.

Vygotsky, L. S. (1962). *Thought and language*. Cambridge, MA: The MIT Press.

Vygotsky, L. S. (1978). *Mind in society: The development of higher psychological processes*. Cambridge, MA: Harvard University Press.

Zimmerman, E. (2004). Narrative, interactivity, play, and games: Four naughty concepts in need of discipline. In N. Wardrip-Fruin & P. Harrigan (Eds.), *First person: New media as story, performance, game* (pp. 154-164). Cambridge, MA: MIT.

Chapter XV

simSchool and the Conceptual Assessment Framework

David Gibson, CurveShift.com, USA

Abstract

simSchool is a game-based simulation developed with funding from the Preparing Tomorrow's Teachers to Use Technology (PT3, 2003) program of the United States Department of Education. The simulation provides users with a training environment for developing skills such as lesson planning, differentiating instruction, classroom management, special education, and adapting teaching to multiple cognitive abilities. This chapter uses simSchool as an example to present and discuss an application of the Conceptual Assessment Framework (CAF) of Almond, Steinberg, and Mislevy (2002) as a general model for building assessments of what users learn through games and simulations. The CAF organizes the theories of teaching as well as the inferential frameworks in simSchool that are used to provide feedback to players about their levels of knowledge and abilities as teachers. The framework is generally relevant and useful for planning how to assess gains made by users while playing games or using simulations.

Introduction

An assessment is a machine for reasoning about what students know, can do, or have accomplished, based on a handful of things they say, do, or make in particular settings. (Mislevy, Steinberg, & Almond, 2003, p. 4)

Assessment is a broad concept. It encompasses small decisions such as whether to have dinner out or eat in (e.g., when we might assess our refrigerator and pocketbook) as well as larger decisions such as whether to become a rock star or an accountant (e.g., when we might assess our lifetime chance of success given our skills). Its essence is that we size up a situation by gathering data, apply some criteria to make inferences that are meaningful to us, and then decide what to do next. When assessing what someone has learned from playing a game or simulation, the same steps are taken, increasingly with automated help from networked computers.

Confusion and debate is often created, however, when the relatively straightforward process of making inferences and decisions expands to include technical issues and the politics of formal educational assessment. Questions arise about audience (who is giving and taking this assessment?), purpose (how will the results be used?), and ownership (who has the control here?), as well as about the fairness, reliability, and validity of the methods. SimSchool has its own answers to these questions. Your situation will most likely be different. This chapter cannot hope to discuss everything about assessment, but will endeavor to provide you with a framework of ideas that you can use in your setting. It will try to do this by calling attention from a detailed level of explanation of how simSchool is thinking about its challenges, to general statements that are valid for most assessments.

The audience for simSchool's assessment has two important constituents: future teachers and the professors guiding them into the profession, which in a general setting might be called users and their supervisors. There are many other possible audiences for assessment, but we do not deal with them in this chapter.

The purpose of the simSchool assessment focuses on making inferences about what the user knows and can do as a teacher. There are other purposes of assessing games and simulations. Program assessment focuses on determining if an investment in a program is paying off. Formative assessments are used to make improvements. Opinion surveys are used to find out how people feel. And there are others. We do not address these alternative purposes.

Concerning ownership, in simSchool the supervisor and user both have access to the assessment information, but the supervisor owns the data. Users see the results, hopefully analyze them, and base their future learning and action on them. But, they cannot withhold their data from the primary owner, the supervisor, who is interested in determining the extent of learning. There are many other ways to make the decision about ownership of assessment information (e.g. an institution, the public, the user), and as with the numerous options for audience and purpose, we understandably cannot deal with them in this chapter.

The plan of the chapter is to present the main concepts of an assessment framework and show in a general sense how simSchool uses the framework to organize its assessment capabilities. Undertaking both of these tasks, the chapter illustrates how games and simulations in general can assess what a user learns.

Conceptual Assessment Framework

Recent work stemming from adaptive testing (Almond, Steinberg, & Mislevy, 2002) expresses and shares a core of ideas with other research on assessment, which holds that every assessment of student learning involves three fundamental components: "a model of how students represent knowledge and develop competence in the subject domain, tasks or situations that allow one to observe students' performance, and an interpretation method for drawing inferences from the performance evidence thus obtained." (Pellegrino, Chudowsky, & Glaser, 2001, p. 2). Mislevy et al. (2003) refer to these as three components of a Conceptual Assessment Framework (CAF): the student model, task model, and evidence model (Figure 1).

Student Model

All simulations and games simplify or exaggerate aspects of the real world. The student model simplifies an ideal user into a handful of variables that are central to the assessment. It represents the ideal configuration or goal state of the variables used in the assessment, for example, what the ideal user would do if they knew what they needed to and could do what they needed to in order to produce evidence of what the game was teaching. The ideal state of the variables is compared to the actual input from the user's interactions to determine rightness, closeness to expert performance, on track, on target and so forth.

The student model can also be thought of as the "ideal user" model. As a real user performs tasks, responds to a prompt, or explores a networked, hyperlinked space of resources, the current state of variables of his or her moves is compared with the ideal user model and used to construct a scoring record that is analyzed using the evidence model. The user performs tasks by interacting with the task model, which in turn documents that performance for the evidence model's analysis (Figure 1).

Figure 1. Initial components of the conceptual assessment framework

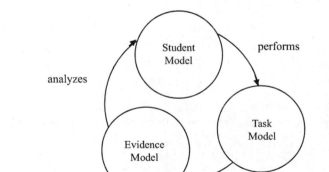

A simple example of the student model can be illustrated by the "objective test," which is admittedly over simplified. In an objective test, the right answers are what an ideal user would answer. A user who knows and can do everything on the test will get all answers correct. The correct answers are the "student model" and are compared to the actual responses of a user to determine a metric distance (e.g., getting 40% correct is further away from the ideal than 90% correct). Since some of the potential answers can be "close but wrong" because they are constructed to distract the user, an analysis can distinguish between the user's guesses, weaknesses in concepts and skills, and right answers. The concept of the student model can be extended to include fuzzy, uncertain, socially determined, and evolving variable configurations, to help deal with situations and kinds of knowledge that are not amenable to objective testing, for example, "soft skills" such as leadership, cultural responsiveness, and forming evidence-based opinions.

In developing simSchool, we created two "student models." This was needed because the concepts we are trying to teach through the game concern how to become better at assessing student learning in a classroom. A good classroom teacher needs to build an accurate mental model—their own private student model—of each of their students. This adds a second layer of complexity (possibly confusion) to the assessment, but we will try to explain. Inside the rule-based artificial intelligence engine of each simStudent, the variables of importance to the teacher's assessment of that student (e.g., emotional and academic variables) have a beginning and current state. The game player can assess how much learning has taken place in the simStudents by comparing the beginning with middle and ending states.

This is similar to what teachers need to do in the real world in order to assess whether a student has learned something from one's teaching. simSchool also makes available variables that are much harder, uncertain, or impossible to track and display in the real world—for example, the emotional stability, extraversion, and intellectual openness of the simStudent. To assess what the user knows and is able to do as a result of playing the game, one of the inferences we want to be able to make is how well the player understands the students and knows what to do to adjust things so that all of them can learn. The simSchool "student model" is thus a picture of how the user develops and uses their own "student model" for each of the SimStudents. This double entendre may not be needed in many assessment plans of games and sims, but is important in assessing many soft skills.

Task Model

The task model is at first glance simply the prompt or challenge given to the user. In general, games and simulations present task situations through a world or project-wide model that contextualizes the game or simulation. The variables associated with the states of the simulated world, objects, and interactive actors collectively represent the potential states of interaction with the user.

But there is another deeper way to look at the task model too. Each situation or task prompt embeds content in the form of theories and assumptions provided by the creators of the game. For example, if there is a ball to pick up, then does it bounce, and if so, does it follow earth gravity or some other rule? In addition to the content assumptions, each task model has other characteristics that impact assessment (Table 1).

Table 1. Example task model characteristics

Prompt or Challenge	How does the game or sim set a context? What is the story line or set-up?
Content	What does the learner need to already know vs. acquire during play in order to succeed?
Validity	What assumptions about the real world are embedded in the game engine's world model?
Performance opportunity	Is relevant performance evidence produced?
Affordance	What does the object, tool, situation allow the user to do that is valid for and maps with the analysis of the evidence?
Rich Picture	Are several kinds and pieces of evidence elicited?
Trustworthiness	Is the user's interaction evidence reliable for making inferences about what they know and can do?
Ideal vs. Real variables	What are the ideal game states for performances that exhibit the knowledge and skills of interest, and how does each user's record compare and change over time?

The job of the task model is to represent the problem space and store and update variables that document how the interactions of the user have impacted the model and changed over time. The variables sent from the task model to the evidence model are more grist for the analysis mill in the evidence model.

Inside the game engine of simSchool, there are currently two forms of tasks faced by each simStudent. There are classroom assignments from and verbal interactions with the user. We plan to add neighbor interactions with other simStudents in the future. The ideal states for maximum learning are tasks that have settings for each variable that are slightly above the current settings of the SimStudent, which can be further enhanced by conversations with a similar profile. When the player understands and applies these facts to improve his or her game score, it reinforces several actions that are central to the main lessons we want the player to get out of the experience—choosing tasks carefully matched to student needs and understanding what kind of supportive interactions students need.

The central challenge for the user, as in all games and sims, is to "figure out how the game engine works," and by doing so, internalize the task model characteristics. Thus, the nature and quality of the task model design determines much of what the assessment can say that the user learned through the game or sim.

Evidence Model

The third stop in the CAF sequence is the evidence model, which contains the inference rules that relate the task and student model variables into an analysis of what the user knows and can do. A simplistic view of the evidence model is that it compares the student model to the current scoring record's storage of variables that were changed by the user's interaction with the task model. The differences are then used to create an output to control new settings and interactions (e.g. new prompts or items in an online testing system, new body positions, attitudes, and language in the simStudents) as well as to characterize the metric distance between what the user has done and what the task called for.

The evidence model specifies analytic conditions and outputs (e.g. a graphic depiction, delivery of messages such as "You've won!" or a narrative about the results of game or sim play) that are called for by clusters of behavioral sequences, timings and game states that are represented in the variables of the student and task models.

In simSchool, a teacher can choose a task that helps some students but causes other students to fail. A key concept of teaching is to understand what needs to change in the task so that the failing students can learn. The evidence model compares what the player actually does with the combination of tasks that would have caused the best results for all simStudents. The analysis engine then prepares scores, narratives, and graphics to help point out what happened, what the failing students needed to have happen, and how it impacted the overall results of the game. More details about this process are described later.

The three elements of the assessment framework—student, task, and evidence models—operate at two levels at least. Level 1 deals with the user experience and the operational level of the models. In the case of a computer-based simulation like simSchool, this amounts to things such as the code, databases, and graphic user interface. Level 2 deals with the evidence-based reasoning that allows us to make inferences from the artifacts of the user's interactions at Level 1. Level 2 reasoning, which we turn to next, allows us to infer what users know and can do based on how they work with and perform in a game or simulation.

Evidence-Based Reasoning

Assessment results are supported by an evidence-based generalization of the scientific method that includes dealing with issues such as observation, inference, and verification. Artifacts made by the user, when observed and classified, become evidence that relate "the particular things students say or do, to what they know or can do as more broadly conceived; that is, in terms that have meanings beyond the specifics of the immediate observations" (Mislevy et al., 2003, p. 1.). Note the Level 1 aspect of the artifact itself a physical object (even if virtual!) and the Level 2 aspect of the "evidence value" of the artifact after it has been classified for use within an assessment context.

Rules of Evidence

Evidence rules classify observables into patterns that can then be used to make inferences or claims about the learner (Figure 2). In both classification and inference there may be fuzzy as well as operationally well-defined rules of evidence present and contributing to the classification or inference. When we say "rules" we mean a set of "If...then..." state-

Figure 2. Rules of evidence

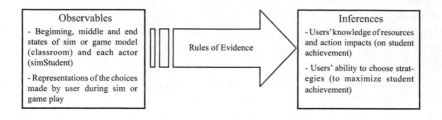

ments that connect patterns or sets of observables into meaningful relationships that allow us to make claims.

Reasoning from evidence in order to support inferences about a learner is grounded in claims about the nature of knowledge for a particular domain, situations that evoke evidence of that knowledge, and how we can connect these to the claims we want to make about learners for the purpose of a particular assessment. This structure of reasoning mirrors the three Conceptual Assessment Framework components, except that the nature of knowledge replaces the student model. In simSchool, among the claims we make about teaching are that one's knowledge of content and how to teach plus one's attitudes or predispositions toward learners influences how one performs as a teacher. We view the simSchool game as an example of someone practicing the skills of teaching and potentially evoking evidence of this knowledge.

All games and simulation assessments that focus on what users have learned have to claim that the evidence created by a user interacting with the application provided realistic evidence of performance in some other context. In other words, it would not be very helpful for an assessment to only be able to say that the learner had learned to "play the game." We want to be able to say that by playing the game, we infer that this user knows and is able to do something in the real world. To create appropriate evidence in simSchool, we place the learner in a classroom of simStudents that evokes or invites realistic behaviors and responses. We then record and classify the responses and artifacts according to our model of teaching. We evaluate the learner's responses against our model of teaching and make judgments about what they know and can do.

In what follows, we attempt to make clear each of these aspects of the relationship of sim-School to the CAF, and by extension how you can use the framework to think about your game or simulation assessment challenges.

simStudents, Users, and the CAF of simSchool

There are two paths we want to follow. In one, the CAF framework is used to analyze the internal alignment of simSchool teaching with its impact on simStudents, and shed light on how the sim models the realities of teaching and classrooms. On the second path, the CAF is the framework by which we can draw inferences about the user's knowledge and abilities as a teacher, and evaluate the validity of our inferences.

To hopefully keep things clear, we will use the term "simStudent" to represent a database profile of a student and "Teacher" or "User" to represent the player who is using simSchool to practice teaching. We want to deal with both analyses, even though there is a chance for some confusion, for two reasons. By focusing on the "simStudents," we can present how the sim embeds theories of instruction, classroom management, learning theory, and psychology aligned with assessment results and other evidence of student learning. By focusing on the Teacher or User, we explain how simSchool can be used as a platform for professional development.

Generalizing to all educational games and sims that want to assess the extent of learning, there will be an internal model of the knowledge and skills intended to be transferred or learned, an interface that leverages important intervention points in the model while representing realistic actions and knowledge needed in an analogous real-world situation, and ways of comparing beginning, middle, and ending states. These data are then used to build a picture of what level of knowledge and skill the user demonstrated. At this point we should be able to answer the question "What did the user demonstrate that they know and can do during this round of play?" There are of course many questions to answer beyond this simplified schema of an assessment. Did the user know these things before playing, or did they develop the knowledge during play? Over how many games did the user's knowledge change and by how much? Were there patterns of change in knowledge such as different speeds of learning under different circumstances? And so on. These kinds of questions require a record of the user that is stored and analyzed over time, but otherwise utilize the same framework we have been developing.

We turn now to the specifics of simSchool as a platform designed to teach teachers, and attempt to continue to draw out generalizable lessons about assessment that might be useful in any educational game or simulation

Level 1: Game Play

At Level 1—the Game Play level—we will explain the internal model of the simStudents and the simulated classroom as a model of instructional planning, teaching, and classroom realities. We will call this the SIMSTUDENT MODEL. It shows how simSchool embeds theories of aligned instruction and assessment, psychology of interpersonal interactions, and cognitive growth. In general terms, this might be thought of as the game world model, the game engine.

We will then focus on a model that we will call the TEACHER MODEL in which the three components of the CAF are intended to build the foundation for making inferences about what the user knows and can do as a teacher. In general terms, this might be thought of as the user model, what we expect users to do while playing the game.

simStudent Model

Table 2 lists the three CAF components (student, task, and evidence models), their definition, and how simSchool basically and broadly embodies the concepts. The definition column is taken from Mislevy et al. (2003). Following the table, we discuss more of the details of each of the framework's models.

Additional Notes About the SIMSTUDENT MODEL

The major factors of the SimStudent personality are independent of one another but can also be clustered or related by rules at different aggregation points. For example agreeableness for working with others and emotional stability operate independently so that a task that requires some emotional risk but does not require social interaction can be differentiated from a similar task in a group context. But when a teacher speaks harshly and in a voice loud enough for the whole class to hear, both factors are impacted as though they are linked.

The representational schema for simStudents is highly flexible, which allows the selection of students for any conceivable school context (e.g., mixtures of race, gender, and performance profiles) and allows a wide range of classroom behaviors. This allows specific teaching strategies and adaptations to be matched for timely, responsive teaching adjustments in special settings such as special education, ESL, low literacy, poverty, within a single class session or across several sessions. Alternative dimensions can be added to the student profile, as needed for particular simulations, for example, learning style, self-perception, and subject-area specifics. There is no limit on the number of dimensions of personality, which in the base game is set at five emotional and one generic academic dimension.

Table 2. Conceptual Assessment Framework for the SIMSTUDENT MODEL

Component Name	Definition	simSchool Features
Student Model (Defines the SimStudent as a personality and learner, how the simStudent "thinks," "learns," and "feels")	Specifies the dependencies and statistical properties of relationships among variables that lead to claims about the knowledge, skills, and abilities of the learner. A scoring record holds the values of those variables at a point in time.	simSchool uses dynamic variables to represent and store simStudent behavior and performance in two broad areas: emotional and academic matters. The state of the simStudent includes representations of each factor as a continuum from –1 to 1, where 0 represents "on grade level" or "the norm" for the factor, 1 is well above, and –1 is well below. The emotional factors are taken from the OCEAN model of personality, also known as the Big Five in personality theory. Academic factors are taken from assessed domains of a subject area (e.g. in mathematics: problem solving, computation, and communication might be used. Or if a finer grain is needed, then specific skills within arithmetic might be used).

Table 2. continued

Task Model (Defines the tasks for the SimStudents determining how they react to the player's choice of tasks and verbal interactions)	Specifies variables used to describe key features of tasks (e.g. content, difficulty), the presentation format (e.g. directions, stimulus, prompts), and the work or response product (e.g. answers, work samples)	simSchool organizes the variables of the task model to map 1:1 with the student model variables (e.g. the specific emotional and academic factors required by a task) and provides an administrative interface to facilitate a variety of settings. Tasks are further organized by Depth of Knowledge levels (Webb, 2002). The task model settings act as "point attractors," causing the student model variables to change over time in the direction of the task model's variables.
Evidence Model (Defines inferences about the simStudents that we want the future teacher to be able to make)	Specifies how to identify and evaluate features of the work or response product, and how to update the scoring record.	Pattern matching routines and relational algorithms are used to compute metric distances between the initial arrays of the student and the arrays of the task and verbal interventions chosen by the teacher. The simsStudents then display by body position and verbal statements how they are doing. If the task is in the sweet spot for learning (what educators call the Zone of Proximal Development) then they stay on task and improve over time. In general there are three ways to get off task; tasks that are completed but then not replaced by other tasks cause "down time;" tasks that are too high to be completed in a reasonable amount of time cause "frustration;" and those that are too low to create a positive learning challenge cause "boredom."

The simsStudents attempt to close the gap between their internal settings and the requirement of the tasks and verbal interventions and if given enough time, will come to rest on the requirements. This approximates student achievement and is made more realistic by the fact that not all of the simStudents can reach those goals in the allotted time of a classroom. Some students reach the task goal too quickly and then get bored; others will take too long to see any improvement and will get frustrated. The challenge for any teacher is getting the balance and mix right so that students remained challenged appropriately for most of the class and do not spend too much unproductive time sitting around.

The "game challenge" in simSchool is that even when many of these variables can be brought up to the surface for monitoring, they are difficult to control. The ideal task for one student is not going to work for all students, and as time marches on in the classroom, everyone can potentially get bored or frustrated. As expertise develops, more of the variables can be hidden, as many of them are in real life, which raises the challenge level.

Teacher Model

Table 3 presents Level 1 issues for the users, for example, teachers who might use simSchool in teacher development programs. The CAF component names and definitions are the same as above, but the analysis of features, rather than outlining how the artificial simStudents learn, points to an evidence-based chain of reasoning needed to make inferences and claims about what the user knows and can do as a teacher.

Table 3. Conceptual Assessment Framework for the TEACHER MODEL

Component Name	Definition	simSchool Features
Student Model (Models the user of the simulation)	Specifies the dependencies and statistical properties of relationships among variables that lead to claims about the knowledge, skills, and abilities of the learner. A scoring record holds the values of those variables at a point in time.	For any selection of simStudents, there are "best choices" of tasks, "best order" of tasks, "best timing" for conversations, and "best attitude" for verbal interactions. These "bests" are generally not repeatable, since the context of the game changes constantly, so the game cannot lead to a simplistic level of "learning the trick" of the game. Instead, the player has to form heuristics and strategies that pay-off most of the time. As the user makes choices of task and talk.
Task Model (Defines the tasks for the user of the simulation)	Specifies variables used to describe key features of tasks (e.g. content, difficulty), the presentation format (e.g. directions, stimulus, prompts), and the work or response product (e.g. answers, work samples).	The player has many options for action, but at the heart of the assessment, there are just two fundamental tasks: matching tasks to students and speaking to students at the right time and in the right ways to help them. Both of these tasks have complex subtask levels, evidence of which is tracked from user movements and stored in a complex time-based scoring record. For example, if the user never "reads" the student profile, we expect to see longer times and inconsistent effects from verbal interactions and more mismatches of classroom tasks.
Evidence Model (Defines inferences about the user of the simulation)	Specifies how to identify and evaluate features of the work or response product, and how to update the scoring record.	Several metrics are used to form a full analysis. For example, total number of simStudents academically gaining and emotionally happy during the lesson, clusters of simStudents and collections of best tasks for each group, specific moment-by-moment timeline graphs that illustrate the impact of player moves. These metrics form sub-analyses that are collected over time and compared with earlier versions, to make inferences about growth of the user.

Level 2: Inferences about the User

A chain of reasoning from Level 1 to Level 2 allows us to make inferences about teaching knowledge. The inferences are based on a claim that a simulated set of typical teaching tasks (making instructional decisions, making adjustments and adaptations during instruction, talking to students) elicits user actions and related artifacts that stand as evidence of knowledge of teaching. The kinds of knowledge that evidence from simSchool game play potentially refers to include:

Knowledge of Students

- Reading and using student records to make instructional decisions
- Pre-planning assessment and instruction to meet individual and group needs
- Observing in-classroom behavior and making inferences about adaptations needed in instruction and assessments

Pre-Planning Instruction

- Knowing what subject one is prepared to teach
- Knowing how many and what kinds of tasks are suited and fit with a subject
- Estimating the number of class sessions needed to teach a particular set of tasks

Making and Using Tasks

- Designing appropriate tasks
- Sequencing tasks for best effect

Making and Using Assessments

- Aligning assessment items to assess a given objective
- Estimating the number of and what kinds of assessment items/measures are suited and fit for a particular set of objectives
- Understanding the data produced by administration of a pre-assessment

Re-Planning Instruction

- Prior to instruction, choosing whole-class instructional strategies based on (aligned with) pre-assessment results

- Prior to instruction, choosing individual strategies based on (aligned with) student records and individual pre-assessment results.

Classroom Decision-Making

- Interpreting in-class performance (on task versus off task behaviors) as academic versus emotional issues
- "Reading" students via participation clues and language
- Speaking to students in effective and appropriate ways
- Grouping students for differentiated instruction
- Adjusting instructional strategies based on in-class performance
- Individualizing tasks
- Focusing talk and discussion on improved student performance

Making and Using a Post-Assessment

- Designing appropriate and aligned test items to assess a given "unit of study" (objectives plus the instructional strategies and adaptations that have occurred during a number of class sessions)
- Estimating the number of and what kinds of assessment items/measures are suited and fit for the unit of study
- Understanding the data produced by administration of a post-assessment

Reflections on Teaching

- Making mental notes (and possibly written records such as grade book notations) about the evolution of a unit of study—the interaction of one's plans with the realities of teaching
- Abstracting and articulating lessons learned from the whole experience

In general, to make a Level 2 claim, there is a mapping of artifacts produced by the evidence model, which aggregates artifacts from the comparison of the student and task models. For example, to make the claim that a user has improved in his or her ability (or now "knows how") to, for example "interpret in-class performance as academic versus emotional issues," we can lookup the current level of the user on several sub-analyses and categorize those levels on a continuum of development (called a rubric in educational assessment). Table 4 shows a partial example of the mapping process for one claim important to simSchool.

The same body of evidence can consistently support multiple claims by clustering parts of the Level 1 evidence into new configurations. For example, evidence of asking a lot of questions of students might show more openness than making a lot of assertions, if everything else is going well. But if the questions are not working to improve student performance, then it is not a good strategy for this particular group of students, and might be a sign of weakness and uncertainty. This points out the ambivalent role of evidence at Level 1. Data is just data. At Level 2, data becomes knowledge with the addition of context that is provided by change over time and point of view applied to various clusters of the data through the "if…then" rules that map the evidence to the claims.

A general rule of assessment is to consider several sources of data when making a claim or assessment decision. The corroborating evidence helps establish the validity of the finding. For knowledge and skills that are complex—such as becoming a skilled teacher—the

Table 4. Example of mapping Level 2 inferences from Level 1 evidence

Level 2 Claims	Level 1 Artifacts	Evidence Model
User knows how to interpret in-class performance as academic versus emotional issues. And so forth [Other claims are proposed to provide a complete picture of the "assessable" knowledge and skills central to the game or sim.]	When a simStudent slumps in the desk: 0—user ignores the student 1—user speaks to the student about their behavior…making an assertion 2—…making an observation 3—…asking a question 4—user speaks to the student about their academic performance…making an assertion 5—…making an observation 6—…asking a question 7—user changes the task, selecting one with more challenge 8—…one with equal challenge 9—…one with less challenge And so forth [Similar lists of artifact options are created for other conditions, such as "When the user selects a task," "When an individual student is grouped with other students," etc.]	Example rules of inference related to the claim include: If the user shows evidence of 0 for most students most of the time, he or she is not exhibiting how to diagnose in-class performance. If the user shows evidence of 1 or 4 and the student does not improve, the user is making assumptions without relating to or understanding the student. If the user shows evidence of 1 or 4 and the student does improve, the user is successful in interpreting in-class performance. If the user shows more evidence of either 1 or 4 with better success as defined above, then if 1, the user interprets behavioral issues or if 4, interprets academic issues more successfully. And so forth [Other Evidence Model sub-analyses are created as rule systems and are used to classify the Level 1 artifacts in clusters that support the Level 2 claims.]

assessment will have many high level claims, supported by a higher number of evidence model rules, that in turn utilize an even higher number of artifacts and artifact clusters. In traditional testing and measurement theory, this structure is described by "item response theory." For assessment in online games and sims, item response theory can be expanded via the CAF to include approaches such as neural net analysis, complex systems theory, semantic Web mechanisms, evidence-based inference, and performance assessment methods. Some of these approaches are explored in other chapters in this book. A full exposition is beyond the scope of this chapter.

Conclusion

Assessing learning in educational games and simulations requires a formalization of familiar everyday reasoning. The assessment of what users know and can do based on artifacts they create involves three basic phases: sizing up the situation based on gathered data, applying some criteria to make inferences that are meaningful to the desired claims and inferences, and then deciding what to do next. The Conceptual Assessment Framework, a broad and flexible way of thinking about assessment possibilities, prompts us to make clear the ideal user model, relationships among the user's actions and states during game play, the affordances of the task model, and the potential inferences we can make from comparing these data sources.

References

Almond, R. G., Steinberg, L. S., & Mislevy, R. J. (2002). Enhancing the design and delivery of assessment systems: A four process architecture. *The Journal of Technology, Learning, and Assessment, 1*(5). Retrieved from http://www.jtla.org

Mislevy, R. J., Steinberg, L. S., & Almond, R. G. (2003). On the structure of educational assessments. *Measurement: Interdisciplinary Research and Perspectives, 1*(1), 3-62.

Webb, N. (2002). *Alignment: Depth of knowledge level definitions.* Retrieved from http://facstaff.wcer.wisc.edu/normw/state%alignment%20page%20one.htm

Chapter XVI

Designing Online Games Assessment as "Information Trails"

Christian Sebastian Loh, Southern Illinois University Carbondale, USA

Abstract

Online retailers make successful use of sophisticated online tracking mechanisms to profile their customers in order to understand their buying habits. Online multiplayer games make use of similar technologies to keep track of gamers' activities, for better management of in-game resources and to settle disputes. However, educators looking to online games as a learning tool lack a similarly powerful strategy to help them reconstruct users' gaming decisions in order to understand the learners and make effective use of games as a teaching/learning tool. Moreover, it is necessary to develop an assessment component for online games to measure its effectiveness, or the return of investment. This chapter outlined a strategy to design the much-needed assessment into online games as "information trails."

Introduction

Follow the White Rabbit. ~ Trinity, *The Matrix* (1999)

The anonymity during the early days of the Internet prompted cartoonist Peter Steiner (1993) to pen, "On the Internet, nobody knows you are a dog." Today, the Internet is far more advanced and far less anonymous than it once was. For example, because Web users expect certain conveniences, like the "Back" and "History" functions, when surfing the World Wide Web (WWW), Web browsers must be sophisticated enough to keep track of the user's online activities. As people click on the Web links to "jump" from one Web page to another, they inevitably leave behind a series of online "footprints" detailing their actions and movements. When harvested from the Web servers, such information becomes the evidence of users' interaction with the WWW services.

The pervasiveness of computing devices, the increasing ownership of personal computers, the near ubiquity of the Internet, and the prevalent use of *cookie* technology have made it easy for Web sites to "remember" and correctly identify every returning visitor (Coleman, 1999). Instead of "blanket marketing" to the once faceless, nameless online customers, retailers can now "target" their online marketing efforts by uniquely profiling each customer based on their browsing behaviors when using the company Web site. The online advertising industry has indicated that they will mine even "more information about individuals" in time to come (Glasner, 2005a). Even though privacy and ethics are legitimate issues, because such information is already being collected of everyone who uses the Internet, the purpose of this chapter is to recommend harnessing the technology rightly for use in education.

The following section presents an overview of online tracking technology, followed by a discussion about online games and education. This is followed by the conceptual framework for the information trail and how the information trail may be designed into games for assessment. Last but not least, a case study using an existing online game is described before the final concluding remarks.

Online Tracking Technology

Tracking Customers in Online Commerce

Peter Drucker (1994) once predicted that an age of "Knowledge Economy" is coming when *knowledge* will become a much sought after and tradable commodity. In today's world, personal data obtained from Web sites' "user registration" (e.g., demographic data, e-mail addresses), Web server logs (e.g., browsers used and IP addresses at time of login), cookies (e.g., categories of merchandise favored, referrer Web sites), and user feedback (e.g., from usability and satisfaction surveys) have all become acceptable sources of revenue. Even virtual game items and monies, such as Linden dollars (currency used in an online game community known as Second Life), are being traded as if they are real commodities (Ackerman, 2004). The knowledge economy has indeed arrived.

Web sites providing just-in-time information (e.g., major newspapers, magazines, and blogs), online commerce sites, and special interest communities are increasingly requiring "user registration" before granting access to their sites. Even though many of these registrations are giveaways—requiring only a valid e-mail address for account activation, others have become subscription-based. Online stores, such as eBay and Amazon, require additional information such as credit card numbers and mailing addresses to facilitate the sales and delivery of their merchandise. These stores also make use of *cookie* technology to identify returning registered users during an online transaction, and to keep track of the merchandise placed in users' online shopping carts.

Advertising firms also employ *cookie* technology in collecting marketing data about Web users' browsing habits and online buying behaviors. Large e-commerce companies have in place elaborate strategies to track users' movement in order to create an accurate profile of their customers—profiles that are likely to include age, occupation, demographic data, IP addresses, and other online traits, such as buying and dining habits, favorite Web-links, chat rooms, movie preferences, and so forth. Done correctly, online profiling can be a valuable tool that allows Web companies to achieve better hit-rates (Glasner, 2005b) and to encourage more online buying through *targeted marketing.*

Amazon.com, the current leader in online tracking technology (Associated Press, 2005a), is known for successfully using its online profiling tool to reach out to its customers. Using sophisticated online tracking technology, Amazon.com monitors its customers' and visitors' online activities by recording the sequences of Web links they click on from the moment they enter the company's Web site until they leave. Accuracy of the customer's profile is maintained and updated each time one makes use of Amazon.com to search for merchandise and make purchases. The liberal use of tracking tactics enables the online retailer to shower its customers constantly with new book recommendations and catalogs of merchandise created just for them! Other online retailers are quickly catching on to Amazon's proven marketing strategy. The explosion of the online music and video market brought about by Third Generation (3G) cellular phones and Apple's iPods will continue to push targeted marketing and online tracking technology to the next level of sophistication. One industry that stands to benefit from all these technological advances is online gaming, for it is also in constant pursuit of new ways to entice more gamers who will pay-and-play.

Avatar Tracking in Online Games

The video game industry has long engaged in information collection, well before the advent of Internet and online games. In the days of DOS games, users' registration records and sales figures from game retailers provided the industry with the customers' information they needed. Because the act of playing already constituted agreement with the terms and conditions set by the game publishers, the extent of information collected during game play (if any) is often undisclosed to the gamers.

The launch of online games played in an online, persistent, virtual world—otherwise known as Massive(ly) Multiplayer Online Games (MMOG)—opened the floodgate to player (or avatar) tracking. In order to ensure smooth game play at all times, the MMOG game engines must not only keep track of the coming and going of a massive number of avatars and what they do during game play, but also what the avatars carry in their inventories, including weapons, armors, gold, quest items, and missions received. Almost all MMOGs required the download of proprietary *game clients* instead of effecting game play within Internet browsers to better control and unobtrusively collect vast amounts of in-game information necessary for dispute resolution, and policing against cheating and loophole exploits. The use of game clients would, of course, grant the game company the legal rights to collect avatars' information throughout the whole duration of the game.

Game consoles, such as the Xbox, made use of unique machine identifiers to pinpoint each sold unit within the network, making it extremely easy for the parent company to monitor gamers' playing patterns. Xbox 360, Microsoft's next generation console, implements a *Gamer ID card* system as part of its new Xbox Live profile, containing gaming feats, trophies, high scores, motto, demographic data, even a player's photograph, for all to see (Game Informer, 2005). The company Web site (http://www.xbox.com/en-US/xbox360/ xbox360console. htm) contained the following information: *"Set up a Gamer Profile, visit the Xbox Live Marketplace, even send voice messages... experience multiplayer games and tournaments, intelligent matchmaking, voice communication... and much more"* (paragraph 4). By capitalizing on the online gamers' need for social interaction with other human players, either to play along with or against one another (Croal, 2002), game publishers have successfully escalated customer information collection and profiling into a desirable gaming experience.

The Business of Video Games and Education

The video game industry predicted that it would eventually outpace the "Internet (advertising), television, radio, motion pictures, music, and newspapers" as the fastest growing industry in the country (Interactive Digital Software Association, 2002). Today, the video game industry is a 10-billion dollar industry. More and more video game players are turning to online games (see Figure 1). Of those who play games online, about 56% are male. Some 34% of the online gamers made use of a wireless device, such as a cell phone or a personal digital assistant (PDA), to play games. About 10% of the total online games played are of the MMOG kind, with an additional 10% being browser-based games using Flash or Shockwave (Entertainment Software Association, 2005; Interactive Digital Software Association, 1999, 2002, 2003).

In the short term, game publishers promised even more Internet-capable games in an attempt to cash-in on the runaway successes of MMOGs (e.g., Lineage and EverQuest) and player-versus-player (PvP) games (e.g., Unreal and Halo). In the longer term, industry driving forces are currently pushing for mobile phone games, to be powered by either Macromedia Flash or Java (more precisely, J2ME), as the next impending wave of change (Trento, 2005; Ward, 2005). Because of its tremendous potentials in economic impact and outreach, the video game has not only captured Hollywood's attention but also that of the academe (Carlson, 2003).

Figure 1. Percentage of gamers who play online games (reported by ISDA & EDA)

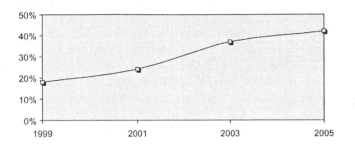

On the education front, the study of the video game is fast maturing into a legitimate academic discipline with more than 50 higher education institutions across the nation offering game-related courses at both the undergraduate and graduate levels (Associated Press, 2005b; Hill, 2005). Several dissertations (e.g.,, Heckel, 2003; Squire, 2004) and books (including this one) (e.g., Aldrich, 2004; Gee, 2003; Prensky, 2001) have been published on various aspects of video games and learning. Other initiatives include the Daedalus Project (http://www.nickycc.com/daedalus/) by Nick Yee, the Education Arcade project (http://www.educationarcade.org/) led by Kurt Squire, and the Game-to-Teach (http://cms.mit.edu/games/education/proto.html) collaboration between Massachusetts Institute of Technology and Microsoft Research.

Educators and researchers have begun the dialogue to discuss the value of "serious play" (Rieber, 1996) in learning, and the potential of games in and for education (Loh, Rieber, Wiley, Van Eck, & Holschuh, 2004). Additional scholarly activities include the initiation for special interest groups (SIGs) within the Association for Educational Communications and Technology (AECT) and American Educational Research Association (AERA) to provide on-going forums for discussion; and professional conferences focusing on video games and learning, including the following: (a) Serious Games Summit, (b) Education Arcade Conference, (c) Games, Learning and Society, (d) the Annual Symposium for Instructional Gaming by AECT, and (e) the International Workshop on Digital Game and Intelligent Toy-based Education (DGTE) by the IEEE Computer Society.

Online Games and Education: Issues

Although there is much potential in using video games for education, and with no shortage of interest, its use in the classrooms, particularly K-12, is still very limited (Rieber, 1996). One problem that received much publicity in the media is, of course, the violence and questionable materials found in certain game titles (e.g., Anderson & Field, 1983; Sherry, 2001), even "E" rated ones (Thompson & Haninger, 2001); which led many researchers and educators to focus on developing more video games that are educationally appropriate (Rosas, Nussbaum, Cumsille, Marianov, Correa, Flores, et al., 2003). However, for many educators, parents, and administrators, he more troubling issue about using games in the classrooms is that of assessment. This is because traditional classroom assessment quantifies student learning through the matching of learning outcomes with indicator-activities stated in the learning objectives. For instance, after a lesson on simple addition, if a child is able to show in some ways—be it verbal, mental calculation, finger-counting, written computation, or correctly choosing the answer from multiple choice (amongst many other assessment methods)—that 13+15 is equivalent to 28, the child is said to have learned how to *add*, particularly if the child was unable to do so before the lesson. Conversely, if the child picked a wrong answer, or was unable to supply the correct answer for whatever reason, the child has failed to demonstrate his or her knowledge in summing 13 and 15. A high rate of failures in one sitting will normally result in the child receiving a poor "test score" for that assessment. Because games are created primarily for the purpose of entertainment, it is almost impossible to design traditional assessment such as the one described above into games without taking out the "fun." Readers are probably well familiar with many early *edutainment* games that had been criticized as pedagogic exercises in disguise (Rosas et al., 2003).

It is imperative that, if and when included, an assessment feature must not detract from the gamers' enjoyment of game play. Yet for the game to be useful for learning, it must have features that will allow teachers to quantify the amount of learning that occurred as the students engage in play! Using online games for learning complicates the design issue with the complexity of technology. Even the task of score keeping within an online environment is a highly elaborated design-level task that requires a lot of pre-planning, often involving a massive and scaleable online database. Even when available online games are already developed with information collection in mind, very little of the information collected can be of use to educators directly because there is no easy (and legal) way of retrieving the in-game data.

Assessment and Online Games

The purpose of assessment is manifold. Most commonly, assessment is carried out by classroom instructors as a means to collect early and frequent feedback from their students for the improvement of teaching and learning, and to prescribe just-in-time remediation if needed. Because assessment can take the form of "any method" (Dietel, Herman, & Knuth, 1991),

it may range from the subjective opinion of a teacher, to a student's blog, to a transcript of students discussion in an Internet chat session, to the test score of a national standardized test. Nevertheless, stakeholders (e.g., parents, principals, school administrators, and policymakers) remain steadfast in viewing *test scores* as the main indicator of learning.

Within a test score-oriented educational culture, setting aside time in the classrooms for (online) games seems ill advised. At best, it will receive a lukewarm support from stakeholders; at worse, it will become an unnecessary burden for classroom teachers who are usually strapped for time to complete stipulated curriculum. If game playing is to receive any support from schools, there will need to be some ways for the educators to record and report on the students' progress when playing games, so as to justify to the stakeholders that gaming is a legitimate way of learning, and not a waste of precious classroom time and resources.

As one begins to consider assessment with online games, it is important to bear in mind that the strength of computer-based assessment still lies very much in repetitive and mechanical tasks, at least at this point in time, meaning it would be *easier* and *faster* for the computer to judge the quality of learners' *choices* (that A is the correct choice) rather than evaluating their *opinions* (why B is not the correct choice, or as good as A). Of course, given the right technology, it is possible for the computer to "record" human interaction as qualitative data for analysis, for example, peer-to-peer chat, after-play blog, thinking aloud, eye movements across the computer screen, and other physiological reactions. Although qualitative data is highly valuable in understanding students' intention and reasoning in making choices within the online games, the data collection and analysis procedure may not be readily assimilated into the information trail conceptual framework. The following section presents the conceptual framework for the *information trail* and its use in assessment with online games.

The Conceptual Framework for Information Trail

If online games must collect information trails for assessment, one must carefully contemplate what kind of in-game data must be collected. More importantly, the incorporation of the information trail should rightly occur in the pre-planning stage (e.g., storyboarding), and never as an afterthought. Using the motion picture *The Matrix* (Silver, Wachowski, & Wachowski, 1999) as an analogy, an instructional game designer (in the role of Morpheus) must carefully plan for the placement of *nodes* (in-game events, e.g., "Follow the white rabbit"), to intrigue and evoke the curiosity of the learners (in the role of Neo) to come along the trail (navigational path) that was predetermined to eventually lead them to the learning objective (discovering what the Matrix is). And as Neo became increasingly immersed in the process of self-discovery, Morpheus would begin to guide him through various learning adventures and mind games. (If only real-world learning were as easy as depicted in the movie: as a direct computer up-link to the brain.)

Trails and Nodes

Consider this scenario: If a child went missing, a detective who was in-charge of the case might enlist the help of specialized agents, such as a canine or a DNA test kit, to uncover scents and hidden clues undetected by human senses at the site of investigation. Based on the broken twigs, torn fabrics, footprints, and other trails left behind by the child, the detective might be able to piece together a likely scenario of what had happened to the child, and even point out the path traveled by the child. The basic idea of the information trail is very similar to virtual detective work and path finding.

Conceptually, the information trail can be defined as a series of agent-detectable *markings* left by another *moving agent* within an information ecology. Operationally, the information trail is the long track of information markings left behind by "people" as they traverse the Internet. Strictly speaking, the *moving agent* is not the human, but his or her online extension. As people traverse the Web, it is their streams of decisions to click on Web links that become the manifestation and representation of their online personas. In the context of games, the moving agents would be the avatars, and nodes are designated areas where special in-game events occur; examples include the Boss room in *Legends of Zelda* series, the (game-saver) typewriter in the *Resident Evil* series, the resurrection altar in *Guild Wars*, and hot-zones such as traps, doors, treasure chests, and others.

Associated with the idea of the trail is the notion of *nodes* (Wheeldon & Levene, 2003), or special points of interest where the moving agent interacts with the information ecology (e.g.,, the many mission-givers in *Dungeon and Dragon Online: Stormreach*). Figure 2 shows a main navigational trail with numerous nodes that divert into (a) unexplored doorways, (b) unexplored pathways (e.g., mission received), (c) dead ends, and (d) new paths that are yet-to-be explored.

Within the context of information trail, nodes are special designated zones that could serve as branching points for new trails. Using *The Matrix* as an example, a node can be a white rabbit tattoo, or the choice of a red or a blue pill. It is the point in time when the players are required to make a choice that could potentially lead them down a different path. Readers who are interested in navigational path finding may want to explore *information foraging theory* (Pirolli & Card, 1999), *information scents* (Chi, Pirolli, Chen, & Pitkow, 2001), and *Web data-mining* (Borges & Levene, 1999).

Figure 2. A navigational path model

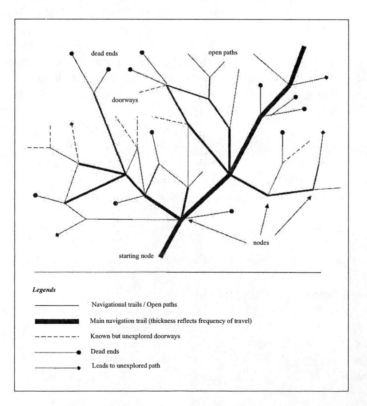

Rethinking Games as Avatar Tracking Systems

Researchers in the field of education are familiar with using Web server logs as assessment tools, and even empirical data for research purposes (e.g., Burton & Walther, 2001; DeBra, 1997; Garrison & Fenton, 1999; Zalane, 2001). Educators interested in using online games for learning need to re-visualize games as avatar tracking systems that allow instructors to better profile players' actions for assessment. An avatar tracking system accessible by educators could help:

- Create better profiles of learners.
- Track how often learners interact with the learning materials (in this case, the online game).
- Assess students' learning based on their achievement in the games.
- Collect quantitative and qualitative data about the students' learning behavior,
- Document meaningful data about the students' learning style.
- Retrieve performance indices of learners based on their interaction with the game-based learning objectives.
- Reward appropriate learner behavior with *free* in-game tokens, such as trophies, badges, special armors, extra lives, and so forth, for all to see.
- Understand student trends of thought and weaknesses to take or suggest appropriate remedial actions.

Depending on the learning and teaching philosophy behind the online game, the information trail can range from:

a.   Open-ended and non-linear (constructivist approach) to close-ended and completely linear (instructivist approach),

b.   Hands-on manipulation (such as virtual frog or virtual chemical lab) to hands-off observation (watching a colony of ants or pre-recorded media),

c.   Guided approach (with virtual mentor and pedagogic agent) to free roaming (exploratory), and,

d.   Team-based game play (collaborative learning) to single player mode (individualistic).

Games as Learning Systems

While the demarcation between game and simulation is not always clear (Gredler, 1996), they are treated as the same in this chapter. Every game has a goal, and it is the learner's prerogative to learn the rules and activities depicted, either to play the game or to operate the simulator. In a first person shooter (FPS), the ability to kill all moving targets, and at the same time to stay alive, is one of the major goals of the game. In many FPS games, the player's goal is to train up to the point where he or she is strong and agile enough to defeat the Boss and win the game. In online games, such as EverQuest, players' goals can be short term, as in defeating the dragon in tonight's campaign, or long term, as in becoming the Guild Master with 300 guild memberships. Therefore, most games are in essence *closed* learning systems (as a truly open gaming system with no clear in-game goal is likely to result in many confused and frustrated players).

If games are regarded as closed learning systems, then the players may be viewed as learners within the systems (i.e. learning agents interacting with the rules within a finite system). How do developers of the games assess the efficacy of the players, or learners of the game system? Because (electronic) games are programs of some sort, mathematics is involved. A winning scenario is a set of fulfilled conditions, most frequently determined by the values of game variables and formulas. For example, suppose in a game, two players, taking on the roles of a paladin and a dragon, engage in a battle. If the life point reaches 0 for the dragon, but is greater than 0 for the paladin, then the dragon avatar loses and the paladin avatar wins.

Game makers planning to incorporate the information trail must first consider what information needs to be monitored during game play before developing the game. Because "storyboarding" is the stage where game flow is commonly decided, it is rightly the place to decide information capturing as well. The instructional designer will need to discuss *event hooks* with script/story writers to plan for adequate tracking to happen. For example, if in a game about the Solar System, the blue ball is taken to mean the Earth, and Sarah picking up the blue ball is taken to mean, "Sarah recognizes the Earth is blue when viewed from outer space," then the action of picking the blue ball is the event hook. The hook is attached to the online database in such a way that when Sarah, the avatar, picks up the blue ball, the event would trigger a value change in the variables associated with "recognizing the Earth is blue" from null to yes, or (0) to (1).

In programming parlance, variables are normally written like this: *myFirstVariable*. Several words that describe the variable are meshed into one word, with the first word beginning in small letter, and subsequent words in capital letters, for easy reading. This is *yetAnotherExample*. Using Tetris as the example, several game variables must first be initialized (or set to 0) whenever a gamer begins a new game, including (a) *score*, (b) *highScore*, (c) *startTime*, (d) *endTime*, (e) *level*, (f) *userName*, amongst many others. The value of some variables, such as *score* and *level*, may change or increase with the passage of time, while others, such as *highScore* and *userName*, will need to be entered when the winning (or losing) scenario is reached. Variables may exist singly, or in an array. The *hallOfFame*, for example, comprises of an array of variables, in sets of two (*playerName* and *highScore*), denoted in the following format:

```
hallOfFame { playerName1, highScore1;
        playerName2, highScore2;
        playerName3, highScore3;
        playerName..., highScore...; }
```

Depending on the purpose of the game, different variables may need to be added, or programmed to behave differently. In a game scenario where the player's team must defend a position for five minutes against an onslaught of enemies (as in Command and Conquer) or non-player characters (NPC), it may be necessary to include *countdownTimer*, *gameOver*, *lifePlayer*, *lifeNPC*, and *winCondition* variables as part of the code, which can look like:

```
countdownTimer = 5 x 60;  (as number of seconds or milliseconds)
lifePlayer = 500;
lifeNPC = 50000; (may also be expressed as arrays of characters)


If
  { lifePlayer = 0; then gameOver = true; }


If

  { countdownTimer = 0; AND lifePlayer ≠ 0; then winCondition = true; }


else

  { gameOver = true; }
```

As suggested by the above algorithm, there can only be one condition for winning: the player must still be alive (*lifePlayer* ≠ 0) when time limit is over (*countdownTimer* = 0). Different programmers may, of course, choose to name their variables differently, or use a vastly different algorithm to reach the end goal. It is suffice to note that a discussion about game programming is beyond the scope of this chapter. Nevertheless, readers should reckon that all computer and video games consist of information collection schemes and that these schemes must be thought out carefully by the developers—even in games as simple as Tic-Tac-Toe and Tetris. In an educational setting, such schemes must be carefully designed for close matching between learning objectives and performance indicators.

Designing Assessment into Games

As stated earlier, educators and researchers must carefully consider the in-game data to be collected so that the information trail laid down can later be used as evidence for assessment. A carefully designed avatar tracking process will open the door for educational assessment in online games. When designing online games for instruction, it is important for educators to work with game developers and instructional technologists to incorporate appropriate learning objectives into the games. The general lack of successful instructional games might well be an indicator of how difficult the process really is. For the assessment system to work, one should design the system "from the very start around the inferences one wants to make, the observations one needs to ground them, the situations that will evoke these observations, and the chain of reasoning that connects them" (Mislevy, Steinberg,

Breyer, Almond, & Johnson, 2002, p. 364). Online games need to be carefully designed and developed with pre-planning to incorporate information trails as the means to game assessment, embedding event hooks for data collection, and user tracking at the appropriate nodes, if they are to be of use for instruction.

Having considered the pedagogic and technological consideration (Salen & Zimmerman, 2004), a game should also be fun to play (Koster, 2005). It is important that educators be mindful of the literature on the impact of motivation on learning and instructional design (e.g., Csikszentmihalyi, 1975; Keller, 1987; Keller & Suzuki, 1988), and to seriously consider including the element of fun in game development. Many educators' handbooks and educational textbooks actually refer to games as "activities," which has resulted in many "edutainment" titles in the past. A game is necessarily more than just an activity (Loh & Botturi, 2005) because a game that is not fun to play is doomed to fail.

Apart from being fun to play, an instructional game must allow an instructor to assess the learners. While it is fairly easy for programmers to create games that will generate much data, instead of simply performing data dumps, an instructional game designer must consider what *useful* information is. Many good programmers pride themselves in elegant programming—using the least amount of code to do the job efficiently—and refrain from GIGO, or "Garbage In, Garbage Out." In other words, unnecessary codes should be eliminated (or better yet, never introduced) so that the program will operate optimally.

"Follow the White Rabbit"

In software development, a typical programming workflow would include (a) analyzing the problem, (b) deconstructing the problem into appropriate data flow diagrams, (c) outlining the algorithm in the data flow diagram with *pseudocodes* (written in structured English for describing the problem), (d) testing for proof-of-concept, (e) code writing (programming), (f) testing and revising. Games programmers follow a similar workflow, but must additionally have a good understanding of *data representation*, or the ability to represent game world or levels using data structure.

The field of instructional technology makes use of a very similar instructional design (general) model known as ADDIE, which encompasses Analysis, Design, Development, Implementation, and Evaluation, for the design and development of instructional materials. Instructional technologists interested in developing online games for instruction will need to transfer their skills from task analysis to game flow analysis, as well as to translate learning objectives into learning nodes in the online games. Each learning task may contain a series of *nodes* (white rabbits) within the game information ecology for the embedding of an information collection mechanism (see Figure 2). An *instructional game designer* will carry out the following design tasks:

a.   Analyze the instructional or learning problem at hand.

b.   Break down the overall learning problems into achievable and measurable objectives using data flow diagrams.

c.   Consider the pedagogic dimension (Reeves, 1997) of each objective to establish a close-match with the game design.

d.   Design and outline the algorithm using pseudocode.

e.   Test for proof-of-concept using storyboard.

f.   Develop the instructional game in-house (or farming-out the development job).

g.   Usability and *beta* test.

h.   Design a teacher interface for the extraction of player progress report.

i.   Implement the instructional game and collect feedback from players and instructors for evaluation.

j.   Revise the game if necessary, plan for new or additional features in future release.

Extracting the Information

Having developed the game with the concept of the information trail, how does one go about retrieving the data? Moreover, what does the collected data tell us about the players? Let us consider two fictitious first grade classrooms where students are learning to distinguish the colors Red, Green, Blue, and White. In the first classroom, Mrs. Jones has decided to assess the learning of her students by asking them to group objects with similar colors together. For every attempt that was performed correctly, her students will receive a score in her score sheet. The teacher of the second classroom, Miss Lee, has instead chosen to use an online version of Bejeweled (http://zone.msn.com/en/bejeweled/) as the assessment tool.

When Miss Lee introduced the game in class, she allowed each student 15 minutes to practice using the game. She then provided the students with the Web site so that they may access the online game from home: to practice grouping objects of similar colors together. She also distributed a unique pair of user IDs and passwords to each of her students, and cautioned them to keep the password confidential and to not share it with anyone else. Now, Miss Lee can distinguish each of her students by name instead of allowing the students to access the online Bejeweled Web site anonymously.

Conceptually, there is no difference between the two assessments because students from both classes are asked to recognize and group objects of similar shape and color together. However, operatively, while Miss Jones applies a scoring rubric whenever Tim correctly matches white circles together, Miss Lee may have a problem expressing the criteria of her assessment and interpreting Johnny's online Bejeweled score as evidence of learning to the principal or to Johnny's parents, even though it is conceivable that Johnny must also exercise strategy planning skills in playing the online game and has consequently demonstrated more "learning" than Tim. Administrators and parents are likely to want answers to some of the following questions:

- How many times did Johnny attempt the matching assessment?
- How many colors were used in the assessment for Johnny?
- How many times did Johnny correctly perform a match?

- How many times did Johnny incorrectly perform a match?
- Did Johnny receive any remedial instruction on the matching task?
- How often did Johnny make use of remedial materials?

Although the answers to the questions listed above can be found among the many variables used within the game, it would be nearly impossible for Miss Lee to extract the information directly from the commercial version of Bejeweled. However, suppose that Miss Lee's brother, Nathan, is the programmer of the online version of Bejeweled; she may request that a special extraction program (teacher interface) be developed to allow her to "read" certain in-game variables and use them to compile a "progress report" for each of her students (Table 1 showed the report for Johnny). This report may further be accessed by administrators, and Johnny's parents, and may contain Johnny's ranking in the "Hall of Fame," rate of improvement, and bonus awards received, if any.

An administrator who reads the report (Table 1) can easily deduce that Johnny was first introduced to the online game in class on June 5 (Monday), when he played for 15 minutes from 9:10 am to 9:25 am. During the week, Johnny spent a total of 430 minutes on the online game, which amounted to 36 rounds of playing. It was rather obvious that Johnny's usual login time was around 8:00 pm, perhaps after dinner and before his bedtime. His biggest improvement occurred on Day 3, when he spent 75 minutes on "beating" the game and nearly doubled his score from the day before. Over the week, his achievement score improved greatly from an initial 20% to the final score of 87.5%. Because Johnny appeared to have some difficulty in telling the color red from the color green (consistent lower combined scores than

Table 1. A 'mock' progress report for Johnny D. Smith (Johnny)

Name of student: Johnny D. Smith				ID: Johnny			Teacher: Anne Lee			
Login Log for the week: June 5-11, 2005										
Day	Login	Logout	Time spent	Round	Scores					
					Red	Blue	Green	White	Total	Final Grade
June 12	7.27 pm	8.47 pm	80 min	9	69/90	89/90	72/90	85/90	315/360	87.5%
June 12	9.01 am	9.58 pm	57 min	4	28/40	36/40	25/40	33/40	122/160	76.3%
June 11	8.05 pm	8.48 pm	43 min	5	32/50	40/50	40/50	38/50	150/200	75.0%
June 10	8.05 pm	8.55 pm	50 min	3	16/30	28/30	18/30	23/30	85/120	70.8%
June 9	8.22 pm	9.07 pm	45 min	3	18/30	22/30	15/30	20/30	75/120	62.5%
June 8	8.08 pm	9.23 pm	75 min	6	30/60	40/60	31/60	43/60	144/240	60.0%
June 7	8.05 pm	8.35 pm	30 min	2	4/20	10/20	6/20	10/20	30/80	37.5%
June 6	8.15 pm	8.35 pm	20 min	2	6/20	10/20	6/20	10/20	16/80	20.0%
June 6	5.20 pm	5.35 pm	15 min	1	2/10	3/10	2/10	3/10	10/40	25.0%
June 6	9.10 am	9.25 am	15 min	1	2/10	3/10	1/10	2/10	8/40	20.0%

blue and white), Miss Lee recommended Johnny for an optical check-up and subsequently discovered that he was suffering from a very mild case of red-green color-blindness. Miss Lee's innovative use of the online game for learning gained her the approvals she needed from the parents and her principal.

"Useful" Data

Having enjoyed the success of the online Bejeweled, Miss Lee decided to ask her brother, Nathan, to add even more features to the online game system. Miss Lee learned from Nathan that the online game contained numerous variables. Nathan insisted that as a trained professional, she must decide what variables are meaningful to her and therefore, should be extracted for use in the reports.

After careful consideration, she asked that the following weekly report be created (see Table 2) in addition to the progress reports she already received. Nathan was able to create the following report using information retrieved from the online game's Web server log. Armed with the report, Miss Lee was able to skim through the data and use it to help her revise her teaching strategy and monitor her students' usage of the online games as weekly learning tasks.

At a glance from the report summary, Miss Lee knew that 10 of her 12 students had logged in at least once for the week, except Timmy55 and Lucy98. Miss Lee took note that this

Table 2. A customized report by Miss Lee that was extracted from the Web Server log

Date	IP Address	Location	Login Time	Logout Time	User ID	YTD Log-in
6-7-2005	122.52.6.156	CompLab1	9.12am	9.38am	Johnny	326 min
6-7-2005	122.52.6.152	CompLab1	9.15am	9.32am	SusanD	733 min
6-7-2005	122.52.6.154	CompLab1	9.13am	9.39am	Tom34	287 min
6-7-2005	122.52.6.134	CompLab2	9.00am	10.00am	LeeAnn	476 min
6-7-2005	122.52.2.100	Library	11.12am	11.50am	Johnny	364 min
6-7-2005	166.44.26.10	Public	1.12pm	1.50pm	NancyP2	60 min
6-7-2005	166.210.34.15	Public	4.05pm	5.10pm	Rq662	138 min
6-7-2005	122.52.2.138	Library	5.12pm	6.14pm	Jones	24 min
6-7-2005	138.24.99.111	Public	9.12pm	9.54pm	Johnny	406 min
Etc...	Etc...	...	...	...	...	...
Summary:						
Total number of students: 12			Student with 0 time: Timmy55, Lucy98			
Highest frequency: SusanD			NewUser: Jones (added on June 7 2005)			
Etc...						

week's highest login award went to SusanD, and made a note to e-mail SusanD with an unlock code to a special in-game bonus token. She would have to send Timmy55 and Lucy98 a reminder to "login and have fun," a much better alternative to "Remember to do your homework." Miss Lee recalled that some of her students were opposed to playing the online games when she designated them as "homework."

Just last week, Miss Jones, a fellow first-grade senior teacher, had requested to be added as a user to Miss Lee's online game system, so that she, too, could find out about using online games as a learning tool in her class. Miss Lee observed that Miss Jones had accessed the Web site from the school library, on June 7, 2005, at 5:12 pm. Miss Lee smiled when she noticed one of the parents, RQ662, had logged in for the first time. Miss Lee hopes NancyP2's dad will become one of her strong supporters in using online games for learning.

Extending the Gaming Idea

During one of the staff meetings, some other teachers had asked Miss Lee if her brother could customize the online Bejeweled, to allow for the following:

a.   Teacher modifiable conditions

- Miss Jones would like to modify the game condition for her students who were targeted for remediation—for example, student A's online game session would contain 30% more Red and Green gems than other students.

- Mr. Roland would like to reward a few of his students—who have attempted over and beyond what they were asked to do—with special in-game tokens. For example, one of his students practiced some 300 rounds and raised her achievement score from 15% to 95% in seven days. He would like to award the student with a special in-game item not obtainable elsewhere to give her due recognition, and at the same time, make playing the online game more fun and rewarding.

Miss Lee's 1st grade students have the following requests:

b.   Student modifiable conditions

- Instead of the 16x16 grid, Tim would like to play a more challenging game using a bigger grid of 25x25.

- Mary would like the online game to use only pastel-colored gems, and she would specifically like them to be Pink, Baby Blue, Lilac, and Aquamarine.

- "Quick-finger" Jason would like his session of the game to carry a shorter response time so he will feel more challenged.

- "Painter" Joe preferred to see real gemstones instead of the current graphics used in the game. He has asked his father to scan photographs of real gemstones to help make the gems look more realistic, which prompted Nathan to add a "skin" feature for the online game

- Two students who play Pokémon on GameBoy Advance (GBA) have requested a head-to-head feature where two players can compete simultaneously on-screen.

- Having visited DirectSong's Web site (directsong.com), Johnny would like to replace the background music of the online game with his collection of music from his favorite anime.

A Superintendent who was present at the staff meeting immediately recognized the potential of the system, and requested that Nathan expand the database to include:

- Names of teachers
- Names of schools
- Names of school district
- Names of states
- Difficulty level of the game
- Subject categories
- Game ratings by teachers
- Game ratings by students
- Amount of time taken in playing the game
- Calculation of difficulty quotient: % of accuracy/time taken to play
- Feedback

The Superintendent was convinced that he could bring this game system to the rest of the classrooms within his school district and had decided to apply for external funding to set up a game server to better manage and analyze all the information collected.

While Miss Lee, Nathan, and the first grade students are all fictional characters, it is indeed possible for the video game developers to create "thin-client" versions of popular MMOGs that fit the educational context. These games can be less complex and smaller in scope, with simplified missions that allow the incorporation of classroom learning objectives and authentic learning tasks. Most importantly, these games must provide instructors with the necessary access into in-game database for extraction of useful information as evidence for assessment. Readers interested in making sense out of complex data for assessment may want to further explore the area of *Network-based Assessment* (Gibson, 2003) and *Evidence-center Assessment* (e.g., Mislevy et al., 2002).

Other Considerations

Implementing online games for learning is not a bed of roses. There will certainly be issues to be contended with, such as the issue of privacy. Privacy policy will need to be drawn up to detail how information is collected and intended for use within the system and to obtain special consent from parents' or guardians of children under 13 years old. Can the information tracked and collected be disclosed, under what circumstances, and to whom? What security systems must be put in place to safeguard the information collected? Since the avatar data collected are likely be stored in an online database, it would be prudent to keep in-game variables apart from identifiable personal information to avoid corruption of database and to protect the hacking of online database and ensuing identity thefts.

Education assessment has always been plagued by cheating, online games notwith-standing. Because games can be a very powerful motivator, educators must guard their students from becoming *grade obsessive*—placing undue importance in test scores and grades (Romanowski, 2004), another common rationale for classroom cheating. Interestingly, when the games become too challenging, many players would resort to cheating in order to "beat the system." It would do well for educators to work with the MMOG developers in the video game industry to control and minimize this problem.

Case Study: Experiencing "Guild Wars"

This section presents a case study using a commercial off-the-shelf online game called Guild Wars, to walk the readers through some of the salient points in this chapter, including avatar tracking in online games, nodes and navigational paths, and possible ways of incorporating information trails. One of the unique features of Guild Wars is the abolishment of the monthly subscription fee commonly associated with MMOGs. This feature could help to extend the number of players engaging in a multiplayer online universe, possibly into some classrooms. The author will describe some of his first-hand experience of GW and suggest what an educational version of GW might be like with information trails embedded into the game for assessment of learning.

Pre-Game Avatar Tracking

After installing the game, a would-be player was shown the "Registration" screen. Several posts of breaking news and updates were shown, followed by a warning as follows:

> *Warning: If you download Guild Wars add-ons like bots, skill calculators, etc., you're likely to have your account stolen. These programs often contain key-loggers that capture passwords and cannot be detected by virus-scanners.*

This was interesting because it once again attested to the reality of the Knowledge Economy and the increasing trend of information tracking and capturing in the online world. Would the "stealers" of game accounts be referred to as *information rogues*, or *terrorists*?

The registration screen was followed by an "Enter Address" screen with the following message:

> *Enter your Mailing Address*
>
> *Regulations in many countries require that we ask you for your mailing address.*

One wonders which countries would require the mailing addresses of online players, and under what regulations? Besides, how could the "law enforcers" from these countries ensure the mailing addresses were not bogus information?

This was then followed by the "Enter E-mail" screen, which concluded the registration process. The user received the following message, somewhat akin to a privacy statement:

> *We will send a message containing your account information to this address.*
> *We will never send you spam, and we will never sell or distribute your e-mail*
> *address.*

Compared with the mailing address, an e-mail address is more likely to be authentic, especially if gamers are expecting to receive a confirmation e-mail from the game company. The IP address of the computer used in registration is likely to be logged at this point, and would be tagged with the registrant's e-mail address as well as the serial number of the game. This information is, no doubt, used for user verification and to prevent game owners from creating more than four avatars per account. While IP address alone may not be hard evidence enough against a player, one copy of the game being used at multiple IP addresses is a highly suspicious activity and may flag the player's account for monitoring.

In-Game Avatar Tracking

After successful registration and login using an appropriate ID and password, a player's avatar would magically appear outside a town where Sir Tydus was to be found. The Ascalon kingdom is at war with the Charr, and Sir Tydus' charge is to recruit brave warriors to Ascalon's defense. However, before Sir Tydus would receive the player into the academy, a player must first receive some basic training. This is akin to a tutorial that helps the player become familiar with the game mechanics. Special in-game trainers might be found in strategic locations to offer missions to the players for level advancing. Every successful mission accomplished would unlock certain dormant skills to give each player a unique combination of skills and to make him or her strong enough to join Sir Tydus for some "real adventures."

One can find "Collectors" in almost every town. These Collectors would ask for a specific number of items (e.g., three fins, four bake husks) in exchange for special in-game items. Many of these items are found only in specific locations, such as on a riverbank, or up on a hill. The "Collector" mission is highly suitable for a simulative classroom because students who are interested in getting the special items from the Collectors must learn how to count. Moreover, they must also learn how to read, and additionally be able to recognize the items of interest. Such skills are also useful in science (recognition of plants and animals) and geography (map reading and topography).

A little girl named Gwen can be found on the outskirts of the first town. If spoken to, Gwen would ask the player to retrieve a lost flute. She enjoyed receiving small gifts, including "small girl's cape" and "red iris flowers," obtainable at the local market and the open field, respectively. A simulative classroom for young children may make use of non-violent missions such as these to teach younger learners the value of friendship, art, music, counting, reading, and even trading. On the other hand, adult players are likely to prefer the hack-and-slash missions for character advancement.

Identifying Nodes and Navigation Paths

All "named" objects within a game are potential *markers* for *information trails*. In GW, for example, merchants, collectors, Sir Tydus, monsters, and even the "red iris flower" are *markers*. Some markers can be designated as *nodes*, or points of interest along the information trail. These nodes are easily identified because they often become congregation sites for game players. In GW, for example, important merchants are often surrounded by a large group of players who are trying to barter for merchandise.

Some *nodes* can be doorways to different sections of the game world, and may be activated by certain events, such as the completion of a special mission, or achievement of a particular level. These *nodes* may also provide clues to the next checkpoint (finding new nodes). In GW, players who have completed a mission are often required to return to the mission-giver for "experience points." Mission-givers (like Sir Tydus) may then redirect the players to a new section of the game by unlocking hidden abilities/special game items or assigning players with a new mission. Similarly, unique mission agents may be used to direct students to a different part of the game world by their class number, level of achievement, school district, subject of interest, ability, learning style, and other suitable criteria. Students can spawn multiple adventures using avatars "designed" for specific guilds, complete with interesting names such as Language and Poet Society, Chemist Clan, Guild of Traveling Bards, and Miss Lee's Little Lion Cubs.

Teacher's Interface

Instructors will need a special "interface" to extract and compile the information trails for *assessment* purposes. The interface should also be simple to use, probably a database-driven online form, by which different pre-formatted templates will be made available to different groups of consumers, including students, teachers, administrators, and parents.

Much like Miss Lee's special reports (e.g., Tables 1 and 2), the purpose of the interface is to enable instructors to easily interpret in-game markers as empirical data for gamers' behaviors and achievement. In that way, even teachers who do not understand how the information trail works will still be able to call up a student's progress report in a moment's notice, without ever needing to know any computer coding or programming.

Game Guilds and Qualitative Research

While many online games have groups (loosely referred to as guilds, or clans) that enlist players for various missions and adventures, GW is unique in the way it implements *guilds*. Players in GW can form their own guild, just as they create their in-game characters or avatars. One guild member is identifiable from another by the color of the capes they wear, as well as the emblem of the Guild (much like use of logo and colored uniforms in competitive sports). Total strangers, colleagues, classmates, close friends, and even family members can login to GW simultaneously to journey as a group. Over time, the sharing of life experiences as a group affords the guild members a sense of camaraderie previously not possible in standalone games.

The Guild feature is useful for collaborative learning using learning tasks that range from pair-work, to small group, to an entire class (guild) of students. It will be possible for qualitative researchers to put on the guise of a player in order to become *participant observer* in a guild (Papargyris & Poulymenakou, 2005), or to play alongside the players in the role of a tutor or a master in order to collect rich data, or in the role of a comrade to triangulate certain observations. Educators finally have a viable context to embody the "sage on the stage" with "a guide by the side," effectively switching between constructivist and instructivist teaching styles at will.

Conclusion

It has been predicted that the imminent Semantic Web and its intelligent agents will bring great changes to our lives (Berners-Lee, Hendler, & Lassila, 2001). Judging by today's Internet technology, one can only expect that more information trails will be left behind by users, with more sophisticated tracking tools made available to track even more customer information. In order for the software agent technology of the Semantic Web to be effective, user profiles may have to be integrated into the Semantic Web altogether. Hopefully, knowledge peddling will be brought under control, with the information being accessible only by authorized software agents.

The advent of agent technology will make online games even more elaborate, with realistic non-player agents acting as gatekeepers of game flow. Using online games in traditional classrooms for daily teaching and learning is not inconceivable. Unless researchers begin to think of games as avatar tracking systems, and unless researchers consider the information they could collect and track for the purpose of assessment, it will be difficult to use games directly in the classroom as a legitimate learning tool.

As I conclude this chapter, I would like to revisit the role-playing game that started it all, Dungeons & Dragons. Invented by Gary Gigax in the 1970s, and named after a dodeca-hedral (twenty-sided) dice, the "D20 game system" successfully attracted players from different backgrounds for 30 years (King & Borland, 2003). Because D&D was created for the tabletop (before the advent of computer), a Dungeon Master (DM) had to first design a game world on paper and then lead a group of adventurers on a game "campaign." Every event that happened during the campaign was a combination of chance (dice throwing) and the story-weaving ability of the DM. Due to the chance element of the game, sometimes the turn of events within the campaign made the imaginary play too hard or too easy, result-ing in players losing interest. Hence, a DM had the power to referee the game to keep the story going and the adventure interesting and fun for the players. Referee actions included rewarding players with special items, introducing calamity, adding more monsters, and subplots—essentially doing whatever was necessary to balance the game play.

Teachers may eventually take on the role of DMs in educational online games and lead their students on weekly game campaigns to conquer new lands, slay dragons, rescue princesses, and learn mathematical and scientific formulas. Certainly a DM can also choose to lead a team on a *picnic* campaign to identify species of flowers and to count the number of *Bufo americanus* (frog) found. While it is perfectly acceptable to use a world created by others, as not all DMs can design game worlds, it is a requirement that DMs be good story-weavers. Similarly, teachers must design (the learning tasks) and lead the game campaign (conduct learning activities) within the online game world created by game programmers and designers. Teachers must be given the power as DMs to *reward* and *punish* gamers with in-game items or events, with the purpose to balance the learning experience for players. Although a DM toolkit is already available with the RPG game NeverWinterNight (http://www.gamespot.com/pc/rpg/neverwinternights/review.html), there is yet to be any report on educational research with the DM toolkit.

The *information trails* left by gamers will provide a DM with the gamers' statistics, revealing their strengths and weaknesses. It is the DM's prerogative to raise the gamers' abilities with appropriate *side* missions, so that the players can survive the ultimate challenge and win the campaign. While some D&D campaigns can be notoriously difficult to win, a good DM's responsibility is to ensure that every player has a wonderful time of adventuring. One expects no less from a teacher. Even as D&D seeks to reinvent itself with MMOG (http://www.ddo.com), it is time for classroom teaching and learning to do the same by closely examining online games for pedagogical ends.

Note

The author has been awarded a Faculty Seed Grant of $20,000 in May 2006 to being work on the "Information Trails for Game Assessment" project. More information is available at the Collaboratory for Interactive Learning Research (CILR) Web site, http://idt.siu.edu/cilr.

Acknowledgment

I would like to thank Kane Gilmour for his help in reading the drafts and providing feedback.

Reference

Ackerman, K. (2004, August 24). *Linden lab and transactions in second life*. Retrieved June 18, 2005, from http://www.frictionlessinsight.com/archives/2004/08/linden_labs_and_html

Aldrich, C. (2004). *Simulations and the future of learning: An innovative (and perhaps revolutionary) approach to e-learning*. San Francisco, CA: Pfeiffer.

Anderson, D. R., & Field, D. (1983). Children's attention to television: Implications for production. In M. Meyer (Ed.), *Children and the formal features of television* (pp. 56-96). Munich, Germany: Saur.

Associated Press. (2005a, March 27). *Amazon knows who you are*. Retrieved June 10, 2005, from http://www.wired.com/news/ebiz/0,1272,67034,00.html

Associated Press. (2005b, September 23). *A generation of game boys, girls*. Retrieved September 26, 2005, from http://www.wired.com/news/culture/0,1284,68964,00.html

Berners-Lee, T., Hendler, J., & Lassila, O. (2001, May 17). The Semantic Web. Retrieved June 14, 2005, from http://www.sciam.com/article.cfm?articleID=0004814410-D2-1C70-84A9809EC588EF21

Borges, J., & Levene, M. (1999, August 15). *Data mining of user navigation patterns*. Paper presented at the WEBKDD'99 Workshop on Web Usage Analysis and User Profiling, San Diego, CA.

Burton, M. C., & Walther, J. B. (2001). The value of Web log data in use-based Web design and testing. *Journal of Computer-Mediated Communication, 6*(3). Retrieved June 7, 2005, from http://www.ascusc.org/jmc/vol16/issue3/burton.html

Carlson, S. (2003, August 15). *Can grand theft auto inspire professors?* Retrieved June 18, 2005, from http://chronicle.com/weekly/v49/i49/49a03101.htm

Chi, E. H., Pirolli, P., Chen, K., & Pitkow, J. (2001, March 31-April 4). *Using information scent to model user information needs and actions on the Web*. Paper presented at the SIGCHI '01, Seattle, WA.

Coleman, G. (1999). *Online tracking: How anonymous is the Internet?* Retrieved June 10, 2005, from http://www.slais.ubc.ca/courses/libr500/fall1999/www_presentations/g_coleman/

Croal, N. G. (2002, November 25). *Sims family values*. Retrieved June 10, 2005, from http://www.msnbc.msn.com/id/3070145

Csikszentmihalyi, M. (1975). *Beyond boredom and anxiety: The experience of play in work and games*. San Franscisco, CA: Jossey-Bass.

DeBra, P. M. E. (1997). Teaching through adaptive hypertext on the WWW. *International Journal of Educational Telecommunications, 3*(2), 163-180.

Dietel, R. J., Herman, J. L., & Knuth, R. A. (1991). What does research says about assessment. Retrieved June 8, 2005, from http://www.ncrel.org/sdrs/areas/stw_esys/4assess.htm

Drucker, P. (1994). The age of social transformation. *The Atlantic Monthly, 274*(3), 53-80. Retrieved June 8, 2005, from http://www.theatlantic.com/election/connection/ecbig/soctrans.htm

Entertainment Software Association. (2005). *Essential facts about the computer and video game industry*. Washington, DC: Entertainment Software Association.

Game Informer. (2005, May). Microsoft talks next Xbox. *Game Informer, 15*(145), 19.

Garrison, S. J., & Fenton, R. J. (1999). Database driven Web sites in education. *Educational Technology, 39*(4), 31-38.

Gee, J. P. (2003). *What video games have to teach us about learning and literacy* (2nd ed.). New York: Palgrave Macmillan.

Gibson, D. (2003). Network-based assessment in education. *Contemporary Issues in Technology and Teacher Education, 3*(3), 310-323.

Glasner, J. (2005a, May 2). *Ad execs want to track every move*. Retrieved June 8, 2005, from http://www.wired.com/news/ebiz/0,1272,67390,00.html

Glasner, J. (2005b, April 28). *Ads that know what you want*. Retrieved June 8, 2005, from http://www.wired.com/news/ebiz/0,1272,67365,00.html

Gredler, M. E. (1996). Educational games and simulations: A technology in search of a (research) paradigm. In D. H. Jonassen (Ed.), *Handbook of research for educational communications and technology* (1st ed., pp. 521-539). New York: MacMillan.

Heckel, H. L. (2003). *Online social interaction: The case of EverQuest*. Unpublished master's thesis, George Mason University, Fairfax, VA.

Hill, M. (2005, September 25). *More colleges offering video game courses*. Retrieved September 26, 2005, from http://www.usatoday.com/tech/products/games/2005-09-25-video-game-colleges_x.htm

Interactive Digital Software Association. (1999). *State of the industry report*. Washington, DC: Interactive Digital Software Association.

Interactive Digital Software Association. (2002). *Essential facts about the computer and video game industry*: Interactive Digital Software Association.

Interactive Digital Software Association. (2003). *Essential facts about the computer and video game industry*: Interactive Digital Software Association.

Keller, J. M. (1987). Development and use of the ARCS model of instructional design. *Journal of Instructional Development, 10*(3), 2-10.

Keller, J. M., & Suzuki, K. (1988). Application of the ARCS model to courseware design. In D. H. Jonassen (Ed.), *Instructional Designs for Microcomputer Courseware* (Vol. I, pp. 401-434). Hillsdale, NJ: Lawrence Erlbaum Associates.

King, B., & Borland, J. (2003). *Dungeons and dreamers: The rise of computer game culture from geek to chic*. Emeryville, CA: McGraw-Hill/Osborne.

Koster, R. (2005). *A theory of fun for game design.* Scottsdale, AZ: Paraglyph Press.

Loh, C. S., & Botturi, L. (2005, October 18-22). *What's in a name? A discussion of what 'game' means to the field.* Paper presented at the annual conference of the Association for Educational Communications and Technology (AECT 2005), Orlando, FL.

Loh, C. S., Rieber, L. P., Wiley, D., Van Eck, R., & Holschuh, D. (2004, October 19-23). *Let's make R.O.O.M. for games.* Paper presented at the annual conference of the Association for Educational Communications and Technology (AECT 2004), Chicago, IL.

Mislevy, R. J., Steinberg, L. S., Breyer, F. J., Almond, R. G., & Johnson, L. (2002). Making sense of data from complex assessment. *Applied Measurement in Education, 15*(4), 363-389.

Papargyris, A., & Poulymenakou, A. (2005). Learning to fly in persistent digital worlds: The case of massively multiplayer online role playing games. *ACM SIGGROUP Bulletin, 25*(1), 41-49. Retrieved September 30, 2005, from http://doi.acm.org/10.1 145/1067699.1067706

Pirolli, P., & Card, S. K. (1999). Information foraging. *Psychological Review, 106*(4), 643-675. Retrieved September 12, 2005, from http://www2.parc.com/istl/groups/uir/pubs/items/UIR-1999-05-Pirolli-Report-InfoForaging.pdf

Prensky, M. (2001). *Digital game-based learning.* New York: McGraw-Hill.

Reeves, T. (1997). *Evaluating what really matters in computer-based education.* Retrieved June 10, 2005, from http://www.educationau.edu.au/archives/cp/reeves.htm

Rieber, L. P. (1996). Seriously considering play: Designing interactive learning environments based on the blending of microworlds, simulations, and games. *Educational Technology Research and Development, 44*(2), 43-58.

Romanowski, M. H. (2004, summer). *Student obsession with grades and achievement.* Retrieved June 13, 2005, from http://www.findarticles.com/p/articles/mi_qa4009/is_200407/ai_n9424194

Rosas, R., Nussbaum, M., Cumsille, P., Marianov, V., Correa, M., Flores, P., et al. (2003). Beyond Nintendo: Design and assessment of educational video games for first and second grade students. *Computers and Education, 40*(1), 71-94.

Salen, K., & Zimmerman, E. (2004). *Rules of play: Game design fundamentals.* Cambridge, MA: The MIT Press.

Sherry, J. (2001). The effects of violent video games on aggression. A meta-analysis. *Human Communication Research, 27*(3), 409-431.

Squire, K. (2004). *Replaying history: Learning world history through playing Civilization III.* Unpublished doctoral dissertation, Indiana University, Bloomington, IN.

Steiner, P. (1993, July 5). On the Internet, nobody knows you're a dog. [cartoon] *The New Yorker* (p. 61). Retrieved July 9, 2006, from http://www.cartoonbank.com/assets/1/22230_m.gif

Thompson, K. M., & Haninger, K. (2001). Violence in E-rated video games. *The Journal of the American Medical Association, 286*(5), 591-598. Retrieved September 30, 2005, from http://jama.ama-assn.org/cgi/content/full/286/5/591

Trento, A. (2005, March 25). Developing a cross-platform flash game for Dolce & Gabbana. Retrieved June 10, 2005, from http://www.macromedia.com/devnet/devices/articles/dolce_gabbana.html

Silver, J. (Producer), Wachowski, A., & Wachowski, L. (Directors). (1999). *The Matrix* [Motion Picture]. USA: Warner Brothers.

Ward, M. (2005, April 18). *Mobile games to "go interactive".* Retrieved June 15, 2005, from http://news.bbc.co.uk/2/hi/technology/4449319.stm

Wheeldon, R., & Levene, M. (2003). *The best trail algorithm for assisted navigation of Web sites.* Paper presented at the 1st Latin American Web Congress (LA-WEB 2003), Santiago, Chile.

Zalane, O. R. (2001, June 27-28). *Web usage mining for a better Web-based learning environment.* Paper presented at the Conference on Advance Technology for Education, Banff, Alberta, Canada.

Chapter XVII

Machine Learning Assessment Systems for Modeling Patterns of Student Learning

Ron Stevens, UCLA IMMEX Project, USA

Abstract

We have developed and validated layered analytic models of how high school and university students construct, modify, and retain problem solving strategies as they learn to solve science problems online. First, item response theory modeling is used to provide continually refined estimates of problem solving ability as students solve a series of simulations. In parallel, students' strategies are modeled by self-organizing artificial neural network analysis, using the actions that students take during problem solving as the classifying inputs. This results in strategy maps detailing the qualitative and quantitative differences among problem solving approaches. Hidden Markov Modeling then develops learning trajectories across sequences of performances and results in stochastic models of problem solving progress across sequential strategic stages in the learning process. Using this layered analytical approach we have found that students quickly adopt preferential problem solving strategies, and continue to use them up to four months later. Furthermore, the approach has shown that students working in groups solve a higher percentage of the problems, stabilize their strategic approaches quicker, and use a more limited repertoire of strategies than do students working alone.

Introduction

Strategic problem solving is a complex process with skill level development being influenced by the task, the experience and knowledge of the student, the balance of cognitive and metacognitive skills possessed by the student and required by the task, gender (Fennema, Carpenter, Jacobs, Franke, & Levi, 1998), ethnicity, classroom environment (Olson & Locks-Horsley, 2000), and overall ability constructs such as motivation and self efficacy (Conati & Zhao, 2004; Mayer, 1998; O'Regan, 2003). The variable contributions of these influences helps account for why it is so challenging for teachers to identify which students are using the knowledge and critical thinking skills presented in class to solve real-world problems, and distinguish them from other students that may require interventional supports (Marshall, 1995). These analyses are complicated as the acquisition of problem solving skills is a dynamic and often gradual process characterized by transitional changes over time as experience is gained and learning occurs (Lajoie, 2003). Given the nature of novice learning, student trajectories are likely to be complex with regard to the heterogeneity of strategies, the pace of learning, and the level of expertise obtained.

One challenge, therefore, is to develop models of student learning that incorporate experience, gender, and other influences that can begin to position students' strategic problem-solving sophistication upon a continuum of experience. When such approaches can be reliably and predicatively modeled, they can then be coupled with deliberate practice (Ericsson, 2004), feedback, and/or interventions such as collaborative learning (Brown & Palincsar, 1989; Webb, 1992) expected to improve the level of competency.

With the development of increasingly powerful online learning environments and the coupling of them to dynamic assessment methodologies, it is now becoming possible to rapidly acquire data with linkages to the students' changing knowledge, skill, and understanding as they engage in real-world complex problem solving. This can be accomplished both within problems (Arroyo, Beal, Murray, Walles, & Woolf, 2004; Croteau, Heffernan, & Koedinger, 2004; VanLehn, 2000) as well as across problems (Stevens, Soller, Cooper, & Sprang, 2004).

While it is becoming relatively easy to capture student performance data, a continuing question is how to best extract the most important features of the student data streams and refine them into models (predictive simplifications or abstractions) that can be used to more accurately position students on learning trajectories and to optimize the form of subsequent interventions. A range of tools are being employed in these analyses including Bayesian nets (Mislevy, Almond, Yan, & Steinberg, 1999),computer adaptive testing (CAT) based on item response theory (IRT), regression models (Margolis & Clauser, 2006), and artificial neural networks (ANN) (Stevens & Najafi, 1993), each of which possesses particular strengths and limitations. One emerging lesson, however, is that a single approach is unlikely to be adequate for modeling the multitude of influences on learning as well as for optimizing the form of subsequent interventions. Technical and conceptual challenges are to develop system architectures that can provide rigorous and reliable measures of student progress yet can also be progressively scaled and refined in response to evolving student models and new interventional approaches.

We have approached these challenges with an online problem solving delivery environment and layered analytic system termed IMMEX (interactive multi-media exercises), where we have been broadly developing and implementing problem solving tasks that require students to analyze descriptive scenarios, judge what information is relevant, plan a search strategy, gather information, and eventually reach a decision(s) that demonstrates understanding (Palacio-Cayetano, Allen, & Stevens, 1999; Underdahl, Palacio-Cayetano, & Stevens, 2002). While IMMEX problem solving supports the three cognitive components described by Sugure (1995) as important for problem solving (e.g., understanding of concepts, understanding the principles that link concepts, and linking of concepts and principles to procedures for application), evaluation studies suggest that the second and third components are most emphasized by the IMMEX format (Chen, Chung, Klein, de Vries, & Burnam, 2002). In this chapter we describe how layers of online machine learning and analytic systems are integrated approach these challenges.

IMMEX: Interactive Multi Media Exercises

IMMEX™ problem solving follows the hypothetical-deductive learning model of scientific inquiry (Lawson, 1995) where students frame a problem from a descriptive scenario, judge what information is relevant, plan a search strategy, gather information, and eventually reach a decision that demonstrates understanding.

Figure 1. HAZMAT:his screen shot of Hazmat shows the menu items down the left side of the main "Hazmat" window on the screen and a sample test result (the result of a precipitation reaction)

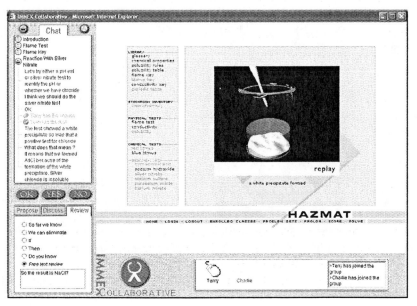

In this figure, the IMMEX problem set has been embedded within a collaborative learning environment, allowing groups of students to chat using sentence openers (left-hand panel of the screen) and share mouse control (bottom panel, see Discussion)

Since beginning online delivery of these cases eight years ago, over 80 problem sets have been constructed in science and other disciplines, and over 500,000 cases have been performed by students spanning middle school to medical school (http://www.immex.ucla.edu).

One, of several problem sets researched extensively is *Hazmat*, which provides evidence of students' ability to conduct qualitative chemical analyses (Stevens et al., 2004; Stevens & Soller, 2005). The problem begins with a multimedia presentation, explaining that an earthquake caused a chemical spill in the stockroom and the student's challenge is to identify the chemical. The problem space contains 22 menu items for accessing a Library of terms, the Stockroom Inventory, or for performing Physical or Chemical Testing. When the student selects a menu item, her or she verifies the test requested and is then shown a presentation of the test results (e.g., a precipitate forms in the liquid in Figure 1). When students feel they have gathered adequate information to identify the unknown they can attempt to solve the problem. To ensure that students gain adequate experience, this problem set contains 38 cases that can be performed in class, assigned as homework, or used for testing.

For *Hazmat*, the students are allowed two solution attempts; the database records these attempts as 2 = solved on the first attempt, 1 = solved on the second attempt, and 0 = not solved. The *Hazmat* problem set is challenging for students with an overall solution frequency for the 38 cases (n = 28,878) of 51%.

IMMEX Systems Architecture

From a systems architecture perspective, IMMEX is a data-centric system centered around a SQL database of both problem and performance data. It consists of Delivery, Data, Analysis, and Modeling components, connected with direct or Web services communications. In the delivery component, options are currently available for a) large scale (~400 concurrent users) individual problem solving and b) for pilot testing (~20 concurrent student groups) for collaborative problem solving.

For collaborative studies, the collaboration client runs in a browser and is managed through Java applets that communicate with the IMMEX Collaboration Server. The Collaboration Server is an HTTP server acting as a proxy, which filters, edits, and synchronizes the IMMEX HTML pages through JavaScript, and sends them to the clients. The IMMEX database server records the student performance data, and the collaboration server records the student chat log. These are subsequently merged during the chat modelling process to associate chat segments with the test selections.

The analytic models that provide the engine for suggesting interventions, focus on (1) effectiveness, as measured by item response theory (IRT) analysis, and (2) strategies, as modeled by ANN and hidden Markov modeling (HMM). We have chosen to model both in real time, but in different software modules, for both efficiency as well as that we think they may be assessing different constructs. The analyzed data can then be propagated and integrated back into the decision models as described below, for providing, or triggering interventions as needed.

Figure 2. Architecture for proposed pedagogical model integration with IMMEX system

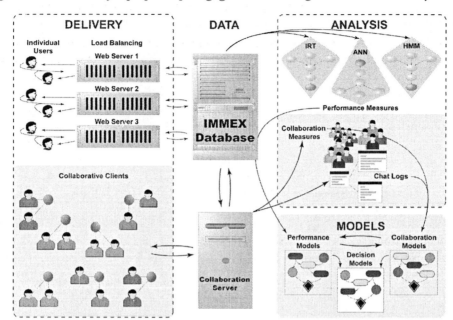

Item Response Theory Estimates of Student Ability

The first layer of our data analytic system uses estimates of student ability (theta) as determined by IRT. Item response theory relates characteristics of items (item parameters) and characteristics of individuals (latent traits) to the probability of a positive response (such as solving a case). Unlike classical test theory item statistics, which depend fundamentally on the subset of items and persons examined, IRT item and person parameters are invariant. This makes it possible to examine the contribution of items individually as they are added and removed from a test. It also allows researchers to conduct rigorous tests of measurement equivalence across experimental groups.

Using IRT, pooled data for students is used to calibrate all of the items and to obtain a proficiency estimate for each student. Using the one-parameter logistic model as well as the two-parameter logistic model, IRT modeling software scales both the items and the individual examinees on the same logit scale. A logit is a standard reference in statistics, known as log-odds, which is calculated as the log of the probability of getting an item correct over the probability of getting an item incorrect:

$$\log\left[\frac{P(x_j = 1)]}{P(x_j = 0)}\right] = \theta - b_j$$

The overall θ is an estimated proficiency based on the number of correctly answered items in a set. The higher the student ability θ, the higher the probability of getting a more difficult item correct. The item difficulties, b_j are the difficulty estimates of each item.

As shown in Figure 3, the cases in the problem set included a variety of acids, bases, and compounds that give either a positive or negative result when flame tested and were of a range of difficulties.

As expected, the flame test negative compounds are more difficult for students because both the anion and cation have to be identified by running additional chemical tests. Overall, the problem set presents an appropriate range of difficulties to provide reliable estimates of student ability (Stevens, Johnson, & Soller, 2005). Item response theory analysis is the first measure of our multi-layered analytical approach, and these estimates are updated in real-time with each case performance (Stevens & Soller, 2005). IMMEX cases are currently delivered randomly to students, however our recent ability to compute IRT estimates in real time after each performance, and to predictably re-estimate these measures based on the next case to be delivered, will provide the opportunity to deliver cases of defined difficulty to individual students in a computer adaptive testing approach.

Figure 3. Levels of problem difficulty

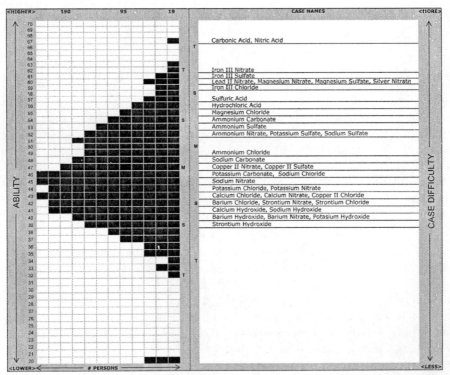

The case item difficulties were determined by IRT analysis of 28,878 student performances, the problem difficulty begins with the easiest at the bottom and increases towards the top, the distribution of student abilities is shown on the left with the highest ability students at the top, decreasing downward, for each graph, M indicates the mean, S, the standard deviation, and T two standard deviations.

Artificial Neural Network (ANN) Classification of Strategies

While useful for ranking the students by the effectiveness of their problem solving, IRT does not provide strategic measures of this problem solving. Here, we use ANN analysis. As students navigate the problem spaces, the IMMEX database collects timestamps of each student selection. The most common student approaches (i.e., strategies) for solving *Hazmat* are identified with competitive, self-organizing artificial neural networks (Kohonen, 2001; Stevens & Najafi, 1993; Stevens, Wang, & Lopo, 1996) using these time stamped actions as the input data. The result is a topological ordering of the neural network nodes according to the structure of the data where geometric distance becomes a metaphor for strategic similarity. Often we use a 36-node neural network and the details are visualized by histograms showing the frequency of items selected for student performances classified at that node (Figure 4a). Strategies so defined consist of actions that are always selected for performances at that node (i.e., with a frequency of 1) as well as ones ordered variably.

Figure 4. (a) Sample neural network nodal analysis*; (b) A composite ANN nodal map that shows the topology of performances generated during the self-organizing training process**

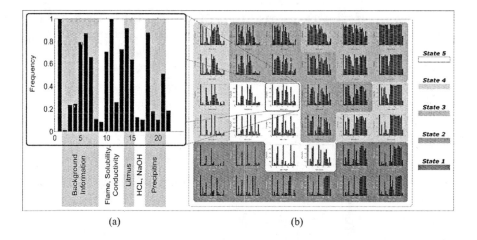

(a)   (b)

*(a) The selection frequency of each action (identified by the labels) is plotted for the performances at node 15, and helps characterize the performances clustered at this node and for relating them to performances at neighboring nodes; (b) This figure shows the item selection frequencies for all 36 nodes, and maps them to HMM states

**Each of the 36 matrix graphs represents one ANN node where similar students' problem solving performances have become competitively clustered; as the neural network was trained with vectors representing selected student actions, it is not surprising that a topology developed based on the quantity of items; for instance, the upper right of the map (nodes 6 and 12) represents strategies where a large number of tests were ordered, whereas the lower left contains strategies where few tests were ordered; once ANNs are trained and the strategies represented by each node defined, new performances can be tested on the trained neural network, and the node (strategy) that best matches the new performance can be identified and reported

Hidden Markov Model (HMM) Strategic Progress Models

On their own, artificial neural network analyses provide point-in-time snapshots of students' problem solving. Any particular strategy, however, may have a different meaning at a different point in a learning trajectory. More complete models of student learning should also account for the changes of student's strategies with practice. To model student learning progress over multiple problem solving episodes, students perform multiple cases in the 38-case Hazmat problem set, and we then classify each performance with the trained ANN. Some sequences of performances localize to a limited portion of the ANN topology map. For instance the nodal sequence {32, 33, 28, 33, 33} suggests only small shifts in strategy with each new performance. In our analytic system we have used Hidden Markov Modeling to extend our preliminary results to more predicatively model student learning pathways.

Markov models are used to model processes that move stochastically through a series of predefined states over time (Murphy, 2004; Rabiner, 1989). In applying this process to modeling student performance, we postulate that a number of unknown states exist in the dataset representing strategic transitions that students may pass through as they perform a series of IMMEX cases. These states might represent learning strategies that task analyses suggest students may pass through while developing competence (Mislevy, Steinberg, Almond, Breyer, & Johnson, 2001). For most IMMEX problem sets, a postulated number of states between 3 and 5 have produced informative models. Then, similar to the previously described ANN analysis, exemplars of sequences of strategies (ANN node classifications) are repeatedly presented to the HMM modeling software to develop temporal progress models. The resulting models are defined by a *transition matrix* that shows the probability of transiting from one state to another, and an *emission matrix* that relates each state back to the ANN nodes that best represent student performances in that state.

The overall solution frequency for the Hazmat dataset (N= 28,878 performances) was 51%, but when students' performance was mapped to their strategy usage as mapped by the HMM states, these states revealed the following quantitative and qualitative characteristics:

- State 1—55% solution frequency showing variable, but limited numbers of test items and little use of Background Information;

- State 2—60% solution frequency showing equal usage of Background Information as well as action items; little use of precipitation reactions;

- State 3—45% solution frequency with nearly all items being selected;

- State 4—58% solution frequency with many test items and limited use of Background Information;

- State 5—66% solution frequency with few items selected Litmus test and Flame tests uniformly present.

The critical components of such an analysis are shown in Figure 5 where students solved seven *Hazmat* cases, and then their ANN strategies and HMM states were modeled. The resulting five different HMM states reflect different strategic approaches with different solution frequencies. In this figure, one level of analysis (stacked bar charts) shows the distribution of the five HMM states across the seven performances. On the first case, when students are framing the problem space, the two most frequent states are States 1 and 3. Moving up an analytical layer from HMM states to ANN nodal strategies (the 6 x 6 histogram matrices) shows that State 3 represents strategies where students ordered all tests, and State 1 where there was limited test selection. Consistent with the state transitions in the upper right of Figure 5, with experience students transited from State 3 (and to some extent State 1), through State 2 and into States 4 and 5, the more effective states. By the fifth performance the State distributions stabilized after which time students without intervention tended not to switch their strategies, even when they were ineffective. Stabilization with ineffective strategies is of concern as described next, as students tend to retain their adopted strategies over at least a 3-months period (Stevens et al., 2005).

From the associated transition matrix State 1 is an absorbing state meaning that once students adopt this approach they will likely continue using it on subsequent problems. In contrast, States 2 and 3 are more transitional and students are likely to move to other approaches as they are learning. State 5 has the highest solution frequency, which makes sense because its ANN histogram profile suggests that students in this state pick and choose certain tests, focusing their selections on those tests that will help them obtain the solution most efficiently.

The solution frequencies at each state provide an interesting view of student progress. For instance, if we compare the earlier differences in solution frequencies with the most likely state transitions from the matrix shown in Figure 5, we see that most of the students who enter State 3, having the lowest problem solving rate (27%), will transit either to State 2 or 4, and increase their solution frequency by 13% on average. Students performing in State 2 are more likely than those in State 4 to transit to State 5 (with a 14% increase in solution

Figure 5. Modeling individual and group learning trajectories

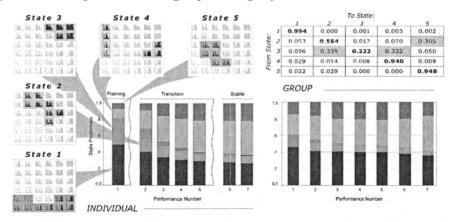

This figure illustrates the strategic changes as individual students or groups of students gain experience in Hazmat problem solving; each stacked bar shows the distribution of HMM states for the students (N=1790) after a series (1-7) of performances; these states are also mapped back to the 6 x 6 matrices, which represent 36 different strategy groups identified by self-organizing ANN; the highlighted boxes in each neural network map indicate which strategies are most frequently associated with each state; from the values showing high cyclic probabilities along the diagonal of the HMM transition matrix (upper right), States 1, 4, and 5 appear stable, suggesting once adopted, they are continually used. In contrast, students adopting State 2 and 3 strategies are more likely to adopt other strategies (gray boxes)

frequency). From an instructional point of view, these results suggest that we might guide students who are performing in State 3 toward State 2 rather than State 4 strategies.

Effects of Collaborative Learning on Strategy Selection and Efficiency

We have examined the utility of this modeling system by exploring the effects of a common intervention, collaborative learning, and by testing the effects of gender on the persistence of strategic approaches.

There are many theories to support the advantages of collaborative learning in the classroom (Brown & Palincsar, 1989), which has the potential to increase task efficiency and accuracy (Thagard, 1997) while giving each team member a valued role grounded in his or her unique skills. Although it is not always the case, groups sometimes even outperform the best individual in the group (Ellis, Klahr, & Siegler, 1994). Here, working in pairs encouraged the students to generate new ideas that they probably would not have come up with alone. These studies suggest that the ability of a group may somehow transcend the abilities of its individual collaborators. Learning and working with peers may benefit not only the overall team performance by increasing the quality of the team product; it may also enhance individual performance. Increasingly, intelligent analysis and facilitation capabilities are being incorporated into collaborative distance learning environments to help bring the benefits of a supportive classroom closer to the distant learners (Barros & Verdejo, 2000; Constantino-Gonzalez, Suthers, & Escamilla de los Santos, 2002; Soller & Lesgold, 2003).

Also shown in Figure 5 is a learning trajectory for 5452 *Hazmat* performances from students working collaboratively in groups of two or three. Consistent with the literature, students working collaboratively significantly increased their solution frequency (from 51% to 63%). As importantly, ANN and HMM performance models showed that the collaborative learners stabilized their strategies more rapidly than individuals, used fewer of the transitional States 2 and 3 and more State 1 strategies (limited and/or guessing approaches) (Stevens et al., 2004). This suggests that group interaction helped students see multiple perspectives and reconcile different viewpoints, events that seem associated with the transitional states. Collaboration may, therefore, have replaced the explicit need for actions that are required to overcome impasses, naturally resulting in more efficient problem solving.

Persistence of Strategies and Effects of Gender

With a smaller set of advanced placement chemistry students (3 classrooms from the same teacher, 79 students) we next explored the short- and long-term stability of students' strategies and the influences that gender plays in strategy persistence. In a standard classroom environment students first performed five *Hazmat* problems to refine and stabilize their strategies. Then, one week (short-term) and 15 weeks later (long-term) students were asked to solve additional *Hazmat* cases.

At the end of the required first-set of performances (# 1-5), the proportions of the five strategy states and the solution frequencies had stabilized. As expected, State 3 approaches

Figure 6. Tracking and predicting long-term term strategic approaches

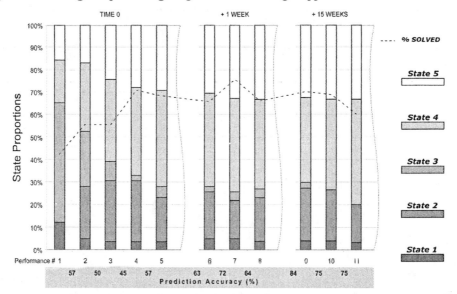

The students (n=79) from three classes with the same teacher performed a total of 868 Hazmat cases at the times indicated, and the state distributions, solved rate, and prediction accuracy were calculated as described in this chapter

were preferred on the early problem solving performances, and these decreased over time with the emergence of States 2, 4, and 5. The proportion of State 1 strategies in this subset of students was lower than the overall population, and this was most likely due to the more controlled classroom nature of this assignment that reduced guessing (Figure 6).

One week, and 15 weeks later the students were asked to perform an additional three *Hazmat* cases in class. The state distributions of the performances at both time intervals were not significantly different from those established after the initial training. It is also interesting that the solution frequency also did not change. Combined, these data indicate that students adopt a preferential approach to solving *Hazmat* after relatively few cases (4-5) and, as a group, they continue to use these strategies when presented with repeat cases, even after prolonged periods of time.

The performances were then separated by gender, and the state distributions were re-plotted. As shown in Figure 7, both male and female students appeared to have stabilized their strategic approaches by the fifth performance, but the state distributions were significantly different, with females preferring the approaches represented by State 5, whereas the males preferred State 4 approaches.

Discussion

These studies were motivated by our interest in understanding students' shifting dynamics in strategic reasoning as they gain problem-solving experience: an understanding that could

Figure 7. Gender-related strategic trajectories; the data in Figure 4 were separated by gender and re-plotted

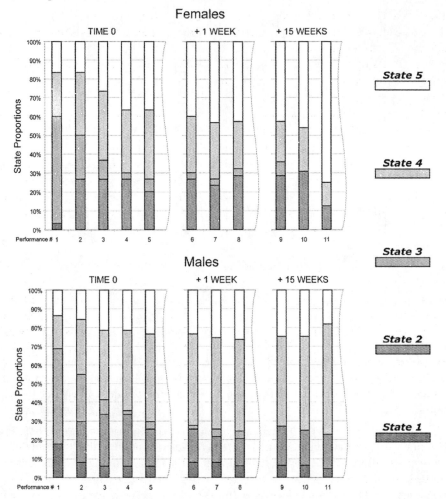

perhaps be extended to develop targeted feedback to teachers and students to improve learning. The analytic approach we chose was necessarily multilayered to address the broad needs set out in the introduction to this paper. This analytic model combines three algorithms (IRT, ANN, and HMM), which, along with problem set design and classroom implementation decisions, provide an extensible system for modeling strategies and formulating interventions. When combined, these algorithms provide a considerable amount of real-time strategic performance data about the student's understanding, including the IRT person ability estimate, the current and prior strategies used by the student in solving the problem, and the strategy the student will most likely use next, all of which provide information important to constructing detailed models of the development of scientific understanding. These findings are contingent, of course, on the validity of the tasks as well as the performance and strategic models developed from the student data.

In these studies we have focused on validating one representative problem set, *Hazmat,* where to date, over 41,000 performances have been recorded by high school and university students. This problem set was created along the frameworks we have published previously (Stevens & Palacio-Cayetano, 2003), and has face validity in that it covers much of the spectrum of qualitative analysis with the 38 parallel cases that include acids, bases, and flame test positive and negative compounds. The tasks also have construct validity in that cases are of different difficulties by Item Response Theory analysis (Linacre, 2004), and these differences correlate with the nature of the compounds (e.g., flame test positive compounds are easier than flame test negative compounds).

The next validation step concerns the data to be collected, and we do this by requiring that students re-confirm each test ordered (for a cost). The deliberate actions also seem to have a cognitive basis as concurrent verbal protocol analysis has indicated that ~90% of the utterances by students can be categorized into explicit cognitive or metacognitive categories (Chung et al., 2002).

In the first modeling step the most common strategies used by students were grouped by unsupervised ANN analysis, and the resulting classifications showed a topology ranging from those where very few tests were ordered, to those where every test was selected, which makes sense given the nature of the input data (i.e., deliberate student actions). The HMM progress models are somewhat more difficult to validate given the hidden nature of the model. One important consideration would be the dynamics of the state transitions as reflected in the transition matrix derived from the modeling process. Here theories of practice and cognition (Ericsson, 2004) would predict that students would change strategies with practice and eventually stabilize with preferred approaches much as we have shown in Figures 5 and 6. Similarly, the general overall shift in states from those representing extensive exploration to more refined test selection mirrors the data reduction effects observed previously with practice (Haider & Frensch, 1996). For instance, most students approached the first *Hazmat* case by selecting either an extensive (State 3), or limited/guessing (State 1) amount of information. The State 3 approaches would be appropriate for novices on the first case as they strive to define the boundaries of the problem space. Persisting with these strategies, however, would indicate a lack of understanding and progress.

As students gain experience, their strategies should change (Ericsson, 2004). Background information that was needed earlier may no longer be needed, and students should begin to develop their own preferred approaches based on knowledge, experience, motivation, and prior experiences.

The states that students stabilize with presumably reflect the level of competence as well as the approach they feel comfortable with. These approaches are the ones that would most often be recognized by teachers and for *Hazmat* were represented by States 1, 4, and 5. State 4 is interesting in several regards. First, it differs from the other states in that the strategies it represents are located at distant points on the ANN topology map, whereas the nodes comprising the other states are contiguous. The State 4 strategies represented by the left hand of the topology map are very appropriate for the set of cases in Hazmat that involve flame test positive compounds, whereas those strategies on the right are more appropriate for flame test negative compounds (where more extensive testing for both the anion and cation are required). This suggests that students using State 4 strategic approaches may have mentally partitioned the *Hazmat* problem space into two groups of strategies, depending on whether the initial flame test is positive.

State 5 also contains complex strategies, which from the transition matrix emerge from State 2 strategies by a further reduction in the use of background resources. State 5 approaches appear later in problem solving sequences, have the highest solution frequencies, and are approaches that work well with both flame test positive and negative compounds. In this regard they may represent the outcome of a pattern consolidation process. Also, State 5 differs from the other states in that the strategies represented are located at distant points on the ANN topology map, whereas the nodes comprising the other states are contiguous.

A final advantage of HMM is that it supports predictions regarding future student performances. By using the current state of the student and the transition matrix derived from training, a comparison of the "true" value of a student's next state, with the predicted values resulted in model accuracy at 70-90% (Stevens et al., 2004). The ability to model and report these predictive measures in real time provides a structure around which to begin developing dynamic interventions that are responsive to students' existing approaches and that aim to modify future learning trajectories in ways that enhance learning.

The validated models appear useful for both documenting the temporal dynamics of strategy encoding, consolidation, and retrieval, as well as for studying the effects of problem-solving interventions. Students working collaboratively improved their problem solving (by IRT) and stabilized their strategies faster than students working alone, begging the usual question about why collaborative learning in this case is effective. Some indication comes from the different state distributions describing individual and group performances. Group performances mainly stabilize with State 1, which appears to be strategically heterogeneous in that it contains student performance representing guessing (with a low solved rate), as well as very limited, but effective strategies. The successful use of this state by collaborating students, along with the decrease in the use of transitional states 2 and 3 may suggest that collaboration with peers encourages students to make the appropriate transitions within states 1 and 2, rather than explicitly transiting through them.

An important next step will be deriving quantitative data on the interactions within groups to gain insights into the nature of the collaborative interactions that result in these learning trajectory changes. We are beginning to develop such Web-based collaboration models by integrating IMMEX into a Web-based scientific inquiry environment (see Figure 2). Collaborative IMMEX allows groups of students to communicate through a chat interface (with specially defined sentence openers), and share workspace control while solving *Hazmat* and other IMMEX problems (Giordani & Soller, 2004; Giordani, Gerosa, Soller, & Stevens, 2005). By monitoring and assessing the collaborative interaction (Soller, 2004), and comparing it to the problem-solving outcomes defined by the HMM strategic models, we hope to not only determine more precisely what aspects of the collaboration modulate problem-solving strategies, but also use this information to strategically pair different individuals in specific combinations that our models suggest will enhance the learning of both partners.

Supported in part by grants from the National Science Foundation (ROLE 0231995, DUE 0126050, HRD-0429156).

References

Arroyo, I., Beal, C. R., Murray, T., Walles, R., & Woolf, B. P. (2004). Web-based intelligent multimedia tutoring for high stakes achievement tests. In J. C. Lester, R. M. Vicari, & F. Paraguaçu (Eds.), *Intelligent tutoring systems, 7th International Conference, ITS 2004, Maceió* (LNCS 3220, pp. 468-477). Alagoas, Brazil: Springer.

Barros, B., & Verdejo, M. (2000). Analyzing student interaction processes in order to improve collaboration. The DEGREE approach. *International Journal of Artificial Intelligence in Education, 11*, 221-241. Retrieved from http://sensei.1si.uned.es/~bbarros/papers/ijaied2000.pdf

Brown, A., & Palincsar, A. (1989). Guided, cooperative learning and individual knowledge acquisition. In L. Resnick (Ed.), *Knowing, learning, and instruction: Essays in honor of Robert Glasser*. Hillsdale, NJ: Lawrence Earlbaum Associates.

Chen, E., Chung, G., Klein, D., de Vries, L., & Burnam, B. (2001). How teachers use IMMEX in the classroom. *CSE paper*. Los Angeles: University of California, National Center for Research on Evaluation, Standards, and Student Testing (CRESST). Retrieved from http://www.immex.ucla.edu/docs/publications/pdf/evaluationforteachers.pdf

Chung, G. K. W. K, de Vries, L. F., Cheak, A. M., Stevens, R. H., & Bewley, W. L. (2002). Cognitive process validation of an online problem solving assessment. *Computers and Human Behavior, 18*(16), 669.

Conati, C., & Zhao, X. (2004). Building and evaluating an intelligent pedagogical agent to improve the effectiveness of an educational game. In *Proceedings of the 9th International Conference on Intelligent User Interface* (pp. 6-13). New York: ACM Press.

Constantino-Gonzalez, M. A., Suthers, D., & Escamilla de los Santos, J. (2002). Coaching Web-based collaborative learning based on problem solution differences and participation. *International Journal of Artificial Intelligence in Education, 13*. Retrieved from http://aied.inf.ed.ac.uk/members02/archive/Vol_13/constantino.full.html

Croteau, E. A., Heffernan, N. T., & Koedinger, K. R. (2004). Why are algebra word problems difficult? Using tutorial log files and the power law of learning to select the best fitting cognitive model. In J. C. Lester, R. M. Vicari, & F. Paraguaca (Eds.), *Intelligent Tutoring Systems, 7th International Conference Proceedings* (pp. 240-250). Heidelberg, Germany: Springer-Verlag Berlin.

Ellis, S., Klahr, D., & Siegler, R. S. (1994, April). *The birth, life and sometimes death of good ideas in collaborative problem solving*. Paper presented at the Annual meeting of the American Educational Research Association (AERA), New Orleans.

Ericsson, K. A. (2004). Deliberate practice and the acquisition and maintenance of expert performance in medicine and related domains. *Academic Medicine, 79*(10), S70-S81.

Fennema, E., Carpenter, T., Jacobs, V., Franke, M., & Levi, L. (1998). Gender differences in mathematical thinking. *Educational Researcher, 27*(5), 6-11.

Giordani, A., & Soller, A. (2004). *Strategic collaboration support in a Web-based scientific inquiry environment*. Paper presented at the European Conference on Artificial Intelligence, Workshop on Artificial Intelligence in Computer Supported Collaborative Learning, Valencia, Spain.

Giordani, A., Gerosa, L., Soller, A., & Stevens, R. (2005, July). *Extending an online individual scientific problem-solving environment to support and mediate collaborative learning*. Paper presented at the 12th International Conference on Artificial Intelligence in Education, Amsterdam, The Netherlands.

Haider, H., & Frensch, P. A. (1996). The role of information reduction in skill acquisition. *Cognitive Psychology, 30*(3), 304-337.

Kohonen, T. (2001). Self organizing maps (3rd ed.) In T. S. Huang, T. Kohonen, & M. R. Schroeder (Eds.), *Springer Series in Information Sciences* (vol. 30). Heidelberg, Germany: Springer.

Lajoie, S. P. (2003). Transitions and trajectories for studies of expertise. *Educational Researcher, 32*(8), 21-25.

Lawson, A. E. (1995). *Science teaching and the development of thinking*. Belmont, CA: Wadsworth Publishing Company.

Linacre, J. M. (2004). WINSTEPS Rasch measurement computer program. Chicago. Retrieved from http://winsteps.com

Margolis, M. J., & Clauser, B. E. (2006). A regression-based procedure for automated scoring of a complex medical performance assessment. In R. E. Mislevy, D. M. Williamson, & I. Bejar (Eds.), *Automated scoring of complex tasks in computer based testing: An introduction* (pp. 123-168). Mahwah, NJ: Lawrence Erlbaum.

Marshall, S. (1995). *Schemas in problem solving*. New York: Cambridge University Press.

Mayer, R. E. (1998). Cognitive, metacognitive and motivational aspects of problem solving. *Instructional Science, 26*(1-2), 49-63.

Mislevy, R. J., Almond, R. G., Yan, D., & Steinberg, L. S. (1999). Bayes nets in educational assessment: Where do the numbers come from? In K. B. Laskey & H. Prade (Eds.), *Proceedings of the 15th Conference on Uncertainty in Artificial Intelligence* (pp. 437-446). San Francisco: Morgan Kaufmann.

Mislevy, R. J., Steinberg, L. S., Almond, R. G., Breyer, F. J., & Johnson, L. (2001). *Making sense of data from complex assessments* (Tech. Rep. No. 538), University of California, National Center for Research on Evaluation, Standards, and Student Testing (CRESST), Los Angeles, CA.

Murphy, K. (2004). Hidden Markov Model (HMM) toolbox for Matlab. Retrieved from http://www.cs.ubc.ca/`murphyk/Software/HMM/hmm.html

O'Regan, K. (2003). Emotion and e-learning. *Journal of Asynchronous Learning Network, 7*(3), 78-92.

Olson, A., & Loucks-Horsley, S. (Eds.). (2000). *Inquiry and the National Science Education Standards: A guide for teaching and learning*. Washington, DC: National Academy Press.

Palacio-Cayetano, J., Allen, R. D., & Stevens, R. H. (1999). Computer-assisted evaluation—The next generation. *American Biology Teacher, 61*(7), 514-522.

Rabiner, L. (1989). A tutorial on Hidden Markov Models and selected applications in speech recognition. *Proceedings: IEEE, 77*(2), 257-286.

Soller, A., & Lesgold, A. (2003). A computational approach to analyzing online knowledge sharing interaction. In U. Hoppe, F. Verdejo, & J. Kay (Eds.), *Artificial intelligence in education: Shaping the future of learning through intelligent technologies* (pp. 253-260). Amsterdam, The Netherlands: IOS Press.

Soller, A., Jermann, P., Mühlenbrock, M., & Martinez, A. (2004). Designing computational models of collaborative learning interaction. In J. Mostow & P. Tedesco (Eds.), *Proceedings of the 2nd International Workshop on Designing Computational Models of Collaborative Learning Interaction (ITS 2004)* (pp. 5-12), Maceio-Alagoas, Brazil.

Stevens, R., & Casillas, A. (2006). Artificial neural networks. In R. E. Mislevy, D. M. Williamson, & I. Bejar (Eds.), *Automated scoring of complex tasks in computer based testing: An introduction* (pp. 259-312). Mahwah, NJ: Lawrence Erlbaum.

Stevens, R. H., & Najafi, K. (1993). Artificial neural networks as adjuncts for assessing medical students' problem-solving performances on computer-based simulations. *Computers and Biomedical Research, 26*(2), 172-187.

Stevens, R., Johnson, D. F., & Soller, A. (2005). Probabilities and predictions: Modeling the development of scientific competence. *Cell Biology Education, 4*(1), 42-57.

Stevens, R. H, & Palacio-Cayetano, J. (2003, fall). Design and performance frameworks for constructing problem-solving simulations. *Cell Biology Education, 2*, 162-179.

Stevens, R. H., & Soller, A. (2005). Machine learning models of problem space navigation, The influence of gender. *ComSIS, 2*, 83-98.

Stevens, R., Soller, A., Cooper, M., & Sprang, M. (2004). Modeling the development of problem solving skills in chemistry with a Web-based tutor. In J. C. Lester, R. M. Vicari, & F. Paraguaca (Eds.), *Intelligent Tutoring Systems, 7th International Conference Proceedings* (pp. 580-591). Heidelberg, Germany: Springer-Verlag Berlin.

Stevens, R., Wang, P., & Lopo, A. (1996). Artificial neural networks can distinguish novice and expert strategies during complex problem solving. *JAMIA, 3*(2), 131-138.

Sugrue, B. (1995). A theory-based framework for assessing domain-specific problem solving ability. *Educational Measurement: Issues and Practice, 14*(3), 29-36.

Thagard, P. (1997). Collaborative knowledge. *Nous, 31*(2), 242-261.

Underdahl, J., Palacio-Cayetano, J., & Stevens, R. (2001). Practice makes perfect: Assessing and enhancing knowledge and problem-solving skills with IMMEX software. *Learning and Leading with Technology, 28*(7), 26-31.

VanLehn, K. (1996). Cognitive skill acquisition. Annual review. *Psychology, 47*, 513-539.

Webb, N. (1992). Testing a theoretical model of student interaction and learning in small groups. In R. Hertz-Lazarowitz & N. Miller (Eds.), *Interaction in cooperative groups: The theoretical anatomy of group learning* (pp. 102-119). New York: Cambridge University Press.

Chapter XVIII

Shaping the Research Agenda with Cyber Research Assistants

Lyn Henderson, James Cook University, Australia

Abstract

Games and simulations in online learning are energizing development in learning and teaching and therefore of great interest to the research community. This chapter reflects on a few of the innovative methods currently in use to capture and report user data for education assessment and sets out new ideas for shaping the research agenda as applications become more capable of effective high level analysis of qualitative simulation and game data. Three areas are briefly explored. Cyber research assistants are defined and their achievements explored. Issues such as longitudinal studies, transference, and international collaboration are discussed. Finally, ethical considerations are raised. A case is outlined for students and teachers in various contexts to have access to the returned data in order to take ownership of subsequent learning and teaching actions. The chapter concludes with a call for the integration of teachers, students, researchers, governments, granting bodies, and computer scientists as important players in the research conversation. The chapter aims to describe the shape of an education research agenda targeting students playing online games and simulations in classrooms from kindergarten through higher education levels.

Introduction

Games and simulations in online learning are energizing developments in learning and teaching and therefore of great interest to the research community. Innovative methods using intelligent agents constructed through complex programming are currently in use to capture and report online simulation and game data for education assessment purposes (e.g., Gibson, 2003; Stevens, Johnson, & Soller, 2005). Although online intelligent agents collect valuable data for researchers, the computerized methods are currently inadequate, on two major counts. One is that they typically target games and simulations in the sciences and math with few directed at the social sciences and creative arts. The other is that the intelligent agents are not yet capable of effective high level analysis of qualitative simulation and game data that involve audio input from students and ascertaining students' thoughts at the time they are choosing strategies or answers. Shaping the research agenda involves solving these and other possibilities. The goal, as always, is to enhance teaching and learning outcomes.

Imagine how enriched researchers' interpretations will be if we can find non-intrusive electronic ways to capture what individual student players are actually thinking as they carry out their game strategies online or as their ideas and strategy planning are discussed with a partner, or partners, sitting beside them or in another country. Imagine online qualitative tools that not only collate and satisfactorily analyze such verbal and text discussion but also do this through triangulation of the results with the other variously mined data. Also imagine if the intelligent agents gathered and reported all this for each individual across various disciplines in order to explore Gardiner's (1999) multiple intelligences at work. Furthermore, it takes time for students to accomplish mastery of increasingly complex skills and remediate their weaknesses. Visualize collecting data as to whether higher order thinking skills, strategies, and processes developed during game and simulation play are transferred to problem solving in the same and different disciplines without, and with, other computerized games and simulations. Next, envisage obtaining electronic longitudinal data for each student and groups of students from one year to the next and the next on more than their overall government and school mandated achievement scores. Such data would be an invaluable teacher, educational designer, programmer, institutional, policy, and researcher tool.

Such innovations will allow researchers, academics, computer scientists, teachers, and students to be students to be part of the conversation about how to support and improve the students' thinking processes and strategies, collaborative and team skills, short and long term outcomes, motivation, transference, and perseverance with learning. The overarching goals would be to promote each student's ability to take on the attitudes and strategies of a life long learner and for the teacher to accomplish this by individual strategic scaffolding. This is the eClassroom vision for the cyber research agenda.

In the course of developing this vision, the chapter does not provide full descriptions of technical terminology and programs in which current and future intelligent agents carry out learner assessments in educational Web environments. Readers will find this background in the previous chapters as well as in the references provided. Three areas of shaping the cyber research agenda are singled out for attention.

The first outlines current cyber research assistant achievements after a brief sojourn to define cyber research assistants. The second focus presents new directions for cyber and human researchers. Issues such as longitudinal studies and transference are targeted, as is international collaboration. Finally, ethical considerations are raised. A case is outlined for students and teachers in various contexts to have access to the returned data in order to take ownership of subsequent learning and teaching actions. The chapter concludes with a call for the integration of teachers, students, researchers, governments, granting bodies, and computer scientists as important players in the research conversation. Through the exploration of these issues, the chapter aims to help shape the education research agenda targeting students playing online games and simulations in classrooms from kindergarten through higher education levels.

Current Cyber Research Directions

Cyber Research Assistants

Although other chapters have defined and discussed the technical aspects of mining online data during educational simulation and game playing, some explanation is warranted to clarify a construct useful for distinguishing between the cyber research assistant and other computerized intelligent agents as well as between the cyber research assistant and human researcher.

"Cyber research assistants" are normally labeled electronic intelligent agents, robots, and avatars that are software programs currently deployed in multi-agent virtual environments (Tambe, Johnson, Jones, Kossand, Lairdand, Rosenbloom, & Schwamb, 1995). A major environment is that of online recreational and educational games and simulations. Other examples of these environments are to be found in Web programs run by NASA, the armed forces, education learning management systems, and e-Bay.

There are also "pedagogic agents" that operate in educational Web contexts (Vasilakso, Devedzic, Kinshuk, & Pedrycz, 2004). Cimolino and Kay (2002) developed a pedagogic agent that infers the students' misconceptions when creating concept mapping tasks in science. Contai and Zhao (2004) created one based on a "probabilistic student model" (p. 7) to provide unsolicited offers of help to the individual student. This occurred when the model, which was constructed on the game inputs from a student, indicated help was needed when solving a factorization problem based on comparison with the probabilistic student model. The *ViSMod* (visualization of Bayesian student models) tool allows teachers and students to access and interact with a Bayesian representation of the student with respect to the levels of cognitive and social guidance used or not used by that student (Zapata-Rivera & Greer, 2004). Johnson, Lewis, Kole, Shaw, and Pain (2003) are developing an animated avatar that, they argue, will "convey empathy and solidarity with the learner, and thus further promote … a positive attitude to learning" (p. 231). It is labeled as a socially intelligent learner-agent that assesses certain learner characteristics and then intervenes by exhibiting social politeness through appropriate attitudinal and emotional sensitivity as it engages in cognitive and motivational tutorial dialog with the student.

Intelligent and pedagogic agents can be team members who "coordinate actions during their distributed task execution. This coordination requires an agent to observe (that is, to monitor) the other agents in order to detect a possible coordination failure of the team" and then direct particular agents to run programs to rectify the problem (Browning, Kaminka, & Veloso, 2002). These agents can learn when they are provided with more examples to increase their database of cases, and thereby improve the reliability and validity of their assessments of students' strategies (Vendinski & Stevens, 2002).

Hunt and Minstrel (1994) employed "diagnostic agents" (my descriptor) that ask a series of questions in order to identify physics students' current conceptual knowledge:

Through an item analysis of the responses the program [Diagnoser] can diagnose students' thinking, and then based on this analysis offer instruction designed to help students refine their understanding to a more precise (higher) level ... This progressive refinement of test, teach with feedback and retest helps students develop a stronger conceptual understanding of the material so they are better able to transfer this knowledge to future settings. (Sabelli & Pea, 2004, p. 107)

Virvou and Moundridou (2000), in effect, developed "tutoring agents" (my descriptor) in a Web-based authoring tool that allows instructors to construct online tutorial exercises within a problem-based learning pedagogy in domains that apply algebraic equations such as chemistry, economics, and physics. These diagnostic and tutoring agents take over the instructor's role to monitor the student's problem solving progress and provide appropriate feedback.

Notice that these non-purposefully selected examples disproportionally target the sciences. There appear to be at least six reasons why the sciences and math are targeted for electronic assessment. First, even though the simulation problem is open-ended, there is still one correct answer. Second, this makes it easier to program. Third, math and science are less controversial than the social sciences, humanities, and the arts with their multiple perspectives and answers. Fourth, the sciences and math are seen to be more difficult areas for a majority of students to develop effective solution strategies. Fifth, people with science and math skills are needed for a county's prosperity. Consequently, sixth, there are significantly more successful and larger grants for the sciences, including computer sciences, and math than for the humanities, social sciences, and the arts.

Returning to the discussion of labels, when these intelligent agents act in teaching, learning, tutoring, and assessment contexts, they are labeled by their usual terms. When they act for research purposes, the array of online programmed agents can be legitimately labeled, "cyber research assistants." The cyber research assistant role specific to this chapter is to monitor, trawl, gather, code, categorize, and return the inputs from educational online Web game and simulation players in ways that are meaningful to the human researcher. In doing so, the cyber research assistants will utilize current and future technical capabilities to "facilitate the discovery, execution, interoperation, composition, and execution monitoring" (Pollock & Hodgson, 2004, p. 9) of the pathways and actions of students as well as their written, speech, and non-verbal affective inputs. More simplistically, the cyber research assistants are trained to carry out "meaningful searches among the vast amounts of data living" (Pollock & Hodgson, 2004, p. 9) within online educational games and simulations as well as data returned when the users go "outside" into other Internet environments. Once gathered these data are stored, coded, categorized, correlated, and presented to the human researcher in ways that provide unproblematic interpretation. In essence, cyber research assistants exhibit the same behaviors as human research assistants administering data collection tools as well as coding, categorizing, and correlating the data. However, they also take on roles that are more applicable to the researcher, such as reporting the research findings and, to some extent, analysis of those findings. Both the cyber and human researchers are in symbiotic collaboration.

Current Cyber Research Assistants

The relevance of the impetus for new cyber research assistants and, ipso facto, computer science directions can be gauged on cyber research progress. This is not to imply that what is occurring with autonomous intelligent agents in the online educational field is meager or mediocre. To the contrary, it is exciting and innovative in terms of what types and in what ways it allows the various intelligent agents to garner and assess data in Web-based learning environments. The following describes a purposeful selection of such current developments in, first, online simulations utilizing the Web-based interactive multimedia exercises (*IMMEX*) system and, second, online education games, thereby enabling a comparison between the use of intelligent agents across different categories (simulations and games) and disciplines with variously aged students. This exploration thus provides a means to demonstrate the level from which cyber research assistants could be utilized in varied ways in the future.

Current Cyber Research Assistants: Online IMMEX Simulations

Various authors (Gibson, 2003; Giordani & Soller, 2004; Stevens, Johnson, & Soller, 2005; Vendlinski & Stevens, 2002) have described the IMMEX environment as an online set of complex simulation problems that have been utilized predominately in K-12 school and university science classrooms for over a decade (see IMMEX Web site, http://www.immex. ucla.edu). The real-life scenario problems utilize constructivist teaching and learning theory (Brown, Collins, & Duguid, 1989; Jonassen, 2000; Seely-Brown, Collins, & Duguid, 1989) for "the hyperthetical-deductive learning model followed in scientific inquiry" (Stevens et al., 2005, p. 43; also see Novak & Gowin, 1984). When solving the problem, the student's path can involve 15 to 90 steps (Vendlinski & Stevens, 2002) depending on the elementary, middle, secondary, and higher education level.

At each step, the student chooses from a menu that, although currently presenting most resources in a more static and concise manner (Stevens & Palacio-Cayetano, 2003), can contain some or all of the following: appropriate articles, definitions, explanations, animations, video, voice-overs, diagrams, graphs, pictures, and science testing tools. However, the menu possibilities must contain more than enough information so that the student has a variety of ways to solve the problem (Vendlinski & Stevens, 2002). For each simulation, the specific steps (i.e., menu items) chosen and time taken by each student to solve each open-ended problem are concurrently recorded and then collected, judged, categorized, and subsequently retrieved and printed as a diagram of their search path map (Stevens, 1991). The search path map delineates each student's linked steps by color-coding the items that were used as well as by segregating these in clusters by type of assessor-judged relevance to the simulation problem as well as by time spent on each resource item (Gibson, 2003;

Stephens et al., 2005). Each search path map can then be compared with all the student's other maps and with other students' search path maps in order to ascertain the types of strategies used over a number of simulations. Crucially for reflective and remedial assessment, the search path maps clearly delineate if there was a predominant strategy employed that was more aligned with a weak grasp of the problem's concepts or with effective and efficient strategies (Gibson, 2003; Vendlinski & Stevens, 2002).

Artificial neural network (ANN) and Kohonen ANN clustering (see index; Kohonen, 2001) provided the individual IMMEX "point-in-time snapshots" (Stevens et al., 2005, p. 48) of the search paths and the students' performance sequences that utilized hidden Markov modeling to train the intelligent agents "to more predicatively model student learning pathways ... across a sequence of performances" (pp. 48, 50; also see index this book). In Vendlinski and Stevens' (2000) study, 1,571 solved and unsolved performances were analyzed from high school biology and chemistry students while Stevens et al.'s (2005) research involved 2,564 performances by 776 sophomore biology university majors. With this quantity of data, these programs consistently clustered the students' strategies and "performed at more than 90% accuracy when tasked to predict the most likely problem solving strategy the student would apply next" (Stevens et al., 2005, p. 53). Consistent with their previous research (Stevens & Casillas, 2004; Stevens & Palacio-Cayetano, 2003; Vendlinski & Stevens, 2000, 2002), Stevens et al., (2005) pointed out that students seemed to stabilize their type of strategy to solve the problem—limited (accessed too few and often an inaccurate selection of resources), prolific (accessed too many and unnecessary resources), or efficient (effectively targeted requisite core resources)—by the fourth case performance even if the students were unsuccessful in obtaining the correct solution approximately 20 percent of the time. Stevens et al. (2005) found no gender differences in the strategies utilized. The studies' results indicate the need for formative intervention by instructors as well as the students themselves.

The preservice teacher education program, the Educational Technology Integration and Implementation Principles (eTIP) Cases project, tracks the users' choices and use of resources within each constructivist multimedia Challenge Case targeting urban, rural, and suburban "sim-schools" with the online capability to score students' essays through a scoring rubric tool (Gibson, 2003; Riedel & Gibson, 2004). There are three rubric criteria: validation, evidence, and decision. Validation requires explanation of "the central technology challenge in terms of case characteristics;" evidence requires identification of "case information that must be considered" in each particular challenge; and decision requires "a justified recommendation for implementing" each aspect of the case challenge (Module 3: eTIP Cases: http://www.etips.info/users/module3/rubic.html). If students did not present, identify, and justify their validation, evidence, and decisions, respectively, they were awarded a zero score; one mark if they gave a limited account in each of the three criteria; and a score of two if they supplied what was required with relevant explanations, examples, and justifications, respectively. Although the numbers were not as large as in other online essay and short answer grading, the reliability of the results of the trained intelligent agents was similar to the 80-97 percent validity ratings supplied in Valenti, Neri, and Cucchiarelli's (2003) comparison of researchers' experiments on 10 off-line or online essay grading systems.

As Foreman and Gibson (2006) pointed out, teacher educators choose "the application which then better guides learners, and learners provide new real world examples as input that teachers validate, which teaches the application how to improve in its estimates" (p. 3). Many eTIP education students access this "semantic Web" (Berners-Lee, Hendler, &

Lassila, 2001; Foreman & Gibson, 2006) essay scoring tool to obtain feedback on draft essay assignments before submitting the final essay to the course instructor (Dexter, 2002; Riedel, Gibson, & Boriah, 2004). A further assessment was conducted to ascertain how the combination of high or low relevancy of the accessed resources with the top and bottom quarter percentiles of individual students' total essay scores related to their IMMEX search strategies (Riedel, Gibson, & Boriah, 2004). This was with two groups of preservice teachers accessing resources in the Curriculum and Assessment Case. They found that the students with high essay scores also had high relevancy for targeting appropriate resources and those with low essay scores had selected low relevance resources.

The research reported by IMMEX researchers, supplemented with ANN, Kohen ANN, and/or essay scoring, did not utilize expert performances as the judging criteria because students are not experts and will take time to become expert. However, the intelligent agents were able to demonstrate how the not or less successful strategies of variously-aged students from the different disciplines compared with successful students, and whether and how students changed to more or less successful strategies over time. This model therefore classifies "successive student problem solving attempts as these attempts move from novice-like to expert-like performances over the time taken" to complete the requisite number of online simulations (Vendlinski & Stevens, 2000, pp. 111-112).

The authors mentioned previously are among the most exciting network-based innovators utilizing online cyber-research assistants' simulation assessments. Of course, none of the authors viewed their artificial neural nets as containing cyber research assistants. Given the definition in this chapter, this is what their intelligent agents did, as these agents returned data to them as the research assistants, rather than just as assessors of the students' problem solving strategies using online case-based and problem solving scenarios.

Current Cyber Research Assistants in Online Computer Games

If the sub-heading were re-worded as a question, the answer would be that cyber research assistants are essentially non-existent. Obviously, online single and multi player computer games utilize intelligent agents and avatars to manipulate the game play, levels of difficulty, story, characterization, motivation, and so forth by keeping track of the player's moves and providing responses. However, they are not utilized as research assistants.

Educational online multi-user virtual environments (MUVEs) and massively multi-player online role-playing games (MMORPGs) have recently been developed either specifically for students of various ages and contexts or the context is such that teachers can confidently allow students in middle and high schools to participate. An example of a MUVE for students is *River City*. It targets middle school students' learning and motivation about biology, ecology, and society in order "to promote learning for all students, particularly unengaged or low-performing students" (Dede, 2005). Its museum-based environment positions the students as scientists who collaborate to identify and solve historically situated cases (Dede, Ketelhut, & Ruess, 2002). The latter category, MMORPG, includes *Whyville.net* with over 50,000 registered players and approximately 4,000 concurrent players. Forty-six Grade 6 students joined this MMORPG to discover how, and what happens when, you catch *Whypox* (Neulight & Kafai, 2005). Another MMORPG, *Apolyton University*, was spawned in order to help players understand *Civilization III* game play. It consists of 25 courses that are managed by volunteers. Participants play saved games, post screenshots, and report on major game events and decisions that are labeled, "during action reports (DARs)" (Squire & Giovanetto, 2005). These two researchers of the Apolyton university game were "participant observers for 6 months, completing courses, keeping journal notes, collecting field notes ...[and conducting] several focused data collection exercises" that included Apolyton's During Action Reports and tracking individual gamers' participation (Squire & Giovanetto, 2005; unfortunately, only the abstract was available).

In *Revolution*, the players' avatars act out the various roles of the people involved in the United States' revolution against English rule in 1776. As a character allocated particular class, occupation, gender, political, and racial characteristics, high school students play a chapter of the overall story within a class lesson of 30 to 40 minutes. This segmentation is what makes Revolution unique from other MMORPGs. Each chapter-event involves pre-assigned tasks requiring individual, collaborative, or competitive solutions to one or more historical circumstances. These have to be negotiated by each student who is forced to make quick difficult decisions. Resolution or non-resolution of their decision-making denotes the dramatic climax of the episode. Players then reflect on their decision-making and chat about their decisions with the other players online. After the students have logged-off, the teacher then leads discussion in order to clarify and strengthen cognitive and collaborative strategies and outcomes (The Education Arcade, 2005).

eCybermission and *Quest Atlantis* are examples of other online computer games for mainly middle and high school students. The first two online games are more specifically targeted to the U.S. context. *eCybermission* is a Web-based science, math, and technology competition for middle school students. Indeed, the U.S. Army sponsors various teams that have a national competition in Washington. In contrast, *Quest Atlantis* has international popularity. One reason is that the multi-user 3D virtual environment is freely downloadable; the other more important reason is the veracity of research findings confirming its ability to engage students across gender, ethnicity, race, ability, and behavior through being personally invested in learning through playing (Barab, Thomas, Dodge, Carteaux, Tuzun, 2005; Whelan, 2005).

Most of the data trails (see index) from the above online computer games are not stored and delivered for assessment let alone research purposes as are the online classroom simulations discussed previously. In all these computer game examples the data were collected by human researchers mainly through interviews, observations, and, where appropriate, pre- and post-testing and/or analysis of the students' text communications with other players using the games' inbuilt text communication function. *MuzzyLane*, however, has developed online *multiplayer* computer game software, for instance, *The Calm and the Storm*, a WWII simulation, that has built-in tools that permit teacher-generated reports, tracking of individual as well as group development, observation and analysis of student progress, and a consistent scoring system among a range of its games (MuzzyLane, http://www.muzzylane.com/games/). Yet "development" and "student progress" are not clarified and probably do not relate to the quality of student understanding strategies and processes but rather to each student's current place in the game vis-à-vis length of time taken and to a count of the number of each student's interactions or discussion postings.

Implications of the discussion so far are obvious. Lessening the work load of human researchers, strengthening the validity of research analysis, and improving teacher and student critique of the students', and ipso facto, the teachers', strategies at strategic points in the teaching-learning cycle are paramount, particularly if reducing student under-achievement is a goal. Cyber research assistants need to be a lot smarter than they are now.

Future Cyber Research Assistant Directions

Developing cyber research assistant affordances to access digital data that can be returned in various collated ways to the human researchers is a priority. This is particularly so, given the dearth of online assessment and research instruments available in non-science games and simulations.

Need for Smarter Cyber Research Assistants

Although fulfilling their current roles as intelligent, pedagogic, and diagnostic agents, the cyber research assistants will become much better at what they do and be trained with new programs to meet the future needs of quantitative and, particularly, qualitative data storage, collection, coding, categorization, correlation, and presentation in easily understandable tables, graphs, cluster maps, diagrams, and, perhaps, animations to show cause and effect. Cyber research assistants need to be asked to do more difficult things and to come back with their findings and analysis two or three days later as do human research assistants. Engaged in automated data mining based on pattern recognition, cyber research assistants would be called on to present all the viable patterns for interpretation, not just those based on the human researcher's queries, but also for those that the human researcher forgot to ask or did not foresee. Indeed, the assistants would generate questions and hypotheses that involve pattern finding, then test the hypotheses and analyze the questions for their potential. Obviously, the cyber research assistants could ask stupid questions because there could be some inability to distinguish good questions from bad questions. Nevertheless, what they "throw up" could be well worth the exploration.

Obviously, these are not simple tasks. But they are also not impossible. The data-to-knowledge (D2K) and the Automated Learning Group are currently working on deep data mining, pattern recognition, and unsupervised classification of data. The amount and complexities of space data suggests that, because the education field is small in comparison, what is being suggested is doable.

Qualitative Cyber Research Assistants

Using Stimulated Recall Methods

Stimulated recall interviews are contextualized within an information processing and mediating processes paradigm as well as introspection theory (Henderson & Tallman, 2006).

Opposed to the process-product paradigm in which researchers interpret what occurred in students' minds based on the input-output variables, mediating processes can be viewed as "the fine-grained elements of cognition through which, and by which, learning outcomes are realized" (Henderson & Tallman, 2006, p. 74). Research attests to the maximized reliability of participants' recall if strict interview protocols are maintained and if recall is obtained as soon after the event as possible, but certainly within 48 hours (Bloom, 1954; Ericsson & Simon, 1999; Gass & Mackey, 2000; Marland, Patching, & Putt, 1992; Meade & McMeniman, 1992; Russo, Johnson, & Stevens, 1989). This method was utilized with 13-year-old youth playing a video game (Henderson, 2005) and with students from Grade 4 through 13 using IMM software and online resources (Henderson & Tallman, 2006). The former study acknowledged the errors in interpreting decision-making strategies and thinking processes from the students' game moves and actions (which the software stored) and from the video for researcher analysis. The latter study demonstrated that the students were not thinking about what the teachers thought they were, or what could be interpreted from their computer actions, queries, and choices. Given stimulated recall's sound theoretical base and data, correlating the cyber research assistants quantitative data with stimulated recall data would strengthen data interpretation. The recommendation is therefore to utilize cyber stimulated recall research assistants without intruding into the student's state of flow (Csikszentmihalyi, 1991).

Oral comments from the player rather than typed or selecting an item from possible text choices would seem to be less intrusive. An avatar could engagingly get a student to provide his/her thinking orally by talking into a head microphone. Various intelligent avatars could be utilized to give clues or bonus points in return for the student telling them what they had been thinking, strategizing, or guessing. When the player had "gone around in circles" too long, Contai and Zhao's (2004) pedagogic intelligent agent would exchange scaffolded help for their thoughts. Of course, technological developments would have caught up to allow all sorts of voices to be decoded into text for coding. The automated meta-tagged data streams utilized to tag and code key concepts and argument turns would naturally be substantially augmented to categorize the discourse transcripts.

The audio suggestions just mentioned would be advantageous when pairs are working together at a computer or multiplayers are collaborating or competing in online educational games and simulations. Even better, a Web cam captures one or two students' non-verbals as they play, while a *SKYPE*-type system captures their oral discussion. Research (Henderson, Klemes, & Eshet, 2000; Pausawasdi, 2001) revealed that students (grade 2 and medical students, respectively) were willing to say publicly in front of the other student that they were thinking something quite different (see Anderson, Howe, & Tolmie, 1996).

Analysis of the findings by the IMMEX studies reported earlier suggest benefits for students if they were enabled to engage in an online dialog intervention with an intelligent agent, also acting as the cyber research assistant, after the first teacher education essay or after the first four science simulation solutions. A weak student's strategies could be verbalized when their path map is compared with a prepared virtual student's path map. Then, a voice-over could explain the differences as animated highlighting of the relevant sections of both diagrammatic cluster maps occurs or, until programming catches up, of the virtual student's path map. This would be particularly useful for distance mode students. The avatars would also retrieve one of the most relevant documents that should have been consulted and stimulate discussion, probably via text choices with meaningful asssociated feedback to each choice as to why this document was more relevant than that chosen by the student. The avatar's voice could again reinforce why the former was more strategically useful than that consulted by the student. The programmed involvement of the pedagogic agent and cyber research assistant would be crucial if a student still chose inappropriate strategies and resources. To augment validity, both qualitative and quantitative cyber research assistants would be gathering additional evidence to provide longitudinal data from (a) each student, and (b) across cases from all students.

Longitudinal Studies

What is gravely lacking in both human and cyber research is long-term data on learning with online (or, for that matter, any type of computerized) games and simulations in classrooms. This recognition is not new (Haertel & Means, 2002). There is a plethora of studies on learning outcomes with online and off-line interactive multimedia and online courses in various disciplines from kindergarten through higher education classrooms, and in industry, government, and armed forces training. Such research is predictably short-term targeting one group of participants. If the research is repeated, it typically targets the next intake of participants. Hedges, Konstantopoulos, and Thoreson (2003) cogently pointed out the weaknesses in current longitudinal studies, especially those conducted by the United States National Educational Longitudinal Study and the National Assessment of Educational Progress. They argued that neither have the design and content sufficient to answer vital questions about computer technology availability, use, and, importantly for this chapter, its impact on various aspects of student learning. As it is cross-sectional, the yearly survey conducted by the National Assessment of Educational Progress is unsuitable for revealing causal relationships between technology and student achievement, particularly when the surveys contain inconsistent questions. We know little about how repetition of interacting with information communication technologies, particularly online or off-line computer games and simulations, affects learning outcomes and teaching.

This is most likely because there are limited instances of the same participants learning with online or off-line interactive multimedia simulations and games over a number of years (Haertel & Means, 2002). For instance, in the Plano Independent School District in Texas (Eshet, Klemes, & Henderson, submitted), the school children are involved with at least one interactive multimedia simulation per year from Kindergarten through Grade 5. Yet there are no comparative data targeting the same students' cognitive and affective outcomes year by year, except for the normal compulsory nation-wide standardized test data by grade and school. This type of data is characteristically reported in comparative terms between schools, school districts, and states that do or do not use online or off-line computer games and simulations; those that have high or increased positive results claim their use of information communication technologies as a causal variable.

When the focus is online games and simulations, it would be a responsible act to research the cognitive, social, and affective consequences when the same students interact with either or both online educational games and simulations on a once-a-term, twice yearly, or yearly basis. Are the individual and group findings consistent or variable when learning in the same discipline, in different disciplines, with multi-disciplinary educational games or simulations year after year? What happens with respect to all the following advantages currently extolled and demonstrated by research when playing recreational computer/video and online games and simulations: motivation, immersion, persistence to complete and improve, shared peer learning and teaching, higher order thinking skills and strategies, parallel processing, understanding of the concepts being taught through game play and simulation, and so forth (e.g., Gee, 2003; Henderson, 2005; Prensky, 2003)?

Cyber research assistants, as described in this chapter, have the capacity to "break the mould" of current and traditional assessments in online and off-line computer games and simulations. It behoves us as online games and simulation educational researchers to rectify the paucity in longitudinal research with the same individual student and groups of students. Cyber research assistants in tandem with computer scientists and human researchers can provide the solution. Strengthening the efficiency and effectiveness of longitudinal research would therefore necessitate engaging and enthusing the various computer science communities and granting bodies. Building on present models and devising new models of coordinated cyber research assistants that collate current, previous, and future online and off-line data, regardless as to whether it was from a game or simulation, whether the structure of the game or simulation was the same or whether the disciplines were different, would be complex, but, given the increasing strides in online data programming, conceivably not impossible. Perhaps more problematic would be compatibility between the older and the latest programming versions of the cyber research assistants and, consequently, the human researcher decisions as to whether using these advances, that also involved programs that self-extracted and overwrote the older versions, would negatively affect the comparative reliability and validity of the longitudinal data collected by the cyber research assistants.

Transference

The ability to internalize strategies about how to solve problems in different and unfamiliar contexts is one of transference. This ability is a valued life long skill. Are the correct or incorrect problem solving skills delineated by the intelligent agents transferred to online games and simulations that are structured differently or in differing discipline areas? Are such skills transferred to in-class activities or vice versa?

The IMMEX research (Riedel, Gibson, & Boriah, 2004; Stevens et al., 2005; Vendlinski & Stevens, 2000, 2002) demonstrated that weak students were not able to transfer successful strategies within the same discipline; indeed, they were more likely to revert to strategies that had proved unsuccessful after completing their first four simulations. Cyber research assistants would be well placed to track students' transference abilities in non-science and math game and simulation play. Then another set of cyber research assistants would compare and contrast the online data across the disciplines with findings from "normal" face-to-face teaching and learning research. Teachers and students could then examine the students' transference across their intelligences and, if needed, put in place strategies to improve their near and far transfer strategies in various contexts.

Obviously, though of significance for learning outcomes, these suggestions are still inadequate. Of importance would be ascertaining if the students' online game and simulation problem solving strategies were different in non-computer class contexts or vice versa. Henderson's (2005) research revealed that teacher-identified low achieving students were able to utilize effectively valued metacognitive skills and inductive, deductive, and hypothesising strategies.

Answers from collaboration between the human in-class researcher and cyber assistant online researchers would offer rich evidence to target rectifying such weaknesses in a redesign of particular online games and simulations and in-class teaching.

Plug-and-Research Cyber Assistant Programs

Development of plug-and-research cyber research assistant programs that can seamlessly gather data from current and future games and simulations would be worthwhile. These programs would be invaluable collecting data from games such as *Whyville, Revolution, Quest Atlantis, RAPUNSEL* (or Realtime Applied Programming for Underrepresented Students' Early Literacy) (see Whelan, 2005), and, of course, such programs as the *Sim Family* series! Tapping into education and popular non-education online games, simulations, and computer/video games with the plug-and-research tool in order to obtain transference and other relevant data would be game researcher heaven! Currently, these may be *pie-in-the-sky* requests. Nevertheless, computer scientists are currently engaged in developing languages to solve incompatibility problems.

National and International Collaboration

Currently there are numerous national and international studies, particularly with the same online educational computer games (such as *Quest Atlantis*), that provide little or superficial comparison with each other. Cyber research assistants can help the research community to engage in *mega reviews* of studies focused on educational online simulations and games, and on both "off-line" simulations and games. Current issues of incompatibility of comparison because of differences in definition, methodology, participants, contexts, research aims and questions, and data coding and categorization could be greatly diminished by utilizing cyber research assistant plug-in programs.

The science and teacher education IMMEX-ANN-Kohen ANN studies discussed previously would need changes—language, scenarios (particularly teacher-education cases to include Indigenous remote community schools and urban schools with Indigenous students), pictures, voice-overs, and video clips—in order to be administered, respectively, in various socio-economic schools and teacher education institutions within the same country and between countries, that is, nationally and internationally. Participant characteristics such as gender, current academic ability rating, second or third language learners, ethnicity/race, age, and school grade level would be included. The improved trained cyber research assistants would handle the large data pools to categorize, collate, and deliver all sorts of data combinations to human researchers and then to the research and educational communities. Because these IMMEX cases provide insights and guidance concerning the critical thinking and problem solving strategies used, that is, how students approach and solve science simulations or the eTIP simulations of technology integration in schools, this national and international data would provide a better understanding of content knowledge and critical strategies than do current standardized testing.

Ethical Issues

Ethical issues arise when using cyber research assistants (e.g., Ess & AoIR, 2002). One is that the students need to know their every move and choice is being monitored, not just for working through the game, but also for feedback to outside researchers. Researchers would need to take into account how this could affect the students playing behaviors. Research (Henderson, 1993, 1996; Henderson, Klemes, & Eshet, 2000) suggests that if there is any sense of "being watched," it quickly dissipates.

There is another perhaps larger ethical issue. Who has the right, other than the researcher with ethics approval, to access this data? Would it be all the data? What would be the purpose of such access? If the teacher has access, the data could be utilized for more targeted scaffolding and modeling within a cognitive apprenticeship approach in individual, group, or class exploration. If it were the student or students when working in pairs or in multiplayer games and simulations, then the data would be powerful for them to deconstruct their own successful and problematic strategies and content understandings. This self-examination could be in conjunction with the teacher-as-guide. Implementing such suggestions would necessitate some sort of training for both the teacher and students so that they could make sense of the mapped data and to interpret the data realistically. This case for students and teachers in various contexts to have access to the returned data is backed by the need to take *ownership* of subsequent learning and teaching actions.

Conclusion

In summary, the transferred agency from human researcher to cyber research assistants provides flexibility when carrying out individual, joint, and monitored online tasks within human set boundaries. It offers a future for cyber research assistants to be trained to a high level of reliability. The possibilities for minimizing the heavy load for qualitative researchers yet maximizing the correlation of different sorts of data are encouraging. The outcome for understanding how learning is occurring at the time it is occurring will provide researchers, teachers, and students with robust explanatory and trouble shooting information.

Previous topics highlighted inadequacies in qualitative, longitudinal, and transference cyber research programs. The issue is one for conversation between the various national and international parties: quantitative and qualitative researchers, the computer science community, online games and simulation producers, instructors, students, granting bodies, and government. This is probably a greater challenge than the previously indicated tasks to fix the cyber research assistants' inadequacies. Nevertheless, it makes sense. Grant monies are becoming increasingly difficult for the low-stakes non-sciences; partnerships strengthen the quality of online game and simulation research across the range of school and university disciplines; teachers can target specific learner weaknesses based on substantiated data; life long strategic abilities do not remain a strength of an elite sub-section of the student population; and international grants lessen the burden on each country and private funding bodies.

References

Alloway, N., & Gilbert, P. (1998). Video game culture: Playing with masculinity, violence and pleasure. In S. Howard, (Ed.), *Wired-up. Young people and the electronic media* (pp. 95-114). London: UCL Press.

Anderson, T., Howe, C., & Tolmie, A. (1996). Interaction and mental models of physics phenomena: Evidence from dialogues between learners. In J. Oakhill & A. Garnham (Eds.), *Mental models in cognitive science* (pp. 247-273). Hillsdale, NJ: Lawrence Erlbaum Associates.

Berners-Lee, T., Hendler, J., & Lassila, O. (2001, May). A new form of Web content that is meaningful to computers will unleash a revolution of new possibilities. *Scientific American*. Retrieved February 2, 2006, from http://www.sciam.com/article.cfm?articleID=00048144-10D2-1C70-84A9809EC588EF21

Barab, S., Thomas, M., Dodge, T., Carteaux, B., & Tuzun, H. (2005). Making learning fun: Quest Atlantis: A game without guns. *Educational Technology Research & Development, 53*(1), 86-107.

Bitpipe. (2004). *Intelligent digital agent: A knowledge agent for dialogue based Web site interaction*. White Paper. Retrieved December 31, 2005, from http://bitpipe.com/detail/RES/1006368856_825.html

Bloom, B. (1954). The thought process of students in discussion. In S. J. French (Ed.), *Accent on teaching: Experiments in general education* (pp. 23-46). New York: Harper & Row.

Brachman, R. J. (2002, November-December). Systems that know what they are doing. *IEEE Intelligent Systems*, 67-71. Retrieved May 28, 2005, from http://computer.org/intelligent

Bransford, J. D., Brown, A. L., & Cocking, R. R. (1999). *How people learn: Brain, mind, experience, and school*. Committee on Developments in the Science of Learning with additional material from the Committee on Learning Research and Educational Practice, National Research Council. Washington, D.C.: National Academy Press. Retrieved May 24, 2002, from http://www.nap.edu/html/howpeople1/

Brown, J. S., Collins, A., & Duguid, P. (1989). Situated cognition and the culture of learning. *Education Researcher, 18*(1), 32-42.

Browning, B., Kaminka, G., & Veloso, M. (2002). Principled monitoring of distributed agents for detection of coordination failure. In *Proceedings of distributed autonomous robotic systems* (pp. 319-328). Springer-Verlag. Retrieved January 8, 2006, from http://www-2.cs.cmu.edu/afs/cs/project/coral/publinks/mmv/02dars-monitoring.pdf

Carbonaro, M., Cutumisu, M., McNaughton, M., Onuczko, C., Roy, T., Schaeffer, J., et al. (2005, June 16-20). Interactive story writing in the classroom: Using computer games. In Digital Games Research Assocation (Eds.), *DiGRA 2005: Changing views: Worlds in play*. Bunbury, Canada: Digital Games Research Association. Retrieved July 10, 2006, from http://www. gamesconference.org/digra2005/viewrecord.php?id=226

Chung, G. R., deVries, L. F., Cheak, A. M., Stevens, R. H., & Bewley, W. L. (2002). Cognitive process validation of an online problem solving assessment. *Computer Human Behavior, 18*, 669-684.

Cimolino, L., & Kay, J. (2002, December 3-6). Verified concept mapping for eliciting conceptual understanding. In L. Aroyo & D. Dicheva (Eds.), *Proceedings of ICCE 2002 Workshop on Concepts and Ontologies in Web-Based Educational Systems* (pp. 11-16), Auckland, New Zealand. CS-Report 02-15. Eindhoven: Eindhoven University of Technology, Department of Mathematics and Computer Science. Retrieved July 10, 2006, from http://www.win.tue.nl/~laroyo/ICCE2002_Workshop/proc-Workshop-ICCE2002.pdf

Contai, C., & Zhao, X. (2004). Building and evaluating an intelligent pedagogical agent to improve the effectiveness of an educational game. In R. Jacob, Q. Limbourg, & J. Vanderdonckt (Eds.), *Computer-aided design of user interfaces IV* (pp. 6-13). New York: Kluwer Academic Publishers.

Csikszentmihalyi, M. (1991). *Flow: The psychology of optimal experience.* New York: Harper Perennial.

Dede, C. (2005). Planning for neomillennial learning styles. *EDUCAUSE Quarterly, 28*(1) [Online]. Retrieved June 21, 2005, from https://www.educause.edu/apps/cq/eqm0511.asp?bhcp=1

Dede, C., Ketelhut, D., & Ruess, K. (2002). Motivation, usability, and learning outcomes in a prototype museum-based multi-user virtual environment. In *Proceedings of the 15th International Conference of the Learning Sciences* (pp. 06-408). Mahwah, NJ: Lawrence Erlbaum Associates.

Dexter, S. (2002). eTIPS-Educational technology integration and implementation principles. In P. Rodgers (Ed.), *Designing instruction for technology-enhanced learning* (pp. 56-70). New York: Idea Group Publishing.

Ericsson, K., & Simon, H. (1984, 1993, 1999). *Protocol analysis: Verbal reports as data* (2nd ed. 1993; 3rd ed. 1999). Cambridge, MA: MIT Press.

Ess, C., & Association of Internet Researchers. (2002). *Ethical decision-making and Internet research: Recommendations from the AoIR ethics working committee.* Retrieved February 2, 2005, from http://aoir.org/reports/ethics.pdf

Foreman, J., & Gibson, D. (2006). *Semantic Web applications for e-learning.* Manuscript draft in private communication.

Gardner, H. (1999). *Intelligence reframed: Multiple intelligences for the 21st century.* New York: Basic Books.

Gass, S. M., & Mackey, A. (2000). *Stimulated recall methodology in second language research.* Mahwah, NJ: Lawrence Erlbaum.

Gee, J. P. (2003). *What video games have to teach us about learning and literacy.* New York: Palgrave Macmillan.

Gibson, D. (2003). Network-based assessment in education. *Contemporary Issues in Technology and Teacher Education, 3*(3), 310-323.

Giordani, A., & Soller, A. (2004). *Strategic collaboration support in a Web-based scientific inquiry environment.* Paper presented at the Workshop on Artificial Intelligence at European Conference on Artificial Intelligence at Computer Supported Collaborative Learning, Valencia, Spain.

Haertel, G., & Means, B. (2002). *Stronger designs for research on educational uses of technology: Conclusion and implications.* Center for Innovative Learning Technologies. Menlo Park, CA: SRI International. Retrieved January 4, 2006, from http://www.msu.edu/course/cep/807/zOld807.1998Gentry/snapshot.afs/*studyrefs/beckersynthe1b.pdf

Hedges, L. V., Konstantopoulos, S., & Thoreson, A. C. (2003). Studies of technology implementation and effects. In G. Haertel & B. Means (Eds.), *Evaluating educational technology: Effective research designs for improving learning* (pp. 187-204). New York: Teachers College.

Henderson, L. (1996). Instructional design of interactive multimedia: A cultural critique. *Education Technology Research & Development, 44*(4), 85-104.

Henderson, L. (2005, June 16-20). Video games: A significant cognitive artifact of contemporary youth culture. In Digital Games Research Association (Eds.), *DIGRA 2005: Changing views: Worlds in Play.* Burnaby, BC, Canada: Digital Games Research Association. Retrieved July 10, 2006, from http://www.gamesconference.org/digra2005/viewabstract.php?id=125

Henderson, L., Klemes, Y., & Eshet, Y. (2000). Just playing a game? Educational simulation software and cognitive outcomes. *Journal of Educational Computing Research, 22*(1), 105-129.

Herderson, L., Klemes, Y., & Eshet, Y. (2000). Under the microscope: Factors influencing student outcomes in a computer integrated classroom. *Journal of Computers in Mathematics and Science Teaching, 19*(3), 211-236.

Henderson, L., & Tallman, J. (2006). *Stimulated recall and mental models: Tools for teaching and learning computer information literacy.* Lanham, MD: Scarecrow Press.

Holland, W., Jenkins, H., & Squire, K. (2003). Theory by design. In B. Perron & M. Wolf (Eds.), *Video game theory* (pp. 25-46). New York: Routledge.

Huber, M., & Hadley, T. (1997). Multiple roles, multiple teams, dynamic environment: Autonomous netrek agents. In W. L. Johnson (Ed.), *Proceedings of the International Conference on Autonomous Agents* (pp. 332-339). Marina del Rey, CA: ACM Press.

Hunt, E., & Minstrell, J. (1994). A cognitive approach to the teaching of physics. In K. McGilly (Ed.), *Classroom lessons: Integrating cognitive theory and classroom practice* (pp. 51-74). Cambridge, MA: MIT Press.

Johnson, W. L., Kole, S., Shaw, E., & Pain, H. (2003). Socially intelligent learner-agent interaction tactics. In J. K. Ulrich Hoppe & F. Verdejo (Eds.), *Proceedings of International Conference on Artificial Intelligence in Education* (pp. 431-433). Amsterdam: IOS Press.

Jonassen, D. H. (2000). *Computers as mindtools for schools: Engaging critical thinking.* Upper Saddle River, NJ: Prentice Hall.

Kohonen, T. (2001). *Self-organizing maps* (3rd ed.). Berlin: Springer.

Leung, L. (2003). Impacts of net-generation attributes, seductive properties of the Internet, and gratifications-obtained on Internet use. *Telematics and Informatics, 20*(2), 107-129.

Lindner, M., Kalech, M., & Kaminka, G. A. (2005, July 30-August 5). *Detecting coordination failures by observing groups: A formal approach.* Paper presented at the International Joint Conference on Artificial Intelligence, Edinburgh. Retrieved January 3, 2005, from http://www.isi.edu/`pynadath/MOO-2005/la.pdf

Marland, P., Patching, W., & Putt, I. (1992). *Learning from text: Glimpses inside the minds of distance learners.* Townsville: James Cook University of North Queensland.

Meade, P., & McMeniman, M. (1992). Stimulated recall: An effective methodology for examining successful teaching in science. *Australian Educational Researcher, 19*(3), 1-18.

Metrick, S., & Epstein, A. (2000). *Emerging technologies for active learning: Part 1: Multiuser virtual environments.* Educational Development Center, Inc. Retrieved June 21, 2005, from http://www2.edc.org/LNT/news/Issue10/feature3a.htm

Mislevy, R. J., Steinberg, L., Almond, R. G., Haertel, G. D., & Penuel, W. R. (2001). *Leverage points for improving educational assessment* (Tech. Rep. No. 534). Los Angeles, CA: University of California, Center for the Study of Evaluation.

MIT, & University of Wisconsin (2005). *Revolution. The education arcade.* Boston: MIT. Retrieved February 2, 2006, from http://educationarcade.org/revolution

Mitchell, W. J. (2003). *Me++: The cyborg self and the networked city.* Cambridge, MA: MIT Press.

Neulight, N., & Kafai, Y. (2005, June 16-20). What happens if you catch Whypox? Children's learning experiences of infectious disease in a multi-user virtual environment. In Digital Games Research Association (Eds.), *DIGRA 2005: Changing views: Worlds in Play.* Burnaby, BC, Canada: Digital Games Research Association. Retrieved July 10, 2006, from http://www.gamesconference.org/digra2005/viewabstract.php?id=283

Novak, J., & Gowin, D. (1984). *Learning how to learn.* New York: Cambridge University Press.

Pausawasdi, N. (2001). *Students' engagement and disengagement when learning with IMM in mass lectures.* Unpublished doctoral thesis, James Cook University, Townsville.

Pellegrino, J. W., Chudowsky, N., & Glaser, R. (Eds.). (2001). *Knowing what students know: The science and design of educational assessment.* Committee on the Foundations of Assessment, Board on Testing and Assessment, Center for Education, National Research Council. Washington, DC: National Academy Press. Retrieved May 24, 2002, from http://www.nap.edu/books/0309072727.html/

Pollock, J., & Hodgson, R. (2004). *Adaptive information: Improving business through semantic interoperability, grid computing and enterprise integration.* John Wiley & Sons. Retrieved February 11, 2004, from http://www.topquadrant.com/documents/Adaptive_information_Book_Preview.PDF

Prensky, M. (2003). *Digital game based learning: Exploring the digital generation.* Washington, DC: Educational Technology, U.S. Department of Education.

Quellmalz, E., & Haertel, G. D. (1999). *Breaking the mold: Technology-based science assessment in the 21st century.* Menlo Park, CA: SRI International.

Riedel, E., Gibson, D., & Borian, S. (2004). *eTIP case analysis paper no. 4: The relationship between eTIP case scores and the actual search of cases.* Unpublished manuscript. Retrieved November 28, 2005, from http://www.etips.info/

Russo, J., Johnson, E., & Stevens, D. (1989). The validity of verbal protocols. *Memory and Cognition, 17*(6), 759-769.

Sabelli, N., & Pea, R. (2004). *Six years of knowledge networking in learning sciences and technologies.* Menlo Park, CA; Palo Alto, WA: Center for Innovative Learning Technologies.

Sauvé, L., Villardier, L., Probst, W., Boyd, G., Kaufman, D., Sánchez Arias, V. G., & Power, M. (2005, June 16-20). Playing and learning without borders: A real-time online play environment. In Digital Games Research Association (Eds.), *DIGRA 2005: Changing views: Worlds in Play.* Burnaby, BC, Canada: Digital Games Research Association. Retrieved July 10, 2006, from http://www.gamesconference.org/digra2005/viewabstract.php?id=122

Seely-Brown, J., Collins, A., & Duguid, P. (1989). Situated cognition and the culture of learning. *Education Researcher, 18*(1), 32-42.

Shinkle, S. (2003). Gardens, games, and the anamorphic subject: Tracing the body in the virtual landscape. *Ezine, 17*(8). Retrieved February 5, 2005, from http://www.fineartforum.org/Backissues/Vol_17/faf_v17_n08/reviews/reviews_index.html

Squire, K., & Giovanetto, L. (2005, June). *The higher education of gaming. Changing views: Worlds in play.* In Digital Games Research Association (Eds.), *DIGRA 2005: Changing views: Worlds in Play.* Burnaby, BC, Canada: Digital Games Research Association. Retrieved July 10, 2006, from http://www.gamesconference.org/digra2005/viewabstract.php?id=328

Stevens, R. H. (1991). Search path mapping: A versatile approach for visualizing problem-solving behavior. *Academic Medicine, 66*(9), S72-S75.

Stevens, R. H., & Casillas, A. (2004). Artificial neural networks. In R. E. Mislevy, D. M. Williamson, & I. Bejar (Eds.), *Automated scoring.* Hillsdale, NJ: Erlbaum.

Stevens, R. H., Johnson, D., & Soller, A. (2005, Spring). Probabilities and predictions: Modeling the development of scientific problem solving skills. *Cell Biology Education, 4*(1), 42-57.

Stevens, R. H., & Palacio-Cayetano, J. (2003). Design and performance frameworks for constructing problem-solving simulations. *Cell Biology Education, 2*(3), 162-179.

Tambe, M., Johnson, W., Jones, R., Kossand, F., Lairdand, J., Rosenbloom, P., et al. (1995). Intelligent agents for interactive simulation environments. *AI Magazine, 16*(1), 15-39.

Valenti, S., Neri, F., & Cucchiarelli, A. (2003). An overview of current research on automated essay grading. *Journal of Information Technology Education, 2*(Special Series), 319-330.

Vasilakos, T., Devedzic, V., Kinshuk, & Pedrycz, W. (2004). Computational intelligence in Web-based education: A tutorial. *Journal of Interactive Learning Research, 15*(4), 299-318.

Vendlinski, T., & Stevens, R. (2002). A Markov model analysis of problem-solving progress and transfer. *Journal of Technology, Learning, and Assessment, 1*(3), 1-20.

Vendlinski, T., & Stevens, R. H. (2000). The use of artificial neural nets (ANN) to help evaluate student problem solving strategies. In B. Fishman & S. O'Connor-Divelbiss (Eds.), *4th International Conference of the Learning Sciences* (pp. 108-114). Mahwah, NJ: Erlbaum.

Virvou, M., & Moundridou, M. (2000). Modelling the instructor in a Web-based authoring tool for algebra-related ITSs. In G. Gauthier, C. Frasson, & K. VanLehn (Eds.), *Intelligent Tutoring Systems, Proceedings of the 5th International Conference on Intelligent Tutoring Systems* (pp. 635-644). Berlin: Springer.

Vu, T., & Veloso, M. (2004, July 19-23). *High-level behavior programming*. In *Proceedings of the AAMAS 2004*. New York: ACM.

Whelan, D. L. (2005). Let the games begin! *School Library Journal, 51*(4), 40-43.

Wood, R. T., Griffiths, M. T., & Eatough, V. (2004). Online data collection from video game players: Methodological issues. *CyberPsychology & Behavior, 7*(5), 511-518.

Zapata-Rivera, J D., & Greer, J. E. (2004). Interacting with inspectable Bayesian Models. *International Journal of Artificial Intelligence in Education, 14*, 127-163.

About the Authors

David Gibson is project co-director of simSchool (www.simschool.org), a classroom flight simulator for training teachers and the Director of the Global Challenge Award (www.globalchallengeawards.org), a new competition and scholarship program for high school students that engages students in studying science, technology, engineering, and mathematics in order to solve global problems. His research and publications include work on complex systems analysis and modeling of education, Semantic Web applications and the future of learning, and the use of technology to personalize education for the success of all students. He is currently involved in translating simSchool and articles into Korean. Dr. Gibson is also the Founder and President of CURVESHIFT, an educational technology company (www.curveshift.com) that assists in the acquisition, implementation, and continuing design of games and simulations, e-portfolio systems, data-driven decision making tools, and emerging Semantic Web technologies.

Clark Aldrich is the co-founder of SimuLearn and the author of *Learning by Doing: A Comprehensive Guide to Simulations, Computer Games, and Pedagogy in e-Learning and Other Educational Experiences* and *Simulations and the Future of Learning*. He recently lead the international team that created SimuLearn's Virtual Leader, the first ever learning experience to follow the development cycle of a modern computer game. Virtual Leader has been featured on CNNfn, on CNet, in *The New York Times*, and in *U.S. News and World Report*, and it has been sold to some of the largest enterprises in the United States.

Aldrich previously worked for Gartner Group, where he was the research director responsible for creating and building the company's e-learning practice. In this position he developed strategies with Global 1000 organizations, vendors, and venture capitalists and published more than 40 research notes. Prior to joining Gartner, Aldrich worked for almost eight years at Xerox, where his responsibilities included special projects for the executive office. Aldrich earned a bachelor's degree in artificial intelligence and cognitive science from Brown University.

Marc Prensky is an internationally acclaimed speaker, writer, consultant, futurist, visionary and inventor in the critical areas of education and learning. Marc is the founder of Games2train, an e-learning company whose clients include IBM, Bank of America, Nortel and Nokia. He is the author of the critically acclaimed Digital Game-Based Learning (McGraw-Hill, 2001). Marc's professional focus has been on reinventing the learning process, combining the motivation of video games and other highly engaging activities with the driest content of education and business. He is considered one of the world's leading experts on the connection between games and learning. His innovative combination of educational tools and game technology—including the world's first fast-action videogame-based corporate training tool—is being accepted throughout schools, government and corporate America. Marc's background includes master's degrees from Yale, Middlebury, and The Harvard Business School (with distinction). He is a concert musician and has acted on Broadway. He has taught at all levels from elementary to college. He worked in human resources and in technology at Bankers Trust Company, and spent six years as a corporate strategist and product development director with the Boston Consulting Group. Marc is a native of New York City, where he lives with his wife Rie Takemura, a Japanese writer.

* * *

Göknur Kaplan Akilli completed her undergraduate degree in mathematics education at Hacettepe University, Turkey in 2001 and ranked first in her graduating Class of Faculty of Education, the same year. In 2004, she earned her master's degree from Middle East Technical University (METU), with her thesis "A Proposal of Instructional Design/Development Model for Game-like Learning Environments: The FID²GE Model," which is nominated to many national and international awards. Currently, she is pursuing a PhD in instructional systems program at Penn State University, USA.

Karen Barton, senior lecturer in legal practice, Glasgow Graduate School of Law, University of Strathclyde, UK, joined the Glasgow Graduate School of Law in 2004. Her research interests lie in teaching and learning and the use of IT within legal practice. She has carried out a number of collaborative research projects in these areas including The Paisley Pattern, a survey of use of ICT within Scottish legal practices, and the development of The Virtual Court Action, a computer-based learning application. Karen is currently working on transactional, Web-based environments as well as multimedia and video lecture environments. She is also a member of professional legal education projects such as The Standardised Client Project in interviewing skills, and a Portfolio Pilot Project involving trainees and trainers within a number of Scottish legal firms.

Katrin Becker, MSc, has been a senior instructor, Department of Computer Science at the University of Calgary, Canada, since 1983 and is currently a doctoral candidate in educational technology at the same institution. Her research interests include serious games, teaching with games, instructional design and technologies, file and data architecture, computer science education, and computer science curriculum. She is an active researcher in the study of digital game-based learning (DGBL), studying the kind of learning that happens when playing computer and video games, how to use this medium as a tool for learning, and how to design games for learning. Her doctoral work focuses on the design of games for learning. Her work in computer science education (CSE) centers on the use of games to teach computer science concepts and skills, as well as the development of games design curricula within computer science programs.

Jonathon B. Beedle is an assistant professor of technology education in the College of Education and Psychology at the University of Southern Mississippi (USM), USA. He teaches technical and occupational education and instructional technology courses at USM's campuses on the Mississippi Gulf Coast. His research interests include the pedagogy of college faculty, issues related to the potential benefits from multiplayer computer gaming in the educational setting, and technology and legal concerns in education.

Thomasina Borkman received her PhD from Columbia University, NYC in 1969 in sociology. She has been a sociology professor at George Mason University, USA, since 1974, who combines teaching and research. Her research and consulting is in her specialty area of health, illness, and disability, especially with self-help/mutual aid groups and nonprofit organizations nationally and cross-nationally. Between 1997-1998 she co-taught the team aspects of an online course titled Taming the Electronic Frontier designed by Brad Cox; the course won the Paul Allen Distance Education national award in 1998 ($25,000 prize). Her major recent book is *Understanding Self-Help/Mutual Aid: Experiential Learning in the Commons*, Rutgers University Press, 1999.

Stephen C. Bronack is assistant professor of instructional technology at Appalachian State University, USA. As a parent and an educator, Dr. Bronack helps organizations use learning technologies to make education a better process for both kids and adults. His research interests include online learning, organizational development, and school, technology, and society. Dr. Bronack's research on online learning has been published widely in books, journals, and proceedings of international conferences in the U.S. and around the world. He is co-creator of AET Zone, a 3D virtual world for learning. Dr. Bronack holds a PhD in Education from the University of Virginia.

Jeff Denton is an Internet application developer and graphic designer for the Teaching Research Institute at Western Oregon University, USA. He has held the role of lead developer and user interface designer on the Cook School District project since June of 2005. His previous experience includes development of consumer and administrative Internet applications for the photography and printing industries as well as data collection and reporting applications for state agencies.

Sara Dexter is an Assistant Professor at the University of Virginia, USA, where she teaches courses on technology leadership for teachers, technology coordinators, and principals. Prior to her arrival she was an assistant professor at the University of Nevada, Las Vegas and before that a research associate at the Center for Applied Research and Educational Improvement (CAREI) at the University of Minnesota. She has also been a junior high and high school science teacher as well as a district staff developer specializing in educational technology. Throughout her career Dr. Dexter has focused her research on the integration and implementation of educational technology in K-12 schools. See also sdexter.net.

Brian Ferry is associate dean graduate at the University of Wollongong, Australia. His research interests include the use of online simulations in initial teacher education, alternative approaches to initial teacher education, and science education. He began his career as a teacher in an isolated rural primary school and later moved to secondary schools before becoming an academic.

Joel Foreman is an associate professor in the english department at George Mason University, USA. He began teaching distance courses in 1996 and subsequently developed expertise in building and assessing Web-based learning environments. As a member of GMU's Program on Social and Organizational Learning from 1995-2001, he performed organizational learning studies sponsored by Hughes Information Technology Corporation, DynCorp, and Media General. He has been researching computerized instructional media since the 1980s, and his applied experience includes documentaries he produced for NBC, public television, the Discovery Channel, and others. His current research is focused on game based learning and mobile learning.

Lisa Galarneau is a doctoral candidate in the University of Waikato's Screen and Media Studies department in New Zealand and a researcher in the university's post-graduate games research lab. Leveraging her previous academic work in education and socio-cultural anthropology, as well as extensive experience in online learning design and development, her research is looking at spontaneous communities of learning in virtual worlds. Galarneau is also an award-winning new media producer and is currently working as a games user research specialist at Microsoft Game Studios while she completes her dissertation. In addition, she acts as consultant and advisor to various organizations looking to leverage interactive media in the design of engaging, effective learning experiences.

Gerald R. Girod is a research professor within the Teaching Research Institute at Western Oregon University, USA. He has been the principal investigator on the Cook School District project. Prior to this work, Girod has been an elementary classroom teacher, professor of teacher preparation, evaluation specialist, department chair, and dean. His research and development interests are in teacher education and, specifically, teacher work sample methodology.

Mark Girod is an assistant professor of teacher education at Western Oregon University, USA. He teaches courses in learning and development, social foundations of education, and research methods in the Master of Arts in Teaching program. His research explores applications of technology to teaching and learning as well as science education.

William Halverson is a specialist in curriculum and instruction with a concentration in educational technology. He has several years experience providing Web-based technology systems planning and implementation, technical assistance, and Web-based project management for educators. He has worked with teaching research (TR) and Western Oregon University (WOU) College of Education (COE) as instructional designer and as the coordinator of educational media and the director of Web technology at the Florida Gulf Coast University College of Education. Bill created and implemented an interactive "portal" for Florida teacher prep professors and pre-service teachers, which indexed technology enriched lesson plans created collaboratively by professors, pre-service, and in-service teachers and linked Florida and National Educational Technology Standards in eight subject areas.

Lyn Henderson is an associate professor of education at James Cook University in Queensland, Australia. She is interested in student and teacher thinking and mental models while learning and teaching with interactive multimedia and the WWW; instructional design and evaluation of educational media and teaching materials; evaluation of information technology diffusion in schools; effects of gender and cultural differences in learning and teaching with computers; learning and teaching with the WWW; open learning/distance education; and recreational computer/video games. Dr. Henderson is involved in international research with the University of Georgia examining the mental models and thinking processes of teacher librarians/media specialists and students as they employ research skills accessing electronic data bases; The Open University of Israel investigating Year 2/3 students learning outcomes using IMM; evaluation of the implementation of information communication technologies in England; and various aspects of recreational computer/video/Internet games with colleagues in England, Israel, and China.

James G. Jones is an assistant professor of computer education and cognitive systems at the University of North Texas, USA. His interest is in expanding the way technology can be used to further the creation and distribution of knowledge and learning. His research focuses on the areas of emerging technologies for learning, which include visualization systems for education, virtual communities, and multi-user 3D online learning environments. These technologies support learning by the distribution of interaction and feedback across both time and space via interactive forms of multimedia. Dr. Jones holds a PhD in Instructional Technology from the University of Texas, Austin.

Lisa Kervin is a lecturer in the Faculty of Education, University of Wollongong, Australia. She has taught across the primary grades and has been responsible for both the literacy and numeracy curriculum areas within schools. She has been employed in consultancy roles within New South Wales education systems. Lisa Kervin graduated in July 2004 with her PhD, and her thesis was concerned with the professional development of teachers in literacy. Her current research interests are related to the literacy development of children, the use of technology to support student learning, and teacher professional learning.

Christian Sebastian Loh is an assistant professor of instructional design and technology at the Southern Illinois University Carbondale, USA, where he currently evangelizes instructional gaming, content management delivery, and instructional design for e-learning. In 2004, he initiated a Special Interest Forum for Instructional Gaming (SIF-IG) [http://igforum.us] within the Association for Education and Communication Technology, and has since been rallying others to think more about educationally useful games through a series of annual Symposia for Instructional Gaming.

Paul Maharg is a professor in law at Glasgow Graduate School of Law, University of Strathclyde, UK. Paul has a background in arts, education, and law, and his research fields include legal critique and legal education. He has published widely on many aspects of legal education and ICT, and is involved in a number of collaborative projects on the subject of transactional learning environments. He is on the editorial board of several journals, is a member of education committees on the Law Society of Scotland, and is chair of the British and Irish Law, Education, Technology Association (BILETA).

Eric Riedel has conducted research and written in a number of areas including social capital and the Internet, political socialization, and educational technology. After receiving his doctorate in political science from the University of Minnesota in 2000, Dr. Riedel served as a postdoctoral fellow at the Center for the Study of Political Psychology at the University of Minnesota from 2000-2001. He then served as a research associate/principal investigator at the Center for Applied Research and Educational Improvement at the University of Minnesota from 2001-2005. Dr. Riedel is currently the director of assessment for Walden University, USA.

Odilo Schoch is a PhD student and a research assistant at the ETH Zurich's chair for CAAD, Switzerland. His theoretical work focuses on the impact of digital technologies on our environment (such as adaptive buildings, cities, etc.). Schoch earned a diploma degree in architectural design, as well as a MAS in housing design, studying at the ETH Zurich and at UCS London. Schoch has gathered work experience in offices such as Ove Arup, IPL (now FormTL), Züblin (Bangkok), GramazioKohler, and at his father's architectural office. At the ETH Zurich, he coordinated the ETHWorld project "Building IP—lecture hall of the future," as well as the Masters in CAAD (2002-2003). Schoch has been lecturing in Europe and Asia. He is a practicing architect with his own company together with his father. So far, his architectural and consulting work comprises the design and realization of houses and facades in Germany, Switzerland, and China.

Karen Schrier is a graduate of MIT's Comparative Media Studies program, USA, where she completed her master's thesis, "Revolutionizing History Education: Using Augmented Reality Games to Teach Histories." Prior to MIT, she worked at an educational media company, where she produced numerous published academic guides and materials for K-12 and college students. While at MIT, Karen worked as a researcher for MIT's media literacy initiative. She also led workshops at MIT, NYU, and local community centers on diverse topics such as mobile storytelling, video editing, educational media design, and architectural software. She is currently working in New York City, where she creates educational animations for college students.

Ron Stevens is a professor of immunology and microbiology at UCLA's School of Medicine, USA. He has over 25 years of university teaching experience and has published over 100 peer-reviewed articles. He is the originator of IMMEX software and as director of the UCLA IMMEX Project, has overseen the implementation of his technology into primary and secondary schools nationwide.

Richard Van Eck is graduate director of the Instructional Design & Technology program at the University of North Dakota, USA. He received his doctorate in instructional design and development from the University of South Alabama. He has also been on the Instructional Design & Technology faculty at the University of Memphis, where he was also a member of the Institute for Intelligent Systems. His scholarly work on games includes 27 publications and presentations, including seven invited presentations/keynotes. He has also developed five original games, and published on intelligent tutoring systems, pedagogical agents, authoring tools, and gender and technology.

Steffen P. Walz is a game designer and game design researcher, currently pursuing his PhD at the ETH Zurich's chair for CAAD, Switzerland. He holds an MA in Social Anthropology and Rhetoric from the University of Tübingen, Germany. Walz is a co-founder of the BA Game Design program at the University for Art and Design Zurich. He has written about and lectured on topics such as pervasive & mobile gaming, the rhetoric of games, and the sociology of computer-integrated environments. His game works include the pioneering pervasive multiplayer game *M.A.D. Countdown* (2002), the advertainment race game *Carplication* (2003), and the city wide location-based spell-casting sightseeing game *REXplorer* (launching 2006). Before concentrating on his academic career, Walz was an award winning creative director for Web agencies, a TV satire journalist, and a power pop musician. In his spare time, he runs his own music label, playbe records.

Vivian H. Wright is an assistant professor of instructional technology in the College of Education at The University of Alabama in Tuscaloosa, USA. In addition to teaching in the graduate program, she works with teacher educators on innovative ways to infuse technology in the curriculum to enhance teaching and learning and has helped initiate and develop projects such as Electronic Portfolios for the Preservice Teacher, Master Technology Teacher, and Technology on Wheels. Her research interests include K-12 technology integration and asynchronous education.

Melanie Zibit is a research associate at Boston College, USA, in the Teacher Preparation Department. Her research focuses on the impact and development of games and simulations in education as well as designing models and strategies for building online learning communities, particularly for professional development environments. Zibit is currently manager of online support services for simSchool, an innovative simulated classroom where teachers practice the complexities of individualizing instruction based on student learning preferences. Zibit has pioneered innovative approaches to education enriched by the power of technology and has received grants from the National Science Foundation, the GE Foundation, and the U.S. Department of Education.

Index